Authentic Childhood: Exploring Reggio Emilia in the Classroom

Susan Fraser

Carol Gestwicki

Central Piedmont Community College

DELMAR

THOMSON LEARNING

Australia   Canada   Mexico   Singapore   Spain   United Kingdom   United States

Adapted from
Authentic Childhood: Experiencing Reggio Emilia in the Classroom.
published by Nelson © 2000

Authentic Childhood: Exploring Reggio Emilia in the Classroom
by Susan Fraser and Carol Gestwicki

Business Unit Director:
Susan L. Simpfenderfer

Executive Production Manager:
Wendy A. Troeger

Executive Marketing Manager:
Donna J. Lewis

Executive Editor:
Marlene McHugh Pratt

Production Editor:
J.P. Henkel

Channel Manager:
Nigar Hale

Acquisitions Editor:
Erin O'Connor Traylor

Technology Project Manager:
James Considine

Editorial Assistant:
Alexis Ferraro

For permission to use material from this text or product, contact us by
Tel   (800) 730-2214
Fax   (800) 730-2215
www.thomsonrights.com

ISBN: 0-7668-2544-2

NOTICE TO THE READER

Contents

Foreword

After Susan Fraser visited the municipal infant-toddler centers and preschools in Reggio Emilia in 1993, she returned to Canada inspired first to explore the principles with her college faculty and early childhood education students at Douglas College in British Columbia, and then with teachers working with preschool children. In the book *Authentic Childhood: Experiencing Reggio Emilia in the Classroom* published in Canada by ITP Nelson in 1999, Sue described the influential ideas from the Reggio approach that she wanted to explore. She also detailed the first attempts and reflections of teachers trying to implement these ideas in three early childhood programs with which she worked: Quadra Island Preschool, Quadra Island Day Care, and the Vancouver Child Study Center. These were programs with which Sue worked closely from 1997 through 1999, visiting the teachers and children at least once a month, documenting various projects, and interviewing the teachers about the progress of their work. The ideas were fairly new to the teachers and this was very much a documentation of an early part of the journey of working with ideas from the example of the Reggio schools. You will read some of the stories and comments throughout the book. Sue was careful to point out that this was not a "how-to" book but a description of the reflection and adaptation process. More detailed accounts of Sue's motivations and descriptions of the programs involved appear in Sue's book.

When my editor at Delmar, Erin O'Connor Traylor, obtained the rights to publish an edition of this book for an audience of American educators, she asked me to create the American edition. I was pleased to accept the assignment for several reasons. One is that I enjoyed and admired Sue's book when I first read it, and felt that it offered a perspective that should be available in America. Moreover, working on the project gave me an opportunity to again read, think, and talk about the essence of the Reggio Emilia approach. Through the early 1990s, I had been building an understanding of the ideas and practices from the schools in Reggio through readings, presentations at the National Association for the Education of Young Children (NAEYC), videotapes, visiting The Hundred Languages of Children exhibit, and sharing in the enthusiastic experiences of a friend and colleague, Betty High Rounds of Sandhills Community College in North Carolina, who had visited Reggio twice in study tours and generously shared her slides with others in North Carolina. I even tried to describe Reggio in a chapter in my book *Developmentally Appropriate Practice: Curriculum and Development in Early Education.* I had worked as part of a committee to bring the traveling exhibit The Hundred Languages of Children to Winston-Salem, North Carolina, in early spring of 1997, along with visits from Lella Gandini and Carolyn Edwards. It was not until I was able to participate in a study tour to Reggio in May 1997 that I more fully began to comprehend the rich complexity of the Reggio system. Conversations with students and colleagues often led to frustration in attempting to interpret this complexity while trying to begin a dialog of reflection. So this new opportunity to reflect on what Reggio ideas could mean to our American practices was very appealing.

I also welcomed the opportunity to explore the work that American educators are doing as part of their own Reggio journeys. Since Americans first began to explore the impact of Reggio ideas, numerous programs became leaders in the process. The (now, unfortunately, closed) Model Early Childhood Center in Washington, D.C., and the work of the school in St. Louis, among others, were closely watched and supported by educators from Reggio Emilia, and documented early for those of us just beginning the learning process. For this book, I chose to visit and talk with educators who are active in their own education, reflection, and process of thoughtful practices, but whose efforts often are less documented. Through a series of visits, interviews, telephone conversations, videos, and e-mails, these thoughtful educators generously shared their insights and experiences with me. They have been on their own Reggio-inspired journeys anywhere from four to ten years, and have thoughtful answers to many questions that are part of the puzzling process for other educators seeking to discover how the example of Reggio may impact practice in America. They also have newly uncovered questions, provoking new thought for us all. Some of them are part of whole schools or programs that are working together to examine their educational experiences. Others are working separately in their own classrooms, hoping to interest others in co-constructing new understandings of teaching and learning. All of them, and others at their schools, would be quick to state that they are not a Reggio classroom or school, but are continually informed and inspired by the work in Reggio Emilia, and are moved to think about their teaching practices. Let me briefly introduce these educators to you.

Patti Cruikshank-Schott teaches five- and six-year-olds in a full-day program at Durham Early School, part of the Carolina Friends' School, an independent school in Durham, North Carolina. She began her Reggio-inspired work about four years ago after nearly thirty years of experiences teaching in programs with infants, family child care homes, public and private schools, and college classrooms. Patti's classroom reflects her interest in creating children's spaces that value home and a variety of cultures, and honor the beauty of the natural world. In fact, it was the Reggio emphasis on environment that first drew her attention. Although she works alone in her classroom with occasional student interns, the other teachers in the school—Cesanne Berry, Carmen Raynor-Waller, and Kate Parker—join Patti in the dialog about their program practices. As Patti says, they are intrigued by the image of the child, as well as the image of the teacher and parent suggested by Reggio. Together, they try to make the children's work and their own processes more visible through their use of documentation. Patti also shares her experiences through consulting with other programs. Beginning in the fall of 2000, Patti became the Director of Preschool Education at the World Bank Children's Center in Washington, D.C.

Margaret Edwards owns and directs Lakewood Avenue Children's School in Durham, North Carolina. After many years of teaching experience, Margaret wanted to open her own full-day child care program. Her dream became a small, family-oriented program located in an old house in a real neighborhood with a front porch children can play on, within walking distance of the grocery store where children can know the neighbors and the garbage man. Lakewood was the first full-day program in North Carolina to receive national accreditation by NAEYC in 1987, and in 1998, Lakewood was named as one of America's Top 10 Exemplary early childhood programs by High/Scope Educational Research Foundation in collaboration with NAEYC. Margaret virtually stumbled onto the example of Reggio. Given a trip on a study tour to Reggio as a gift from her family, Margaret says that she went with "Plan B in mind": to visit Bologna and Florence if the experience proved to be nothing new in early childhood education after the 30 years she had been in the field. She comments that the jargon was foreign to her, that she felt like a freshman in an upper level course, overwhelmed, exhilarated, and racing to keep up. She came home from Reggio ready to get her staff and the parents of her children excited about the Reggio ideas. The parents at Lakewood are closely involved in the program. Together, they created a beautiful environment using many ideas she had seen in the schools on her trip. Her staff, all with at least bachelors' degrees in early childhood education, has visited the schools in St. Louis, and several will visit Reggio in the near future. More about Lakewood Avenue Children's School can be found at www.lakewoodavenue.com.

Jeanne Goldhaber teaches in the early childhood teacher education program at the University of Vermont in Burlington, Vermont. Together with Dale Goldhaber, director of the Campus Children's Center, Dee Smith, director of the infant-toddler programs at the center, and other faculty and teaching staff at the center, Jeanne has been engaged in a ten-year exploration to incorporate the vision of Reggio's best practices into the work of the Children's Center and the teacher education curriculum. Recently, the entire Children's Center staff went on a study tour to Reggio. The Campus Children's Center functions as a lab school for the PreK–3 teacher education program, and also is a full-day, year-round child care program. The teacher education program has been restructured to provide students and faculty with opportunities to build collaborative relationships.

Documentation is something that has helped Jeanne, the faculty and teaching staff, and the students in the professional development program reflect together in meaningful ways. Jeanne is now involved in efforts to include leaders in her community and state in the reflection process.

Marty Gravett teaches preschoolers at the Sabot School in Richmond, Virginia. When she joined the teaching staff at Sabot five years ago, her knowledge and enthusiasm about Reggio practices influenced director Irene Carney to begin to change the curriculum directions of the school. Founded by parents in the early 1970s in an attempt to replicate British Infant School practices, the school already had an excellent program for young children. Now that all of the teachers are working together on implementing ideas adapted from Reggio, the school offers a working model of collaborative reflection and a community of relationships that are enriched by relationships with children and their families. Sabot also has been able to create a studio and hire a part-time studio teacher. An additional teacher in each classroom has allowed teachers to work more closely with small groups. Each year, the teachers at Sabot School create declarations of intentions by identifying the curriculum issues they will work on together during the year.

Lynn Hill is curriculum coordinator and studio teacher at the Child Development Lab School at Virginia Tech in Blacksburg, Virginia. When she was hired four years ago, she and Victoria Fu, professor of child development, began to work to integrate and blend the early childhood student coursework with what they were learning from Reggio. They reworked how they did things in the traditional course structure. They brought the students together in core groups based on relationships to work for six hours a week for the whole year with the lead teachers in the center. They began to negotiate curriculum based on abundant observation and written notes. Together, they and the students were coming to understand what it really means to be a teacher-researcher. Then the collaboration was extended to other teachers beyond the college and the preschool. Teachers at all learning levels, from preschool through college, collaborated on a year-long project called The Great Duck Pond Project. Meeting regularly, they formed a Reggio learning community and explored how to implement Reggio-inspired practices with their students in various negotiated investigations.

Pam Oken-Wright has been an early childhood educator for over 20 years, and currently teaches five-year-olds at St. Catherine's School in Richmond, Virginia. Pam works with occasional parent volunteers and an assistant. Other teachers in the private girls' school follow traditional teaching approaches, so Pam does much of her reflection and collaboration with more distant colleagues who are interested in the Reggio approach. She says she first realized she was following Reggio inspirations four or five years ago. She was already a cognitive constructivist and oriented to engaging the children in project explorations. She had begun to change the ways she mediated in the children's learning experiences. Pam's environment, a series of large, interconnected rooms with a glass-walled studio in one corner,

lends itself to individual explorations and activities. Pam found the documentation aspects of Reggio tremendously helpful in giving her a beginning point to an
image of powerful children that made so much sense. Pam shares her daily documentation notes with families over an e-mail link. Pam also consults nationwide
and writes when she has time.

Ann Pelo has taught preschoolers at Hilltop School, a full-day child care program in Seattle, Washington, since 1992. Her early teaching experience was in a
program that used a High/Scope curriculum, and influenced her to value play and
child-centered teaching. In the early years at Hilltop, Ann taught alone with her
own group of ten children in a small room. After an introduction to Reggio ideas
and practices, she began to think about what was important to the children and
to build the curriculum around their interests. In what Ann calls an example of
"synchronicity," several years later Sarah Felstiner came to teach at Hilltop. Sarah
also had been deeply impacted by Reggio. Their conversations began to center on
how they could collaborate in their work. A first decision was to combine their
groups, creating one group with eighteen children and two adults. They knocked
down everything but the walls, opening up their thinking and practices. The
smaller classroom became the art studio, a space for children to get involved with
representation of their learning. Together, the teachers learned how to use their
respective strengths, to focus together on really listening to the children, and
figure out what was going on in their play. Some of their extended project work
can be seen in the videos "Setting Sail" and "Thinking Big." After several years,
other staff became involved in sharing the Reggio-inspired vision. Ann teaches
other teachers, leading workshops about emergent, Reggio-inspired curriculum
and antibias practices. Her book, *That's Not Fair: A Teacher's Guide to Activism With
Young Children*, coauthored with Fran Davidson and available from Redleaf Press,
focuses on the intersection of the antibias curriculum goal of supporting children
to take action in the face of injustice with emergent, Reggio-inspired curriculum
practices.

Jane Watkins is the director of a half-day program for children ages two
through five at First Baptist Kindergarten in Greenville, South Carolina. The program was established as a kindergarten in 1952, and is one of the oldest programs
in the South. The program is quite large, with 36 teachers and 220 children. Jane
and her staff have been working with Reggio ideas and inspiration for nine years.
Jane recalls the enthusiasm while being present in the room at NAEYC's annual
conference where educations from Reggio shared their experiences. Soon after,
Jane and a number of staff and parents participated in a Reggio seminar at the
University of New Hampshire, what Jane refers to as "a week that changed us forever." The change came as they visited other Reggio-inspired programs and continued the dialog, moving away from familiar home turf. One of the teachers
commented that changing from where they were has been a bumpy journey, but
there is excitement in the building that radiates down the hallways filled with

documentation of past explorations. Everyone on staff is on the Reggio journey, taking the children and families into exciting new territory. For the last two years, the school has offered a symposium to share their experiences with others.

Other teachers noted in the book are those who worked with Sue Fraser in exploring Reggio ideas in their classrooms in British Columbia. These include several teachers from the Quadra Island Day Care, located in a rural setting on a large island across from Vancouver Island in British Columbia. Those teachers are Dee Conley, now the administrative director; Sherrie Fudikuf, whose early background included a major in education; Barb Lee, originally trained as a Nursery Nurse in England; Susan Emery, who had trained in Montessori; and Lise Burnett, whose early education included special education.

In the same community, Sue worked with Baerbel Jaeckel, a teacher at the Quadra Island Preschool, whose early education was in Munich, Germany. She had taught at the Quadra Waldorf School and the Quadra Island Day Care.

In Vancouver, in an urban setting, Sue worked with teachers at the Vancouver Child Study Center. When the University of British Columbia closed the laboratory school at the Child Study Center, a group of parents and some of the teachers ran the preschool under the administration of the university campus day care group. The teachers there are Patricia Breen, Gloria Rolfson, and Vivian Urquhart who all came to early childhood education from other backgrounds when their experience as parents interested them in the way young children learn. Together, they all had education in early childhood, and years of experience in the UBC Child Study Center before its transition from a lab school. Another teacher, Chava Rubenson, had studied in early childhood education in Stockholm, Sweden, and also had taught for a number of years at the lab school.

These are the teachers and schools that will help illuminate the principles and practices of the Reggio Emilia approach discussed in this book. For those new to the study of ideas from Reggio, the glossary may help clarify commonly used terms. It is the example of excellent theory-based practice developed in Reggio Emilia over fifty years that has inspired these educators and many hundreds more in schools and university programs around the country to reflect on what happens in their classrooms to best support children's learning. As Lilian Katz reminds us, rather than being concerned to adapt, adopt, interpret, translate, or transform Reggio in our classrooms,

> if we focus our collective and individual energies *on the quality of the day-to-day interactions of children and their teachers* in their moments together so that they become as rich, interesting, engaging, satisfying, and meaningful as we can see in the preprimary schools of Reggio Emilia, we will be shaping a pebble that could have very large consequences. . . . Their work is a challenge to the whole field around the world: the challenge to provide early childhood education that is worthy of all children (Katz, from the lecture "Images from the World," Reggio Emilia, June 1994, reprinted in *Rechild,* June 1997).

Every one of these teachers is doing her particular integration of theory and practice in her unique circumstances and setting. Every one states that hers is a work in progress, that the essence of a Reggio journey is that there is no place you finally get to; the process is the product. Studying and learning about the schools in Reggio Emilia opens the door to insight about one's own teaching and creates individual plans for one's next steps. It is the process of reflecting and acting that nourishes these teachers intellectually and emotionally. It is the hope of Susan Fraser and myself that their experiences will encourage other teachers to reflect on how best to work with the young children and families in their particular world.

Acknowledgments

As I complete this work for publication, there are a number of people whose contributions and assistance deserve acknowledgment. First is Sue Fraser, whose energy and vision created an example of trying to turn inspiration into practical reality. Then I must offer respect to the teachers who generously shared their time and insights about Reggio-inspired work with me, and cheerfully continued to respond to questions by means of e-mail. There was never the least hesitation in wanting to join in the conversation. Their ideas and experiences were intellectually stimulating and emotionally moving. It also is important to acknowledge others who helped me find these particular teachers: Victoria Fu, Betty High-Rounds, Irene Carney, and Diane Watkins. I feel certain that the teachers named also would want to acknowledge the collaborative work of the other teachers and directors with whom they work. I found it an awe-inspiring and somewhat humbling experience to learn what heroic efforts at change have involved all of these professionals.

I am also grateful for this current generation of early childhood education students at Central Piedmont Community College who confirm for me the importance of integrating theory with practice, and for my colleagues there who give me an environment for collaboration and reflection. I especially want to thank Charlotte Pfeifer who helped me with the children's books and who shares excitement about exploring Reggio. And always, I am grateful to my family who continue to teach me, as Malaguzzi said, that it's all about relationships. My personal wish is that my granddaughters Lila and Rose, indeed all children loved by their families and their society, will find a place to learn inspired by such teachers.

—*Carol Gestwicki*

This book would not have been written without the help of an amazing group of people. First, I must acknowledge my debt to Loris Malaguzzi and the educators in the municipal preschools in Reggio Emilia: their vision has become our inspiration. Among so many other things, they taught us the value of collaboration which is what writing this book has been all about. I would like to thank my colleagues at Douglas College: Cathleen Smith, who showed us the way, and Pat Brown, Elva Reid, Linda Moncur, Susan Swanson, and Ronnie Cahen, who shared their ideas and thoughts about Reggio Emilia with me and read each chapter, giving me suggestions about how it could be improved. I would like to thank Diana Stewart, our ECE technician, who does all the legwork for Children Teaching Teachers and makes sure that it functions smoothly. I would like to thank the Douglas College Daycare and the neighborhood centers that bring their children to our classrooms. Above all, I would like to thank teachers Dee Conley, Barbara Lee, Susan Emery, Lise Burnett, and Sherrie Fudikuf from the Quadra Island Day Care; Baerbel Jaeckel and the parents in the Quadra Island Preschool; and Chava Rubenson, Patricia Breen, Gloria Rolfsen, and Vivian Urquhart who have let me peer over their shoulders as they bravely embarked on this journey with me. I must thank Pat Tarr who also gave me many suggestions for improving the text, other contributors such as Betty Exelby, Mabel Higgins and Alex Doherty, and Linda and Craig Smith who lent me a room in which to write. I cannot leave out my family, especially my husband, Hugh Fraser, and his computer (who together did most of the work!), and my daughter, Joanna Annett, and her two children, Katrina and Amanda, who introduced me to the preschool and daycare center on Quadra Island. Perhaps the biggest thank you should go to the children themselves who so joyfully made this book possible.

—*Susan Fraser*

The authors would like to thank the following reviewers, enlisted by Delmar, for their helpful suggestions and constructive criticism:

Marion Fox Barnett, Ed.D.
Buffalo State College
Buffalo, NY

Audrey Beard, Ed.D.
Albany State University
Albany, GA

Nancy Carlson
Orange County Community College
Middletown, NY

Pamela Davis, Ph.D.
Henderson State University
Arkadelphia, AR

Kathleen Fite, Ed.D.
Southwest Texas State University
San Marcos, TX

Meryl Glass
San Francisco State University
San Francisco, CA

Tracey Keyes
Kutztown University
Kutztown, PA

Cindy Leigh, Ed.D.
The University of Mississippi
University, MS

Chapter **1**

Experiencing Reggio Emilia

The Reggio Emilia approach produces for the adults, but above all for the children, a feeling of belonging in a world that is alive, welcoming and authentic.

—*Loris Malaguzzi*

Questions to Consider:

- What leads delegations from all over the world to visit Reggio Emilia, a small city in northern Italy?

- What makes the greatest impression on delegations as they observe the preschools and listen to the educators in Reggio Emilia describe and explain their approach?

- What are the major historical and cultural factors that have shaped the Reggio Emilia approach?

- Which theorists have influenced the educators in Reggio Emilia in developing their approach to early childhood education?

- What pedagogical principles are part of the Reggio Emilia approach?

FIRST IMPRESSIONS OF THE REGGIO EMILIA PRESCHOOLS

For many educators, their first exposure to the principles and practices of the Reggio Emilia approach to early childhood education elicits an emotional response. Ann Pelo recalls being moved to tears at a first viewing of the video "To Make a Portrait of a Lion" at a staff meeting. Her words are: "It was like coming home and leaving everything; I was coming home and having my deepest feelings as a teacher being named. There was a pleasant tension, with some ideas so resonant, and some so revolutionary." Patti Cruikshank-Schott recalls going into what she and others have referred to as "the Italian room" at the National Association for the Education of Young Children (NAEYC) annual conference in Washington, D.C., in 1990, and feeling the incredible energy in the room. "It felt like angels had come, who were saying things no one had said about teaching before." Jeanne Goldhaber describes it as being "pretty knocked out, as Reggio offered us a vision of how we might strengthen what we did." Sue Fraser attributes her deep emotional response to the way the Reggio experiences connected with her memories of childhood and what she wanted for all children, as described fully in her book, *Authentic Childhood, Experiencing Reggio Emilia in the Classroom,* published by Nelson Canada in 1999. Margaret Edwards visited Reggio without a great deal of prior knowledge about the philosophy and practices, but with an initial belief born of thirty years of teaching experience that "there was not a lot that wasn't the same ideas being re-named." She came home ready to excite her staff about the new vision. Each experience was unique, and each echoed the feelings of many other educators in discovering in the practices and articulated philosophy from the schools in Reggio Emilia something that resonated within their best ideas of working with children and families. Most American educators share the theoretical foundation of the schools in Reggio so the experience is not starting from the beginning. But the vision of excellence in teaching and learning has inspired many teachers to want to learn more and to revisit their own practices. For many, the inspiration from Reggio and the emotion it engenders become the beginning of a journey of discovery started anew.

For many, the journey will be through reading, videos, dialog, and reflection with colleagues. For some, the journey includes a trip to see the programs first-hand. After a long airplane trip and an hour's bus ride from Milan across the fertile plains of the Po Valley, thousands of early childhood educators from around the world arrive each year in Reggio Emilia, a small city in industrial northern Italy. Over 600 foreign delegations from 35 countries, a total of over 10,000 people, have visited the preschools and infant-toddler centers in Reggio Emilia since 1981. Such notable individuals as Howard Gardner, Jerome Bruner, Lilian Katz, and many others have come to learn about the early education system that has been developed in this city over the past 50 years. Many others have seen and marveled at the touring exhibit, "The Hundred Languages of Children," that has traveled around North America since 1987. What is the reason for the focus of this interest in the schools in this city? The reasons are complex, and unfold slowly as visitors experience and reflect.

Arriving visitors begin to explore the old historic city in the heart of Reggio Emilia, a place where the Italian flag was born over 200 years ago. They stroll the square, by day the site of the bustling market for goods of all sorts from fresh vegetables to elegant clothing. In the quiet evening when the market stalls are gone, the square is presided over by two majestic stone lions guarding the entrance to an ancient church at the far end of the square. The lion statues are very old and are believed to have been brought to Italy from Egypt by the Romans. The statues hold particular interest for those who have seen the video of the children in the Diana School investigating the lion in a long-term project (To Make a Portrait of a Lion, 1987). For many, it was the photographs of the children's concentrated study and amazing representation of these lions in pencil, ink, and clay that made them want to come to Reggio Emilia and see the schools for themselves.

Figure 1–1.   The ancient statues of the lions are familiar to the thousands who have seen the video To Make a Portrait of a Lion. (*Courtesy:* Betty High Rounds.)

After gazing at the lions and touching the ancient, worn surface of the stone, visitors continue to walk through the narrow, winding streets of the city, passing many small shops. When stopping to gaze at the goods beautifully displayed in the windows, they marvel at the value placed on aesthetics in this culture. They may enter the public gardens and walk through the grass to the far end of the park. They linger to look at an old stone fountain covered in moss, recognizing it as the one studied by the children from La Villetta school in the videotape "Amusement Park for Birds" (Performaneutics Press, 1994).

The children in La Villetta school showed particular interest in the birds that visited the large meadow surrounding the school. In 1990 to 1991, the children made birdhouses and built an environment showing the meadow from a bird's perspective with the help of their teachers and *atelierista* (a curriculum specialist with art training), Giovanni Piazza. George Forman of the University of Massachusetts visited Reggio Emilia in 1992, and he and Lella Gandini asked Amelia Gambetti, one of the teachers in La Villetta school, and Giovanni Piazza to help them understand how a project (progettazione) is carried out. The teachers realized from their conversations that the children were interested in making things that the birds would enjoy. One child suggested building an amusement park for the birds. Other children then came up with ideas such as a ticket booth, a waterwheel that the birds could use as a diving board, an elevator to return baby birds to their nests, fountains, and a lake for the birds to sail on. Giovanni and the teachers made a flow chart of all the ideas from which they selected two main ones, fountains and waterwheels, that they felt would be particularly interesting for the children to develop further.

They took the children to the park to see and sketch the fountains. When they returned to school, they encouraged the children to draw their ideas about fountains and how they worked. The teachers projected onto an easel a slide of the fountain the children had sketched in the park so they could draw their ideas of how the water circulated inside the fountain. The children built clay models from their drawings of the fountains. They made graphic designs of waterwheels and then transferred their ideas by building wheels first with paper and then with construction materials. They tested their wheels in an indoor water tank they had constructed earlier, attached to the sink in the atelier. Giovanni helped the children solve problems such as how to attach the paddles at the correct angle so the water turned the wheel. They built pinwheels to help them understand how water and air could act as a source of energy to make wheels turn. Eventually, the weather was warm enough to start building the amusement park outside in the meadow. More and more people became involved in the project. The municipality provided water pipes to the meadow so the children could attach hoses to fill the lake they made for the birds, work the fountains, and turn the waterwheels. The children and Giovanni built a large table to feed the birds and a blind for bird-watching. Members of the local Audubon society helped the children place birdhouses high up in the trees to attract more birds to the park. The parents also helped build many of the pieces of equipment the children had designed. An invitation was placed in the local newspaper announcing the time when the mayor would open the Amusement Park for Birds. People in the community, families, children, and teachers from all the other schools in Reggio Emilia, and even the children's pets came to the opening of the park. The cooks made an enormous layer cake in the shape of a fountain to celebrate the occasion. Still years later, when delegations visited La Villetta school, they see the amusement park and are able to read from the documentation displayed on the walls the story of how the children and their teachers, with the help of the atelieriste, Giovanni Piazza, built the Amusement Park for Birds. A long-term project of this kind is one of the distinguishing features of the curriculum approach in the preschools in Reggio Emilia. In Chapter 7, we will continue to consider this amusement park project to help us understand the method of developing curriculum.

Later in the journey around the town, visitors come upon a squat building surrounded by a fence. This is the famous Diana School, designated by *Newsweek* magazine in 1991 as the best nursery school in the world. Walking around the building, many are surprised at how similar the building is to many of the child care centers in America. Diana School is housed in an unpretentious building that might have been designed for any purpose. There is a playground, but unlike most centers in North America, it has no large, brightly colored plastic climbing equipment.

Figure 1–2.
These delightful fountains and
waterwheels in the Amusement
Park for Birds at La Villetta School
are part of one of the long-term
projects for which the schools in
Reggio Emilia are known.

Instead, there are gnarled trees ideal for climbing and a large concrete tunnel covered with a mound of earth.

Even visiting several schools during the week of the typical study tour, visitors often are overwhelmed by how much there is to see and learn. It takes much reflection to begin to understand the approach and even more to uncover the implications for one's own practice. What is perhaps most impressive is how well the philosophy, theory, and practice are integrated into a cohesive program that so clearly reflects the values of the Italian culture.

As Howard Gardner said in a CNN interview when asked how well the Reggio approach could be transported to other parts of the world: "I think that it's a

Figure 1–3.   The Diana School, in the middle of a public park in Reggio Emilia, was called one of the ten best schools in the world.

mistake to take any school approach and assume, like a flower, that you can take it from one soil and put it into another one. That never works. This doesn't mean at all that Americans can't learn a tremendous amount from it, but we have to reinvent it" (Rechild, April, 1998). Immersion in the images of Reggio, whether by means of a visit, or by study and dialog at home allows educators to begin to understand what aspects of the approach are important to our practice, and what changes have to happen to make those aspects thrive.

The educators in Reggio Emilia welcome visitors to observe the programs and listen to lectures about their philosophy, principles, and practices, but they stress that the Reggio approach is not a method that can be taught; it is "a way of thinking about children, schools, education, and life. You may learn more about Reggio, and also learn more yourself and your experiences." (Rinaldi, Presentation in Reggio, May, 1997). And in the spirit of circular reflection and dialog that typifies the Reggio approach, they welcome the opportunity to see themselves through visitors' eyes and questions as a mirror, hoping it will help them find even more new questions to explore. They also warn that it would be impossible to duplicate the approach elsewhere because the Reggio Emilia approach evolved in a particular cultural context, was shaped by historical forces, and was nurtured by social conditions present only at that time and place. These forces came together to enable the educators in the municipal preschools in Reggio Emilia to develop what is likely the highest-quality early childhood practice in the world today.

THE HISTORY OF REGGIO EMILIA SCHOOLS

The experience of the schools in Reggio is rooted in the reality of that particular city. In the spring of 1945, only days following the end of World War II, the people of a small village called Villa Cella several miles from the town of Reggio embarked on a courageous and visionary task. Out of the devastation left behind by the war, men and women were determined to build a school, beginning the construction with money "from the sale of an abandoned war tank, a few trucks, and some horses left behind by the retreating Germans" (Malaguzzi in Edwards, Gandini, & Forman, 1998, p. 50). Loris Malaguzzi's words:

> I am lucky enough to remember it all very clearly. The news was that the people at Villa Cella had started to build a school for children. They were taking bricks from the bombed-out houses and were using them to build the walls of the school . . . My modest preconceptions were blown away: that the idea of building a school would even occur to ordinary people, women, laborers, workers, farmers, was already traumatic enough. The fact that these same people, with no money, no technical assistance, authorization or committees, no school inspectors or party leaders, were working side by side, brick by brick to construct the building was the second shock . . . It turned logic and prejudice, the old rules of pedagogy and of culture upside down. It set everything back to square one, and opened up completely new horizons . . . I perceived that this was a formidable human and cultural lesson from which extraordinary things would spring. We just needed to join forces and work together. (Malaguzzi in Barazzone, R, 1985. Reprinted in a pamphlet from the Scuola Comunale dell'infanzia, XXV Aprile).

From the beginning, Loris Malaguzzi played a central role in the development of the schools, providing much of the inspiration and leadership as the schools evolved their own philosophy over the years. Incidentally, that first school is still part of the Reggio Emilia system of municipally operated preschools. Named April 25th School in honor of the day of Allied liberation from the Fascist regime, the plaque out front bears this stirring inscription: "Men and women working together, we built the walls of this school because we

Figure 1–4.   The April 25th school has an important place in the history of the preschools in Reggio Emilia.

wanted a new and different place for our children. May 1945." That first school began with the sense of community and shared purpose that is so evident today in the schools of Reggio.

Political equality enabled women to play a powerful role in the community in this part of Italy. The women in Reggio Emilia used their experience of working in informal networks to organize and seek rights for themselves and for their children. In addition, an organized group, the Union of Italian Women, contributed to the formation of the first schools by providing child care for the children of working women. Reggio Emilia historically has had a high level of employment of women (Sandra Piccinni, oral communication, May, 1997).

The Sociocultural Perspective

The municipal preschools in Reggio Emilia evolved in a unique social system. For a long time, there had been a strong movement toward democracy in this region of Italy; in fact, the first declaration of democracy was made in 1797 from the balcony of La Posta, a building that is currently a hotel used by visiting delegations. Since World War II, Reggio Emilia has had a socialist municipal government. The philosophy that is the foundation of the Reggio Emilia system has emerged from this sociocultural perspective. The social constructivist approach to education, the high level of community participation in the preschools, and the emphasis on collaboration among children, teachers, families, and the community are examples of the Reggio Emilia philosophy put into practice.

The belief in society's collective responsibility for young children is apparent in the importance given to issues such as child care in Reggio Emilia. Many of the practices in the schools such as the lack of a hierarchy in the staff and the emphasis placed on collaboration, reflect the policies of the elected municipal government and the socialist leanings of the people of the region.

In 1963, the first municipally run school (as differentiated from parent-run schools) for preschool children was opened in Reggio Emilia. This represented a major step for the people, affirming the right for secular schools rather than those run by the Catholic Church in a rather exclusive monopoly. A debate raged all over Italy for the next few years about the right of the state and municipalities to establish such secular schools. Finally, in 1967, a national law was passed that entitled every child between three and six years of age to attend a publicly supported early childhood education program. Parents were given the choice of enrolling their children in national, municipal, or private preschools. That same year, the municipality of Reggio Emilia took the lead in Italy by assuming the administration of the parent-run schools.

In 1970, Reggio Emilia educators also became innovators by opening the first infant–toddler centers (called *asilo nido*) one year before the provision of child care for children under three became law in Italy (Edwards, Gandini, & Forman, 1998, pp. 44–54). By 1997, the municipality supported 19 preschools and 13 infant–toddler centers, serving about 50 percent of the children who attended preschool in the city. Today, although the municipality seems to have a strong commitment to early childhood education, teachers have had to become strong advocates, and fight for funds and services that support the quality of education to which they believe young children are entitled. In 1998, 12 percent of the city budget was spent on providing child care for children six years and under. The school committee, *La Consulta*, which includes administrators, teachers, and elected community members, debates many of the issues relating to child care. This committee is able to influence policy at the municipal level (New, 1998).

Theoretical Influences

Loris Malaguzzi, philosophical leader of the Reggio approach, when speaking to a delegation in 1993, said, "Here all theorists are put together in an unusual way." He told the delegation that the educators in Reggio Emilia had used many theoretical perspectives in building their philosophy. He said that they were interested in studying Piaget to learn "how the individual constructs knowledge," but that they also were interested in studying Vygotsky's theory to understand how children co-construct knowledge in social situations.

Loris Malaguzzi visited the United States early in his career, and he took back to Reggio Emilia many of the principles he had seen put into practice there, including the ideas of John Dewey. John Dewey (1859–1952) believed that a child should learn "through and in relation to living." Dewey, according to Malaguzzi, "urged a method of education combining pragmatic philosophy, new psychological knowledge, and—on the teaching side—mastery of content with inquiring, creative experiences for children," while also "seeking a new relationship between educational and sociocultural research" (Malaguzzi in Edwards, Gandini, & Forman, 1998, p. 78). Dewey developed a child-centered curriculum in which children were educated for living in the reality of the modern world. He felt that education was a process of living instead of a preparation for future living. Like Friedrich Wilhelm Froebel, who founded the first kindergarten in 1837, Dewey believed in the value of play in education; however, Dewey's concept of play was more open. He felt that the gifts such as the spheres, cubes, and cylinders that Froebelian teachers used with children were too artificial and abstract for children to relate to. He recommended that teachers create a dramatic play corner in the classroom, and that children be given real materials such as carpentry tools and cooking utensils to dramatize everyday living experiences. He called these "real, familiar, direct, straightforward materials." Dewey also believed that children should be encouraged to reproduce their own experiences in imaginative form and that children should be allowed to practice and learn how to live in a democratic society. Dewey encouraged teachers to plan the program based on the children's interests and, at the same time, to be responsible for weaving traditional subject matter into the child's school experiences (Dewey, 1897). He felt that children would develop the inner motivation to learn if teachers gave them the freedom to construct knowledge from their own investigations. This was the beginning of the project approach, a method implemented in many early childhood programs today.

These ideas of John Dewey would have been apparent in many of the early childhood programs that Loris Malaguzzi visited in the United States. For instance, Malaguzzi probably would have seen children actively involved in play, and using real materials and tools. He would have noted "democracy in action" as children interacted in the social group and were encouraged to solve their own problems with the teachers' support. He would have seen the children engaged in activities such as using a carpenter's bench in constructing a birdcage or setting up a grocery store for dramatic play in the classroom. The teachers would have chosen these experiences because they had relevance in the children's lives. Loris Malaguzzi shared these ideas with the teachers in Reggio Emilia, and eventually Dewey's principles became an important part of the philosophy of their schools. Malaguzzi told the delegation in 1993 that "Dewey and Reggio Emilia are similar [because] . . . the unity of the social life and subject matter are related."

This philosophical position uniting the life in society and the content of learning in the schools, brought Dewey's philosophy in as a crucial element of the Reggio approach, and was an important connection, for it embedded the Reggio Emilia approach within the mainstream of educational ideas that reach back to Jean Jacques Rousseau (1789–1802) through to Johann Heinrich Pestalozzi (1746–1827), and on to Friedrich Wilhelm Froebel (1782–1852). This connection with other philosophies gives the Reggio Emilia approach an organic root that is shared with early childhood education in other parts of the world. Instead of becoming a closed system, as in the Waldorf and Montessori schools, the Reggio Emilia approach is free to grow and develop, and crossfertilization can happen between programs. The principles that have evolved in the preschools in Reggio Emilia, therefore, have meaning to many other early childhood programs. Indeed, it is because of the shared theoretical understandings that most American educators can consider the Reggio Emilia approach without major philosophical or intellectual leaps, and they can focus on the vision of excellence in applying those mutually understood theories.

GUIDING PRINCIPLES OF THE REGGIO EMILIA APPROACH

The following are some of the concepts of the Reggio Emilia approach that became increasingly evident during a visit to Reggio Emilia:

- *the image of the child*—the cornerstone of Reggio Emilia experiences conceptualizes an image of the child as competent, strong, inventive, and full of ideas with rights instead of needs

- *environment as a third teacher*—preparing an environment that acts as a third teacher carefully designed to facilitate the social constructions of understanding, and to document the life within the space

- *relationships*—seeing the importance of relationships physically in the way objects are displayed in the classroom; socially and emotionally in the interactions of the people in the environment; and intellectually in the approach to learning that is always seen in context and depends on co-construction of knowledge

- *collaboration*—working together at every level through collaboration among teachers, children and teachers, children and children, children and parents, and the larger community

- *documentation*—providing a verbal and visual trace of the children's experiences and work, and opportunities to revisit, reflect, and interpret

- *progettazione*—this difficult to translate Italian word means making flexible plans for the further investigation of ideas, and devising the means for carrying them out in collaboration with the children, parents, and, at times, the larger community

- *provocation*—listening closely to the children and devising a means for provoking further thought and action

- *one hundred languages of children*—encouraging children to make symbolic representations of their ideas and providing them with many different kinds of media for representing those ideas

- *transparency*—creating transparency through the light that infuses every space and in the mirrors, light tables, and glass jars that catch and reflect the light around the classroom; and metaphorically in the openness to ideas and theories from other parts of the world, and in the availability of information for parents and visitors

This is not a finite list of the principles fundamental to the Reggio Emilia approach but a selection of some of the important ones that many visitors take away with them after visiting the preschools in Reggio Emilia. These principles will be discussed in more detail in subsequent chapters.

The Environment as a Reflection of Reggio Emilia Principles

Each of the schools in Reggio has a different flavor with its own culture evolved over time. For example, the buildings in which the schools are housed vary; some, like Diana School, are public buildings, and others, like La Villetta, are formerly private houses. The educators in Reggio Emilia have created environments for children that are truly beautiful. Every space, whether the floor, ceilings, windows, or hallways, reflects a concern for providing children with an aesthetic and stimulating environment. There are many surprises including unusual arrangements of furniture. For example, two small armchairs are placed in a curtained alcove in front of a series of large pictures telling the story of "Little Red Riding Hood." Later in the day, the municipal puppeteer will perform the story for the children. And there is a little mattress with piles of soft pillows tucked into an alcove at the top of the stairs with a small window looking out to the roof, and a mural of clouds that suggests cloud-gazing and dreaming. The use of materials is also unexpected. Colored tubes connect classrooms, spinning disks hang on walls, masks hang from the ceiling, and leaves are pressed against the windowpanes. Mirrors are placed everywhere including on the ceiling, floor, and lining the sides of a large prism-shaped house built for children to climb in and see unexpected images of themselves.

Food plays an important part in Italian culture, and this value is reflected in the time spent making the presentation of food attractive and enjoyable for the children. Tables are set with brightly colored tablecloths, candles, and small bowls of flowers. A water container shaped like a wine bottle and glasses are provided at each table for the children to serve themselves. The menu, consisting of large photographs of different kinds of pasta and fruit, is displayed prominently on the wall. One menu shows a photograph of tuna molded into the shape of a fish with eyes and fins made from sliced red peppers. The dining room is designed to look like children's homes, with dried peppers and garlic hanging on the walls, and attractive arrangements of glass bottles containing beans, oils, and herbs displayed next to colorful pottery and plants on a large credenza.

Respect is shown for the families of the children in the way the space is planned to welcome their presence in the school. The schools are easily accessible from the street, rather than surrounded by vast parking lots. Many children arrive on foot and on the back of a bicycle (but more often on the front so they can see where they are going). The entrance hall is furnished with comfortable chairs for parents to invite them to take the time to make the transition between home and school gently. Shelves display the children's work, and a portfolio for each child is available in the infant and toddler classrooms so parents can see what their children have been doing in school. Documentation displayed on panels on the walls of the classrooms also shows parents and visitors the children's experiences in school. These documentations include commentaries, photographs, and examples of the children's work to provide a record of the process the children and teachers follow as a learning experience unfolds. On the floor below the documentations or on shelves nearby are indoor plants, bowls of flowers, or a few beautiful objects to examine. Windows in the interior walls of the buildings allow parents and visitors a view of the classrooms within. Light is everywhere—clear natural light or light reflected by mirrors and through colored glass infusing every space—because transparency is an important principle in Reggio Emilia schools as well as a metaphor that explains the philosophy of openness to families, the community, and to ideas.

Another principle reflected in the design of the environment is the importance of social relationships. Reggio Emilia, like other Italian cities, has a piazza, or public square, that is the hub of the city. Here, people gather for events, meet to discuss politics or other issues, or just linger to socialize. At lunch time and in the evening, the piazza is filled with groups of people absorbed in earnest discussions and families strolling around, chatting, and greeting friends. This social practice is clearly reflected in the way the schools have been designed. Many of the classrooms open onto a piazza providing a familiar place for children, teachers, and visitors to meet socially. The piazza allows freedom of movement between the classrooms and other areas of the school. The children are not confined to their own classroom, but can mingle with the children in other rooms in the school. For instance, the children from all three classes in Diana School are able to use the piazza and, if they wish, to dress up in the clothes arranged on circular dividers in this central meeting place.

The arrangement of space has been carefully thought out so that every part of the building has a purpose. There are places where children can work together in small groups or in larger groups with a teacher. For example, platforms are built into corners of the room to provide a separate space for small groups of children to build with blocks of various sorts. Clear plastic strips hanging from the ceiling form a transparent curtain that separates the platform from the rest of the open space in the room. Low bleachers are built in the classrooms and provide an area where larger groups of children and teachers can meet to share experiences and discuss their plans for the day. Loris Malaguzzi, in emphasizing the importance of interaction, said, "I believe there is no possibility of existing without relationship. Relationship is a necessity of life" (Kaufman, 1993, p. 287). The support of a complex variety of relationships is the enduring focus of decisions in the schools.

Routines are minimal in the Reggio schools. The children are not interrupted by unnecessary transitions from one activity to the next as so often happens in schools in other parts of the world. In a Reggio Emilia classroom, there are times to eat, sleep, and meet with the group, but there are few unnecessary interruptions in the children's day. This is thought to be one of the reasons the children can become so absorbed in a lengthy project such as the Amusement Park for Birds. The teachers and children arrive in the morning, spend some time socializing or playing, and then gather to plan the day. Some children may already be working on a project and after the group meeting, leave together to carry on with it. Other children may have a new idea they want to pursue or may decide to do one of the activities that are available every day such as painting at the easels, building with the many different kinds of blocks available, or playing with the beautiful natural objects set out in the housekeeping area of the classroom.

The children who have been chosen to help the cook leave the classroom a little earlier than the others to help set up the lunch tables or to prepare and serve the food. Some teachers eat with the children, but most teachers eat on their own or, sometimes, with visitors to the preschools. The auxiliary staff supervises the children during this time.

After lunch, the children usually have a long siesta and spend a relaxed afternoon playing outside if they stayed inside during the morning. Most children are picked up by four o'clock unless parents have made special arrangements for them to stay later. The teachers then have additional time to meet and discuss the observations they made of the children, and to go over any problems that may have arisen. This is also a time to make future plans based on their observations during the day.

The environment in all the classrooms gives the visitor a sense that it is a good place for children to be. There are many activities that are similar to those in early childhood centers in other parts of the world such as blocks, housekeeping materials, games, and puzzles on shelves beside low tables, but some areas such as the atelier, or studio, are unique. The atelier on the top floor of the house at La Villetta school is filled with interesting materials beautifully displayed and work that the children are doing with the atelierista who is a part of the teaching team in every school in Reggio Emilia. Each atelier seems to reflect the unique character of the atelierista. At La Villetta, for example, the atelier is filled with mechanical constructions that the children built with atelierista Giovanni Piazza, whereas at Diana School, the atelier displays the beautiful clay pieces the children were doing with atelierista Vea Vecchi. The documentation on the walls of the ateliers and in the classrooms tells the story of the children and teacher's investigations. The viewer sees not only the finished products, but the steps in the process as well.

The teachers are intensely involved in what the children are thinking, saying, and doing. They are present for the children and actively engaged with them in their activities. The teachers are either helping the children as they work with the materials, sitting beside them discussing something of interest, or sitting close by, observing and recording their actions and conversations. Sometimes, the teachers set up a tape recorder to capture the children's conversation or they videotape the children at work. This level of awareness and involvement of the teachers with the children contributes to the high quality of the programs that amazes visitors to the Reggio Emilia schools.

The social relationships that are developed in the schools of Reggio Emilia are the fabric into which everything else is woven. These social relationships go beyond the classroom walls to reach out to families and the community. Each school has a parent–teacher committee that meets every month. There are also meetings arranged throughout the year to provide an opportunity for parents and teachers to get to know one another and exchange ideas. The teachers try to create a community that uses the parent's particular skills. Lella Gandini has said that in

Figure 1–5.   These photographs show an outdoor atelier at La Villetta School
with natural materials carefully
displayed to provoke exploration
and creativity.

Reggio Emilia, "parents have a sense of belonging and their voices are visible. We believe in the potential of parents and we as teachers should help this to emerge."

Therefore, the environment in the schools in Reggio Emilia reflects the layers of meaning in the whole philosophy. As the educators in Reggio Emilia frequently tell us, the various aspects of the program are an intricately connected system; it is impossible to work with only one aspect without affecting the whole. No matter what entry point is used by educators trying to work with Reggio ideas, they find themselves and their practice being influenced in multiple and interrelated ways.

The entry points have been uniquely individual. For Jeanne Goldhaber at the University of Vermont Campus Children's Center, after a first visit to the schools in Reggio, the beginning was in consideration of the environment. At the time, they were changing from preschool lab setting to a newly configured child care program, and with everything new, it was the perfect time to begin considering the environment. The environmental changes led to beginning investigations with the children, very tentative at first. Within a couple of years, when going back to Reggio for a second visit, she knew that what she wanted to focus on was documentation, to create a program based on observation and reflection moving to see how to provoke children's understanding.

Margaret Edwards of Lakewood Avenue Children's School also began with the environment. After a trip to Reggio, she shared her slides of the schools with a group of parents. Three parents were particularly interested in architecture and design, and they poured over the slides with her, pointing out features of light, connections between spaces, and aesthetic components. Margaret says with a smile, "Everybody always says don't copy, but copying worked for us. We got our ideas from the slides about light, transparency, connections, beautiful and home-like setting, and that was our beginning. Everything came from those changes." Together, they began to transform the environment, and then to see the incredible impact of environment on the children's behavior and explorations. As curriculum emerged, parents were draw into the process, and documentation became a necessity for sharing ideas back and forth with them. This is an example of not imitating in a merely superficial way—adding a light table and several mirrors and expecting instant transformation—but of opportunities to revisit previous understandings and engage in ongoing dialog and reflection.

It also was the work on the environment that contributed to the sense of collaboration and reflection as Lynn Hill worked with the other faculty at the Child Development Lab School at Virginia Tech. "We rolled up our sleeves and all pitched in. But the important piece was being able to articulate to each other why we were doing things." It became a tangible way of working and reflecting together.

When Louise Cadwell spoke of arriving at the College School in St. Louis after a time of working in the schools in Reggio, she described her heart sinking as she entered through "heavy, darkly stained wooden doors into a small, windowless room," and then into the "predominantly dull beige and dark, cavernous space of the preschool" (Cadwell, 1997, p. 60). "How do I tell them that we can't do it here? We can't make something from nothing. How can we try to put an approach that is centered around light, order, and beauty into practice in a dark, ugly space?" (p. 61). Nevertheless, Cadwell went on to speak of beginning with three aspects of the Reggio ideas: learning how to have conversations of quality with small groups of children; working to enhance children's natural abilities in using the languages of artistic expression; and creating an environment that was beautiful, filled with light, inviting, and orderly.

Other teachers began with documentation, finding that as a vehicle to form their understandings of powerful, strong children and their own role in co-constructing knowledge with children. Patti Cruikshank-Schott of the Carolina Friends School was first attracted to Reggio ideas because of the attention to the environment, finding that a match for her own ideas and practice about creating beauty for children. But beginning the process of documenting the traces of children's minds held particular power for her, making her watch what she did in a whole different way. Pam Oken-Wright of St. Catherine's School also found her beginning point in documentation. Her daily journal entries allowed her to revisit the learning process and come to new places in her thinking. Parents came to almost demand participation as they followed the progress of explorations through daily e-mail communication.

In a recent Internet dialog on the Reggio list, many other teachers agreed that documentation was an important entry point for implementing Reggio ideas because it contributed to transformation of the environment, support of learning, communication, and relationships of all participants, and required deep reflection on children's thinking and investigations. One of the participants in the dialog argued that a great deal had to go on before documentation could happen: that teachers first had to understand the image of the strong child and let go of the teacher role of dispenser of information. The answer of several teachers was that it was, in fact, through the process of critical thinking, note taking, and recording— in short, documentation—that they were able to change their image of the child and reflect on their own practice. One said: Documenting is to Reggio work as turning the soil is to gardening.

Ann Pelo of Hilltop School and Marty Gravett of Sabot School each tell similar stories of individually beginning with the intent of thoughtful planning around their curriculum. Marty said "The curriculum was not emerging. The art was on the level of decoration or design, not representation." Ann loved the idea of sparking children's interest and building projects around them. But this led to the taking of copious notes and transcribing tapes as each searched for the threads that would allow investigations to grow out of the children's actions and questions. This led to, as Marty called it, "the culture of engagement" as adults came together to reflect. For Ann, it led to an increased emphasis on revisiting and representation. Later, the opportunity to work with another teacher meant rethinking the environment, with lots of practice in collaboration on thinking about the space that could then lead to reflecting on what was going on with the children in the space.

No matter what the entry point, the philosophy of the Reggio approach is so intertwined and circular that, when teachers inspired by the model begin to change practices, they find themselves eventually working with all components of the complex system. Nothing can work in isolation.

The Image of the Child

The cornerstone of our experience, based on practice, theory and research, is the image of the children as rich, strong and powerful. The emphasis is placed on seeing the children as unique subjects with rights rather than simply needs. They have potential, plasticity, the desire to grow, curiosity, the ability to be amazed, and the desire to relate to other people and to communicate.

—Carlina Rinaldi

Questions to Consider:

• What are the major theoretical perspectives that have influenced the image of the child in Reggio Emilia?

• What image of the child emerges from an understanding of each of these theoretical perspectives?

• How have the educators in Reggio Emilia interpreted their image of the child based on these theories?

• What important principles relate to the inclusion of children who need extra support in Reggio Emilia?

INFLUENCES ON THE REGGIO EMILIA APPROACH

Each of us holds deep down an image of the child. This image has many reflections. First, there is the subjective, personal one, the one known from our individual experiences as a child. Then there is the objective, empirical one, the one constructed from observing and thinking about the children we meet in our journey through life. But the strongest image of all is the cultural one, the one that is shaped by the values and beliefs about what childhood should be.

Every society has particular hopes for children and certain expectations of children. As Carlina Rinaldi said, "Each society creates its image of childhood and of its child" (Rinaldi, Spring 1999, p. 1). Several questions necessitate reflection on basic social ideas: Who is the child? What is childhood? How does a child learn? What is the meaning of education? The answers to these questions are socially constructed and culturally situated (New, 1999). The first schools in Reggio Emilia were created, as discussed in Chapter 1, in the wake of the destruction of World War II. The mayor of Reggio Emilia in the 1960s commented that the fascist experience had "taught them that people who conformed and obeyed were dangerous, and that in building a new society it was imperative to safeguard and communicate that lesson, and nurture and maintain a vision of children who can think and act for themselves" (Dahlberg in Dahlberg et al., 1999, p. 12). The Reggio image of the strong, powerful child, rich in resources, was created in this social context. In Reggio, they are aware that this construction is a choice they have made, a choice that reverberates in all directions through their philosophy.

Reggio educators continually indicate the central position to their pedagogical philosophy and practices of the image they hold of the child. As Rinaldi said in the quote that began this chapter, the cornerstone of the Reggio philosophy is the strong, competent, rich image of the child. And the rich child produces other riches. "They argue that 'if you have a rich child in front of you, you become a rich pedagogue and you have rich parents', but if instead you have a poor child, 'you become a poor pedagogue and have poor parents'" (Dahlberg et al., 1999, p. 50). A rich child is not an empty vessel waiting to be filled, but is one born equipped to engage actively and immediately in learning. As such, young children must be treated with seriousness, recognizing that their ideas are worth listening to and exploring with them. Therefore, embedded within this image of the strong, competent child are implied all the principles of an appropriate educational system. Tiziana Filippini, another pedagogista in Reggio Emilia, says: "Our image of the child has evolved out of our collective experience and a continually reexamined understanding of educational philosophy and psychological theory" (Filippini in Edwards, Gandini, & Forman, 1998, p. 128).

When Loris Malaguzzi himself was asked about sources of inspiration for the philosophy of the schools in Reggio Emilia, he listed some twenty-five names, some familiar to American educators, others less so (Edwards, Gandini, & Forman, 1998, pp. 59–60).

This is important when trying to understand the image that the educators in Reggio Emilia hold of the child. The philosophies and theories of a number of people, including Erik Erikson, John Dewey, Jean Piaget, Barbara Biber, and Lev Vygotsky, have been integrated into the Reggio Emilia approach. It is necessary, therefore, in trying to understand the approach, to first understand the image of the child at the core of each of these theories or philosophies.

The first section of this chapter will attempt to define the image of the child from the perspective of the developmental theorists that Loris Malaguzzi identified as important in the evolution of the Reggio Emilia approach. The chapter then turns to how teachers, parents, and community members can define a common image of the child, including the child with disabilities, in a particular setting.

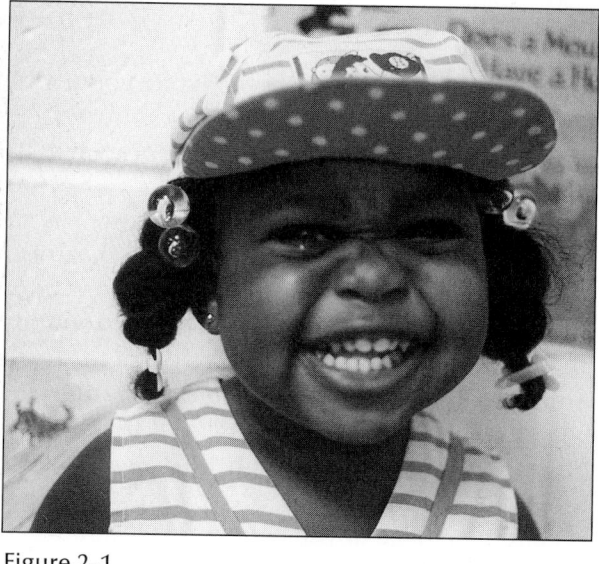

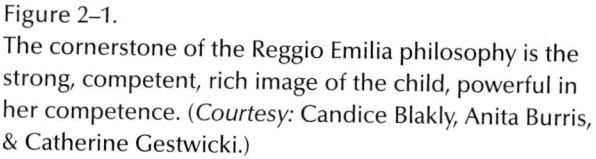

Figure 2–1.
The cornerstone of the Reggio Emilia philosophy is the strong, competent, rich image of the child, powerful in her competence. (*Courtesy:* Candice Blakly, Anita Burris, & Catherine Gestwicki.)

John Dewey's Image of the Child

John Dewey influenced the educators in Reggio Emilia with his positive view of human nature. Dewey saw the child as "spilling over with activities of all kinds," and he saw education as "taking hold of his activities, of giving them direction." He felt that a child should be given the materials to "reproduce in imaginative form his own experience" (Dewey, 1915).

There is an echo of Dewey in the way teachers in Reggio Emilia listen closely to children to help them take hold of their ideas and give them direction. The educators in Reggio Emilia have expanded Dewey's emphasis on the role of play in representing ideas in their concept of the hundred languages that a child can use for symbolic representation. John Dewey also stressed the importance of viewing the child in the context of the family and society that has become a key principle in the Reggio Emilia approach.

Erik Erikson's Continuum of Achievement

Erik Erikson was a theorist who wrote about children from a cultural and developmental perspective. His theory is examined in detail here because, like the Reggio Emilia approach, its roots are European but it continued to evolve after it was transplanted in North America.

Erikson began his work with children in Germany in the 1930s. As a young man, he was interested in becoming an artist and spent some time wandering around Europe. However, after meeting Anna Freud, the psychoanalyst and daughter of Sigmund Freud, he began to study psychoanalysis, especially child analysis. Anna Freud introduced him to a group of teachers who ran a small American school in Vienna. He agreed to teach art to the children in the school, but in the 1930s when the threat of the Nazis became too overwhelming, he and his Canadian-born wife, Joan Erikson, left Germany to live in the United States where he continued to practice psychoanalysis. In the following years, he began to expand his image of the child as his awareness of the cultural diversity of the role culture plays in the child's developing personality increased.

After studying the child-rearing patterns of Native Americans, Erikson wrote *Childhood and Society* in which he outlined his theory of the eight ages of man. The first four stages of Erikson's theory deal with childhood from birth to the teenage years. Each stage identifies the task the child needs to achieve for healthy personality development to occur and includes a description of the consequences if the challenge is not met. Erikson believed that each task in the eight ages of man could be metaphorically measured on a continuum of achievement. Erikson's image of the child is based on identified personality traits that can be measured on a continuum from positive to negative. In the development of a healthy personality, children need to have traits found at the positive end of the continuum, balanced by a small amount of the traits found at the negative end. These personality traits are trust versus mistrust, autonomy versus shame and doubt, initiative versus guilt, and industry versus inferiority.

The first stage of development involves achieving a balance of trust and mistrust. In the first two years, the infant develops a basic trust if the people who care for him are responsive to his needs. The child's sense of security grows as he develops "the recognition that there is an inner population of remembered and anticipated sensations and images which are firmly correlated with the outer population of familiar and predictable things and people" (Erikson, 1950, p. 247). If, however, the child is never allowed to cry and every wish is anticipated, he grows up to be too trusting. A little mistrust is healthy, but if too much mistrust develops, the child may have difficulty forming close relationships later in life. The healthy personality, therefore, is more trustful than mistrustful. The educators in Reggio Emilia have adapted this idea of a balance between trust and mistrust by emphasizing responsive interaction with children that can be symbolized by a game of ping-pong. Imagine a teacher repeatedly throwing the ball to the child and then catching it when the child throws it back. This turn-taking, or responsive interaction with children is essential in the development of trust, the foundation for healthy development at this stage.

Autonomy versus shame and doubt is the second of the eight ages of man. Erikson stated that "this stage, therefore, becomes decisive for the ratio of love and hate, cooperation and willfulness, freedom of self-expression and its suppression. From a sense of self-control without loss of self-esteem comes a lasting sense of good will and pride; from a sense of loss of self-control and of foreign control comes a lasting propensity for doubt and shame" (Erikson, 1950, p. 254). It is during this stage that the child who is growing up in an environment that "allows him to stand on his own feet" and is "firmly reassuring" develops a strong sense of self, balanced by a willingness to cooperate (p. 252). This stage lays the groundwork for a sense of right and wrong. If the child has been given opportunities to explore within safe limitations and to develop autonomy, the child begins to show pride in doing what is right and shame for doing wrong. Eventually, this trait will become a sense of fairness, tempered by a realistic doubt that everything in life will work out perfectly. A sense of security enables the child to act autonomously, an essential component of an image of a child who is competent. For example, toddlers in the asilo nido in Reggio Emilia are put to sleep in baskets on the floor with small openings through which they can climb in and out. This practice respects the toddlers' right to be autonomous and responsible for their own rhythms of sleeping and waking. The toddlers are not confined to cage-like cribs as is the case in most other toddler centers.

In the third stage, the child builds on autonomy to develop a sense of initiative. "He is eager and able to make things cooperatively, to combine with other children for the purpose of constructing and planning, and he is willing to profit from teachers" (Erikson, 1950, p. 252). This stage adds to the image of the child the ability to be inventive and full of ideas. Baji Rankin describes the process that unfolded as the children in the Anna Frank School in Reggio Emilia studied and represented their ideas about dinosaurs. She describes how, after much discussion and research, four girls selected materials and used their initiative and inventiveness in collaborating to create a three-dimensional representation of Tyrannosaurus Rex:

> The girls chose styrofoam as their medium. The material turned out to be rather easy to work with as it was easy to handle and the shape and size of the styrofoam pieces suggested to them different parts of the dinosaur. . . . A satisfying, three-dimensional, approximately 4-foot high, highly decorated Tyrannosaurus Rex resulted along with a stronger friendship among these particular girls. (1998, pp. 223–24)

In the fourth stage, industry versus inferiority, the child adds the quality of deep and sustained engagement. According to Erikson, "the child must now be a worker, he learns to win recognition by making things" (Erikson, 1950, p. 252).

This image of the child accurately describes the children in Reggio Emilia as they collaborate with the teachers to create the amazing work on display in the municipal preschools.

The educators in Reggio Emilia believe that if parents and teachers focus on only the negative traits, the child will be viewed as needy, and a dynamic will be set up that responds mainly to the child's deficits rather than strengths. If the child is viewed in a positive light, teachers will focus on her strengths and build on these. Erikson's positive image of the child and his view of the child in the context of the family and society have been integrated in the Reggio Emilia approach. These two perspectives, in particular, give Erikson's theory and the Reggio Emilia approach relevance to early childhood educators in the North American setting.

Jean Piaget's Stages of Development

Jean Piaget was born in Neuchâtel, Switzerland, in 1896. Initially, he was interested in biology, and by the time he was 21 years old, he had published over 20 scientific papers on mollusks. On completing his Ph.D. in 1921, he was hired to work with Alfred Binet in France on the development of intelligence tests for children. His early work in the natural sciences led him to make many important inferences from his observations of the children taking these tests. He found that children were able to adapt to the testing procedure with experience, and when he compared the performance of older and younger children, he found that the older children did not know quantitatively more than the younger children. Instead, there was a qualitative difference in their results; that is, they thought differently about problems. This discovery led him to explore the field of epistemology, the study of the process children and adults undergo to become knowledgeable.

Three key parts—order, structure, and process—of Piaget's cognitive developmental theory form a basic framework on which other ideas can be built.

Order. Children progress through four stages of development: sensorimotor (birth to 2 years); preoperational (2 to 7 years); concrete operational (7 to 11 years); and formal operational (11 years and up). Children progress through each stage in the same order but their rate of progression varies, depending on cultural factors, previous experience, and individual differences.

The sensorimotor stage is the preverbal stage. Children before the age of two use their senses and physical actions to explore and make sense of the environment. The second stage, the preoperational stage, is divided into two substages, preconceptual and intuitive. In the first substage, children use symbols, especially language, to order and derive meaning from their experiences; however, they still use their own perspectives as a frame of reference. In the second substage, children use their intuition to solve problems as in the example below of Patrick and Adam blowing bubbles at the water table. By the third stage, the concrete operational stage, children have formed simple concepts and can begin to use thinking skills such as classification and seriation, to organize their environment, and solve problems. Finally, the formal operational stage is reached when children use logical and abstract thinking processes.

Structure.   Intelligence develops as children build notions or ideas from their experiences in the environment. At first, they form the information from these experiences into preconcepts or schemas that are somewhat workable but primitive views of the world. Later, with more experience, children refine these schematic understandings to form more complex, abstract concepts.

Process.   Assimilation, accommodation, and equilibration are three parts of the process of learning. Assimilation occurs when children absorb information from experience to form schemas. Accommodation takes place when the child adapts these schemas learned from previous experiences to meet new assumptions. Equilibration is a self-regulatory process children employ in an attempt to maintain a balance between their cognitive structures and experiences of the external world. When children strive to reach equilibration by seeking satisfactory solutions to problems arising in their environment, they develop intelligence. This dynamic process creates a spiral of learning that is experienced differently in each of the four stages of development. In the first stage, the child will explore, for example, a square block physically by putting it in the mouth. When the block is no longer a novel experience, the child has reached a state of equilibration. In the second stage, however, the child's desire to label the block and use it in symbolic play will cause a new state of disequilibration as the child strives to meet the challenge of transforming the block into a symbol. At the third stage of cognitive development, the concrete operational stage, the school-age child will be presented with the challenge of performing simple operations such as measuring the four external surfaces of the cube. In the fourth, formal operational stage, the child will again experience disequilibrium when challenged to carry out abstract operations such as determining the cubic area of the block.

According to Piaget, thinking originates in a gradual internalization of action. Children in the sensorimotor period of development use their senses to explore the environment. Their actions on objects and the world around them form the basis for concept development in later stages. The child, like the one above who has had many opportunities to discover all the properties of a square block, will develop an awareness of angles and planes, equidistances between points, area, and volume that eventually will develop into an in-depth understanding of the cubic properties inherent in a square block. "The learner's structures, as they interact with the environment, first do simple assimilations and accommodations but eventually—at a nonpredictable threshold or bifurcation point—combine to make a sweeping change *(toute ensemble)* transforming themselves into new and more sophisticated structures" (Doll, 1993, p. 71).

Piaget was the first to pay serious attention to what children could do as opposed to focusing attention on what they lacked. He also demonstrated that

Figure 2–2.   Douglas creates a bubble-making machine.

learning is qualitative instead of quantitative. For educators, the open-endedness of this image of the child required a change in the teacher's role from directing learning to facilitating it. The kind of environment that teachers provide for children, therefore, has changed from being a structured environment in which the teacher delivers the content to one that fosters the children's exploration and investigation. This new environment has generated an image of the child as an active discoverer and inventor who constructs knowledge from experiences in the environment. The following observation of children, recorded at the Vancouver Child Study Center illustrates how active exploration of materials provides children with many opportunities for learning about physical science.

Patrick and Douglas stand opposite each other at a water table. Patrick is filling a cylinder with water, pushing his arm into the cylinder, and watching the water squirt out of the top of the cylinder.

The teacher passes by and asks, "Is that a bubble machine? What do you think a bubble machine would be like?" Patrick starts squeezing a soapy sponge and looks at the bubbles forming on his hand. He empties a bucket of soapy water into the water in the water table. "Look! A bubble machine!"

Douglas connects two long plastic tubes together, puts one end in the bucket, and starts to blow. He makes a face, but he continues to blow through the tube. He attaches the two ends to make a circle and pushes it down into the soapy water in the water table, carefully positioning the circular tube to keep it horizontal. He gently raises the tube to the surface, and there is a soap film attached to the circumference of the circle. He blows an enormous bubble downward from the soap film.

"Look, Chava," he calls out to his teacher.

Chava asks, "How did you make it? Aaron, come here and check this out." She calls another child over to look at the bubble. Aaron gently pokes it with his hand. The bubble bursts, and Patrick lowers the circular tube gently under the soapy water, raises it, and blows a bubble, which connects to a bubble in the water, making a long, tubular shape.

Adam joins him.

Patrick says, "Watch this, Adam. Don't spoil it! See the bubble. You put your hand in the bubble. Look, you do it."

Adam tries to raise the tube but is not successful in forming a bubble.

Patrick says, "Adam, go in my spot." They change places, but Adam still can't get a bubble to form. They leave the tube in the soapy water and pour water in the water wheel. They start to spin the water wheel, squealing as it splashes their faces.

Two of these boys clearly reflect a Piagetian image of the child. They investigate the water, soap, and tubes. Patrick eventually invents a bubble machine which he tries to teach Adam to use. He demonstrates intuitive thought (specifically, transductive reasoning) by suggesting that they change places; presumably, he thinks the position at the table will have an effect on Adam's ability to make the bubble. The teacher, Chava, by asking the boys the question, "What do you think a bubble machine would be like?" provoked the boys to think about different methods of making bubbles that led Douglas to invent the pliable hoop and successfully blow a long, tubular bubble. This invention, in turn, led to more discoveries of how soap film could be manipulated. The episode ended with disequilibration because Adam still was unsuccessful in blowing his bubble, even though he changed places with Patrick.

Loris Malaguzzi acknowledged the contribution the cognitive-developmental theory of Piaget has made to the Reggio Emilia approach. "We maintain intact our sense of gratitude towards Piaget. . . . Howard Gardner describes Piaget as the first to take children seriously" (Malaguzzi in Edwards, Gandini, & Forman, 1998, p. 81). The Piagetian view that development occurs in conjunction with experience is well supported in the schools in Reggio Emilia. The rich and stimulating environments in these schools provide many opportunities for children to transform materials and use symbolic representation to express their thoughts and ideas. These opportunities are part of the generative or emergent curriculum fundamental to the schools in Reggio Emilia.

Malaguzzi lists a number of aspects of Piaget's theory with which the educators in Reggio Emilia disagree. They agree with the Piagetian image of an active, self-motivated child, but they contest the view of an egocentric child who constructs knowledge in isolation from the social group and without the support of adults. Malaguzzi and the educators in Reggio Emilia also question a basic tenet of Piaget's theory: the lockstep progression through the four developmental stages. Their experience in supporting children in the realization of their thoughts and ideas lead them to agree with Lev Vygotsky's theory that children have a zone of proximal development that enables them, with the support or "scaffolding" of adults, to achieve more mature levels of functioning than Piaget identified as possible (Edwards, Gandini, & Forman, 1998, pp. 81–84).

Lev Vygotsky's View of the Child's Learning

Lev Vygotsky was born in Orsha, Belarus, in 1896, and grew up in a prosperous Jewish family in Gomel, Russia. He was a successful student and graduated as a lawyer from Moscow University in 1918. Because racism made it difficult for a Jew to practice as a lawyer at that time, he returned to Gomel and taught at the secondary and postsecondary levels. He had a passionate interest in psychology, and in his short career, before he died of tuberculosis at the age of 38, wrote seven books and numerous articles. His ideas were suppressed in Russia after 1936 but were rediscovered in the 1960s, and in the last 30 years have gained increasing attention all over the world.

Four of Vygotsky's ideas are particularly important for educators of young children. The first is that children actively construct knowledge. Vygotsky studied Piaget and agreed with this aspect of his theory. The second point, however, conflicts with Piaget's theory. Piaget stated that development is invariant and that learning follows development. For instance, Piaget wrote that children first must have a foundation of sensorimotor experience on which they can build concepts, which, in turn, are shaped by language. The child in the sensorimotor stage of development needs many opportunities to explore elements such as texture, shape, and color before he can learn the words to describe these elements. Vygotsky, however, stated that learning leads development. Vygotsky believed that if the child is given labels first such as the names of colors, this will hasten the child's ability to understand the concept of classifying by color. According to Vygotsky, learning is not invariant as Piaget believed, but relevant to experience. If an adult tells the child the name of the color of a pencil she is drawing with, this information will enable the child to recognize other objects of the same color and to become aware of relationships of objects grouped by color.

Vygotsky's third point is that learning cannot be separated from its social context. Learning is enhanced when children are able to interact with others who assist and support them in the learning process. His fourth point is that language plays a central role in intellectual development because it is through language that the higher mental functions such as symbolic thought are transmitted. Vygotsky identified three lower and three higher mental functions. The lower functions are inborn and similar to those functions found in the more advanced species of animals such as mammals. The three lower functions are reactive attention, associative memory, and sensorimotor thought. The higher mental functions are unique to humans and are developed through interactions with other humans. The higher mental functions are focused attention, deliberate memory, and symbolic thought. In the example above, an adult would support a child's greater understanding of the concept by focusing the child's attention on the color of the pencil, asking questions to help the child recognize the color in other situations, and encouraging the child to use the concept at the symbolic level.

According to Vygotsky, the child has two levels of performance: the first is the level that the child is capable of achieving independently, and the second is the level of performance that the child reaches with assistance. The distance between these two levels is known as the *zone of proximal development*. For example, an adult sitting beside a child who is drawing with colored pencils might focus the child's attention on the green color of the grass in the child's picture. The adult might then ask the child what color the leaves will be on the tree that the child has begun to draw. In this way, the adult moves the child from the level of unassisted learning to the level of assisted learning within the child's zone of proximal development. The child, with help from an adult, may now begin to use accurate representational colors when drawing whereas previously, he would have randomly chosen the colors for depicting objects in the picture (Bodrova & Leong, 1996).

Vygotksy, like Piaget, acknowledged the importance of play in a young child's development. Both theorists saw value in play, especially for the opportunities it provides children to engage in symbolic representation and symbolic action. However, whereas Piaget saw the value of play in the freedom it provides children for active engagement, Vygotsky believed that play is important for the constraints it imposes on free expression of the child's will. Vygotsky felt that the greatest value of play lies in the demands it imposes on children to master their own behavior. Each episode of play has a set of roles and rules that children are required to follow if they are to be successful participants. His views differed from those of Piaget, therefore, in that he believed that play is not entirely spontaneous. He asserted that play imposes certain constraints and limitations on children that are essential in the development of what he terms self-regularization (Bodrova & Leong, 1996, p. 125).

Malaguzzi said: "We seek a situation in which the child is about to see what the adult already sees. . . . In such a situation, the adult can and must loan to the children his judgment and knowledge. But it is a loan with a condition, namely that

Figure 2–3.   Schools in Reggio emphasize the Vygotskian idea of the child as a member of
the social and cultural group.

the child will repay" (Edwards, Gandini, & Forman, 1998, p. 84). The "repayment"
comes in the form of increased skills and independence. The view of the child from
a Vygotskian perspective is of a social child who is intelligent, strong, creative, and
competent. The image of the child in the Reggio Emilia approach is of a child who
is securely embedded within the social and cultural group.

Barbara Biber and the Whole Child

Barbara Biber, an educator and psychologist in the United States, was instrumental,
particularly during the 1960s and 1970s, in forming a link among the ideas of
Erikson, Piaget, and the evolving educational philosophy in the preschools in
Reggio Emilia. Biber was among the early educators who first perceived development from the perspective of the "whole child." She integrated the psychosocial
view of Erikson with the cognitive constructionist view of Piaget in an attempt to
discover "how to make knowledge and the experience of learning available to
growth processes; how not merely to keep children interested in their lessons but
to make the process of learning functional at deeper levels of the total process of
integration; in other words, how to make the experience of learning (1) yield ego
strength and (2) contribute to positive feelings and attitudes toward self and
others" (Biber, 1972, pp. 313–314).

Biber believed that relationships are central to the child's education; therefore, she stressed the importance of a child's sense of belonging and active participation in the social group as critical factors in the development of a positive sense of self and in the ability to learn successfully. The important principles of collaboration and a positive image of the child in the Reggio Emilia approach have been influenced by her work. Further connections between the educators in Reggio Emilia and the work of Barbara Biber exist in the kind of learning environment considered important for children. She writes about the importance of providing children with rich sensory experiences, helping them to become aware of "the light of the afternoon in wintertime; the bong of drums and the whisper of triangles" (Biber, 1972, p. 315). She and the educators in Reggio Emilia believe that children need a rich sensory environment to heighten their aesthetic awareness, to develop their thinking skills, and to encourage representation at many levels. Her contribution to the Reggio Emilia approach may be summed up by understanding her statement that "by helping the child penetrate experience, concrete and abstract, to the level of relationships, the school is preparing the child to order and deal with his world in terms of his society's logic and perception of reality. . . . The child creates and recreates the world around him, building a pattern of coherence for his impressions, concepts, roles, and relations, and integrating knowledge and feeling" (Biber, 1972, p. 316).

The teacher's relationship with children in the schools in Reggio Emilia was influenced by Biber's view of a teacher as "the intellectually resilient researcher, the one who can enjoy the intriguing course that the young mind takes in ordering the world of ideas, can perceive and accept the importance of the underlying thought processes while she supplies information and experience relevant to the correction of errors of fact and inference. . . . On this level, teacher and child are interacting cognitively: communicating" (pp. 317–18). She spoke of the teacher "mediating" the learning environment for children and supporting the children in "transforming information, knowledge, skill, and competence into ego strength" (p. 321). This statement also describes the relationship the teachers in Reggio Emilia develop with the children in their classes. However, the teachers in a Reggio Emilia classroom view the child as competent whereas Biber saw the teacher as leading the child toward competence.

Barbara Biber's major contribution to early childhood education was in integrating the separate areas of development, psychosocial and cognitive, into a holistic image of the child. Also, by placing relationships at the center of the child's learning experience, she saw the teacher as taking a supportive rather than authoritative role in the classroom. This change in perception allowed the teacher to play a partnership role with children as in the Reggio Emilia preschools. It also enabled educators to appreciate the work of Lev Vygotsky who had established earlier the importance of the adult's role in supporting the child's learning.

CONSIDERING THE IMAGE OF
THE CHILD IN TEACHER EDUCATION

Students entering an early childhood education teacher preparation program have been influenced necessarily by a number of factors in forming their personal images of childhood. Their own childhood experiences and the parenting belief systems, as well as larger cultural norms, values, and beliefs that informed the practices of their own parents have been strong determinants. For example, has the student's cultural experience influenced him or her to believe that it is good for children to be independent or to build interdependent ties? Historical, political, and economic factors also impact to create contemporary assumptions that influence their ideas about children's realities and potential. More than one contemporary writer has noted it is often expedient for many harassed working and/or single parents to believe that their children are competent enough for self-care because the social and economic realities demand that children be able to care for themselves in their parents' absence. Faced with ideas of various theorists, it becomes a necessary task for students to integrate their already existing images of children with those inherent in the views of each theorist.

One way to do this is to focus observations of students in child growth and development courses in interpreting their observations of children from the perspective of the three main developmental theorists, Erikson, Piaget, and Vygotsky. The following extracts are selected from student observation reports.

Example 1—Erik Erikson

> **N:** (30 months) Grabs the airport from another child who has started to play with it when N left it. The other child starts to cry.
>
> **N:** "Mine, mine!" She gets into a tug of war over the airport. The other child shouts back, "No, mine!"
>
> **N:** Pays no attention to this child's words and continues to pull.

The above example presents a powerful image of two young children both trying to establish their autonomy.

Example 2—Jean Piaget

> **M:** (42 months) is able to recognize and use a variety of symbols. To her, dressing in a fancy dress and shoes symbolizes getting married. A wooden block is used as a gun on another occasion, and cornmeal in a container represents variously apple juice and a cupcake.

The image portrayed by this student is of a child who engages in rich episodes of pretend play. The child is able to function effectively at a symbolic level, transforming herself and objects as she engages in imaginative play.

Example 3—Lev Vygotsky

S: (teacher) to N (30 months) "You're playing with the lift, N You'll have to wait your turn."

N: Goes back to examining the lift; she seems puzzled as to how it works.

S: "I am going to try something." She puts a car into the lift. "Here's the car, down, down."

N: "Let me, let me, it's inside." She carefully lets the car come down the ramp.

This image shows how the teacher supports the child by refocusing her attention on the task, enabling the child to overcome frustration and begin to solve the problem by learning how to make the toy work.

When students understand the image of the child from different theoretical perspectives, they can begin to absorb this information into their own image of the child. This is often a challenge for students because they have to integrate their own subjective view of children with the objective theoretical perspective.

Students may be challenged to draw up a list of terms that characterize their image of the child, then transform their ideas into a visual representation. These representations may take many forms and be constructed from a variety of media. For example, one group of students wrote a prose poem and illustrated it with a collage of children's photographs. Many of the groups used a variety of materials to create large posters illustrating their ideas. And one semester, a group of students made a mobile that when hung from the ceiling, twirled around, reflecting on each of the four sides one area of physical, social, emotional, and intellectual development. The four sides of the mobile, when seen together, reflected a view of the whole child. As students learn more about the children in their groups, they are encouraged to revisit and revise their initial image of the child.

SHARING AN IMAGE OF THE CHILD

The view of what a child is and ought to be has deep roots in the culture, society, and family values of the people involved. Because we live in a multicultural society and the people we work with come from many different backgrounds, the images we hold of children will reflect this diversity. This disparity in point of view makes it difficult for the adults working with the children in a center to share a common vision of what a preschool child is really like. However, a shared understanding of the preschool child is essential in designing programs that are congruent with the values and beliefs of all the parents, teachers, and members of the community involved in an early childhood program.

The key question to ask teachers, parents, and others who are involved in the program is, "What is your image of the child?" The answers to this question should be given after careful reflection because the labels that first come to mind often need to be explored further to get to the truth of their meaning. Later, when everyone has had a chance to reflect on the answers, they can begin to work as a group to develop their shared understanding of the image of the child. This may be time consuming because there may have to be much negotiation before the group as a whole reaches a common vision of their image of the child.

The Quadra Island Preschool provides an example of how teachers, parents, and the community evolved a common vision. The group of parents in the preschool work very closely with the teacher and take turns working as the parent assistant in the classroom. It was essential for them, therefore, to explore as a group their image of the child to ensure consistency in the program. After they had discussed each person's ideas about children, they drew up the following list of characteristics that define their image of the child.

They stated that preschoolers are imaginative and curious: whereas three-year-olds tend to be observers, four-year-olds are much more energetic. They noticed that preschool children are forgiving of adults' mistakes. The children's behavior has the quality of fluidity. For example, they observed the group of children becoming more sociable as they turned four. One parent said, "They [preschoolers] are clever, more so than you think." Another parent noticed how excitable behavior contrasted with "deep and sustained activity." The parents noted how the children like to play with language and how their ideas, at times, are surprisingly sophisticated. One parent said, "The amount of creative play the children engage in and how much they learn by imitation is a continual source of amazement to me." The group stated that the overriding characteristics of the preschooler are powerfulness, loudness, and forcefulness. This image of the child matches the Reggio Emilia educators' image of a child who is "rich in resources, strong, and competent" (Rinaldi, 1998, p. 114).

The parents and teacher in this preschool have worked as a team to provide the children with a program that matches the list of characteristics they drew up together. For instance, they have removed barriers such as long circle times and adult-imposed theme lessons that interfere with the children's natural bent for fast-paced, energetic, and fluid activity. The daily schedule they have devised allows the children to engage in deep and sustained activity. It is flexible to avoid unnecessarily interrupting the children's natural rhythm and engagement in learning and play. However, the schedule also provides time for the teacher and the parent assistant to meet in small and large groups to discuss ideas and topics of interest with the children.

The participants also agreed with the parent who said that children are more clever than we think, so they decided that it was essential the adults take the time to listen to the children and support them in finding a means of expressing their ideas. Loris Malaguzzi stated that children have a hundred languages of expression. The teacher and the parents decided that one of their goals for the year would be to provide the children with many different media for expression.

IMPLICATIONS OF THE IMAGE OF THE CHILD

When teachers accept an image of the child as strong, capable, and filled with resources, this image changes the way they work with children and the way they encourage children to work with one another. Teachers who see children as capable are more likely to encourage them to stay with their efforts, knowing they have abilities to move ahead when given support and specific assistance. Rather than just standing back and assuming children will move ahead when they are ready, a teacher with an image of a strong child might be more likely to push her to try again.

In an example from Ann Pelo, this might look like the teacher offering a specific strategy for shaping a figure in clay as she watches a child struggling to realize in clay her vision of a woman with flowing dress and long hair. The teacher might encourage the child to try a strategy that she knows will help the child move closer to what she's trying to achieve, critiquing her work gently but clearly: "Actually, I think you ought to try again; look how wobbly her arms are. Let's look at why they're wobbling, then fold the clay in and start again." The image of the strong child helps the teacher realize the child's capabilities, and offer her the necessary support and technique to move to success. The teacher with an image of a strong child may ask children to stick with their work longer than they are initially inclined because of a certainty that children are capable of one more big intellectual or physical push.

The image of the strong child also helps teachers allow children to give each other feedback and new ideas, knowing that children are capable enough to help one another on the one hand, and strong enough not to crumple under criticism on the other. This might look like the teacher not stopping children when they critique each other's work, not suggesting that the critical feedback be avoided lest it crush the other, as in "Everyone's work is beautiful; that's what a spaceship looks like to him." Instead, a teacher believing in a strong image of the child might be more likely to encourage children to formulate their feedback so that it is potentially useful: "Tell him what you think is missing from his spaceship" or "Instead of telling him 'That's not what a spaceship looks like,' tell him your idea of what a spaceship looks like." Knowing that children are capable of co-constructing their understandings, teachers encourage such interaction.

When children are treated as strong and capable, it follows that they adopt this image of capability in their personal vision of themselves. In Patti Cruikshank-Schott's classroom, a particular practice indicates Patti's image of powerful children.

Each child takes a turn at being the "Peacemaker". When conflicts arise between children in the classroom, they call the Peacemaker over to help them. The Peacemaker uses the communication skills of conflict resolution that Patti has taught all the children, encouraging first one, then the other, of those involved in the dispute to explain their perspective. Then the Peacemaker encourages the children to suggest possible solutions; the Peacemaker does not go back to his own play until a solution has been agreed on. In many classrooms, adults play the role of referee, stopping most conflicts. In others, teachers are the mediators in such conflict situations. But in Patti's classroom, children who are seen as strong and capable learn to play such a role, and other children accept these efforts, seeing each other as able to fulfill the peacemaker role. When children are treated as strong children, in accordance with adults' images of them, they absorb this image themselves.

PRINCIPLES OF INCLUSION

The educators in Reggio Emilia have been instrumental in shifting the image of the child from a child with needs that adults meet to a child with strengths. The Reggio Emilia educators stress the image of a competent child who is a producer as

Figure 2–4.   Peacemakers help their peers find solutions to the conflict. In this documentation, Patti shares an example with parents. (*Courtesy:* Patti Cruikshank-Schott.)

opposed to a consumer of resources, one who has a right to a quality early child-hood education, and one that provides the child with relationships and experiences that promote learning and foster development. This shift in image has had a powerful impact on the education of children who are challenged in one or more areas of development. It has forced educators to think carefully about how they can provide children with disabilities with an education that enables them to reach their full potential. These educators have become aware of how important it is to include these children with their peers, giving them the same opportunities to form relationships and the same quality educational experiences as other children. The educators in Reggio Emilia have become world leaders in their advocacy for the rights of all children to experience a quality early childhood education. The phrase "children with special rights" has come to stand for inclusion of all children in preschool programs and for a guarantee that they will receive the support they need to maximize their potential development. This phrase invokes awe in people who have been trying to figure out how to support their children, especially children with disabilities (Smith, 1998).

Italy was one of the first countries in the world to recognize that all children have the right to a quality education. From 1960, when orphanages and institutions for children with disabilities were closed and the children returned to their families, the rights of these children have been given increasing consideration. At first, they were educated in special classes, but in 1971, children between the ages of six and fourteen were given the right to a desegregated education. In 1995, a law was passed that guaranteed infants under the age of three a place in infant-toddler centers.

Children with special rights are given priority in being accepted into the municipal preschools in Reggio Emilia, and only one child with disabilities is accepted in each class. Once the child is enrolled, the two classroom teachers meet the psychologist-pedagogista to decide if they will need the support of a third teacher to work with all the children in the classroom.

The process of orientation, or *inserimento,* is carried out slowly and carefully. Ivana Soncini, the psychologist-pedagogista specializing in special education for the municipal schools in Reggio Emilia, explains that beginnings are considered very important. A long and gradual entry period is designed to ease the separation process for children and families. In the case of children with special rights, this period may be even longer (Soncini in Smith, Edwards, Gandini, & Forman, 1998, p. 203). Soncini says that the child's behavior is observed for a long period and long dialogs are held with families; no diagnosis is made before the team has a thorough understanding of the child's situation. Even then, no special curriculum is developed for children with disabilities, and they are expected to participate in the same program and classroom routines as the other children in the class, at a level that is comfortable for them. An agreement, or declaration of intent, is written to ensure that communication is ongoing with other health professionals, with families, and with the teachers working with the child. This declaration includes ideas about the methods and materials that probably will be part of the child's educational plan, all subject to the same kind of flexibility and revision by teachers and pedagogistas as with any other classroom plan. The educators in Reggio Emilia have found that the practices of documentation used for all children also are very important for children with special rights, to reflect children's progress as well as the collaboration among teachers, other professionals, and family.

Ivana Soncini states that one of the biggest advantages in the Reggio Emilia system is that the different learning styles of children are accommodated because the hundred languages of children approach allows children a wide variety of ways to express themselves. This is particularly important for children with special rights.

> Our basic theoretical approach is to value differences and to bring out as much potential as we can. Each of us is different; this is considered positive. We acknowledge that a handicap brings with it a difference, but that it is just one of many differences. As we recognize our differences, we develop knowledge of who we are and who others are. . . . We gradually synthesize our own identity. There are many ways to look at ourselves in order to construct our own images (Soncini in Smith, in Edwards, Gandini, & Forman, 1998, p. 205).

When discussing children with special rights, educators from Reggio Emilia again circle back to the importance of relationships with others, and to give the children opportunities to see themselves in authentic relationships with other children and adults. The child should want to come to school, and the family should feel positive about their child's experience in school. The educators in Reggio Emilia believe that the image of the child as rich, strong, and powerful encompasses all children including children with special rights, and that all children deserve to be given the support they need to reach their full potential.

The foundation of an early childhood education program is a shared understanding of the image of the child, an image that is informed by theory and co-constructed through observation, reflection, and discussion. When the child is seen as "a producer of culture, values, and rights, competent in living and learning" (Ceppi & Zeni, 1998, p. 117), the adults who are creating the spaces in which children learn ensure that "children's learning paths and processes thus pass through the relationship with the cultural and scholastic context which, as such must be a 'formative environment,' an ideal place for development" (p. 117).

Chapter **3**

The Role
of the Teacher

*The central act of adults . . . is to activate, especially indirectly, the meaning-making
competencies of children as a basis of all learning. They must try to capture the right
moments, and then find the right approaches, for bringing together, into a fruitful dialogue, their meanings and interpretations with those of the children.*

—Loris Malaguzzi

Questions to Consider:

- How has the role of the early childhood teacher evolved?

- What philosophical and theoretical principles shape the role of the teacher?

- What is the job description of an early childhood educator at the beginning of the 21st
  century?

- What does a teacher using ideas from the Reggio Emilia approach need to understand about the
  role of the teacher in that system?

- How are these ideas about the teacher's role interpreted in practice?

- How do the roles of pedagogista and atelierista support teacher roles in Reggio Emilia?

THE CHANGING ROLE OF THE TEACHER

A hundred years ago, no one would have been able to foresee how much growth
and change there would be in early childhood education in the 20th century. In
the second half of the 19th century, industrialization and immigration brought
many families to work in the cities of North America. Many of the women in these
families became working mothers and no longer had the support of the extended
families who traditionally took care of their young children.

The earliest nonreligious child care in North America, aside from orphan care or
child welfare, was probably the Nursery for the Children of Poor Women in New
York City in 1854. The growth of child care in Canada was much slower than in the
United States, probably owing to Canada's smaller population. By 1898 the United
States had 175 day nurseries. The purpose of these early child care programs was to
provide children with a clean, safe environment in which the teacher's role was to

ensure the children's health and moral behavior, a role that today would be seen as custodial caregiver. The change in the role of the teacher from custodial caregiver to early childhood educator did not begin until public school kindergartens based on Froebelian principles were opened in the United States and Canada.

The Evolution of the Role of the Teacher

In 1856, Margaretha Schurz, a student of Froebel, opened the first kindergarten in the United States in Watertown, Wisconsin. Although this was a private school for German-speaking children, it inspired educators such as Elizabeth Peabody to study the Froebel method. After her return from observing Froebel kindergartens in Germany, Elizabeth Peabody persuaded William Harris, the superintendent of schools in St. Louis, Missouri, to open the first public school kindergarten in North America in 1873. Susan Blow, who had trained in the Froebelian method, was hired as the first teacher. The following excerpt from a lesson notebook from 1881 presents a typical schedule for the morning in one of these schools:

Opening exercises (prayer, hymn "God Is Love")

Songs ("Good Morning, Kind Teacher," "Thumb & Fingers")

General ball exercise

Modeling

Third gift with children

Sticks and tablets

Folding

Sewing (vertical in red, connect with sticks)

The circle

Games

Closing song (Dixon, 1994, p. 8)

The Froebelian interpretation of the importance of learning through play, as can be seen from the schedule above, allowed the children hands-on experience in using materials such as by paper folding, sewing, and weaving using paper cut into strips. Teachers, however, were required to follow a carefully prescribed procedure in presenting activities to the children and the learning was a structured experience for children. Froebel designed didactic tools called *gifts* and *occupations* which teachers used to teach concepts such as color, shape, number, symmetry, and proportion as well as skills such as weaving, threading, and paper cutting. In his system, there were ten gifts consisting of materials that children were to use in specific ways. For example, the third gift mentioned in the lesson plan above consisted of eight one-inch cubes. A child received the gift from the teacher and after playing with it, was expected to learn number concepts, specifically division, and the value of self-activity. The occupations that Froebel advocated were more open-ended and designed to allow children to practice useful skills. Sewing, the occupation listed in the lesson plan above, was designed to increase the child's awareness of lines and to practice the art of embroidery (Froebel [1887], 1974, p. 286).

It was not until the early part of the 20th century, when John Dewey adapted Froebel's methods in founding the progressive school movement, that the role of the teacher became less teacher directed and children were allowed more freedom to follow their own ideas.

The child study movement also had an impact on the role of the teacher. In the 1920s and 1930s, many college and university campuses in Canada and the United States opened laboratory schools. Disciplines such as home economics, psychology, and education needed a setting where children could be studied in order to gain more knowledge about child development and child psychology. It was during this period that Dr. Arnold Gesell founded the Gesell Institute at Yale University for the purpose of studying children and identifying the "norms" of development. Graduates from child study programs filled important positions in early childhood education. Not only did the child study movement create a solid theoretical foundation for early childhood education but also provided teachers with a greater sense of professionalism in their work. As teachers began to study theories about child development and methods for observing children, they increased their understanding of children's behavior and development. This knowledge enabled them to see children as individuals and to plan programs to meet the needs of each child. The grounding student teachers receive in the study of child development and in the philosophy of learning through play (reaching back to Froebel and Dewey) are the tenets that make early childhood education a discipline separate from teaching older children.

World War II provided the next impetus for early childhood education. Child care centers were opened across the United States and Canada to care for the children of mothers who were recruited for war work. The United States Congress passed the Lanham Act creating Lanham Act child care centers funded by federal dollars. There were also centers opened by private industry to provide child care for the women who worked in their factories. The most famous of these private child care centers were the Kaiser Nurseries in Portland, established to enable mothers to work in the shipyards. At the end of the war, many of these high-quality programs were closed and women returned to their homes. It was not until almost two decades later that there were any further advances in the field of early childhood education.

In the 1960s, the work of Jean Piaget became more widely known in North America. His theory of cognitive development caused major changes in every aspect of early childhood education such as in the delivery of the program, the use of space, and the kind of educational materials used in the classroom. His theory also caused a major change in the role of the teacher. Jean Piaget said that "if the aim of intellectual training is to form the intelligence rather than to stock the memory, and to produce intellectual explorers rather than mere erudition, then traditional education is manifestly guilty of a grave deficiency" (1969, p. 51). These words had a powerful impact on the way teachers delivered the content of their lessons. In the second half of the 20th century, teachers increasingly began to change from seeing children as empty containers who need to be filled with information to viewing them as active agents who construct their own knowledge from their experiences in the environment.

Typical programs at that time were based on the principles of nursery school education of Rachel and Margaret McMillan, imported from England earlier in the 20th century, and the principles of John Dewey. Programs were based on the theory that children learn through play, but the curriculum also provided the children with many real experiences such as cooking in the classroom and cultivating a garden in the outdoor playground. The classroom was divided into areas for specialized activities such as art, woodworking, block building, and dramatic play. The room had a library corner, water and sand play areas, and shelves stocked with puzzles, games, and small blocks for fine motor development. The first hour of each morning and afternoon session was scheduled as free play with special activities such as preparing fruit to make a salad which was set out on one or two tables in the classroom. Children then gathered together for about half an hour for circle time when they listened to the teacher read a story, sang a few songs, and had a short discussion about some topic of interest. Finger plays such as "Eeenzy Weenzy Spider" were frowned on, as were books that were not didactic. The stories by Lucy Sprague Mitchell that dealt with the "here and now," and the books of Ezra Jack Keats such as *The Snowy Day* that explored a specific concept, were considered the most appropriate books for children. The last hour, no matter what the weather, the teachers took the children outside to play.

It was during circle time that the conflict in the role of the teacher emerged. Some teachers believed that it was their responsibility to teach the children specific skills and content; for example, how to develop memorization strategies. A teacher might set up an exercise during circle time in which the children were required to memorize the names of the animals whose pictures were pinned on a board. She would take one picture away, and the children would have to identify the missing animal. She taught the children strategies to help them with this activity by sorting the animals and counting the number of animals in each group. Each day, she had a specific lesson plan based on a concept she wanted to teach the children. In one lesson, she asked the children to come up to the front, one by one, and place pictures of vegetables in the correct position on a chart that was divided in two sections, the lower half representing underground, and the upper half aboveground. Other teachers believed that these lessons were too structured because there was very little opportunity for the children to engage in the activity. They suggested that a more appropriate aid to memory would be to help the children remember what seeds they had planted in the spring when they harvested the vegetables from their garden in the summer. In addition, they felt that a more appropriate time for the children to learn the concepts would be when they were picking or digging the vegetables out of the ground. It has always been difficult for many teachers to give up the responsibility of teaching children content and allowing them the freedom to investigate and develop skills on their own.

The work of Diana Baumrind looked at different styles of parenting and also had an impact on the role of the teacher in the latter half of the 1960s. She termed these styles authoritative, authoritarian, and permissive (she later divided permissive into permissive/indulgent and permissive/neglecting). Authoritative parents, according to Baumrind, are consistent, affectionate, interested in their children as individuals, and able to communicate clearly their expectations for responsible behavior. Authoritarian parents are controlling, and offer little nurturance and affection. Permissive parents are inconsistent in their expectations and expect less of their children. Baumrind stated that authoritative parents are the most effective in raising children who have good social skills and are self-confident and self-assertive (1967). This research helped teachers find a balance between having a too-authoritarian role or being too permissive as the style of teaching became less structured in the classroom. The 1960s were an exciting time for early childhood education. Everything the teacher did seemed to come into question, especially any form of authority. What emerged was a new role for the teacher, one that was far more democratic and less didactic. The emphasis changed from teaching children content to preparing a stimulating environment, then standing back and observing the children's play.

The 1970s added new dimensions to the role of the teacher. This was a time when issues such as poverty and multiculturalism came to the fore. In the United States, the Head Start program, which had begun in the mid-1960s, began to have a major impact on early childhood education. It began as an attempt to give children who were outside the cultural mainstream an opportunity to catch up with children who entered school better prepared to cope with the demands of public school education. Advocacy became an important part of the teacher's role as educators struggled to get adequate resources to provide children with quality early childhood education programs. The freedom of the 1960s began to disappear, and accountability became a key word. Planning programs based on themes such as spring or community helpers enabled teachers to demonstrate that they were doing more than just providing baby-sitting services.

This brief history of early childhood education in this country shows how the change over the last hundred years from an image of the child as needy to a view of the child as competent has raised questions about the teacher's role. Before the turn of the century, the child in the early child care centers was seen as needing protection. This view was followed by an image of an ignorant child who needed instruction, and more recently by a view of the child who learns by finding things out for herself. There are, however, still strong echoes of an earlier age when children were seen as weak and needing protection such as when labeling children who need extra support as "children with special needs" or when using the common phrase "meeting the needs" as opposed to considering the abilities of children in our care.

At each phase in the history of early childhood education, there was a major change in the role of the teacher. First, teachers were mainly concerned with the child's health, safety, and moral development; then followed a time when teachers emphasized prescribed information and skills. More recently, teachers have focused on providing children with an environment that stimulates exploration. Finally, teachers added the notion of rights for the child to their image of the child as they found they had to act as advocates for children in need of resources. The educators in Reggio Emilia believe strongly in the right of children to a fair share of the resources in an affluent society and in the right to an "authentic" childhood, one in which children are expected to be, as Gianni Rodari said, "no longer a consumer of culture and values, but a creator and producer of values and culture" (1996, p. 116). In the schools of Reggio Emilia, the belief is that children have the right to a world in which they are respected, and their childhood is valued as a time when they lay down the foundation that will enable them to grow into adults who are creative thinkers and responsible citizens in a democratic society. Recalling the strong image of the child discussed in the last chapter, it is not possible to speak of the teacher's role in isolation but only as a complementary image of adults who can support that growth.

There is another point that needs to be added to this idea in considering what teachers' roles are to be in relation to children. That is the Reggio idea that children are able to educate themselves and adults through their relationships with them. Adults in the Reggio schools value interacting with children as opportunities to develop their own personal potential. The concept of reciprocality of adult-child relationships is emphasized as an alternative beyond the two more usual types of relationship between adults and children: either teachers dominating the learning process or children having complete freedom within the learning relationship. In the third (Reggio) view of adult-child relationships, both child and adult grow to fuller potential as partners and co-constructors of learning. "A strong image of the child is also a strong image of the teacher and of the school" (Rinaldi, Spring 1999, p. 2). The consideration of children as protagonists requires "parallel expectations and possibilities for adults" (Edwards in Edwards, Gandini, & Forman, 1998, p. 180).

THE STRUCTURE OF SCHOOLS IN REGGIO EMILIA

The Reggio Emilia municipal preschools have developed in the last half century into a clearly delineated educational system with defined roles and responsibilities. There are thirteen infant–toddler centers (for children four months to three years) and nineteen preschools (for children three to six years) serving about two thousand children or about 35 percent of the resident children in the city. The elected superintendent of the department of education in Reggio Emilia oversees these centers. A department director heads two sectors, the administrative and pedagogical sectors. The administrative manager heads a team of ten administrative personnel, and the director of the pedagogical sector coordinates the team of nine pedagogisti, one of whom is an expert in special education. Each pedagogista supervises three or four schools and infant centers, supporting the teachers and staff in each school team, interpreting the philosophy, and acting as consultant and mediator when necessary. There are eleven teachers, one cook, and three full-time and three part-time auxiliary staff in each infant–toddler center. The preschools usually have three classrooms, one each for 25 three-, four-, and five-year-old children. There are two coteachers for each preschool classroom, one cook, and two full-time and three part-time auxiliary staff members. Also, each preschool employs an atelierista who specializes in the visual arts curriculum (how young children relate to materials and use them to represent their ideas). Parents play an integral role in Reggio Emilia schools, and are seen as the third protagonist by participating in activities and serving on classroom or school committees. They also have representation on the school advisory council, composed of ten to fifteen parent representatives in addition to members of the school staff in rotation. The advisory council does not have decision-making powers but it is influential because it is represented by the general coordinating committee that works together with the municipal administration to determine the educational, political, and cultural aims and objectives of the infant–toddler centers and preschools.

While it is immediately obvious that this structure is different from the typical organization and functioning of most American preschools, to say nothing of financial resources to support such staff, this does not mean that American teachers cannot learn from considering how the additional support positions enhance the efforts of the teachers and help expand their roles.

The Teacher's Role

Central to the role of the teacher in the schools in Reggio Emilia is the responsibility for forming a circle of relationships. Teachers work with one another, with the parents, and with the children to form "a mutual community of learners" among all protagonists. This means that the children's learning is shared in reciprocal connections. When this basic tenet is understood, other essential components of the teacher's role become obvious, especially the importance of communication. Communicating with children means listening carefully to their ideas and participating with them in conversation.

"Listening" may be too simple a word to describe the complex process of attempting to be involved, to follow and enter into the active learning of the child, acting as a resource and sometimes a provoker. Tizianna Fillippini uses the analogy of being able to catch the ball thrown by children and throwing it back in such a way that they want to continue the game with the adult, and perhaps develop other games as they proceed. Moreover, this is not a fast-paced game where children are frustrated in their attempts to keep up, but a game where child novices are trying to play, assisted and supported by an adult expert. The adult is trying to help keep the game going. Sometimes he or she steps in to return the ball, or puts the ball back in play, or coaches children on technique, or fixes or adjusts the materials, or even calls a break (Edwards in Edwards, Gandini, & Foreman, 1998, pp. 181–182).

From their careful listening and interpreting as they play this ball game, teachers have the task of finding interests that are both challenging and satisfying to explore. Through the process of *progettazione*—an Italian concept that suggests a very complex form of the ideas of webbing that many American educators use to predict directions for possible learning experiences—teachers hypothesize the potential for exploring the children's ideas. This process of trying to identify directions for emergent curricula is at once exhilarating and surprising for teachers, and involves the capacity to listen and interpret continuously.

This interpretation of teachers and other staff involves a high level of collaboration at every level, such as in discussing the observations of the children, interpreting these observations, and making *progettazione* through negotiation with children for future directions. Documentation has to be done in collaboration with all the participants involved to capture a complete picture of the experience. Collaboration and communication are essential skills when learning in relationship is at the core of a teacher's role.

An aspect of this role of the teacher as listener is to act as co-constructor of knowledge. The belief is that for children to be able to co-construct knowledge they must be able to find the right environment and a partner who can facilitate this learning. The adult in this partnership cannot be a teacher in the traditional sense; he has to be a provocateur who can support and help the children build their own knowledge. Jerome Bruner states,

> So back to the innocent but fundamental question: how best to conceive of a sub-community that specializes in learning among its members? One obvious answer would be that it is a place where, among other things, learners help each other learn, each according to her abilities. And this, of course, need not exclude the presence of somebody serving in the role of the teacher. It simply implies that the teacher does not play that role as a monopoly, that learners "scaffold" for each other as well. (Bruner, 1996, p. 21)

This statement illustrates a major shift in the traditional relationship between the teacher and the learners. The teacher in Reggio Emilia is not viewed as the expert or sole dispenser of information; rather, the role of the teacher becomes one that is shared equally among members of the group. There is an implicit acknowledgment that all the participants can make a worthwhile contribution to the learning experience. The teacher's role is to create a partnership with the learners, to walk beside them as together they launch themselves into the experience and begin the process of the co-construction of knowledge. At times, however, the teacher will have to act as a provocateur, to prod the learners to move forward or in a new direction. Sometimes, it may become necessary to take stronger action, to put children in crises and allow them the opportunity for confusion so they can come up with solutions. This idea is similar to Piaget's concept of disequilibrium when a teacher sets up a situation in which the child has to adapt to a new set of circumstances. Carolyn Edwards has used the term traffic jam to describe the same idea of disentangling all the jumbled pieces so that the child is free to move forward again, perhaps in a different direction.

Helping the children sustain their interest may come from the teacher's identifying "knots," the sticking points that may be productive in creating dialog and comparison of cognitive understandings and points of view. The example that comes to mind here is of the scene in the video "Amusement Park for Birds" where Giorgia and Simone are working in the atelier with the support of Giovanni, the atelierista, to translate their drawings of the fountains into versions of clay. Giorgia and Simone have an extended disagreement—that is increasingly articulate and loud—about Giorgia's plan for creating the separate streams of the fountain. Their misunderstanding stems from the fact that Giorgia is counting the streams that remain to be made from her plan of 10 streams when she has finished making three; Simone is focused on the total number instead of on the number remaining that is being counted by Giorgia. In fact, the atelierista had suggested that Simone look at Giorgia's work, evidently seeing that their different viewpoints might create a "knot" that could expand their understanding of the different cognitive perspectives each was taking.

Sustaining work also may come from the teacher's decision to intervene—or not—so as to let children find their own way and continue on the journey they redefine. In the video segment described above, Giovanni allowed the dialog to continue for long minutes with no intervention at all (often to the discomfort of some viewing American students). When he does join the conversation, it is primarily in a listening role, and only to help them summarize their discoveries of the differing perspective of the other, and to reinforce the idea that they "both agree, right?" now that they have been able to discover the source of the misunderstanding. Decisions about intervention mean that teachers are trying to strike a balance, afraid to miss a "hot moment," but unwilling to enter where children may be quite capable of managing their own ideas and exchanges.

The teacher's role is to observe children and judge when to supply the technical information they require to carry out their ideas. In an observation in Reggio Emilia, for example, a teacher worked with a child to help her make a clay drawing of a dancer. It was a challenging task for the child to place the rolled coils of clay to form the dancer's body, showing how the legs, feet, arms, and hands moved as she danced. The child also had made the dancer's long hair from thin coils of clay. The teacher discussed with her how to place these coils on the dancer's head, making them appear to swing above her shoulders to suggest the movement of the dancer's body. The teacher stayed beside the child for almost half an hour, offering support and giving technical suggestions. She showed the child how to mix slip, a soup clay mixture that acts like cement in joining pieces of clay together. When the clay figure was complete, she helped the child carefully lift it onto a sheet of cardboard to dry. This is truly "lending" children knowledge and technique.

The adult has to understand that children do not have "the strength to sustain work." It is the role of the teacher, therefore, to help the children stay interested in their work, and bring their thoughts and ideas to fruition. Pam Oken-Wright, in a journal entry to her families describing the children's project work, uses the phrase "borrow a bit of adult control to stay with the project." The theory of Vygotsky is at work here. "The discrepancy between a child's actual mental age and the level he reaches in solving problems with assistance indicates the zone of his proximal development . . . with assistance, every child can do more than he can by himself—though only within the limits set by the state of his development." (Vygotsky, 1962, p. 103). Bruner uses the term scaffolding to describe this process (Bruner, 1996, p. 21).

Sometimes, the teacher has to break up a temporary idea that may not be a lasting solution. Amelia Gambetti demonstrated this notion at La Villetta School in the early stages of the Amusement Park for Birds project. The children had been building their theories about how a fountain works when suddenly they were sidetracked into talking about electric currents.

Filippo: Or one can die because the current (electricity) can get into the water.

Andrea: And one gets a shock. The current is in the water because the current comes, gets wet, and then one dies.

Simone: In the fountain there is water that runs, not the current (electric).

Amelia: How does the water arrive to the fountains?

Filippo: There is a pipe underground. (Forman & Gandini, 1994).

Amelia did a number of things here: she listened carefully to the children's discussion, intervening when she felt she needed to break up the temporary idea of electric currents. She provoked the children to think beyond the limit of the fountain itself, and she questioned them about how the water gets into the fountain. This example demonstrates that a teacher who adapts the Reggio approach has to be more than just an observer. She takes an active role in the discussion, provoking the children to think more deeply about the ideas they are working on.

The Pedagogista's Role

A role that is parallel to, supportive of, and intertwined with these teacher roles in Reggio Emilia is that of the pedagogista. Pedagogisti are not unique to Reggio Emilia schools since they function throughout Italy; however, the uniqueness of their position in the Reggio schools is their integration into a system in which everything is seen as connected and interrelated. Although there are some administrative functions of the *pedagogisti* in terms of maintaining coherence and quality of the municipal schools, and having a specific area of responsibility within the system (such as overseeing the plans for children with special rights), the pedagogista is included in the network of relationships within the school. Each pedagogista is responsible for a number of infant/toddler centers and preprimary schools. Through regular meetings and continual dialog with teachers and parents, the pedagogista facilitates reflection about all sorts of educational issues and problems. The overall task is to support teachers in their daily work with children and their relationships with families. Pedagogisti play active roles in formulation of long-term explorations in projects, engaging in the dialogue that contributes to the design of projects. "Rather than acting as an expert, the role of the pedagogista is that of an active discussant, in a position to sustain the teachers' critical interpretations, to suggest possible questions which might bring out the teachers' narrative and interpretive abilities in relation to their ongoing projects" (Cavazzoni, 2000).

The pedagogista is also responsible for working with the teachers to identify new ideas and experiences for continuous professional development, sustaining and nurturing their desire and need to reflect on their work. The complex teacher roles discussed earlier are supported by providing experiences where teachers can continue to reflect and puzzle together. The dialogs with the pedagogista and among teachers facilitate the understanding that all learning is in a continual process of change and growth. Pedagogista Tizianna Filippini expresses it this way:

> A culture of the school based on negotiation requires educators to be active participants. We cannot approach our own learning and growth passively . . . Instead we reflect on our practice . . . As we discuss and share reflections, we create culture. . . . Without these reciprocal relationships and processes of sharing, each one of us would remain isolated within his or her own perspective and our system would remain fragmented. . . . Working to create a shared culture of education within the pedagogical team and the schools is basic to all the other elements of the pedagogista's role (Filippini in Edwards, Gandini, & Forman, 1998, p. 133).

The pedagogista's role appears crucial in teachers' learning to play the various roles of the teacher defined by the Reggio philosophy.

The Atelierista's Role

Another network of relationships within each preschool is added by the atelierista. The atelieristi in the municipal preschools in Reggio Emilia have specialized training in the visual arts. They also have a deep understanding of children's relationships with materials and how they learn from them. In each of these schools there is an atelier, a studio where children work with the atelierista. These areas are supplied with many art materials beautifully displayed for use. The atelier serves two purposes: it provides a place for children to be supported in learning the techniques for expression in "the hundred languages." It also is the center that allows adults to see the processes by which children learn (Vecchi in Edwards, Gandini, &

Forman, 1998, p. 140). The atelier becomes the repository for documentation of past investigations.

In the atelier, groups of children work on extended projects such as the lion project and the Amusement Park for Birds. The atelieristi work closely, becoming part of the circle of relationships in each school, and part of the dialog that develops the *progettazione* for long-term projects.

Figure 3–1.   Studios in Reggio-inspired preschools are supplied with a rich assortment of art materials, beautifully displayed to invite creativity. (*Courtesy:* Patti Cruikshank-Schott.)

The atelierista meets several times a day with the teachers. It is the atelierista's particular responsibility to help in the development of the children's aesthetic awareness and technical skills. They also provide the children with opportunities for using the hundred languages, and collaborate in developing and displaying the documentation of the children's experiences. The role of the atelierista is critical in supporting the teachers' roles in creating emergent curricula and long-term projects.

The Teacher in Reggio Emilia and in North America

There are many similarities between the typical role of the teacher in North America and in the municipal preschools in Reggio Emilia. However, the teacher's role in Reggio Emilia is different in several significant ways, some of which are listed below.

The role of the teacher as an observer is extended to documentor and researcher.   Observation is an important skill for most early childhood teachers, but the educators in Reggio Emilia have taken it a step further. Observation, for them, is only the first step in collecting the data that are used in developing documentation that captures the story of the children's experiences in the classroom and the progression of their developing understandings. Documentation becomes the basis for ongoing dialog to plan curriculum directions. The teacher then uses the documentation to revisit the experiences with the children and to communicate with parents and other visitors to the classroom. Documentation is taken a step further as it becomes a tool for teacher research, reflection, and collaboration.

The role of teacher as program planner emphasizes the role of creator of the environment as a third teacher.   Preparing a stimulating environment that fosters play, communication, and exploration is an essential part of the work of a teacher of preschool children. Creating an environment that acts as a third teacher in the classroom, however, is a new and challenging task for those who accept the challenge of Reggio educators to understand how the environment supports both interaction and focused communication.

The role of the teacher as curriculum planner changes to the role of the teacher as a co-constructor of knowledge.   Teachers usually plan experiences and activities for the children collaboratively with other teachers in the school. In considering the Reggio Emilia approach, however, the program is perceived as emerging from the children's interests and ideas, and in negotiation with them. Long-term *progettazione* guide the thinking of adults in creating meaningful learning experiences. This means that teachers need to meet often to discuss and reflect on their observations and on the transcriptions they make of the children's conversations. Planning is done in cooperation with others, but it becomes more spontaneous, has to be done more often, and involves more collaboration and negotiation with others.

The role of the teacher as parent educator changes to the role of the teacher as a partner with parents. Early childhood educators always have understood the importance of communicating with parents. For school to be a positive experience for children, there has to be congruence between the children's experiences at home and at school. In exploring ideas from the Reggio Emilia approach, however, teachers will find themselves working even more closely with parents. The concept of transparency allows parents to enter their children's experiences at school. In turn, they will understand how valuable their contribution is to their children's education, and become more aware of the many different ways they can partici- pate in the program.

The role of the teacher as communicator changes to the role of the teacher as listener, provocateur, and negotiator of meaning. Communication, in its myriad forms—written, visual, and verbal—has always been important in early childhood settings, but the emphasis on collaboration and documentation in the Reggio Emilia approach has greatly increased and changed the way the teacher communicates. Listening to children's conversations, interpreting their meaning and questions, knowing how to help them elaborate on their ideas, negotiating with them in furthering these ideas, reflecting on practice with other teachers, interpreting the program to parents verbally, and documenting the children's experiences have made communication one of the most essential parts of the teacher's role.

The role of the teacher in providing guidance changes to the role of the teacher as a supporter of the competent child. Traditionally, early childhood teachers spend much of their time guiding the children's behavior. During indoor and outdoor play, teachers use various strategies to guide the children's behavior; they supervise the children at transition times and help them with daily routines such as bathroom, lunch, and snack time. Bruner, in his study of Oxford preschools, noted that "a high proportion of adult-initiated interaction with children was given over to the boring stuff of petty management" (Katz, 1993, p. 28). Implementing principles of the Reggio Emilia approach brings the greatest rewards when teachers begin to see children as competent, when the environment begins to act as a third teacher, and when collaboration is in effect. The amount of time managing the classroom diminishes as the teacher becomes a partner with the children in the co- construction of knowledge, and teachers become free to do the things they really find rewarding such as engaging with children in real conversations about things that are important and pursuing exciting ideas with the children.

The role of the teacher in maintaining the social relationships in the class- room changes to the role of the teacher in supporting the social relationships in the classroom. Establishing a positive social environment in the classroom and beyond in the community is another essential part of the teacher's role in early childhood settings. A sense of belonging is at the core of every early childhood classroom. Without this sense, young children simply will not thrive. The first task of every teacher is to create what Carolyn Edwards calls "the circle of we" (1998). The educators in Reggio Emilia have helped us understand how important it is to provide children with opportunities to co-construct their knowledge in the social group. This creates what Bruner calls "a mutual community of learners" (1996, p. 81). The social relationships, or "the circle of we," not only includes children but also is expanded to draw in teachers, parents, and the community.

The role of the teacher in facilitating play changes to the role of the teacher as an exchanger of understandings. Learning through play is the foundation of the majority of early childhood programs with philosophical roots reaching back to Froebel, Dewey, and more recently, Piaget. Teachers spend time and effort creating environments that foster play in all areas of the program. Play is believed to be critical for physical, emotional, social, cognitive, and moral development. Teachers learn how to promote early math and literacy skills through play, as well as science and social study concepts.

Play is also considered an important part of the Reggio Emilia approach, but it does not seem as central to their program as in other early childhood settings. For instance, one does not hear the educators in Reggio Emilia extolling the values of learning through play. Children certainly have many opportunities to play freely in the Reggio Emilia preschools, but educators do not stress play as the most important medium for learning. What they do stress is "an exchange of understanding between the teacher and the child: to find in the intuitions of the child the roots of systematic knowledge" (Bruner, 1996, p. 57). This emphasis encourages teachers to listen to children, to engage in conversation with them, and to observe, record, and reflect on their behavior and words. Moreover, the work at Reggio Emilia focuses firmly on the sociocultural context that increases opportunities for children engaged in activities to "experience various, conflicting, and sometimes confusing perspectives. Thus they create 'disturbances' in the physical environment, and they support children's predispositions to challenge one another's views" (New in Edwards, Gandini, & Forman, 1998, p. 271). This view sees children as playmates and peers, but also as provocateurs. Play is expanded to its most serious dimension.

American teachers influenced by the ideas of Reggio Emilia have also changed their thinking about teacher roles.

Patti Cruikshank-Schott, Carolina Friends School:

I was the curriculum queen. I had literally hundreds of ways to teach the color "red". Every day it was something different, some new activity that I planned. The thinking from Reggio transformed the whole nature of being the curriculum queen, turned it upside down. Actually, children had been teaching me that for a while [before the Reggio influences]. I'm a producer. But now my production goes into the many hours I spend each week on producing the documentation. And now I'm fascinated by the traces of children's minds that I can get through the process of documentation. My way of documentation is very accessible. It provides windows, answering the questions of how to show children's development and interests, how to reflect on my own growth. The documentation makes me watch what I do, helps me to examine my practices. I finally get it about being a teacher/researcher. I thought that by being a practitioner I had to reject the role of researcher. Now I embrace the idea of practitioner as protagonist.

Margaret Edwards, Lakewood Avenue Children's School:

Reggio has expanded, more than anything, my ideas as to the role of the teacher. This notion of collaboration between teachers, children, and parents is so powerful. And I find that when teachers think of themselves as collaborators, rather than the person in charge, the whole nature of their relationship (and therefore their role) changes with both children and parents. It becomes less hierarchical and more lateral in nature. Also, something Malaguzzi said—"teachers should 'lend' their knowledge to children"—really changed us from teaching in a hands-off role, to occasionally a much more very hands on, quite directive role. Teachers here are now not so afraid to step in and demonstrate something to the child, or say, "Here, watch me. Then see if you can do that." This notion of "lending your knowledge" to the child (and parents too) seems to have given us as teachers permission to go down heretofore uncharted roads, and we love it!

Marty Gravett, Sabot School:

For many years I have felt what we as early childhood educators were able to do with children was not enough. We hadn't gotten it right. At first I thought it was me, that I didn't have the right education or enough education, or maturity, or enough resources. As I attempted to remedy these problems I found a philosophical home within progressive education. But still there was a ghost of a vision, a vapor trail I was following towards more integrity, more substance, more meaning in my work. And then I got a glimpse of the vision in its concrete incarnation—it was the work of the teachers in the municipal preschools in Reggio Emilia.

Now, eight years into pursuing that vision, I see myself as one of many active players in the classroom. My roles now include collaborator, provocateur, scaffolder. In the past as a teacher I had, at separate times, both taken the reins of control in the classroom and had given them over to the children. Both were incomplete ways of working. Today, I value my own and colleagues' contributions as much as I value the children's. The result is a dance between teachers and children where the lead changes as the steps become more familiar or more intriguing to one person or the other. It is a dance that no one knows, no one has seen in full; it is being choreographed by the dancers as we dance. This is a thrilling way to work.

While team teaching was a concept that long appealed to me, I had not understood its real potential until I began to work in a team inspired by the Reggio approach. Now my role as a teacher includes being an organizer, a communicator, and collaborator with colleagues. I spend a significant part of each day in the classroom in conversation with my colleagues making decisions about what next step to take to move individual children and small groups forward. The team concept also includes taking on leadership when my strengths are needed, or when I am challenged by a particular line of inquiry that opens itself to me. This is required of all the teachers, and so to support each other's leadership we each take on the important, corollary role of ally.

Another role I have just begun to identify is that of the inverse magician. The task in this job is to make the invisible, visible. The task includes making the work of teachers and children visible to parents, making visible the elements and wonders of the environment to the children, making the teachers' intentions visible to the parents, and the children's intentions visible to themselves. The inverse magician is an observer first of all, a documenter, a reflector, and a provocateur.

Ann Pelo, Hilltop School:

In my earlier teaching, I saw my work primarily as offering children learning opportunities—nudging them towards particular insights or knowledge by setting out particular activities or leading small groups. I watched their play for evidence of particular sorts of learning and thinking.

I now approach my work with a broader and deeper understanding of my roles as a teacher. I observe children's play with curiosity, seeing myself as a researcher learning about the children's insights, understandings, misunderstandings, questions, passions, worldviews. I'm not so much looking for evidence of particular learning as I am watching for glimpses into the children's minds and hearts; it's a much more open and humble posture, with an empty pad of paper waiting for my notes and questions, rather than a checklist of learning experiences to watch for.

Another idea from Reggio that has impacted me is the idea of the master/apprentice relationship between adults and children. Earlier in my teaching, I lived in the tension between the typical U.S. "hands-off" attitude towards children's work and my inclination to teach—to offer information and skills. Now, I try to stay anchored in an awareness that I have more experience and skill than the kids and that I can offer that to them, AND in an awareness that the children have unique and potent ideas and insights that I want to honor and learn from.

I sometimes describe the relationship between teacher and child as a slow game of catch. It is a mutual relationship, one shaped by both people. The teacher isn't throwing balls hard and fast at the child, nor is she standing back and watching the child toss balls in the hope that someone will catch them. Both are actively involved in creating what happens in the classroom. It demands mindfulness, openness, respect, and self-awareness in the teacher and the child.

Reggio has influenced my understanding of the role of a teacher in relationship to other adults as well. I'm pushed to explore genuine collaboration with families and with co-teachers, moving out of the role of expert or ultra-competent manager, and into the role of collaborator, sometimes an expert and sometimes a learner.

Pam Oken-Wright, St. Catherine's School:

As Reggio ideas inform our ideas about children and learning, they of course also inform our image of what it looks like to support children's learning. Perhaps the biggest change for American teachers would be that, in our desire to be researchers of children's thinking and learning, we have to become observers and analysts, rather than transmitters. It is a major role shift, I think. We look for children's intent, their theories, confusions, and passions, and that informs our next "move," whether it is a conscious decision to observe and document some more, or a decision to offer a new provocation. Our planning becomes fluid, responsive, and reciprocal—no longer arbitrary or "subject" oriented.

In documenting, we make experiences visible, keeping memory of those experiences alive for all involved. In a sense, we act as memory proxy: to help children find common impressions around an experience, to make it visible and therefore accessible to the children in the community, and to keep it alive long enough to invite further investigation later. This is part of setting up an environment full of provocation, inspiration, and invitation—also a vital role of a teacher in a Reggio Emilia-inspired classroom.

In direct interaction with children, our role as supporter is enlarged and refined under Reggio inspiration. Once we have developed the skill to read children's intent (what is the child really trying to do here? What does she need to make her idea visible?), our support becomes more specifically responsive. If Annie is stuck trying to sculpt a giraffe out of clay, and we can work with her to determine what bit of help would get her unstuck, we are accomplishing a number of things. Yes, she develops a deeper understanding of "giraffe," but she also learns to trust that she CAN make her ideas visible, no matter how big or elaborate they are (and that adults will help her do so), and so she does NOT learn to put aside those big ideas just because they are big. Our role in supporting that learning is key, I believe, especially if children have already had experience with the "culture of impossibility," as many as young as five years old have already had.

EARLY CHILDHOOD EDUCATORS TODAY

What is the role of the teacher in early childhood education at the beginning of the 21st century? More children, for the first time in the history of parenting, are cared for outside the home. With both parents at work in an increasing number of homes, early childhood educators are providing children with a major portion of their care. Therefore, all aspects of the profession have to be given serious consideration because of the impact this will have on future generations.

It is important to understand that the hierarchy in the work of an early childhood educator is fairly horizontal: there are not many levels in the job that require different sets of skills. The work is both complex and multifaceted. Many early childhood teachers are expected to manage the center operations including budgeting, hiring staff, enrolling children, and fund-raising. They also plan the pro-gram and the physical space in the classroom. A large part of the job involves over-seeing the social relationships in the classroom, supervising the children, communicating with children and their families, and acting as an advocate in the community for quality programs for children. The graduate of a two-year program in early childhood education is expected to be knowledgeable in subjects as far reaching as child development, early childhood curriculum, multiculturalism, antibias advocacy, group dynamics and interpersonal communication, inclusion of children needing extra support, and business management.

Over the last century, the role of the early childhood educator has become more clearly defined. It has evolved as a separate discipline, perhaps somewhere between social work and education. For those of us studying the Reggio Emilia approach, there seems to be another change in the wind, a shift in the paradigm, especially when looking at relationships. If we think of the role of a teacher as a prism with many different facets, it seems likely that in the 21st century, relation-ship will be the side of the prism that is turned to face us, the one that will be given the brightest focus.

It is evident why the educators in Reggio Emilia place so much importance on relationships with children, coworkers, parents, and the community. The high quality of care in the infant–toddler centers and the preschools in Reggio Emilia is a result of the emphasis that has been placed on building relationships so care-fully and solidly at every level of the program. The concern some people express about placing children for long periods in their early years in child care will be lessened if society sees it not as a necessity only, but as a positive choice. If child care can be viewed as a natural part of the web in family relationships, then gen-erations of young children will reap the benefits. This view means shifting the emphasis in the teacher preparation programs from learning how to manage early childhood settings to creating a community of people working together for the benefit of the children.

THE PREPARATION OF TEACHERS

As the focus of teacher education programs turns to creating a setting where stu-dents can experience the development of relationships for reflective collaboration, restructuring, and rethinking of existing programs becomes necessary. No longer can preparation consist of students completing a prescribed sequence of courses that are expected to give preservice teachers all the required knowledge and skills to take into future solitary classrooms where they will follow defined steps to pass knowledge on to their students. Instead, teachers must be prepared to understand how knowledge is co-constructed and how reflective communication among all participants in a learning setting facilitates learning for all. The teacher education program itself must allow students opportunities to become members of learning communities where relationships focus on supporting one another's learning. How are teacher education programs beginning to meet this challenge? Examples of two programs follow.

Lambton College, Sarnia, Ontario

Mabel Higgins, in her article "Come, Join the Journey" (1999) describes how her interest in the Reggio approach began when she read the following quotation in the November 1994 edition of *Exchange:* "What we do every day celebrates children and the work of teachers. With great care, we create a friendly, responsive environment for children, an environment that invites children to action and exploration" (Gandini, 1994). Higgins writes, "The words and the visions on these few pages stirred something inside me . . . *this is the way it ought to be but is not always the case.*" Higgins, an instructor in an early childhood education program at Lambton College in Sarnia, Ontario, began to incorporate ideas from the Reggio approach in her work with college students.

The invitation to college students to join her in her journey of discovery of the Reggio Emilia approach required that the curriculum be built from the students' concerns and interests in the same way that the curriculum arises from the interests and questions posed by the children in Reggio Emilia. Mabel states in her article: "I wanted to do this with *my* students while teaching within the framework of the recently established *Ontario Standards for College Early Childhood Education programs.* We know that learning occurs when the learner has control over what they are learning. I once heard someone say that . . . *We teach best, that which we most need to learn!* I was ready to do some learning alongside my students." As a result, the faculty began to make modifications to the curriculum design courses and field experience courses. Mabel notes that "a review of the program was occurring at the same time so the 'mood' or desire for change was already rolling in and the 'fit' became natural." One of the major changes they made in the field experience course was in the way observation is taught. They installed a video lab where students and faculty could observe children and teachers at the campus school. "Prior to this," Mabel states, "we taught students observational techniques in a traditional classroom and then sent them off to observe on their own. Together we now work through the questions that arise as we observe."

The program began to employ Vygotsky's theory in supporting the students' learning. Knowing that the students were at varying levels of ability, the instructors provided them with the tools to enable them to climb from their current level of understanding to a higher threshold in the zone of proximal development.

Mabel notes that it was easy to inject lectures on Reggio Emilia into the curriculum courses because the approach had always been to offer students a smorgasbord of educational approaches. She writes, "No matter what lesson I was presenting, little bits of this approach would seep into our discourse. I soon began to bring in books on the subject, then videos and now whilst still presenting a variety of approaches, my bias [toward the Reggio Emilia approach] becomes rather evident."

The Reggio Emilia approach was also introduced into the students' final field experience in the fourth semester. In this semester, students were prepared for life after graduation. The college instructors modified earlier assignments in this semester and added two new components implementing some elements of the Reggio Emilia approach: community outreach projects and student-initiated placement experience. Mabel writes,

> "The results have been astounding. In both assignments the faculty role was one of protagonist and guide. The challenge was unleashed and the students were supported in every way possible to meet it. Our students, like the children, were given the space, time and materials to develop their project. They collaborated with faculty, peers and community."

Early Childhood PreK–3 Teacher Education Program, University of Vermont

The lab school at the University of Vermont has a long history having begun as a half-day preschool program open only during the academic year. In 1990, the program was restructured to create a full-time, full-year program for children from infancy through age five. Because the center is a lab school, it has the dual mission of providing an excellent early childhood program for children and a learning setting for the university's early childhood education majors. A collaborative program unites the faculty of the teacher education program with the teaching staff of the center; all work as a team in terms of the child care program and the teacher education program. "Faculty work with teachers in the classroom, teachers participate in undergraduate courses, and core courses in the program are team taught between faculty and the two Head Teachers in the program" (Visitors' Guide, p. 2). Such collaboration not only suggests the influence of the ideas of Reggio Emilia on the program but also has been the means for creating an educational system based on relationships and reflection.

About the time of the restructuring, Dale Goldhaber, director of the center, and faculty including Jeanne Goldhaber, Dee Smith, Barbara Burrington, and Susan Sortino began to study ideas from Reggio. They participated in a study delegation in Reggio and came home inspired to see what could be incorporated into the center and the teacher education program. With each visit to Reggio, they return with new concepts to investigate. Recently, the entire teaching staff of the center participated in a study tour. Jeanne Goldhaber attributes this joint trip as the source of providing a true vision of excellence to work toward: "When only two or three had been, it had been more difficult to work on a shared vision."

The center's environment gives testimony to putting ideas of excellence into practice. There are separate spaces for infants that include play and sleep areas, a room for toddlers, another for older toddlers, and a multiage preschool classroom. There is a welcoming sense of physical and social comfort, with attention paid to light and physical softness, pictures of families and staff, intriguing areas for active exploration, and delightful surprises such as the pattern of mirrors on the ceiling in the infant room. Relationships are nurtured and strengthened as the teaching staff moves on with their particular group of children as they change classrooms during the first three years. This provides continuity for children and families, and opportunities for deep collaboration. Observations and reflections form the basis for making

Figure 3–2.   The toddler area looks very home-like, with comfortable furniture, family photos, and flowers. (*Courtesy:* University of Vermont Campus Children's Center.)

Figure 3–3.   This intriguing addition of mirrors on the ceiling of the infant room gives a different view. (*Courtesy:* University of Vermont Campus Children's Center.)

decisions about directions for curriculum to emerge. Children's active exploration is documented and shared in panels lining the hallways outside the classrooms, and in notebooks found in the entryways to the classrooms, presenting the notes and artifacts of each extended project. The Reggio principles of relationships, collaboration, environment as third teacher, extended investigations about topics that emerge from the interaction within the classroom, and documentation of children's growth and learning processes are seen in action in the center.

The theoretical base for the work in the center is acknowledged to be the child development theories of Jean Piaget and Lev Vygotsky. The vision is acknowledged to be the work in Reggio. The faculty point out that the ideas from Reggio are not unique; "What *is* unique to Reggio is that you see early childhood education being done as it should be done. In particular, you see a program whose vision of the child comes as close to being perfectly translated into practice as is perhaps possible" (Visitors' Guide, p. 7).

It is the program's mission to offer this same vision to a new generation of teachers in the Early Childhood PreK–3 Teacher Education Program. The same developmental theorists who inform the idea of constructing knowledge influence the structuring of the teacher education program. "This Constructivist theme serves as the unifying and integrating element of the program—one that cuts across both course and field experiences" (Visitors' Guide, p. 12). Students participate in a coherent, integrated program of professional development rather than simply a sequence of classes. The purpose of the program design is to offer students experiences that will help develop knowledge and skills to work with children from infancy through the primary grades. Students are eligible for licensure for PreK–3 from the state of Vermont.

The sequence of professional development work begins with child development and observation courses. In the observation course, students begin to participate in the campus center. Then follows a 10-credit hour block course in which small groups of students spend two mornings a week working in either infant/toddler classrooms or the preschool. The groups of students will remain a constant, building relationships with fellow students and within the classroom. Four hours of seminar work each week help students begin the process of collaborative reflection about their observations of children. Each observation includes a series of questions generated in the seminar or by individuals.

The following semester, students have a full-semester, full-time student teaching experience (a 12-credit hour block) in the same classroom. Again, a continuity of relationships for students, children, families, and mentor teachers is maintained. This structure reflects the program's recognition of the critical role of relationships, something not accounted for in typical student placements. Jeanne Goldhaber comments, "We often shoot ourselves in the foot when we keep changing placement sites." Part of the time is spent in two-hour segments apart with the mentor teacher to work on documentation. A documentation workroom with computers and other materials is down the hall from the children's classrooms. Jeanne made the comment that one of the hardest things early on in addressing some Reggio ideas had been teachers' initial discomfort with some of the necessary technology, as well as the concept of going public with what they thought. Finding time to free the teachers for this documentation was always a challenge.

The students may join the classroom teachers in following the threads of their investigations with children, or may follow the thread they have noticed, gaining experience in individualizing curriculum to support children's explorations. An example of this was seen on a documentation recently posted in the hallway outside the preschool classroom. The ongoing activity had involved sewing, something that challenged and intrigued many of the children. The board, labeled "Sewing Stories," included transcriptions of the children's dialog as they created, pictures of the children at work, and of the individual products they had made including a pillow for an expected sibling and a little purse. Some reflections about the impact of the sewing process were also included. A student had been interested in watching the sewing work and looked for other ways to extend the experience. She found some plastic sewing grids and offered them to

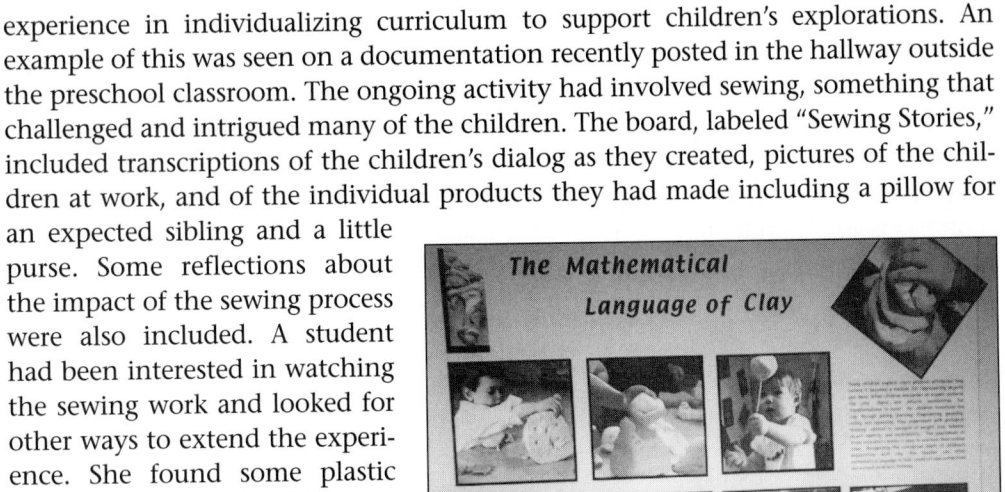

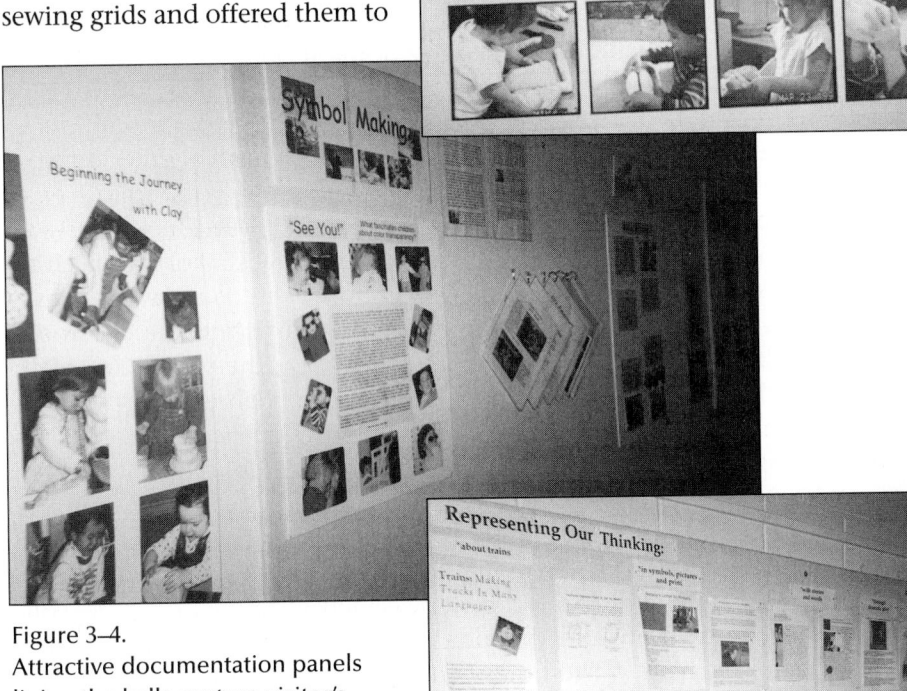

Figure 3–4.
Attractive documentation panels lining the halls capture visitor's interest. (*Courtesy:* University of Vermont Campus Children's Center.)

the children. Her documentation panel included pictures and descriptions of the process of choosing particular grids and working with them. Other boards outside the toddlers' rooms illustrated individual work students had done in exploring music and block building with toddlers. Ongoing work is described on observation sheets and reflections bound together and hanging on the board outside the room. Later in the semester, these ongoing documentations likely will be synthesized into a final documentation panel. Surrounded by meticulous and thoughtful documentation, it would be difficult for parents and visitors not to become engaged in exploring the intellectual life of the children within. Through this professional development sequence (another similar sequence focuses on experiences with the primary grades), students are participating in long-term experiences involving collaborative exploration, learning to observe, reflect, and build curriculum based on those reflections, and to make their work public to build a community of adults supporting children's growth.

The teacher education program's use of ideas from Reggio has evolved over a period of time. In a chapter "Observing, Recording, Understanding: the Role of Documentation in Early Childhood Education" in *First Steps Toward Teaching the Reggio Way* (Hendrick, 1997), Jeanne Goldhaber and two faculty colleagues describe some of their first efforts to incorporate principles of collaboration in the process of documentation they were introducing to their students in the early 1990s. What is immediately obvious in their description is the increased collegial collaboration that the program changes necessitated; college faculty were no longer merely involved in parallel but separate teaching practices. As the faculty experimented with introducing various documentation techniques to their students, their primary goal was to increase students' skills and knowledge. Even though there were frustrations and difficulties with the process, the faculty perceived that student learning about components of best practice was enhanced.

The first assignments for documentation called for two students to be assigned for two-hour periods every week in the preschool on two-week rotations. One student was to interact primarily with the children on tasks such as play dough or blocks; the other was the primary observer/documenter. They were to document an experience of a child involved in an investigation, using at least three Polaroid pictures with short written observations or transcripts of children's conversations attached. The panel was to be created in 20 to 30 minutes of the two-hour block of time. The faculty's first discovery was that the time pressure in a situation where students were not already familiar with the children or classroom produced panels where ideas about what to observe and document had been chosen too quickly and superficially. A second series of assignments to make audiotapes of children at work in a writing/drawing center produced the more positive results of students "listening more intently" to children. Allowing more time to create the panels allowed students to give more thought to what was included, and improved the quality of the panels. Later that semester, faculty introduced video prints as another documentation strategy. They discovered that the reviewing of the tapes caused students to rethink their ideas about children's experiences. At this early stage, faculty developed a list of essential elements for documentation panels, noting that it was a tentative list.

As the program has evolved, with students' semester long and intensive involvement in the classrooms, the emphasis is on the documentation of the process of investigations without focusing so much on the final piece to be created. And the process of documentation continues to be revisited within the center and the teacher education program. Recently, a new teacher in the center raised the question whether there were any rules for documentation. This led faculty and center teachers to review their current definition of documentation, to consider whether it reflected who they are and what they are doing, and how they now consider the role of documentation. Each submitted a definition. They are now analyzing the definitions to find common threads and a new definition probably will be devised. The journey of investigation and co-construction of meaning continues. And through the process of reflection, students begin their own journeys. One student said:

> This then is the greatest "discovery" I've made thus far: there are no easy answers. . . . They really do come from the interactions and observations we make. This shouldn't sound so revealing, since it is what we study, but somehow I never really connected the philosophy to myself. It really is a process. You said this all along and I nodded and agreed and said "Yes, yes it is," and I thought I knew what you meant. But I didn't. And I don't know if I do now, either (but I think I do). And I am on the road, finally, and that is what I wanted (Goldhaber et al. in Hendrick, 1997, p. 209).

And Jeanne Goldhaber and her colleagues say, "That is what we want, too; to be on the road together."

It seems appropriate to conclude this exploration of the expanded thinking on teachers' roles suggested by the Reggio Emilia approach with words from Loris Malaguzzi:

> The teacher's task is to be a mediator, offering carefully measured and pertinent loans of knowledge and skills, periodically producing summaries of the children's convergent and divergent elements and the points of arrival of their work . . . and to solicit the participation of each and every child through increasingly cooperative and productive interaction. In one essential concept, the teacher's task is to preserve, as far as is possible, the naturalness of the children's creative and practical processes, in the conviction that children have the necessary resources for going much further than we might think (Malaguzzi, 1995, pp. 20–22).

Chapter **4**

Relationships

*I believe there is no possibility of existing without relationship. Relationship is a neces-
sity of life.*

—Loris Malaguzzi

Questions to Consider:

- What are the underlying theoretical perspectives that guide an understanding about relationship?

- How is relationship woven into all parts of the program?

- What roles do communication and documentation play in establishing relationships?

- How does the emphasis placed on relationship affect the facets of the program, such as children, co-workers, community, program, play, space, time, and materials?

- What are the challenges in making relationship central to the program?

- What indicates that relationship has become a fundamental principle in the program?

When teachers study children, either for the purpose of observation or in planning curriculum experiences, they consider the uniqueness of each child in the class, and they also view children in the context of their family, peer group, and community. Ask any teacher of young children what her goals are for children, and she will probably say to ensure they develop a strong sense of self and reach their full potential physically, emotionally, socially, and intellectually. This is one of the reasons play in childhood is considered so important: it is in play that the development of the whole child is fostered. Learning through play has been an important philosophical perspective in early childhood programs since Froebelian kindergartens were founded in the early part of the 20th century. Later, Piagetian theory reaffirmed the value of play, especially its role in promoting young children's cognitive development. The development of play behavior and how it evolves from a solitary to a social behavior has been described by Parten (1932) and Smilansky (1968). More recently, researchers such as Elizabeth Jones and Gretchen Reynolds (1997) have examined the role of the teacher in play. However, only in more recent years, as we have become more aware of the role that relationship plays in early childhood, have early childhood educators emphasized children's development in the context of the social group.

One of the earliest social relationships develops between mother and infant at birth. The typical suck/pause pattern of feeding forms the basis for the turn-taking rhythm, an early form of communication between mother and infant. When mother and child establish a synchronous rhythm, they form a positive relationship. Development of the relationship, however, will not proceed as smoothly if factors such as early trauma or a mismatch in temperament between the mother and child interfere with the formation of this rhythm. This early relationship between the mother and child is an example of the interdependence of children and adults in all areas of development (Brazelton, 1981).

The work of Vygotsky and Bruner has increased awareness of the importance of the quality of the relationship between child and caregiver in fostering the child's intellectual development, especially language development. In the following example of an interchange between a mother and child, Bruner observes how a mother instinctively uses language to further her child's thinking. He describes how the mother uses "little 'formats' or rituals" to help the child learn the words for the pictures in the book they are reading together:

"Oh look Richard! What's that?"

"It's a fishy."

"That's right."

She then encouraged the child to think about the meaning conveyed by the pictures. "What's the fishy doing?"

Bruner observes how the mother seems to know intuitively when to raise the ante, or to challenge the child to think and use language at a higher level. He notes that "she remains forever on the growing edge of the child's competence" (Bruner, 1986, p. 77).

As Bruner's example shows, interactions between children and either an adult or a child who is more competent act as scaffolding to nudge children to go beyond what they can achieve on their own. They now enter what Vygotsky termed *the zone of proximal development,* the area in which the child is able to perform with assistance at a higher level of mental functioning. Vygotsky believed that when children receive the right kind of assistance from others, they reach beyond their present level of ability and move forward in their development. The major difference between the theories of Piaget and Vygotsky lies in the importance given to the role of the relationship between children and their teachers or caregivers. In a Piagetian world, children construct their knowledge mainly on their own; in a Vygotskian world, children co-construct knowledge with others. The quality of the relationship established with teachers or caregivers becomes critical in the child's growth and development. In the past, early childhood programs in many parts of the world were based on the philosophy that children learn through play. But since the work of Vygotsky (and later Bruner) identified the critical role of relationship, and especially reciprocity, in the child's development, there has been a shift toward making relationship a fundamental principle in programs for young children. Before Vygotsky's theories became generally known in Western society, however, the educators in the Reggio Emilia preschools understood the importance of relationship and made it central to their programs.

The challenge for early childhood educators is to ensure that all children who receive care outside their homes are able to form quality relationships with their teachers and caregivers. Think of a child as at the center of concentric rings of relationships, the ring containing family, school, and child care being the closest. Bronfenbrenner terms this ring the *microsystem*. Surrounding this is the *mesosystem*, the ring in which different microsystems interact; for example, the quality of the relationship between home and school or center would be considered here. These interactions will be influenced by how adults at home and at school perceive the child, and by how the child-rearing beliefs at home match the teacher's image of the child. The next ring is the *exosystem*, the community in which the child lives. The formal or informal social structures in the exosystem affect the child's experiences within the first circle of relationships. For example, the policies in the preschool or center have an impact on the quality of care the child receives outside the home. The final, surrounding ring is the *macrosystem*, comprising the culture and subculture in which the child is reared. When links between these circles of relationships are strong and communication flows freely between them, the child benefits; however, if the links are weak or nonexistent, the child's development will suffer. For example, if the child is secure within the ring of family relationships, communication between the school and the family is strong and the community and culture are supportive of the child and family, then conditions for the child's development are optimum (Bronfenbrenner in Yeates et al., 1994, p. 5).

Creating a sense of belonging is fundamental to the Reggio Emilia approach. For the program to function successfully, everyone involved—children, families, and teachers—needs to feel that they play an integral part in what Carolyn Edwards calls "the circle of we." If we agree with the educators in Reggio Emilia that we will be able to provide the highest quality of child care and education only by making relationship the foundation of the program, then we will have to review every aspect of our programs to see how we can strengthen relationships. In a preschool program, relationship takes place at many levels: between children and children as discussed further in the co-construction of understanding and working together on long-term projects; and also between teachers and families, teachers and children, teachers and colleagues, and ultimately teachers and the surrounding community.

RELATIONSHIPS WITH FAMILIES

The initial contact that families have with the school will set the tone for future relationships between home and school. Therefore, the educators in Reggio Emilia believe that beginnings, or *insermento*, are critical. In Reggio, a good deal of thought

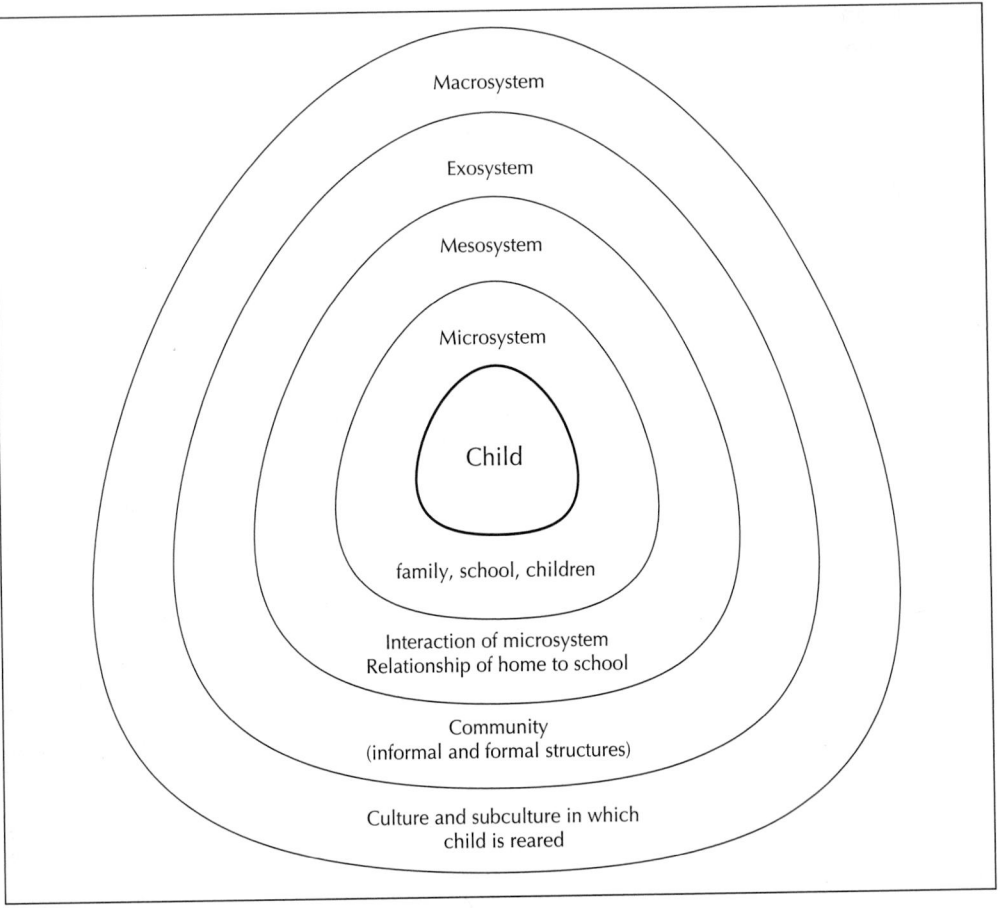

Figure 4–1.   Multiple rings of relationships affect children.

and attention is given to the families' first days at the centers to communicate the impression that parents and children are welcome and very important. The first beginnings are to be shared by parents, children, and teachers together to create a pattern of communication and reciprocity. Teachers and parents together construct a sense of belonging and trust. In Reggio Emilia, the transition is considered as part of the cycle of exchange that is not just limited to the child's entry. There have already been numerous opportunities for parents and children to meet with teachers and to participate in informal events long before the child's actual entry. During the first week of school, parents come together with their children to the center; mothers and fathers work closely with the teacher to help the child explore the new environment. As children gradually become comfortable, parents move into nearby rooms where they work together on creating classroom materials, plan for later parent meetings, and discuss menus with the cooks. Reggio Emilia's edu-cators have a goal of ensuring that new parents also develop relationships with other parents and with other parents' children (New, 1999). So, too, at Lakewood School, the parents arrange parties to welcome the incoming families.

Educators need to review the orientation procedure to ensure that at each of the stages in introducing the child and family to the school, a strong relationship between the teachers and the family is fostered. The process cannot be rushed because there has to be enough time for the child and the parents to build trust in the teachers and the school. Teachers need to respect the attachment of the child to the parents at every stage and should separate the child from the parents only when the child feels secure in the new surroundings. The principles listed below can help teachers build strong relationships with families.

Make families feel welcome. The entranceways in the preschools in Reggio Emilia are designed to make families feel welcome and to encourage them to linger, rather than rush their children's transition from home to school. These spaces are furnished with comfortable chairs. Portfolios of the children's work and experiences in school are arranged on shelves nearby, and documentation is displayed on the walls to inform parents and visitors about what the children are experiencing in school. American programs inspired by Reggio

Figure 4–2.
These attractive entryways at Lakewood Avenue Children's School welcome parents to enjoy the children's work.
(*Courtesy:* Lakewood Avenue Children's School.)

practices also structure their entryways to create warm and welcoming first impressions. The main entrance at Lakewood School is actually in the back through the kitchen where kitchen utensils and information about the program adorn the walls. Here, a round table enables parents and/or teachers to sit and chat under a large mural created by children and a community artist that surrounds the door to the classroom. Plants and a large mirror reflect the whole classroom in the entryway of the two's classroom. The entryway at First Baptist Kindergarten in Greenville, South Carolina, offers the mission statement, children's artwork, and smiling pictures of all who work within, including the custodian, an important part of the children's world. Intriguing photos and quotes of past events are on the walls on Pam Oken-Wright's entry, along with a board filled with post-it notes where parents have written individual answers to the question: "What are your hopes and dreams for your child?" The University of Vermont Campus Children's Center has a central piazza connecting faculty offices, children's classrooms, and teachers' work rooms; the piazza has places for children to play and stories on the wall for families to enjoy. Classroom entryways welcome visitors with photos of all the children, families, and teachers. In thinking of ways to make families feel more closely connected to the center, the staff at Quadra Island moved the children's attendance sheet that parents sign every day from an outside entrance into the classroom itself so that parents spend a few minutes each day with the teachers and children. They hoped that in this way, parents would become more familiar with the center.

Communicate clear expectations. Expectations are usually stated in a handbook that teachers give to parents when they enroll their children in the program. The parents at Quadra Island are expected to serve on the nonprofit board that administers the school. They also contribute their skills by chopping wood for the woodstove that heats the center, maintaining the buildings and playground, and building and repairing the equipment. Parents volunteer their time to the program by preparing food and materials for the children to use. A number of people who serve on the board are people in the community who do not have children in the center but who volunteer to help with its administration.

The center has a documentation panel displayed prominently at the entrance to the school, showing photographs illustrating previous parent involvement. The teachers find that it helps to remind parents of the importance of their involvement and shows them ways in which they can participate in the program.

There is no requirement for parent participation at Lakewood Avenue Children's School, but most parents participate fully in the two scheduled workdays each year. Margaret Edwards comments that there had always been expectations of parent involvement in her program, even before her staff began to implement Reggio ideas. "But that was primarily to hold fees down and keep the place clean and attractive. Now it's about real partnership and a sense of ownership." Jane Watkins, at First Baptist Kindergarten, says that their parents feel needed, essential to the process of the program for their children. With 13 parent committees to choose among for participation, parents can always find something interesting to do. Such active roles draw parents fully into the life of the school, along with their children and the teachers.

Reggio philosophy speaks of parents as equals among the three protagonists in teaching and learning: child, teacher, and parent. This implies clear expectations that parents will do far more than auxiliary volunteer tasks to support the program. The focus on the life of the classroom and the careful documentation of the dynamic learning processes at work draws parents into deeper connections. Documentation itself communicates the clear expectation that parents will be interested in trying to understand the deep sense of what their children are thinking and learning, and invites them into the dialog with their children and the teachers.

A story from Lakewood illustrates how parents become involved in the dialog: Several years ago, the children became interested in the doves in their neighborhood. There was a great deal of discussion about doves and investigation that involved finding pictures of a dovecote. The children became interested in the dovecote and wanted to get one. The teachers could not find one for sale or plans on how to make one. As they wondered who could help them, the children's response was "our parents." They dictated a newsletter for teachers to send out to parents, and the parents responded. Some parents with medical connections wondered whether the doves might be a source of a virus that could present a hazard. They all consulted a veterinarian and learned more about the potential difficulty. Ultimately, they decided not to work with the dove idea any further, but this one experience established a baseline for families getting directly involved in the life of the school. This kind of dialog cannot occur when teachers maintain absolute ownership of the learning process in their classrooms. Teachers have a vital role in creating the kind of classroom culture—the phrase used at Sabot School is "culture of engagement"—that conveys an expectation of teachers and parents communicating and working together as equals.

Provide parents with information about their children in the program. Documentation of the children's experiences makes the program visible to the parents. A portfolio for each child in the program is an essential tool for communication with the parents. The teachers in one center decided that to ensure this task was done, they would each take responsibility for a small group of children. Each teacher would then observe and record information about the children in her group, discussing the observations with the other staff members and communicating with the parents of the children in her group every day.

It is important to realize that for teachers in Reggio Emilia and those schools in North America inspired by Reggio practices, there is a desire to interest parents deeply in listening to and understanding their young children. Usually, they begin the process of listening because journals and newsletters identify children's ideas and words by name, and they are interested in reading about their child; later, teachers hope parents will continue to listen because it has become interesting to have insights into children's minds.

The following is an excerpt from a center newsletter.

On Friday, we had the following discussion at circle time:

Mrs. Stewart: What holiday is coming up soon?

Class: Valentine's Day!

Mrs. Stewart: Who brings us valentines?

Barrett: The mailboxes man.

Mrs. Stewart: What else do you call that person?

Class: Mailman.

Mary Kate: Mail girl.

Barrett: Mail lady. Mail carrier.

Mrs. Stewart: How does the mail carrier bring mail to your house?

Barrett: They drive to your house and put it in your mailbox.

Abigail: If it's big, they leave it at your door.

Barrett: They come in a white truck.

Austin: I have a new house and it has a thing you put mail through your door. He puts it in there and it drops on the floor and we go get it.

Zachary: We go across the street and somebody has to hold your hand.

Mary Kate: My mailbox has bricks all over it.

Mrs. Stewart: What are other mailboxes made of?

Barrett: They are made out of wood. Mine has a place in the front where the mailman puts the mail and a door in the back and you open it and go get the mail out.

Figure 4–3. This documentation panel reveals ways that parents become involved in the Quadra Island Day Care program.

Megan: My door is on the front.

Elise: We found mail on our steps.
(More about the ensuing project later. Thank you to Kathy Stewart at First Baptist Church Kindergarten for the newsletter.)

There is a sense that as parents read transcriptions of conversations and discover that children are thinking about things and creating their own understandings, parents will learn to take the time to really listen. Sharing the words and ideas of all children is an important part of the information provided to parents. Newsletters in Reggio-inspired classrooms are no longer basic reports of what children have been doing; instead, they often include verbatim conversations that point the way to later activities. At first, parents eagerly skim the letter to find their own child's name. Later, they learn to value the opportunity to receive insights from children's thoughts, even when they are not the thoughts of their own children. American teachers often find that American parents focus specifically on their own child's progress; the idea of reporting on learning experiences of all in the group may lead us closer to the shared sense of responsibility for all children that is part of the Italian culture. Even more important, it may help parents come to value the seriousness of young children's work and ideas.

Listen and communicate honestly with parents.   Open communication is possible only when trust has been established between teachers and parents. Careful orientation of parents to the program is essential to enabling this trust to grow. Teachers also have to nurture trust daily by making it possible for the parents to feel a sense of belonging and commitment to the school, with regular, honest communication. Patti Cruikshank-Schott says that after several years of using the daily journals to communicate with the families in her classroom, she now journals *everything.* Initially, the journal reported only positive learning experiences. Now, the tears and conflicts also are reported and reflected on. She comments on the fact that some teachers and parents have had difficulties with such frank reporting, with parents not wanting teachers to write things that seemed to show their child in a negative light, and teachers uncomfortable with going public with a very human classroom. This again is the learning process for parents and teachers; realizing that such documentation is not an evaluation but an opportunity for reflection.

Plan creative ways of involving families in the program.   Parents often participate by doing the essential jobs of serving on committees and driving the children on field trips. It is important, however, to involve the parents in creative ways as well. For example, following the mailbox conversations that were reported above, the teachers asked parents to participate in the subsequent exploration. They sent an envelope home with a disposable camera for parents to take a close-up picture of their mailbox, perhaps with their child standing by it. The envelope also contained a list of all the children in the class so that parents could

Figure 4–4.   Peter, a parent helper, makes pizza with the children.

pass the camera along to someone who lived close to them, or send it back to school to go to the next name on the list. The final comment in the newsletter request was "We don't know where all of this will lead, but we'll keep you posted." When the pictures were developed, they were posted in the classroom near the children's mailboxes.

Accept differences in the value systems of families in the school. The diversity in modern society presents a challenge for teachers and provides a rich source for learning experiences in the classroom. When diversity is viewed as an asset, it becomes a wonderful medium for forming relationships with children and families.

In the Sexsmith Multicultural Preschool in Vancouver (a program that was developed to help children and their families adjust to Canadian culture and learn English as a second language), the teachers observed that the children's play frequently centered on pretend cooking in the housekeeping corner. The teachers asked the parents if some of them would like to volunteer to cook a simple dish from their culture with the children in the class. This cooking experience then became the basis for further learning experiences. For example, one mother who had recently emigrated from Hong Kong offered to help the children cook stir-fried Chinese vegetables. The adults planned a field trip to buy vegetables at a nearby Chinese grocery, and the mother showed the children how to cook the vegetables in a wok. A family who owned a Chinese restaurant invited the class to have a meal at their restaurant. Following this experience, the children made egg drop soup at school. The teachers placed the recipe and materials for cooking and eating Chinese food such as a wok, bowls, and chopsticks in the dramatic play corner for the children to use.

A few days later, the teachers observed the children pretending to be waiters and serving the food to other children who were pretending to be the customers. The children asked for a chalkboard, on which they wrote up the menu for the day, and for white napkins which the "waiters" threw over their shoulders as they served the "customers." This group of children was particularly knowledgeable about serving food because many of their families worked in restaurants or in the cafeteria of the local hospital. After observing the children's interest in preparing and serving food, the teachers asked them if they would like to convert the classroom into a restaurant and invite the parents to be their customers. The children helped write a simple menu of celery sticks stuffed with peanut butter or cream cheese, and apple or orange juice. The teachers and children attractively set a few tables with tablecloths and cutlery, and when the parents arrived, the children took their orders and served the food. This experience proved so successful that the participants repeated the activity, creating meals typical of other cultural groups; for example, one Punjabi family helped the children make roti and curry. The parents' involvement in the program increased and became an integral part of the program as they became aware of how much their contribution was appreciated. Sometimes, it is difficult to find ways to involve parents who do not speak English as a first language, but the teachers in the Sexsmith Multicultural Preschool were able to do this successfully by following the lead of the children. It was the children's interest in food and restaurants that formed the basis for inviting the families to share their skills with the children in the preschool (Fraser, 1992, pp. 27–30).

Challenges in Forming Relationships with Families

A number of factors besides culture such as socioeconomic differences or too little time and energy because of stressful conditions in the family, the workplace, or society make it a challenge to form strong relationships between home and school.

Accommodating differences in values.   Differences in values of the parents and teachers, especially if these affect the beliefs concerning how children should be raised, may block communication between the school and the family. There may be differences in the teachers' and family members' image of the child that can lead to conflict in child–adult relationships. Even if parents and teachers agree on the view of the child as competent, how does this view translate into practice? The interpretation of competency may differ among cultures and across socioeconomic groups. As Sue Bredekamp points out, "overemphasis on children's competence can lead to abuses: If infants are so competent, why is parental leave necessary? If preschoolers are so smart, why not start formal reading instruction at two? If kindergartners are competent, what could be wrong with push-down (developmentally inappropriate) curriculum?" (1993, p. 14). To establish relationship as central to practice, teachers need to implement the principle of the image of the child as competent with careful thought and consideration. In some cultures, parents foster children's dependence on family members and discourage children from showing initiative or asserting their independence. Teachers, therefore, may need to keep the doors for communication wide open. Communication is not only for the purpose of learning about children's family lives but also to engage in active dialog about the purposes and goals of all in the education process. In Reggio, they say that no one person has the right to make all the decisions regarding children's education. This is indeed a useful attitude for teachers.

Understanding stressors on the family. The educators in Reggio Emilia, through the support they give to working parents, have eliminated a great deal of the stress parents experience related to child care. Support begins by having in place a procedure for orientation that ensures that before the child is separated, trust has been established between the teachers and all family members. The educators in Reggio Emilia slow down the process of separation to ensure that the child and family are made comfortable in each stage of the transition from home to school. They go so far as to check that the food prepared for children at school has the same taste as it does at home. The teachers realize how important it is to establish good communication with the family. They take the time to talk to parents when they leave their child in the morning and when they pick up the child in the afternoon. The practice of documentation informs the parent about the child's experiences in school so that the family stays closely connected to what the child is doing every day. Collaboration is a strong value and parents are expected to participate at many levels in their child's school activities, whether by serving on committees, volunteering in the classroom, helping with the preparation of materials, or construction of equipment. The strength of the relationship established between teachers and families serves as a support if stress emerges in other areas of family life through divorce, illness, or other misfortune.

The formation of strong relationships with families also depends on the parents and teachers having enough time and energy to initiate and maintain the relationship. This is particularly hard for parents who work in stressful and demanding jobs. When some parents were asked how they could be made to feel more involved in their children's preschool experiences, their responses indicated less emphasis on collaboration and partnership. "Do people who are working all week really want to be involved in child care?" "Child care provides me with the time I need to work. I will participate, but I need to feel it is for my kids, and it needs to be enjoyable, not more added work." "To get a better sense of community in the child care center would take a few people really committed to community building. They would have to spend a lot of effort getting all the parents involved." The parents agreed that for the children to feel a strong sense of belonging, they would have to get to know the other families and begin to build a "community of we."

Many American programs trying to use ideas from the Reggio approach admit that they struggle with the aspect of strengthening teacher-parent relationships to full partnership. There may be a number of factors at work here. One is the cultural difference between Italian and American values. Rebecca New notes that her experiences have shown her that in Italy there is a "strong sense of shared responsibility for children that is expressed at the individual, local and state levels" (New, 1994, p. 32). Such a value may translate more readily into forming collaborations to nurture and educate young children. American tradition has placed primary responsibility for the care and education of young children solely within the family; there is still an uneasy sense of separation and division when children are cared for outside the home. It may be this lack of comfort with shared responsibility that contributes to attitudes such as those expressed by the parents above, feeling that if the responsibility for care is being given to (and paid for) the child care program, parents will save their energy for resuming their responsibilities when they have the child at home. Perhaps what is needed here is a move away from the "restrictive, dualistic thinking to which the belief in exclusive maternal care has given rise: *either* maternal care, which is good, *or* non-maternal care, which is bad or, at least, an inferior substitute" (Dahlberg et al., 1999, p. 52). In reconceptualizing childhood as a time where there are many relationships and possibilities, the home and the early childhood program are recognized as having different but complementary roles to play. The struggle may be related to the narrow view of *either/or* and can be broadened to consider *both/and*.

Another factor may lie in the difficulty of reconceptualizing the teacher-parent relationship as partnership instead of the more dominant professional inviting the parent to enter the school as a guest, not a fully participating "protagonist," to use the Reggio phrase. One teacher expresses this quite frankly: "Philosophically I believe in having parents, and I involve parents in lots of ways, but do I truly welcome them as a third protagonist? I'm not yet feeling safe enough to let in the full force of their ideas." There may be a distance to go before American teachers come to the point where teacher-parent relationships are viewed as truly reciprocal and strong.

Lilian Katz makes an interesting hypothesis about the nature of parental involvement as seen in Reggio Emilia (Katz, 1994). Her conjecture is that it is the extraordinary quality of children's experiences in the schools in Reggio that cause parents to become involved, and that the quality of experiences is not simply the consequence of the high degree of parent involvement. In other words, her suggestion is that attention to improving the quality of children's school experiences may be the means to gaining parent support.

> Perhaps there is a dynamic phenomenon in this matter such that good work with children brings in the parents, and their involvement leads teachers to strengthen their work with children. In other words, I am hypothesizing a kind of cyclic phenomenon such that good in-classroom practices engage or capture the parents' interest and provide a context for their involvement, and that these parental responses encourage teachers' continued experimentation, growth, and learning, which further invite and entice the parents' involvement, which in turn supports teachers' commitment, and so forth, in a positive cycle (Katz, 1994, p. 13).

It is this dynamic cycle that creates the complexity and power of the teacher-parent relationship, centered on creating excellent learning experiences for children. This might be a place for American teachers to place their emphasis in considering full parent partnership.

Loris Malaguzzi stated, "Of course, education is not based solely on relationships; however, we consider relationship to be the fundamental, organizing strategy of our educational system. We view relationships not simply as a warm, protective backdrop or blanket but as a coming together of elements interacting dynamically toward a common purpose. The strength of this view of education is in expanding the forms and functions of relationship and interaction" (1993, p. 10). As early childhood educators, therefore, we have to reassess "the form and function" that relationship plays in our programs by asking the following questions:

- Are we engaging in culturally sensitive interaction with the families in the center?
- Are we supportive and able to make families that are under stress feel that they still can be involved in the program?
- Are we exploring ways of involving all families in the program?
- Are we including the richness of the community in the program?
- Are we making clear the options that are available for families to participate in the program?
- Have we established reciprocity as a core principle in our relationship with families?

RELATIONSHIPS WITH CHILDREN

Many teachers may ask themselves how their relationship with the children in the classroom will change when the teacher's role becomes one of a co-constructor with the children of the learning experiences in the program. Acceptance of the children as competent learners will in itself bring about a style of relating to children that is different from seeing the children as empty vessels that need to be filled with knowledge. When reciprocity is seen as the basis of the relationship between teachers and children, the relationship will be more respectful, more equal, and more interactive.

Opening Channels of Communication

When reciprocity is placed at the core of relationships, it changes the patterns of communication in the classroom. For example, one of the biggest changes occurs in the teacher's traditional role of controller of all communication in the classroom. The teacher's role is now shared equally among all the participants in the classroom. Teachers who form reciprocal relationships with children find themselves wanting to listen to the children's conversation to find out what they are thinking and what ideas they have on the topics of current interest. They want to consider seriously the children's suggestions for effective ways of solving problems that have arisen in the classroom. They also want to create opportunities to listen to the children's responses to their suggestions. Children have to feel that their ideas are valued and will be listened to. Teachers influenced by the Reggio Emilia approach set the stage for productive conversation by making changes in the following areas:

1. *The physical space in the classroom by*
   - creating quiet environments where meaningful conversations can take place
   - making places where small groups can meet undisturbed by activities in the main area of the classroom

2. *The daily schedule by*
   - removing all unnecessary interruptions in the daily schedule
   - providing for flexible planning so that if children are discussing a topic, there is enough time to explore it in depth
   - adapting group time to enable it to be more interactive than teacher-directed

3. *The program content by*
   - listening to children, recording their conversations, and following up on their interests
   - encouraging children to express their ideas
   - building on the children's ideas
   - allowing for input from the children in planning the content
   - accepting different perspectives and conflict as a positive dynamic, and using them as a source of energy in the creation of new ideas for program content

4. *The teaching team by*
   - collaborating with other adults in the room to observe and record the children's comments
   - making time for reflection
   - meeting frequently to discuss observations and plan further directions
   - preparing questions beforehand that can be used to stimulate further discussion and possible action

- accepting that conflict is a necessary and dynamic factor in making change effective
- selecting children who work well together to collaborate with teachers in carrying out a project

5. *The peer group by*
   - emphasizing the importance of listening to and respecting one another's ideas and opinions
   - helping children learn to value the different perspectives that other children hold
   - accepting conflict in a positive way so that it can be used as a means of untangling the blockage and perhaps taking a new direction to solve the problem that caused the initial conflict

6. *Parent helpers by*
   - maintaining the communication links between home and school deliberately and regularly
   - providing cues to continuing the conversation at home that began at school, and vice versa
   - encouraging parents to serve as a memory for the child during and after a conversation
   - encouraging parents to discuss topics at home, and to extend and expand on the children's thoughts

At Symposium 2000 at First Baptist Church Kindergarten, several teachers explained how this cycle of home-school listening deepened learning experiences for children and adults. One example came from a year-long project that had grown from children's classroom symbols. On the first day, families came to the classroom and were asked to choose a symbol from available choices selected from the natural world (for example, flamingo, eagle, star). This would be the symbol used, along with the name, to identify the individual child and family throughout the year. From this selection came an early sense of ownership as children knew when they arrived at the classroom that was their particular symbol. Notes were then sent to families asking them to do some research with their children, to learn more about the symbol, and then to find a time where they would represent to the large group what they had discovered.

A whole curriculum resulted. Teachers discovered that children were representing the star as yellow with the traditional five points. After classroom conversations, teachers invited parents to explore the evening sky at home with their children to see what they could discoverer about stars. Parent were encouraged to listen to their children and see where their thoughts led them. Several parents wrote the carefully listened to accounts of children's remarks about the stars, and these became part of the documentation of the on-going dialog and exploration. Teachers listened at school, identified this as an area to explore further, and invited parents to continue the listening at home.

The following ideas come from teachers thinking about how to really listen to and communicate with children.

> Stop talking so much yourself. Observe children's play from the sidelines more often. Find out what they are doing in their own play before it becomes too influenced by your presence, comments, or ideas—then come in with an idea for an extension, a provocation or to assist the children in gathering materials." (Pat Breen, Vancouver Child Study Center)

> For me, asking questions is a natural part of developing relationships with each child; therefore, they vary according to which child I'm talking with, as well as the situation. Looking at the example of the conversation [below] with Jack, who was drawing on the sidewalk, I'm sure this wouldn't have worked with any of the others who would have felt I was sticking my nose into their activity in a most intrusive way. But I know Jack loves to share information and to show what he knows. He enjoyed and was very confident in this exchange.

> *Jack:* I'm going to draw a balloon, a blue one.

> *Susan (teacher):* And a long string I see?

> *Jack:* Yes, a long string and some bolts.

> *Susan:* What are the bolts for?

> *Jack:* To bolt it to the ground so it doesn't float away. And under it I'm putting a book to weigh it down more.

> *Susan:* It looks very secure now, Jack. What are these things on the side?

> *Jack:* They're snippers to cut the string when it's time to take the balloon home.

> (Susan Emery, Quadra Island Day Care)

> Pay enormous amounts of attention to kids' conversations. I always listened to children, but I listen differently now. It is less about recording sound bites, and a more open-ended listening to the whole conversation. I take copious notes, tape and transcribe, and think deeply about what is important (Ann Pelo, Hilltop Children's Center).

> Learn to slow down. In order to listen, teachers must spend more focused time with individual children or small groups of children. This often means changing old patterns of constant movement from one table or activity center to another in order to monitor and manage behavior, and to facilitate with brief comments. It also means rethinking earlier values about equity. When teachers are concerned about fairness about spending a lot of time with a few children, the implication is that other

children are being neglected, and that they should be available to all children at all times. Slowing down is not as simple as it sounds, as it requires that teachers reorganize their time, environment, and functioning with colleagues (Ideas from Brenda Fyfe, 1993).

Sit and observe and try to write down exactly what the children say. Read your notes back to the children and ask a few questions—ones you honestly wonder about—in relation to what they were doing. Reflect back what you think they are saying to see if you've got it right. Tape a complete conversation with a child or group of children, and then transcribe it yourself. The act of transcribing can really help you see/hear/interpret differently—our minds may work differently when we write than when we talk. Mark all the places where you went in a different direction than a child might have been wanting to go, all the places where you didn't quite understand what a child was saying, all the place where a child is "off track." Then think about what you could have done to get "on track" with that child. Or ask a colleague to read the transcripts to see what they notice, and what they would have said instead. Or revisit the conversation with the children; go back to a place where you noticed you went one way and you noticed the child might have had something more to say about something else. Try letting go of the "right answer" and the "lesson" and see what wonderful places children will take you (Patti Cruikshank-Schott, Caroline Friends' School).

We listen more. We think more about what things mean. We now catch on to a child's idea and think about it, reflect on it, and act on it. We also ask more questions as a result of respecting children's thinking. We have also learned how to shut up. Now we don't always have the answer, but we probe them with a question so that they look to themselves for an answer. (Detroit Head Start Teachers in *Innovations* 4[2]).

In order to have "real conversations" with the children, a teacher has to really listen. I notice when I ask a question and already have the answer in my head and am waiting to hear that answer, it does not stimulate real conversation. It seems to be useful to paraphrase back to a child the ideas they are expressing. Ask them "tell me more about it." Ask them to express their idea in another language such as drawing or clay. This allows you to understand their thought process better and in turn allows them to further clarify their idea. Developing meaningful relationships between teachers and children, and between the children themselves is a key component to having "real conversation." Everyone has to feel respected and feel that they make worthwhile contributions to the group. Children need to learn how to listen to each other, and see the power of bouncing ideas off one another and how that deepens one's understanding. (Barbara Lee, Quadra Island Day Care)

As Carlina Rinaldi reminds us, listening is much more than attentiveness with the ears; it is being attentive with the whole being.

Listening means being open to and welcoming differences, recognizing the value of the points of view and interpretations of others; listening as waiting and expectation. Listening means the capacity to respect others, to take them out of anonymity, to give them visibility, enriching both those who listen and those who produce the message.

Listening as a prerequisite of any teaching-learning relationship that is focused on learning . . . a context in which each individual feels welcome (Rinaldi, January 1999).

The following list provides examples of ways that teachers can communicate with children to guide their learning:

Giving words or encouraging children to give words to concepts: (Adult identifying concept) "Anne Louise, I see that you parked your truck between the red and blue cars." Asking child to give words to a concept: "Goodness, where did that green color come from? I only gave you yellow and blue paint."

Outlining steps to problem solving: (Adult modeling) "Christian doesn't want to put on his snowsuit. What should I do? I could get mad or I could try to change his mind. I think it is better to try and change his mind. I could remind him that when he has his snowsuit on he can slide down the playground hill, or I could tell him. . . " (Asking child to outline) "Carol, I see you did a lot of stamping. How did you get such a nice clear picture with this dinosaur stamp?"

Naming, expanding on knowledge, and encouraging observation: "Yes, you may have an orange. This is called a navel orange. Another name for your belly button is a navel. Why do you think they call this a navel orange?"

Asking open-ended and figuring-out questions: An older toddler has just drawn his umpteenth noseless face. "Nicholas, does your person know what is cooking for lunch?" "No." "How could he find out?" (Educator, after giving sufficient time for answers, may touch nose or sniff the air as a clue.) This assisted development will probably never have to be repeated. Faces will generally always have noses after this discovery.

Encouraging talking aloud (inner speech): For self control (child to self): "I will sit down. I will fold my hands. I will wait until everyone is given a snack. Then I can eat." To practice a skill (i.e., scissors): "Open, squeeze, open, squeeze. . . ." For memory skills: "Where did I leave my book, first I went to see Francois. Then I went to the sand table. Then I. . . " (Mouzard, 1997, pp. 38–39)

Meeting Times to Enhance Relationships

When teachers consider relationship a fundamental principle and weave it into all aspects of the program, they will approach the more structured times such as meeting or circle time from a different perspective. The typical format for circle time still is based on the procedure that evolved in the Froebelian kindergartens early in the 20th century. The children sit in a circle and the teacher reads a story, sings songs, and leads the group in discussing a topic of general interest. Froebel believed that children need to be gathered together under the direction of the teacher at least once a day to create a sense of group cohesiveness. He chose the circle as a symbol of unity with the universe: the children are the stars that circle the teacher who is the sun. Froebel felt it was important for children to feel spiritually connected to the world around them. The "gifts" and "occupations" (the materials and activities) he created for children to use in circle time have long since disappeared, but the ritual of circle time must still hold its meaning and significance to have persisted in early childhood programs.

The idea of unity, or connectedness, that Froebel believed so important for young children becomes the principle of relationship in the Reggio Emilia approach. Circle time in the Reggio Emilia preschools, however, has become a less formal group time—a meeting time—when the children and teacher join together in a discussion on subjects that hold relevance for the group. In most classrooms for preschoolers in Reggio Emilia, there is a tier arrangement of seats that can be used for this initial gathering in the morning as children share experiences and plan for the day's work. The tier arrangement, usually a set of three tiers, may provide ample individual space as well as allowing children to see one another clearly. When Margaret Edwards built a similar seating arrangement into the two-year-old room at Lakewood, she observed that attention span was extended and children's participation enhanced. During work times, the tiers may be used for construction or other activities. The gathering is still acknowledged as an important time for creating a sense of belonging, when children and teachers gather together, but the ritualistic aspect has disappeared. The activity during this time has become more informal and more responsive to the interests of the children; therefore, it is more spontaneous and interactive. It has become an important time for teachers to listen to children and draw ideas and suggestions for the program from them.

Louise Cadwell describes a morning meeting at the Diana School:

Marina (one of the teachers) begins, "Well, how was your weekend? Who picked those beautiful flowers? Where were you? Carla, you were away for three days. Tell us about your trip to the mountains. What did you find? What did you bring back?"

Children and teachers chat, catch up, and share the pleasure of each other's company. There isn't any rush; there isn't a feeling that there is a need for control on the teachers' part. It is just a pleasure. "Well, what do we have going today? . . . "Carla, you, Agnese, and Elise were working on the class newspaper you had organized. Would you like to continue? . . . Some children have been invited to help the three-year-olds with working with wire. Who would like to do that?" (Cadwell, 1997, pp. 17–18).

During group time, much of the co-construction of knowledge between children and teachers takes place. At meeting time in Pam Oken-Wright's classroom one day, the children passed blocks from one hand to the other while they counted as far as they could go; one child helped the group get over 120. Then they invented a game of thumping the block on the fifth beat as they counted in sets of 5. Children more sure of numeric skills supported their classmates in the group venture. In allowing more flexible use of time and equality in the child-teacher relationship, and child-child relationships, flexible curriculum practices enhance relationships in the classroom.

In reflecting on how teachers were beginning to reassess past practice when implementing a Reggio inspired approach, one of the teachers at the Vancouver Child Study Center wrote the following comments:

> I think we all need to work at being less directive and more sensitive to the children. I would like to reexamine the format of our daily schedule and the benefit of circle time. It does not work for about half the children. Perhaps make circle time shorter—five minutes. This would allow for more small group explorations, which could occur more spontaneously. We need to examine what is developmentally appropriate and provide more able children with opportunities to demonstrate their abilities while allowing younger children the freedom to feel competent and successful at the level they have reached—i.e., Don't make J repeatedly fail with his inability to remain focused during long circle times. Reduce times of "management" challenges, while facilitating times of increased focus for children who are ready for it." (Gloria Rolfsen)

Linking Play, Projects, and Relationship

For the last hundred years since the Froebelian kindergartens were established in North America, play has been given the central position philosophically in most early childhood education programs. The key question for early childhood educators in adapting ideas from the Reggio Emilia approach is this: If we are to place relationship at the center of the curriculum, how will this affect our belief in the importance of play? Loris Malaguzzi said, "We should not forget the relevant role of make-believe play. This type of symbolic play is pervasive in young children's experience and has an important role in the social development of intelligence, development of the skills needed for reciprocity among children, the potential for children to persist in activity and conversation together, and development of the ability to create symbols" (1993, p. 12). Children in the preschools in Reggio Emilia spend much of their time engaged in play, but the teachers in Reggio Emilia do not focus their attention on the children's play as do educators in many other programs.

In preschools where play is the central philosophical perspective, teachers spend much of their time and energy creating environments that foster play. Then, when children become fully engaged in play, the teachers tend to withdraw and observe. Therefore, the teacher is more of a facilitator than a participator with the children in the play. For example, the teachers at the Sexsmith Multicultural Preschool described earlier observed that the children used the cooking theme most frequently in their play in the dramatic play area. The teachers then used this theme as the foundation for building the content of the program. The children, as they prepared the food for the restaurant, wrote the menu, took orders, served the food to their parents, developed their social and literacy skills, learned new concepts, and developed their vocabulary.

The teachers at the Sexsmith school developed the theme of cooking food from different ethnic groups over six months; in this sense, the project was similar to those carried out in Reggio Emilia because the topic was explored in depth for a long period of time. However, the project differed in the way the teachers used their observations of the children's play, then took the lead in developing the project further. Unlike the teachers in Reggio Emilia, who work collaboratively with the children in developing a project, the teachers at Sexsmith Multicultural Preschool took control of the direction the project followed. They proceeded to organize the children's cooking activities, decide on the menu, and transform the classroom into a restaurant. If the children had had more say in the project, the menu may have offered a wider choice of cultural foods than celery sticks stuffed with cream cheese or peanut butter (Fraser, 1992). The educators in Reggio Emilia use their observations and conversations with the children as an entry point into the process of developing a project further. Then they work *together* with the children throughout this process. The emphasis is on relationship and reciprocity, and the outcome of the project emerges as it unfolds.

One teacher describes how her perspective changed as she began to implement the Reggio Emilia approach and as relationship became more of a guiding principle in the program:

> There is a wish, a desire, an interest to connect, to establish or rather point out webs of connection, of interrelationships—of widening circles, i.e., what a child draws can be related to an earlier event, a book, an experience, etc.—and it becomes more than an individual act. It can be related . . . to another child on that particular subject or situation—thus establishing and/or confirming a contact, a relationship, a common interest among the children. Always, or at least often, there is a sense of wanting to bring things—ideas . . . and people into context—with previous events, other suggestions, etc.—so that there is a link, a connection not only between ideas, information, etc., but also a connection between people; i.e., a child who usually may not relate to another child on an interpersonal level will find a bridge to that child via a similar thought or by problem solving. Earlier in the year E was often quite solitary; when I related another child's interest and remarks about the rainbows (created by the crystals), this interest became a bridge that linked her to another child. If this is done for and with the child quite frequently, then isolation can be opened up.
>
> I just generally look for more collaboration—the so-called teachership steps into the background; when I feel really connected, I am just part of what is happening. Some parents need a lot of affirming of their qualities as co-creators (Baerbel Jackel, Quadra Island Preschool).

These reflections illustrate the change in perspective as a teacher considers ideas from Reggio Emilia and changes from viewing the curriculum as external to the daily experiences in the classroom to viewing it as internal, as an integral part of being and connecting to others. The program content is derived from the dynamic interaction of adults and children with one another and with the environment. It emerges spontaneously out of the relationships in the environment, and it is always fresh and interesting. "Expect the unexpected" is how Loris Malaguzzi described this way of experiencing curriculum.

The educators in Reggio Emilia perceive play as an important medium for fostering relationships because as children interact in the play group, they are given many opportunities to develop their social and cognitive skills. In Reggio Emilia, children are given plenty of time to play, but the focus seems to be on the relationship between adults and children as they participate together in the co-construction of knowledge. Reggio Emilia educators also acknowledge play as one of the hundred languages used by children in symbolic development.

Lilian Katz has suggested that one of the important lessons to be drawn from observations in Reggio Emilia concerns the content of the relationship between children and adults. Her basic point is that "individuals cannot just relate to each other; they have to relate to each other about something" (Katz, 1997, p. 36). When teachers simply communicate with children about routines, rules, and minutiae of classroom life, or give occasional feedback about children's performance, most of the content of the relationships between teachers and children is about the children themselves.

But in classrooms in Reggio Emilia, and those inspired by Reggio, adults and children communicate about the ideas and progress of project work and investigation of theories. Because the projects are of interest to both teacher and child, both are truly engaged in a rich dialog. The projects developed in classrooms inspired by Reggio ideas area both the vehicle and outcome of genuine adult-child relationships.

Presenting Materials

One of the joys of being an early childhood educator is working with a wide variety of materials, but even more rewarding is sharing the experience with children. There is nothing as satisfying for preschool teachers as arriving in the morning before the children and setting up the classroom with the materials the children will have available during the day. The teachers have to consider which materials need to be offered in each area of the room. In the art area, for example, there is paint to mix and place on the easel, collage material to select and set out on the tables, and perhaps special materials such as finger paint or clay ready for the children when they arrive. The teachers check that pieces of equipment such as the blocks are arranged neatly on the shelves and that puzzles and table toys are put out on the tables. In the science area, the teacher may want to prepare an area where the children can experiment with water, magnets, or any of the other science materials the children are interested in at the moment. In the Quadra Island Preschool, the children had planted horsetails, ferns, and moss in the indoor sandbox to create a landscape for the dinosaurs that one of the children had drawn and cut out of paper. Each day, the teacher brought in different books on dinosaurs and placed them beside the sandbox to capture the children's attention. In this way, she hoped to focus their interest on dinosaurs and stimulate further investigation of what they looked like and how they lived.

In the spring, following many gardening experiences and opportunities to notice the flowers blooming in the neighborhood, the preschool teacher at Lakewood created a drawing area with blank paper, glass jars of freshly sharpened colored pencils separated by color, and the book *Planting a Rainbow* by Lois Ehlert beside the drawing materials, as a provocation.

When the teachers at Hilltop noticed the tall buildings children were constructing in the block area, they added pictures of tall buildings from Seattle and pictures of the children building their tall structures. Much to their delight, they observed the children building a cityscape right below the pictures they had added.

In preparing the room, the teachers' main concern is in making the materials appealing and easily available. This task involves thoughtful reflection about which materials might stimulate the children's interest. In recent years, there has

Figure 4–5.   The presentation of a colorful book about spring gardens, along with blank paper and freshly sharpened colored pencils, is an inviting provocation for exploration. (*Courtesy:* Lakewood Avenue Children's School.)

been a change in preschools from a theme-based to an emergent curriculum that has made the preparation of learning experiences for the children more spontaneous and flexible. In an emergent curriculum, teachers base their selection of materials on previous observations and discussions about which materials the children will need to further their investigations and representations of their ideas.

The Reggio Emilia approach has made early childhood educators more aware of how relationship deepens the meaning of experiences in the classroom. Teachers in Reggio inspired classrooms no longer set up materials or experiences in isolation; instead, they think carefully about the interconnection between materials and children, and how this relationship deepens the meaning of activities.

Aesthetics is an aspect of relationship that needs to be considered in presenting materials in the classroom. To foster aesthetic awareness means to help children appreciate the beauty in the world around them. It also means to heighten their awareness of the links between things in the environment and the emotional response that the objects evoke. Teachers need to consider how they can bring objects and materials into relationship with other aspects of the environment in the classroom to foster the children's aesthetic sense. The educators in Reggio Emilia have gone further than any other early childhood education program in showing us the value of aesthetics in the education of young children.

Teachers inspired by Reggio value aesthetics in their programs and incorporate this value into their decision-making. Relationships are enhanced by the attention to beauty in the environment. Margaret Edwards made the comment that she had always appreciated a beautiful environment and assumed the children would as well. But Reggio helped her realize what a major role aesthetics could play in the program, and that it was important to focus on beauty and art. The attention to detail and beauty is a metaphor for the care in the relationships. Aesthetics truly create an "amiable" environment where relationships can flourish.

COLLEGIAL AND COMMUNITY RELATIONSHIPS

One of the greatest benefits of using ideas from the Reggio Emilia approach is in the way collegial relationships are improved by the need to collaborate. The fundamental principle of relationship ensures that all participants in the program have to collaborate to make the program function successfully. This collaboration, in turn, increases each member's commitment to work toward strengthening the group as a whole. Decisions are no longer made by one person but in collaboration with others. Team members share their observations and reflections, and plan the program as a team. Documentation, in itself, cannot be carried out effectively unless all the participants have shared in its development. There is joy and support in becoming part of a community of learners. Sarah Felstiner says, "I figured

Figures 4–6a,b,c.
Attention to detail and beauty in the environment is a metaphor for the care in relationships. Notice the unusual containers for materials, adding to the aesthetics. (*Courtesy:* Patti Cruikshank-Schott.)

out pretty quickly that this isn't something you can do alone. It takes somebody brave enough to be on the journey with you as a co-teacher." This seems an appropriate place to repeat the words of Marty Gravett, first seen in her discussion of teacher roles in Chapter 3:

> While team teaching was a concept that long appealed to me, I had not understood its real potential until I began to work in a team inspired by the Reggio approach. Now my role as a teacher includes being an organizer, a communicator, and a collaborator

(c)

with colleagues. I spend a significant part of each day in the classroom in conversation with my colleagues making decisions about what next step to take to move individual children and small groups forward. The team concept also includes taking on leadership when my strengths are needed or when I am challenged by a particular line of inquiry that opens itself to me. This is required of all teachers, and so to support each other's leadership we each take on the important, corollary role of ally.

In moving to a new paradigm of teaching as an activity of collegial reflection, teachers move into new territory, leaving behind an isolated, silent mode of working as Malaguzzi foretold:

> Co-teaching, and in a more general sense, collegial work, represents a deliberate break from the traditional professional and cultural solitude and isolation of teachers. This isolation has been rationalized in the name of academic freedom, yet wrongly understood. Its results, certainly, has been to impoverish and desiccate teachers' potential and resources and make it difficult or impossible for them to achieve quality (Malaguzzi in Edwards et al., 1998, p. 71).

And because this mode is new, it can be frightening and challenging as well as rewarding and inspiring. Collegiality requires shifts in both thinking and practice.

Even teachers who work alone in their classrooms try to engage other teachers in their work. Patti Cruikshank-Schott frequently discusses ideas with other teachers downstairs who try to incorporate Reggio inspirations in their work with younger children and says that collegial work has transformed the way they do their end of the year reports. Writing their summaries without using any evaluative words, discussion, and the editing by a peer helps reach this goal.

Karen Haigh (1999) reflects on essential elements of collegiality and collaboration. These include having a common goal or purpose, meeting together regularly, doing something together—not just talking about experiences—but doing them, allowing time to reflect and revisit at meetings, thinking of ways to be inclusive with all staff members, valuing and having ongoing dialogs, having unequal positions and equal voices at the same time, having leadership that is involved and connected with the staff, developing and supporting the individual and group simultaneously, having many ways for people to collaborate (children and children, children and teachers, teachers and parents, children and parents, teachers, directors, coordinators and family workers), and having hopes and dreams for the future.

Exciting potential for meaningful changes occurs when educators build relationships with other educators and with others in the community beyond the school. Certainly, Reggio Emilia gives us a vision of what can happen when the community offers a resource of interest and financial support for implementing their philosophy. The educators at the University of Vermont have included public officials and other interested citizens such as a state senator, the associate deputy of social services, the early childhood consultant for the state, the dean of the college, a teacher from a vocational education center, faculty from other disciplines on their most recent delegation to a study tour in Reggio, with a plan to take an even larger group in the future. Their hope is that by involving state and local officials in the exploration of excellence in early childhood education, they can build the base for influencing the public will and financial resources to support the development of their vision. Collaborative relationships can bring powerful change.

Relationship in the Preparation of Teachers

There are numerous teacher preparation programs in colleges and universities that have been inspired by Reggio to restructure their curricula to incorporate principles of relationship and collaboration.

Children Teaching Teachers, the core curriculum experience in the early childhood education program at Douglas College, has proved an effective way of preparing students to work collaboratively. Relationship is a fundamental principle in this method of preparing students to work with young children. The groups of five or six students who work together in planning and presenting activities to the children discover very soon that for their session with the children to be a success, the members in their group have to learn to work as a team. The students have been together for one semester at the college before Children Teaching Teachers begins. But it is not until they begin the process that they really understand the importance of team work. They have to get to know one another well and learn about one another's strengths and weaknesses. They have to build trust and learn to communicate effectively, individually, and as a group. If the members of the group develop a strong relationship, they usually have a positive and enjoyable experience in Children Teaching Teachers. When there are difficulties because of personality conflicts or lack of an equal sharing of responsibility, the experience becomes a challenge for everyone. Often, the students themselves are able to resolve their own problems, but sometimes the instructor who is assigned to each group has to step in and help the students overcome their problems to avoid a negative effect on the visiting children. The instructor helps the students see that conflict can be positive, and that the experience they have gained in collaborating and resolving problems with other students will help them develop the skills they need to be a member of a team at work. The following example, taken from a student's reflection paper, describes how members of her group learned to work together as a team.

> I tend to take on the role of leader in many group situations, and in this experience there were two other people who usually take on the same role. We quickly learned that in order to work productively as a group we would have to share the leadership role. Once this transition was made our group functioned smoothly. I found it helpful to share this role with others because it took some of the pressure off each of us who felt we had to take charge. We took turns facilitating productive discussion and keeping the group on topic.

One of the main goals of a co-teaching experience is to give students practice in building strong relationships in their work. Students build relationships within each group and with a sister group of students with whom each team collaborates. Each group of students is paired with another group that works with the same children on alternate weeks. The sister groups support each other in setting up the environment, debriefing the experience, and analyzing the video they make each week of their session with the children. The students learn to appreciate the support they receive from their sister group, realizing how much it can contribute to the successful outcome of their sessions with the children. Each group keeps a journal of the week's experiences in collaboration with the sister group. Relationships evolve as the students have long and involved discussions within their group and with members of the sister group in creating the documentation of each session for their journal. This process is described in the extract below, taken from a student's reflections in her journal:

> During the evaluation and debriefing, I shared my opinions and thoughts about that day's experience. I felt that I was reflective in my comments and shared positive and negative experiences with the other group debriefing with us. I found it helpful to debrief with another group because we shared what was working on a much broader basis than later in the day during video analysis. During video analysis it was again a collaborative effort with both sister groups participating. I contributed my thoughts as to what portion of the video to use . . . I was always eager to not only share my own

ideas but to acknowledge others. I feel that I was a positive member of the group and may have helped others feel as though they were too.

The students began to value collaboration as they saw it at work in practice. They also observed how the instructors collaborated in integrating the course content to make it more relevant for the early childhood college students.

Students at the Child Study and Development Center of the University of New Hampshire also work in teams to implement projects with young children. The Project Approach Framework for Teacher Education (PAFTE) places undergraduate early childhood students randomly into teaching teams working with the same group of five or six children throughout a semester. Mary Jane Moran (1997) points out that this model is built on two theoretical perspectives about teaching. Both of these theories also inform the Reggio approach. The first idea is that children and adults socially construct knowledge, co-constructing as group members learn from one another. Such learning can happen only if members of the group "are able to listen to one another, negotiate, and accept different perspectives while remaining in relation" (Moran, 1997, p. 408). The second idea is that teachers are learners, researchers, and collaborators together. Collaboration allows those on the teaching team with different strengths, personalities, and perspectives to come together, often challenging each other to create new perspectives and knowledge. A student expressed this idea: "We worked as a team to produce both of our panels, and working together helped us combine our perspectives. We collaborated our efforts and developed combined work, rather than individual work" (Moran, 1997, p. 409). This collaborative structure for early education students creates a community of learners who can support and challenge each other to develop new understandings and skills.

The descriptions of the PreK–3 Teacher Education program at the University of Vermont, discussed in Chapter 3, indicates how the program restructuring to give students large blocks of time throughout a semester to work together was designed specifically to develop collaborative relationships.

Collegial relationships may be developed beyond the classroom when teachers are drawn together with the goal of learning together. The Great Duck Pond Project from Blacksburg, Virginia, is a testimony to community-wide collaboration and learning relationships. As described in this video, subtitled "A Learning Community Venture Inspired by the Reggio Emilia Approach" (Hill, 1998: see audiovisual references for complete information), the project involved year-long efforts from teachers at all educational levels in the town to investigate long-term projects related to the duck pond on the campus of Virginia Tech. Several of the university faculty and child development lab school staff, inspired by a visit to Reggio and by the university's mission to emphasize a community of learners, sent an open invitation to all the teachers in the town, from preschool up through the college level. When they had their first meeting, there were representatives from every grade in town, as well as professors representing eight different university disciplines. As they studied the principles of the Reggio Emilia approach together, they realized that the concepts could be applied to all ages. The video went on to document how teachers at the individual levels worked with their students to create meaningful topics for investigation, all centered on the duck pond, long a community focus. Investigations included collections of materials found at the duck pond by the preschoolers in the lab school, and a nesting on the playground and subsequent hatching of a mallard duck family. Projects by an after-school program included creating a papier-mâché model of the mallard and a play that illustrated the pond's history. In addition, environmental awareness projects by the sixth graders, creation of a book documenting the pond's history obtained by taping alumni stories at homecoming, high school chemistry class explorations of water quality, a high school photography class' creation of a multimedia visual exploration of the pond, and a college art class exploring physical sculpture around the pond were covered. All of the investigations were documented in a joint exhibit at a local museum so the larger community could share in the effects of the collaborative learning.

Victoria Fu, a faculty member at Virginia Tech and one of the project participants, summed up the experience as "experiences of joyful learning built on caring relationships." The teachers came together to learn how to be members of a learning community, learning from each other and building intersubjectivity. These dispositions could then be transferred to their students. Together, this group of educators studied how to adapt and reconstruct the Reggio Emilia approach in their particular context. Later, a 15-member group of educators from this community joined in a study tour to Reggio, and continued to deepen their understanding and collaborative relationships. A very interesting spin-off from this is the school board approved restructuring at the middle school level at Blacksburg Middle School where a Reggio-inspired program opened its doors in the fall of 2000 (Hill, 1999, p. 2001). By creating a wide network of relationships and community within the educational process, the educators of The Great Duck Pond Project have given an example of moving from "I" to "we."

SEEING THE RESULTS

The building of strong relationships in every aspect of an early childhood program is the key factor in providing quality care and education for young children. It starts with the first contact in the process of orientation when the relationship between the children and parents and the teachers begins to develop. It is important that this introduction of the children to school happens slowly and carefully, so that the children's attachment to their families continues to be nurtured, and the children and families are given the time to develop trust

(d)

Chemistry Testing at the Duck Pond

Figures 4–7a,b,c,d,e,f,g. The many community projects involved collaboration among teachers at all levels (a); and included (b) exploring the pond in all seasons; (c) preschoolers making collections of materials found at the duck pond; (d) exploration of the pond's water quality by junior high students; (e) a book of the pond's history by sixth-graders, obtained from interviews of alumni at homecoming; (f) testing of the water by a high school chemistry class; and (g) physical sculpture around the pond by a college art class. (*Courtesy:* Lynn Hill and the Great Duck Pond Project at Virginia Tech.)

in the new environment. It then becomes important to have strategies in place to develop and sustain the relationship with families. Parents need opportunities to get to know one another and the other children in the school so that they feel they are an integral part of the program.

The relationships among the staff also have to be nurtured so that they feel a sense of belonging to the school community. Staff members need to trust one

(f)

(g)

another so that they can communicate openly and honestly. There has to be enough time set aside for meetings and discussions so that everyone has the opportunity to voice their ideas and concerns. If every person feels that they are valued members of the team, their commitment to the program will grow, and the children will receive the quality program they deserve.

Perhaps the biggest change in using ideas from the Reggio Emilia approach has been in the teacher's relationships with children. Teachers come to unwind their agendas, listen more to children, and build a program that evolves from the ideas and interests of the children in the class.

The decision to make relationship central to a program requires that teachers examine the strands in the web of relationships in the school, test their strength, and see how they can be extended into every aspect of the program. The principle of relationship extends beyond the human level as it is woven into every part of the program including the design of the space, the choice of equipment, and the presentation of materials in the classroom. As the quality of the physical and social environment improves, the people involved feel more satisfaction, there is a sense of joyfulness, and the school, as Loris Malaguzzi says, becomes an amiable place for the children, teachers, and families it serves.

Chapter 5

Environment as the Third Teacher

The wider the range of possibilities we offer children, the more intense will be their motivations and the richer their experiences.
—Loris Malaguzzi

Questions to Consider:

- What is the rationale for creating an environment that acts as a third teacher?

- What are the major similarities and differences in the way the environment is planned in Reggio-inspired schools in North America and in other parts of the world?

- What are the key principles that need to be considered in creating an environment that acts as a third teacher?

- What are the challenges in creating and working in this kind of environment?

- How does the creation of an environment that acts as a third teacher affect the quality of programming in an early childhood center?

The space we live in has a powerful influence over us, particularly the space we grew up in. Often, we try, without even being aware of it to recreate in our adult lives the places we remember from our childhood. For example, long ago, the immigrants from Europe brought the images of the gardens they had played in as children to their new homeland where they recreated the rose gardens and flower borders filled with European flowers such as delphiniums and foxgloves.

When teachers plan an environment where children will spend long periods of time, they need to think of the effect this environment may have on their adult lives. When graduates of the Reggio Emilia preschools remember their time there, they speak of a particular atmosphere of deep affection, a feeling of family, lasting friendships, images of light and color, and strong relationships with teachers. Alexis, a student of literature at the University of Parma and head of a theater group, told a study group in Reggio, "It gave me a particular sensibility to face the world" (Wien, 1997).

The spaces that teachers create for children seem to hold enduring memories for them that have a powerful influence on what they will value later in life.

Therefore, it is important that teachers think carefully about their own values and how they affect the decisions they make about the arrangement of space, equipment, and materials in the classroom. Teachers often are unaware of the messages the environment communicates to children and visitors to the classroom. Visitors to preschools can know immediately a great deal about the philosophy of the school after walking in and seeing the children's work, photographs, and other messages displayed on the walls.

- When there are pictures of children engaged in meaningful activity, the message of active learning is heard.
- When those same pictures sometimes show teachers working alongside children, the image of teacher as supporter of learning and co-constructor of knowledge is suggested.
- When there are pictures and introductions of teachers and staff, the message is of staff taking the initiative to reveal themselves to visitors, reaching out to open doors for communication.
- When there are pictures of children with their families, the message is of respect for the primacy of the family, and the staff's desire to include them in the daily life of the center.
- When children's work is displayed attractively, the message is that aesthetics are valued.
- When children's words and questions are recorded for others to ponder, the message is that their work speaks of their growing understandings and urgent desire to find answers.
- When each documentation of children's journeys speaks, it shows the need for adults—parents and teachers—to collaborate together in trying to find children's meanings and ways to support continued growth.

Space does indeed speak.

One can understand why the educators in Reggio Emilia have termed the environment a third teacher because the power of environments such as these inform and shape the kind of learning that will happen in the room. As Lella Gandini wrote,

> The schools in Reggio Emilia could not be just anywhere, and no one of them could serve as an exact model to be copied literally elsewhere. Yet, they have common features that merit consideration in schools everywhere. Each school's particular configuration of the garden, walls, tall windows, and handsome furniture declares: This is a place where adults have thought about the quality of environment. Each school is full of light, variety, and a certain kind of joy. In addition, each school shows how teachers, parents, and children, working and playing together, have created a unique space that reflects their personal lives, the history of their schools, the many layers of culture and a nexus of well thought out choices. (Gandini in Edwards, Gandini, & Forman, 1998, p. 177)

American educators who explore ideas from the Reggio Emilia philosophy often begin by trying to develop a unique space that reflects the lives of the people involved and the culture of the community.

THE ENVIRONMENT AS A REFLECTION OF VALUES

Visitors to the schools in Reggio Emilia are amazed at the care and attention that have been given to the preparation of the environment. It would take a long time, if it were even possible, to become aware of all the details and to comprehend the thinking that has gone into every aspect of the space in the schools in Reggio Emilia. Space has been carefully thought about so that the environment truly reflects the values and beliefs that have evolved in the schools over the last 50 years. Recall those principles stated in Chapter 1: the image of the strong child; the importance of relationships and of collaboration; the use of one hundred languages; the curriculum as progettazione and provocation, with documentation; transparency in the environment and as a metaphor for openness; and the environment as third teacher.

Respect for the image of the child as rich, strong, and powerful is fundamental to preparing an environment that allows the child to be actively engaged in the process of learning. Given this belief in the active exploration of young children, the space must encourage investigation and be open to change to respond to the demands of active learners. Attention is given to promoting "relationships and collaboration in the group, but also to highlight individual identities and personal space. We try to stimulate investigation and exchange, cooperation and conflict" (Rinaldi, *Innovations*, Spring 1999). The initial impression of the attention to environmental preparation is one of expectation, as the stage that is being set for the protagonists to enter and begin.

The importance given to building relationships with children, families, and the community means that learning is viewed as a collaborative process that does not take place in isolation. Spaces, therefore, are designed to welcome children, families, and other visitors. Furniture and wall hangings are placed in the entrance halls to make parents and other visitors feel comfortable and to encourage them to take the time to inform themselves about the school. The documentation displayed on the walls or in portfolios on the shelves in the entryways provides a record of what has been happening in the program. Visual documentation conveys mini-stories about what recent activities and explorations have taken place.

The value placed on relationships is translated into the sense of "we" in the documentation, the care in communication and welcoming in the entry spaces, the tiers of seating in classrooms for children to come together to chat and plan project work, and the careful creation of spaces for small groups to work together. The notion of provocation is found in the unexpected juxtaposition of materials that surprises and compels exploration. The course of the progettazione is shown in the displays of past and ongoing work. The space in the classrooms is designed to encourage children to work with others, sometimes in a large group but more often in small groups of four or five children. There are low platforms built above the floor where a small group of children can work on a project such as building with blocks, undisturbed by the activity in the rest of the room. Mini-ateliers provide an area adjacent to the main classroom where children can work separately with art and construction materials.

Consideration of aesthetics is evident in every aspect of the program. The thought that goes into creating beautiful spaces for children reflects the belief that children deserve the very best and that their aesthetic sense needs to be nurtured in the early years. As Carol Anne Wien wrote in her diary of her visit to Reggio Emilia, "the beauty, serenity and deep affection in the schools stays with the children as a foundation," perhaps throughout their lives. Loris Malaguzzi envisioned Reggio Emilia classrooms as being "transformed into one large space with market stalls, each one with its own children and its own projects and activities" (Edwards, Gandini, & Forman 1998, p. 87). This layout has similarities with the way many early childhood programs organize their space. In most preschools and child care centers in North America, certain areas of the room are designated as places where children can do specific activities such as creating artwork, building with blocks, and working with puzzles and other table toys. There is an area, usually called a housekeeping or dramatic play area, where children can use props for role play. The traditional curriculum areas such as music, literature, art, and science each have their own area of the room where children can use the materials for each aspect of the curriculum. The library corner is stocked with books that may reflect the current topics the children are exploring. On closer inspection, however, a visitor notices that there are subtle differences in the way environments are planned in traditional and Reggio Emilia schools.

Perhaps the greatest difference between preschools in Reggio Emilia and other traditional preschools lies in the personal stamp that is given to each environment. Although there are housekeeping areas, construction areas, and spaces for books and writing, the attention to presenting opportunities in unusual ways means they look very different. Thought has been given to creating an environment that is unique, even though it may contain elements found in other preschools. Amelia Gambetti may have expressed this best with a comment made when visiting the College School in St. Louis early in their work of trying to interpret Reggio principles. Looking at the housekeeping area, she said: "Try to do something special with that area—something that can be identified with your personality in this school and that is unique to you. Everywhere I go in this country they all look the same. Do you all order from the same catalog?" (Cadwell, 1997, p. 93). Teachers in Reggio try to create an environment that truly reflects what is pleasing to those who inhabit the environment.

One housekeeping area in La Villetta school has a full-size wooden dining room table, with full-size chairs and two tall cabinets that store real dishes and glassware, definitely reminiscent of family dining rooms. Blocks are not just for building on the floors, but on a variety of shelf, loft, and step arrangements, some with mirrors or Plexiglas on top to produce a different view. Legos don't just go on a table; they also go on a carpeted step arrangement. Bathrooms are for utilitarian tasks, but they also display interesting objects such as shells or photos from vacation trips, contain huge sinks with available ponchos for water play, or to explore how fluids flow in complex overhead plastic tubing arrangements. A dining room at the Aprile XXV school includes a rocking horse and shelves full of clay figures made by the children. The folding door is open to the kitchen and food preparation area, while a teacher works with a small group of children, writing down their comments as they draw. The piazza at the Aprile XXV school includes a puppet theater, a wood and rope climbing apparatus, and a mirror that distorts real images. The piazza at the Diana School, opened by large windows to the outdoors and into the classrooms, has a circular wall where dress-up clothes hang along with the mirror triangle that permits many views of oneself. The sleeping rooms for toddlers at Peter Pan Infant-Toddler Center have small, flat wooden cots, beautifully made up with bedspread and pillow, blue gauze curtains, and a swirl of blue gauze hanging from the ceiling. The usual clutter of stored strollers and humidifier is hidden from view behind a bamboo blind. Attention is given to making the environment pleasing, comfortable, organized, and amiable. As Louise Cadwell comments, the difference in environments in Reggio teaches us that "no space is marginal, no corner is unimportant, and each space needs to be alive, flexible, and open to change" (Cadwell, 1997, p. 93).

Creating an environment that acts as a third teacher supports the perspective that knowledge is constructed not in isolation but within the social group. Teachers implementing ideas from the Reggio Emilia approach have to think differently about the way they plan the environment. It needs to be designed to provide opportunities for the people involved to interact with one another and with the environment to co-construct knowledge. Lella Gandini quotes Loris Malaguzzi:

> We value space because of its power to organize, promote pleasant relationships between people of different ages, create a handsome environment, provide changes, promote choices and activity, and its potential for sparking all kinds of social, affective and cognitive learning. All of this contributes to a sense of well-being and security in children. We also think that the space has to be a sort of aquarium that mirrors the ideas, values, attitudes, and cultures of the people who live within it (Gandini, 1998, p. 177).

In order to mirror ideas of people within, space and environment cannot be fixed and set but seen as a process of change and growth. The space must change in relation to children who live within that space. Christina Bondavalli, a teacher in the Reggio municipal schools, offers an example of this necessary change:

> We had a space in the classroom that the teachers intended for symbolic play with dolls. We soon noticed how the children in that classroom were particularly interested in the space that was devoted to construction with building blocks and other

materials. We reflected about the children's interest with other teachers and with the parents of those children. As a result, we decided to widen the space that had been devoted to building and called it the Construction Space. The classroom changed its appearance completely. The symbolic play area became the additional space for building. The parents started to bring material to school: plastic tubing, pieces of wood, cardboard tubing of various dimensions. The classroom changed because of the children who inhabited that space (Bondavalli in Gandini, Spring, 1998).

Loris Malaguzzi acknowledged the role the environment plays in the education of young children and its power to communicate beyond the classroom walls. He tells the story of how in the early days when the schools were struggling for their existence, once a week the children and teachers set up their equipment in the center of town so people could see the school in action. The municipal schools in Reggio Emilia have understood and put the power of the environment to work in programs involving young children, parents, and the community perhaps more effectively than in any other kind of school. As Gandini describes it, "The environment is seen here as educating the child; in fact it is considered as 'the third educator' along with a team of two teachers" (Edwards, Gandini, & Forman, 1998, p. 177).

Identifying Shared Values

To plan an environment like that of the preschools in Reggio Emilia which so closely reflects the philosophy and values of the families, teachers, and community involved, is a challenging task. As in all aspects of implementing the approach, teachers have to begin with small steps and then build on these as they feel more confident. The first step in planning the environment is to identify the values that are at the core of our work with young children and those of the families, and the wider community surrounding the school. This means that teachers, in the early stages of planning, arrange meetings with all the people involved in their programs to clarify the values that are important to the group.

This task sounds easy, but when the abstract values that the group has identified are translated into concrete factors, such as the selection of materials and equipment, and the programming of each day, the task gets harder. The team may struggle with such questions as what materials, equipment, and routines are congruent with the identified values. For example, if authenticity is identified as a core value, this will affect the choice of materials set out for dramatic play. Is it congruent with the stated value to provide the children with plastic models of food and utensils, or should real objects be set out in the play kitchen? In the art area, should playdough be used as a modeling material, or is clay a more authentic artistic material? These are the decisions the group will have to make to ensure their program truly reflects their values. As stated above, one of the distinguishing characteristics of the programs in the preschools in Reggio Emilia is the way practice reflects the beliefs and values of the community. Collaboration is highly valued and is seen in operation from the highest level of community-based management of the schools to the partnership in learning between children and teachers in the classroom.

Teachers wishing to explore the Reggio Emilia approach may find it helpful to begin the process of planning an environment that acts as a third teacher by thinking of their own values. Once they have done this individually, they can share their values with the team and members of the community. When the teachers in the child care program on Quadra Island decided to reorganize their environment to make it reflect more closely the principles learned from Reggio Emilia, they began by identifying the values that were important to them. The teachers met once a week in the evening and made a list of ideas they valued and felt passionate about. They then reworked the list until the whole group shared ownership of it. Some of the values the group listed on a chart include aesthetics, light, coziness, comfort, tidiness, organized space, softness, safety, challenges, open spaces, and clutter-free space. On a separate chart they listed their passions. These included children, music, plants, solitude, travel, food, reading, learning, exploring, nature, animals, laughter, outdoors, arts, dress-ups, building, and designing landscapes.

The teachers then began to examine the space in their environment to see what needed to be changed to reflect the things they had identified as important to the group. Because they identified aesthetics as a central value, they looked at every corner of the classroom to see whether it met the criteria for this value. They decided that the heaps of puzzles and games on the shelves in the classroom would have to be stored in a less conspicuous place. These items were replaced with a display of branches and wood collected with the children in the forest and arranged attractively in flat dishes on the shelves. An interesting assortment of shells were placed in glass jars and filled with water of different colors. The children were invited to bring in objects that they were excited about to display on the shelves. Very soon, a dull, uninteresting space became a focus of attention in the room.

Light was also considered an important value, so the group examined the environment to see how it could be used to further advantage. They moved a refrigerator away from a window and replaced it with a painting easel. There was now space and light for a plant to be placed on the windowsill beside the easel. A beautiful, quiet place was created where children could spend long periods of time creating.

The environment demonstrates respect for the children and their ideas in many ways. For example, the teachers asked the children to help plan the housekeeping corner. A child-sized bed with a soft mattress was built at the children's request. The bed also addressed qualities of softness, comfort, and coziness that the group felt should be present in their setting. The art area in the classroom was

Figure 5–1.   Quadra Island Day Care shelves before introducing ideas from Reggio Emilia.

reorganized to form a mini-atelier. In the past, all the art materials had been set out haphazardly on the shelves but were now carefully selected and displayed aesthetically in attractive containers. Documentation of the children's work was displayed on the walls to celebrate the children's ideas and to make their thinking visible.

The teachers kept asking themselves the following questions as they began to reorganize the classroom space to reflect first, their own values and passions, and second, the principles they had learned from Reggio Emilia.

- How well does the room reflect the values we have identified as important to us?
- What overall messages will the room convey to children, parents, and other visitors to the classroom?
- How will the environment mirror an image of the child that is rich, powerful, and competent?
- How well does the arrangement of the room reflect our respect for children, families, and the community?

The search for answers to these questions led the teachers to gradually reevaluate their use of space in the classroom and make profound changes in the physical space, the decoration of the rooms, and the availability of materials. They began to include the parents and the community in their discussions. At one well-attended meeting of parents and community members, the staff asked for specific suggestions about how they could make the space more welcoming to families and other visitors. The parents told the staff how much they valued the documentation in

Figure 5–2.   Quadra Island Day Care shelves after considering Reggio Emilia principles.

the entrance and how it was "drawing them more into the program." They suggested that a special place be created in the entrance hall where the staff could jot down things that needed to be done (small or big) so parents would know how they could help and volunteer if they had the time and the skill.

Figure 5–3.   The staff in the Quadra Island Day Care moved a refrigerator away from the window and replaced it with an easel.

Figure 5–4. The children asked for a child-sized bed and soft mattress in the house-keeping corner.

IMPLEMENTING REGGIO EMILIA PRINCIPLES

A number of principles including aesthetics, active learning, collaboration, transparency, "bringing the outdoors in," flexibility, relationship, and reciprocity need to be addressed to create an environment that acts as a third teacher. Although these principles are discussed separately here, it is important to keep in mind their interconnectedness.

Aesthetics

Louise Cadwell describes the way Amelia Gambetti worked with the teachers in the College School in St. Louis, Missouri, to improve the aesthetics in the environment and how they "transformed our classrooms from dark, dismal places into beautiful, inviting, light-filled, orderly spaces" (1997, p. 61). She describes Amelia looking at a mural of a tree in the entryway to the school:

> "Let's give this tree more of a reason for being," said Amelia. "What about moving that flight cage of finches that is in the hall in here in front of it. That could solve several problems . . . it would give the tree a purpose—a backdrop for the birds; it would make the birds feel closer to the out-of-doors near the colors and image of a tree." (1997, pp. 99–100)

Sue Fraser tells how this concept gave her the courage to approach parents about removing a mural that had been painted some years before on one wall that ran the length of the preschool. This cartoon of an enormous, smiling sun frolicking with small children dominated the room. It smothered the children's "voices" and took up space that could be used for documentation. The parents agreed: "the mural has outlived its time," it came from another era." Over the holidays, they arranged to have the wall painted a warm off-white. It became an area where the children could see their work displayed, and where parents and visitors could read the documentations of the children's experiences in the room. Now it feels as if the real children and their voices are now being heard in the room.

Active Learning

This principle reflects the underlying value of respect for the child, particularly for the image of the child as competent and able to construct learning either

Figure 5–5.   The Quadra Island Preschool classroom with the outmoded mural.

alone or with the support of others. The principle of active learning requires that the classroom have a stimulating environment that offers children many choices, provokes them to engage in many activities, and encourages them to explore a wide variety of materials. There also should be many opportunities for children to represent their ideas in different media. These materials, generally, need to be open-ended to allow the children to act on and transform them in many ways. Actually, the concept of open-ended materials may have at least one developmental exception. Margaret Edwards at Lakewood Avenue Children's School noticed that her two-year-olds' habitual pattern of play in the dramatic play kitchen area was to come in, take out the materials, and carry them somewhere else. She decided that the play kitchen furniture was just too open-ended and abstract in its appearance. She had a cabinetmaker make a very realistic kitchen including drawers that open, a kitchen sink with real faucets, a real mini-refrigerator, a stove with real knobs, and open shelves for plates. The real kitchen elicited real kitchen play, leading Margaret to conclude that the youngest children need materials that suggest reality for them to act on.

The classroom at the Vancouver Child Study Center provides children with a rich and stimulating learning environment. In the fall, the teachers had observed that the children in their group this year were very interested in construction. Over the next few weeks, in addition to the blocks, Legos, and Duplo regularly

Figure 5–6.   A realistic kitchen stimulated more productive play with two-year-olds.
(*Courtesy:* Lakewood Avenue Children's School.)

available in the classroom, the teachers provided the children with many different kinds of blocks such as small, brightly colored wooden blocks of various shapes and sizes, mosaic tiles, and so on. They also brought in carpentry tools and high-quality wood for the children to hammer and nail. The teachers encouraged the children to create many drawings, paintings, collages, and three-dimensional objects representing their ideas about construction. The teachers also brought in a selection of books about building.

One group was particularly interested in the story "The Three Little Pigs," so the teachers decided to ask the children if they would like to build houses for the

Figure 5–7.
Godfrey drew the Wolf
from The Three Little Pigs.

pigs. The children sketched how they imagined the houses might look. They decided to use cardboard boxes as a base for the houses. The children took a walk in the forest behind the school to collect materials to build the houses. A small group of children formed a core group who stayed with the project for the whole time but many of the other children came and went during the three weeks the project lasted. The children made the first two houses by attaching straw and sticks they had collected in the forest to the

Figure 5–8.
Sally drew the straw house for the first little pig.

wooden boxes with "mortar" they had made with flour and water. The children experimented with food coloring and paint to make the glue they had mixed look more like mortar. Then came the more challenging job of constructing the house made of bricks. The teachers put the cardboard box on the table, one surface of which had been shaped to form the roof, and cut a door and a window out of the sides of the box. The teachers showed the children a real brick and discussed how the pigs would have used bricks like this one to build their houses. They set a large block of red clay out on the table and helped the children cut the clay into small, square bricks. The children began to build the bricks up the side of the house to make the walls.

Gloria (the teacher): It looks as though it is going to be strong. If it isn't the right size you need to make it yourself. Which size do you need?

William (age 4): Fat and little ones.

Gloria: What is that coming out of the top of the roof?

William: The chimney. We are making a brick house.

Gloria: Look at the heavy, heavy brick here.

William: I have made one [brick]. I need a paintbrush. (He begins to use the paintbrush to apply "mortar" to cement the bricks he had made.)

William: I am making a brick house, but it is clay, but when the clay dries it will be brick. The water makes it stick good. It is almost going to be a brick house. How does the door close? How does it stay closed? You can close it if it is almost going to dry. If it is starting to be hard it won't open. (He cuts some more square bricks. He measures the size of brick he needs and fits the one he made into the space. It doesn't quite fit. He tries cutting the brick with scissors.)

William: A strongman tool. We need a skinny brick for that corner.

Gloria: Godfrey, can you help us on this corner? Which house is the strongest?

William: Look it is strong. I can't blow it down.

Gloria: But what if a wolf came along?

William: That is strong paper. It is called cardboard. Special little bricks. That is a middle-sized brick.

Gloria: It looks pretty strong.

(William calls out to two children who are pounding the clay bricks into a mound: "You have to make a brick house!" He goes over and joins them at the clay table.)

Figure 5–9.   William announces
that he is making a
"brick house."

This example shows how the experience of constructing a brick house provided the child with many opportunities to actively explore, investigate, and solve problems with the support of Gloria, his teacher. She stayed with him until he put the finishing touches to the house. The transcription gives an insight into how Gloria supported William's thinking process as he estimated the size of the bricks he needed and considered the properties of the clay. He made choices about tools and decided the scissors would be a better tool for cutting the clay than the knife the teacher had suggested. He thought about the strength of the house ("I can't blow it down"). He tried to keep the other children on task, saying, "You have to make a brick house." Gloria gave him the freedom to use the material in another way when he decided to join the children exploring the red clay at the next table.

By the time the three little pigs' houses were nearly complete, only William was left working on the house, and he, too, seemed to be losing interest. Was there any point in bringing out the brick house the next day? The teachers discussed this and decided to bring the project to a close. They put the three houses the children had made for the little pigs on a low shelf below a display board with many drawings, photographs, and written commentaries that documented the experience. The teachers, remembering the way the children had used the clay to make a volcano the day before, wondered if the children were really interested in pursuing this topic further. They had observed that the red clay had made the children think of hot lava. The next day they put out the clay again and observed what the children did with it. The children stated that they wanted the volcano they had made the previous day to explode. The teachers and the children set about figuring how they could make this happen. A small group of children carried on this investigation about volcanic explosions for the next few days.

An environment that stimulates learning and is responsive to the children's input is essential to creating an environment that acts as a third teacher. As Lella Gandini states,

> In order to act as an educator for the child, the environment has to be flexible: It must undergo frequent modification by the children and the teachers in order to remain up to date and responsive to their needs to be protagonists in constructing their knowledge. All the things that surround the people in the school and which they

use—the objects, the materials, and the structures—are not seen as passive elements but on the contrary are seen as elements that condition and are conditioned by the actions of children and adults who are active in it (Edwards, Gandini, & Forman, 1998, p. 177).

Collaboration

Collaboration is one of the strongest messages that the environment in its role as the third teacher communicates. An environment planned to act as a third teacher is particularly effective in helping children learn skills for working with others in a group. The approach, for example, requires that teachers encourage children to contribute their ideas and efforts to group projects. Children learn the value of individual contributions in building the strength of the group. The environment must allow space for working individually or with other children and adults in groups. As Vygotsky says, "With assistance every child can do more than he can by himself— though only within the limits set by the state of his development" (1962, p. 103). The large murals that are painted on acetate and hung from the ceilings in the Reggio Emilia schools are created in collaboration with others.

At Quadra Island Preschool, the teacher, parents, and children collaborated in celebrating the Chinese New Year. One of the children in the preschool, Emma, had been adopted as an infant and brought from China to live on Quadra Island. Her parents are determined that she retain her cultural heritage so the celebration of the Chinese

Figure 5–10.   Emma shows us how to use chopsticks.

New Year became a particularly important celebration for the preschool. Emma's mother shared many of the beautiful objects that she had brought back with her from her trip to China to adopt Emma. A beautiful display was arranged in front of a magnificent wall hanging of a fiery gold dragon. The parents and teacher discussed how they could construct a dragon for the Chinese New Year's parade. One of the fathers offered to help the children build the dragon's head out of a cardboard box. The teacher helped the children make the dragon's "skin," using a sheet and food coloring. Parents made many contributions: one mother cooked Chinese food with the children for snack time, and another showed the children how to do calligraphy. The children also made red money envelopes and lanterns to decorate the room.

Figure 5–11.   Children paint the skin of the dragon.

At last the day of the parade came. When the parents arrived, the preschool was empty; there was not a sound. The children had decided that the dragon should hide very quietly until everyone had arrived. They all huddled in a back room in total silence under the dragon skin, in line behind the child who had volunteered to be under the dragon's head. The parents stood around looking puzzled until suddenly there was a loud boom from a gong and out tumbled the most magnificent dragon anyone had ever seen. He paraded round and round the room, accompanied by the booming of the gong.

The richness of this experience resulted from the collaboration of everyone in the program. It could not have happened the way it did without the children, teacher, and parents all contributing their ideas and skills. It is essential that in creating an environment that acts as a third teacher, children are given the opportunity to work with others in the co-construction of

Figure 5–12.   Des and his mother do calligraphy together.

knowledge. The room also should communicate respect for the families and community, as well as for the cultural background of the people involved in the program and in the community served by the school.

Transparency

In the preschools in Reggio Emilia, transparency is evident at many levels in the program. On the surface, transparency is seen in the importance that light plays in the environment of every municipal preschool in Reggio Emilia. Light is everywhere; it not only shines through windows and internal glass walls but also is used in playful ways. It is captured and changed by colored, transparent film attached to the windowpanes; it is caught on the shiny mobiles that break up the space between floor and ceilings; and it shines through glass objects that reflect it around the room. Light is reflected in mirrors hung from the ceilings and on the classroom walls. Mirrors are found in unexpected places such as attached to the floor and on the ramps for climbing. Mirrors are formed into pyramid-shaped kaleidoscopes into which children can climb and observe their reflections from many different angles. Light is used as an art medium. For example, the children paint and arrange collage materials on the glass surface of light tables. The children's artwork is also projected onto walls by overhead projectors. Light shines through the murals that the children have painted on large plastic sheets that may be hung from the ceilings as room dividers or displayed on the walls of the classrooms.

Transparency is seen in many of the Reggio-inspired environments in America. In the Lakewood Avenue Children's School, there are small windows that connect the toddler, middler (twos), and preschool classrooms so children may watch other children at work and play. Large windows connect the indoor and outdoor environments. Shelves have been chosen that allow children to look right through them at adjoining spaces. In Pam Oken-Wright's classroom, the studio wall is of many glass panes so children working within and in the classroom are connected visually. Pam has added a translucent panel for painting in the playground fence. In Patti Cruikshank-Schott's classroom, glass containers store art materials and other objects to explore. Glass bottles filled with rainbow hues glow at the window as the sun shines through them. In a warm southern climate at First Baptist Kindergarten, the glass classroom doors are often open to connect the indoor and outdoor areas for exploration. On a large window at Sabot School, a large buttercup is painted, echoing the explorations with buttercups going on inside and outside in the meadow where they grow. In the Campus Children's Center, mirrors reflect children's activity at many levels, including at the top of the climber for the toddlers and in a crawling space for infants.

Transparency is also a metaphor for communication, especially in the documentation that informs parents and visitors of what is happening in the program. This information is made transparent through the documentation of the children's work that is displayed in the entranceways and on the classroom walls. On a deeper level, transparency is seen in the openness of the educators of Reggio Emilia to learning from the ideas of others working in the field of early childhood education, and in their willingness to share their approach with visitors from all over the world.

Figures 5–13a,b,c,d,e,f,g,h.   Transparency appears in the environment in many ways: in the sheer colored fabric that reflects light at the window in (a); in the windows that connect children to other classes in (b) and (c); in the reflection of mirrors in (d),(e), and (f); in the open shelves that allow children to see through to the outdoor world in (g); and in the yellow buttercups connecting inside and out in (h).

(*Courtesy:* (a) Caroline Friends School; (b), (c) and (g) Lakewood Avenue Children's School; (d), (e), and (f) University of Vermont Campus Children's Center; (h) Sabot School.)

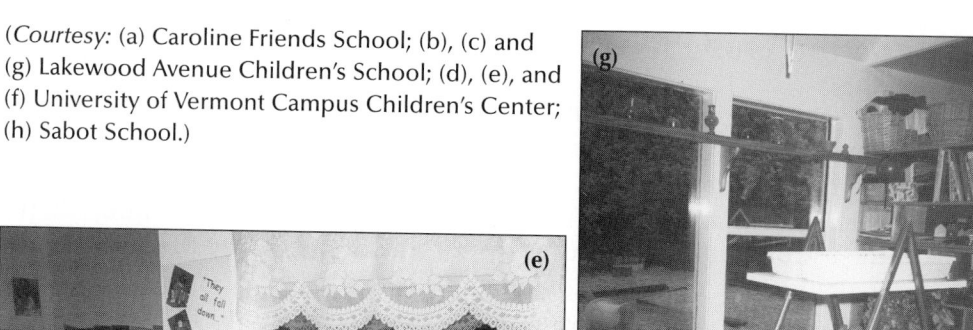

Bringing the Outside World In

Another principle in creating an environment that acts as a third teacher, bringing the outdoors in, heightens children's awareness of the natural, physical, and social environments in which they live. This awareness helps to strengthen the children's sense of belonging in their world. This principle has two levels of meaning. On the surface, the use of natural materials is seen in the decoration of the room and in the materials available for investigation and creativity. On a deeper level, it connects children to their roots, and gives them a sense of value and respect for their community and culture.

Patti Cruikshank-Schott of the Carolina Friends' School reports on a conversation she had with some parents about the environment in her classroom. At a Back to School night, parents were asked to explore the room with seven choices of tasks to work on: adding their child's name to the Making Connections Web on the bulletin board; building a fort with big blocks and fabric; creating a small piece of art and a note for their child's new mailbox; making a block creation using all the blocks to leave as a surprise for the children in the morning; turning a block of clay into orange-size balls for the children's use; exploring the various tools and making a tiny creature for display (also writing a short description of what had been made and making a drawing of it); or using sticky notes to make several comments on children's work displayed throughout the room. When the projects came to a stopping point, the teacher and parents discussed what their favorite things in the room were, including things they would not have thought of using with children. A mother who had grown up in China during the Cultural Revolution reflected on the choices in the environment, something she had not been used to as a child, and chose as her favorite object a metal teapot from China, one of two in the Home Living area.

> "Tea plays such a role in my Chinese background . . . It's not usual to have this . . . I would not think to give it to a child . . . sometimes to teach or force doesn't work . . . that's not what she (her daughter) might think was important . . . she grew up here. But in the surroundings, being surrounded with things with which I'm familiar, this may interest her. So we can talk about things, rather than it being some kind of textbook information."

Patti comments that this mother's statement describes her own beliefs about multicultural education. Her intention is to create a background of concrete daily experiences for the children, not necessarily to talk about it but to lay the foundation of the beauty and uniqueness of objects from other cultures, so that when "a child sees a woman in a Guatemalan huiple they will have a positive response from having worn a similar blouse at school." In the home living area there are bamboo steamers, woks, and other Chinese cooking utensils such as small china tea cups and porcelain spoons, a Scandinavian wooden dish rack, lengths of African and

Figure 5–14.   Surrounded by beautiful objects used by other cultures, children absorb a
sense of value and respect for differences. (*Courtesy:* Patti Cruikshank-Schott.)

South American fabrics, wooden shoes, and huaraches. The outside world comes
into this classroom influenced by Reggio ideas to connect children naturally with
ideas of value and respect.

Flexibility

One of the joys of the Reggio Emilia approach is the spirit of creation that infuses
all experiences. Everyone involved in the program is motivated by this extraordinary energy that becomes part of every experience. Old, tired practices disappear
of their own accord, and everyone, to their surprise, discovers new and more interesting ways of doing things. Being flexible with space, time, and materials, and in
the way people relate to one another and their work, is essential to making beneficial change happen.

Teachers implementing the Reggio Emilia approach have to think differently
about the way they plan the environment. In particular, they need to plan for the
flexible use of space and materials. Art and science materials are no longer segregated in certain areas of the room but are available for use wherever they are
needed, indoors or out. This is one of the reasons the schools in Reggio Emilia
adopted the idea of the atelier as a place where children can work with materials

from all areas of the curriculum including art, literature, and science to produce their ideas in collaboration with the atelierista. Participants in programs influenced by Reggio Emilia principles have to be flexible and able to change their expectations of the preschool program.

Patti Cruikshank-Schott recalls the comments of parents viewing the changes she had made in her environment during the first year in her classroom. The room had been a fairly typical preschool classroom, well stocked with the usual Fisher-Price® toys. Patti says that she had always had a goal of removing all plastic items from her life and classroom. Her classroom, which now truly resembles a studio with abundant quantities of creative materials beautifully displayed throughout, contains many natural items, intriguing artifacts, and beautiful junk. There are attractive woven baskets filled with stones and bits of colored glass, odds and ends of hardware, and small pieces of wood. The art area has open colored boxes, each filled with items such as buttons, small spools, corks, colored pegs, small wood beads in two sizes, pieces of bark and gumballs, and bits of broken shells. There is a ribbon rack dispensing rolls of ribbons and crepe paper next to glass jars of different colored paper scraps. Home Living has a shelf with wooden bowls of various sizes, a small bamboo steamer and bamboo trays, a hanging collection of wooden spoons and utensils, a hanging wok, a nutmeg grater and nutmeg, tiny glass bottles filled with spices, and small taper candles hanging on a dowel by the window.

When parents first saw the new environment with the typical toys removed and the new materials for exploration, they worried that their children would be bored since "there was nothing to play with." Now, after more than three years of serious work and creation and joyful play, parents are coming to value the potential of the environment that invites investigation. At the recent Back to School night, one father commented "You could get lost in here, there's so much . . . and there are niches." Another father agreed: "There's such a variety of things to be involved with . . . and the freedom to move about . . . children choosing their interests for the day." One mother enjoyed the things from the outdoors brought inside—"the twigs, birdhouses and hives . . . the little things that make the room pretty neat . . . another aspect of beauty, this time from the natural world, with most things combined in groups with varying sizes or collections with similarities and differences." One parent summed it up: "There's so much richness and so much simplicity . . . It opened my mind to what good preschool teaching is." Certainly, these parents have changed their perceptions and expectations of the preschool.

Flexibility may also involve teachers having to rethink traditional ideas about the use of space and materials. In the video "Thinking Big" (1999), Ann Pelo and Sarah Felstiner, influenced by ideas from Reggio Emilia, describe their own evolutions in thinking about appropriate uses of environmental space and materials as they attempted to respond authentically to the children's on-going interest in building really tall structures. This required the teachers to open up the traditionally divided space of the classroom and to rethink the usual prohibition on building "anything taller than your shoulders." This ability to open up their thinking came as they really paid attention to what was going on in the children's play. As they saw what the children were building and how they were building, Ann and Sarah came to see why they were building, finding that the building was really about exploring the idea of height, about changing perspectives, and about being powerful. The teachers then could trust the children's building skills, along with their intuition that this was an important theme to pursue in their play. They describe how they had to support each other in letting go of traditional thinking about organization and rules in the environment. One evidence of the letting go came as they responded to the children's idea of going to the local hardware store to test out the available step stools and to purchase one to facilitate the taller buildings. Sarah makes the comment that two things allowed the extended project exploring height to develop: one was opening up the physical space, and the second was in the teachers coming to understand the play at its deepest developmental levels. Ann adds: "I learned to experiment with changing the environment. Changing the physical space is a metaphor for being open and responsive to the children generally" ("Thinking Big," 1999). This extended project will be described in detail in Chapter 9.

Flexibility also involves an unexpected use of materials and equipment. For example, as the children in La Villetta school worked on the Amusement Park for Birds, they used material and equipment from all areas of the curriculum. They used books to find information about birds, they needed science equipment for building the fountains and windmills, and they employed art materials for decorating the objects created for the birds to enjoy. The children and teachers had many ideas for ways to use space: they built a bird blind to watch the birds in the playground, a completely unexpected object to find in a preschool setting.

Relationship

The emphasis the educators in the schools in Reggio Emilia place on relationship, discussed in Chapter 4, also affects the presentation of materials in the room. Objects are shown in relation to other materials. Lego blocks may be laid out with pieces of driftwood on the surface of a mirror. This brings the artificial and natural worlds into relationship. It also gives children a different perspective when they see what they are building reflected upside down in the mirror. Clay for the children to work with is attractively laid out on a table with a flower arrangement and examples of finished clay pieces displayed in the center of the table. Collage materials are kept in clear plastic containers or spread out on trays for use. The abundant jars of brightly colored paint, the aprons, and the paintbrushes are placed on a cart beside the easel.

Relationship is also a key principle in the development of documentation. Documentation is designed to help the observer see the relationship between what the children are doing and the underlying theories and philosophical principles that provide the rationale for the experience.

Reciprocity

The notion of the environment acting as a third teacher gives the classroom the qualities of a living being. As such, it must be as open to change and responsive to the children, parents, and community as any good teacher would be. This reciprocal, dynamic environment, designed to play the role of a third teacher in the room, is a powerful idea. It means that in adopting principles of the Reggio Emilia approach, teachers will have to think more critically about what kind of environment they provide for children. They will have to examine each element and think about its purpose. For, as Lella Gandini said, "All the things that surround the people in the school and which they use—the objects, the materials and the structures—are not seen as passive elements, but on the contrary are seen as elements that condition and are conditioned by the actions of children and adults who are active in it" (Gandini in Edwards, Gandini, & Forman, 1998, p. 177).

SUPPORTING REGGIO EMILIA PRINCIPLES IN THE ENVIRONMENT

The first step for teachers planning their classroom space, whether they are starting from scratch or reorganizing existing space, is to decide what values they want their environment to communicate. The next step is to plan the physical layout of the space. The experiences of students in the Children Teaching Teachers program provide examples of how the space in the classroom can be planned to support the values of the participants and the principles of the Reggio Emilia approach.

After reaching a shared understanding of their image of the child (see Chapter 2), the students then begin to think about what kind of learning environment will support the image they have identified. Students consider questions such as the following while planning the environment:

- Does the environment match our image of the child?
- How effective is the environment in acting as a third teacher?
- How are aesthetics addressed in each aspect of our environment?
- What messages are being communicated to children and other visitors to the classroom?

To help them find answers to these questions, the students are given an exercise in which each group is asked to identify the principles they consider important in planning an environment to act as a third teacher. They identify principles such as aesthetics, transparency, relationship, reciprocity, bringing the inside out, and bringing the outside in. Each group then creates a mini-environment to illustrate the principle they have chosen to work with.

Each week, the janitors move the tables and chairs out of three classrooms in the college. The students then convert these spaces into environments for children. The "before-and-after" effect is mind-boggling. A dull, sterile room is suddenly transformed into a beautiful, rich, and stimulating environment filled with comfortable child-sized furniture, bright colors, stimulating materials, paintings, collages, natural objects, and musical instruments.

Once the students have prepared their environments, they present their ideas to the class and invite students from other groups to experience some of the activities they have planned. For example, the group that selected transparency as a principle prepared activities using transparent materials such as cellophane, tissue paper, and sheets of acetate film as surfaces on which to draw and paint. They used an overhead projector to project images on the wall, and they set up the light table with translucent paper and ink for painting over a surface of light. They also experimented with mirrors, using them in unexpected ways. Following the presentation to the class, each group created a documentation panel to display in the hall outside the classroom. They used Polaroid photographs and written documentation to explain what they had learned about the principle they had selected to demonstrate to the class.

The instructors observed that each week, the environments the students created for the visiting children became increasingly stimulating and reflected more closely the principles learned from the Reggio Emilia approach. In the following weeks, as the students prepared environments for the children, they revisited the documentations to ensure that they included principles such as aesthetics, transparency, reciprocity, relationship, and the use of natural materials in their planning of environments to act as a third teacher. One student describes her experience with this process:

> We learned a variety of things from the children. We learned about the "whole child," including . . . open-ended art and literature. Using the environment as the "third teacher" really helped us. Allowing the child choices and time to explore was really beneficial. . . . We seemed to step back and support the children when it was needed. In using more of the (principles of the) Reggio approach, the children found their own purpose for the cardboard box and seemed to find great enjoyment in doing this also. We learned that aesthetics play an important part in the environment. Because our room is small and has no windows, we felt it needed extra effort in making it [aesthetically pleasing]. To have the children explore and experiment we needed to get their attention first. To do this we focused on making the room bright and colorful. The activity centers were set up to look interesting and inviting, and we tried to use natural materials as much as we could. Most of all, we learned to follow the children's lead, and not to have complicated, structured activities, but rather to simplify and go with the flow. We tried to show the children we respect them as competent human beings. (CTT Journal)

Observations of the children's interests from the previous week are used as a basis for planning the following week. One group of students, before the first session of Children Teaching Teachers, found out from the teacher that the children who would join them the next week were interested in what was under the ocean. The following extracts from the documentation in the journal kept of their experiences illustrate how the Reggio Emilia principles served as a guide in providing the children with a quality program. It is interesting to observe how the theme approach in the first week gradually changed to an emergent curriculum.

> Planning and Preparation: Our focus for CTT#1 was an aesthetically pleasing, theme-based program with the environment being the third teacher. . . . Our sister group decided to work together [with us] to develop our plan and do all the preparation. The initial preparation time was long and involved. We spent many hours making decorations and continuing to plan. We planned for treasure chests, painting on paper on the wall, a quiet area, playdough, sand, and water. Early literacy was incorporated with signs hanging above or near every center stating what the activity was in clear printing.

The analysis of the first experience shows how the students began to be aware of a conflict between their theme approach and the implementation of the Reggio Emilia approach.

> Our first CTT went fairly well, all things considered. We all went into CTT with high expectations but no idea of what would happen. . . . Our entire environment was fairly structured, with treasure chests for an art activity on one large table, playdough on a small table, painting on paper on the wall, a quiet corner with books, and water and sand on the floor. All areas of the room were used throughout the morning and explored by the children but were fairly structured . . . there was not a lot of room for creativity in some of the activities that we had set out. Most of the interactions were teacher/child or teacher/teacher with very little child/child interaction. Our small group (of children) could have been a reason for that.

> What We Learned: We learned from our first CTT that we need to be flexible and go with the children's interests instead of planning such structured activities. Circle could have been . . . more [of] a social activity instead of being so structured. This may hold the children's interest and attention for a longer period of time. We learned to simplify our activities as well as our preparation. We spent far too much time on decorating the room and not enough time concentrating on what the children would enjoy. We definitely learned we need to do planning from now on from a child's perspective and not a teacher's. Our sister group will continue to have sensory experiences for the children because they were successful but will make provisions for a better space for the water and sand. They will carry on with circle, including songs, but will follow the children's lead. . . . They will allow the children to move freely and expel some energy.

The students, remembering their identification of their image of the child as "competent and resourceful," were now beginning to listen more closely to the children and follow their lead as they planned the next session with the sister group.

Planning and Preparation: We put up large pieces of plain paper on the wall once again [for the children to paint on], we kept the treasure boxes, and brought in beach towels, sun umbrellas, sand, and rocks [as sensory materials]. Everyone from both groups collaborated well, and we helped each other out immensely while planning and setting up the room. We also had the privilege of being the first group to incorporate the brand-new light and water tables to our environment.

What Worked Well and What Didn't: The atmosphere was welcoming and non-threatening, our environment was aesthetically pleasing, and the interactions were generally very good. The materials set out were well used except for the treasure boxes (we found that they were not age-appropriate). We found that a structured circle was not necessary, and the "train" around the room, which was initially a cute idea, did not work for this group of children. The set up of the light and water tables was also questionable as they were set against the wall, which limited the space for the children to play. But overall we were pleased with this session's outcome.

What We Learned from the Children: We learned to be prepared for anything and to be flexible. Keeping in mind the children's interests and individual needs is always important. In addition, clear, positive communication with the other teachers and with the children is very beneficial and helps to prevent misunderstandings.

In the third session, the students had returned after six weeks out on practicum in centers in the community. They seemed much more resourceful and confident in their presentations.

Planning and Preparation: We planned for a Spring theme . . . flowers, birds, kites, and brought in a large cardboard box to decorate. We had a free art table with paper, markers, and scissors . . . we set out a light table with watercolors enabling the children to explore the combination of light and paint together. In [the] circle, we discussed with the children what they enjoyed about CTT.

What Went Well and What Did Not: The box was the biggest hit; the children decorated and played in it. (They said it was a puppet theater at one point.) They also enjoyed the umbrella picnic table, which stimulated interesting conversations.

The students were beginning to conceptualize their role less as a teacher controlling the class and more as a partner with the children in the social construction of knowledge. They also were respecting the children's ideas and trusting in the children's resourcefulness and competence. One sees them empowering the children as they allowed them to take the lead in transforming the cardboard box, not into something the students had planned, but into a puppet theater the children could go in and out of.

Summary: We changed the cardboard box into a puppet theater (based on observations from the previous week). The children spent a fair bit of time performing puppet shows and playing in the cardboard box. We also put our documentation on the wall, which interested the children. We changed the format of the session to allow more free play, as we felt it was better to let the children play than pull them away from activities to eat and then return. Our transitions seemed to naturally blend together, and everything ran very smoothly. We worked really well as a team and knew when to step back and not overcrowd the children.

In this session, the students were becoming more flexible in their use of space and in how to use time. They were beginning to be more sensitive to the natural rhythm of the children, following the children's lead in making the transition from free play to snack.

The following extract is taken from the final entry in their journal:

Children Teaching Teachers not only gives students the opportunity to apply their knowledge in practical situations, it allows us to explore the endless possibilities when we allow children to be children. It helps us to understand that we have a special role to play in children's lives. We are not here to "teach," but to guide, scaffold, and facilitate learning. CTT helped us to better understand what roles we play in children's lives. We came to understand the importance of providing children with a consistent environment—one that acted as a third teacher. This consistency allowed the children to feel a sense of trust and familiarity toward CTT. This sense of trust and safety became the foundation for their exploration and discovery.

In terms of planning, we learned that flexibility is key. During CTT we focused on providing open-ended activities that would meet the needs of the "whole child." We followed the children's lead and built on their interests. When the children seemed to enjoy something we carried it into the next CTT, and we learned that when trying to implement an emergent curriculum, it is important to be able to think on your feet and be able to adapt the activities to include all children.

The most important aspect of CTT was what the children taught us. They surpassed any and all of our expectations. They opened up a world of limitless opportunities, and they allowed us to be part of it. CTT and the children helped us to challenge ourselves to try new things and not be afraid to fail! The children made us see what it truly means to be a child.*

*With thanks to Groups 2 and 5 (who shared their journals with Sue Fraser), the children, and the teachers who participated in Children Teaching Teachers in the winter of 1998.

During the six weeks the students participated in Children Teaching Teachers, it was obvious how deeply they were thinking about their practice, how they strived to provide the children with more authentic experiences based on the image of the child they had identified earlier, and how the quality of their programming improved as they implemented some of the key principles such as aesthetics, provision for active learning, collaboration, transparency, flexibility, relationship, and reciprocity, the heart of the Reggio Emilia approach.

An important resource for teachers and programs wanting to explore possibilities in their environments is *Children, Spaces, Relations: Metaproject for an Environment for Young Children,* eds. J. Ceppi & M. Zini, available from Reggio Children.

Chapter **6**

Documentation

Stand aside for a while and leave room for learning, observe carefully what children do, and then, if you have understood well, perhaps teaching will be different from before.
—*Loris Malaguzzi*

Questions to Consider:

- What is the purpose of documentation?
- What are the different formats that documentation can take?
- What are the criteria that indicate high-quality documentation?
- What is involved in the process?
- What are the challenges?
- What might be some of the solutions?

THE PURPOSE OF DOCUMENTATION

Documentation is the visible trace of the process that children and teachers engage in during their investigations together. It provides a record of the learning experiences in the classroom, reveals connections between events, and provides children, parents, and teachers with an opportunity to review and plan future experiences. Documentation does not refer just to creating a final report or collecting documents that help to remember or evaluate learning activities. Documentation is a vital part of the process of *progettazione,* the word used in Reggio to convey the complex web of hypotheses, observations, predictions, interpretations, planning, and explorations. There is a sense of flow in the process of documentation, a sense that it is an open and living system, a basic daily action of communication as natural and pervasive as breathing, completely integrated into the everyday work of the classroom, not lying outside it. Documentation then comes to mean a way of making concrete and visible the "interweaving of actions of the adults and of the children . . . It is in fact a process of reciprocal learning. Documentation makes it possible for teachers to sustain the children's learning while they also learn (to teach) from the children's own learning" (Rinaldi, 1998, p. 120). Documentation is a mind-set about an active desire to learn, to represent and reflect on what is being learned, and to enter into dialog with others.

Teachers are amazed at how documentation heightens their level of awareness of what actually happened during the experience. Virtually every American teacher inspired by ideas from Reggio speaks of the profound importance of documentation in the classroom. The following comments were made by some of these teachers.

Patti Cruikshank-Schott: "Documentation allows the children's words to come to the front. You can be in the same room and hear it, but there is such a difference when you write the words down and reflect on their meaning. Documentation gives me windows to show development and the children's interests, and windows to reflect on my own growth."

Jeanne Goldhaber: "Documentation was our real entry point—of course, Rinaldi's right. It's a system. As soon as you begin to tweak one part of the system, it is all affected. We knew we had to focus on documentation so we could have a program based on observation and reflection, moving to see how we could provoke understanding. Initially we got stuck on the product piece of documentation, but came to understand how the documentation process promotes inquiry and a sense of community, and supports collaboration."

Jane Watkins: "We began to listen to children, really listen—listen with our ears, with cameras, and with written dialogs of conversations. We take a lot of dialog down and the directions for projects come from that. Documentation of the projects reflects the value of the child's work. Documentation allows for an interweaving of the family and the school, to help families see the process."

Pam Oken-Wright: "I keep a daily log with all the day's documentation data— photographs of children working and of their work, transcripts, scanned images of children's work, narrative, and often some of my own first-impression reflections or interpretations. I review the logs periodically to pull out what I know has become a topic of deep interest, what I suspect are episodes in a pattern of some sort, and to look for patterns I may not yet have seen. Making documentation panels (a TINY part of this process, by the way) involves choosing and reformatting images and the usual construction work, but I get to spend most of the available time in the thinking piece: interpreting, seeing and making connections, looking for children's intent and understanding. It is a second opportunity for understanding, something I suspect we may not give ourselves enough time for."

Ann Pelo: "One way we aim to highlight children's daily work is with our "curriculum boards," the bulletin boards outside each classroom. This is a way to reflect that the curriculum is the daily life of the classroom, and that the children's play is rich and provocative. Most every family in the group of kids that I teach reads the board every day, usually when they drop off and pick up. Many families have commented to me that they look forward to reading the board, which gives them a window into their children's daily lives that they treasure. It has developed a profound sense of community among the families in our group; often parents stand at the board and chat with each other as they read. It gives families a shared starting place for conversations, a shared window into the classroom."

Margaret Edwards: "The documentation process transformed the program more than anything. The documentation allowed parents to get directly involved in the curriculum. But more, our teachers are so much more observant since we decided to do documentation panels. There is something about that device that has really helped them learn to look and listen and see the children in a more penetrating and perceptive way."

More recent comments from teachers on the Reggio list include:

- *"I think the image of the child cannot be changed except by documentation. It isn't having panels on the wall that brings about the change; it is making choices about what to put on the panels, thinking about the photos and the tapes to learn what they reflect. The big difference that comes about with documentation is more teacher reflection than without documentation."*

- *"The whole process of making a documentation panel requires meaningful interactions with the children, and reflection on their thinking. Panels themselves emerge from a process that necessitates a certain kind of teaching experience. They are the result of research and reflection."*

- *Documentation is "Listening made visible: to the children, the families, the administration, and to the community."*

Documentation enables teachers to be more effective in their work by opening up possibilities and deepening their own and the children's learning experiences.

Teachers use documentation to record the experience of entering the time frame with children and to keep track of the interests that emerge. Documentation is similar to a system of gears that sets the curriculum in motion. Making visible the children's ideas and experiences in some form of documentation provides the teachers with a means of revisiting them with children, discussing them with colleagues and parents, and making hypotheses and flexible plans for further action. The teachers and children can discuss the documentation together, reflect on the experiences, and perhaps get an idea of how to proceed further with the topic.

Documentation is central to emergent curriculum. When children and adults review the earlier experiences together through representations such as children's drawings or recorded comments, the children are moved to a higher level of mental functioning in which they are encouraged to focus their attention and remember in detail past experiences (Bodrova & Leong, 1996). In retracing their experiences, children may correct and expand earlier understandings, and compare their ideas with others.

Parents and other visitors should be able to read a story of what has been happening in the classroom from the documentation and the theory, philosophy, and purpose that underlie the experience. Parents can hear what actually happened

Figure 6–1. Making families feel welcome is an important part of the communication process.

during the experience. In this way, parents are learning what their child has been doing and are getting an intimate view of how and why the activities were important to the child's learning. And it is a way for families to stay connected with what is happening in their children's lives at school at a level that goes deeper than just superficial chitchat with the teachers. Reading the story of their child's experiences at school might suggest to parents ways of contributing to the program or give them topics to discuss at home.

Every child is not necessarily part of every documentation story, but reading the story of other children's experiences is important for families for several reasons. Because their child is part of a learning community, he or she is impacted directly or indirectly by everything that occurs in the classroom. Learning to be interested in other children besides their own helps extend families' idea of community. Stories about other children also give families insights about how teachers think about their work and how they make their decisions about how to extend children's learning. In learning to listen to children other than their own, parents come to realize the importance of really listening.

Above all, documentation makes a statement of respect for children and their ideas. It shows the outside community the high level of commitment the teachers have made to the education of the children in their classroom and the seriousness of the role they play in the children's lives. From the documentation, the larger community can learn what excellent child-centered work looks like. Documentation is the representation of information for purposes of communication, and communication may lead to understanding and support.

The challenge of documentation is to make explicit in an aesthetically pleasing and easily accessible record both the complexity of the children's experiences and the ever-increasing depth of understanding that occurs during the process. Documentation should capture the depth and breadth of a developmental sequence or learning experience, and make the stages in the process visible to others. To produce documentation that is of the high quality achieved by the educators in Reggio Emilia, teachers require skills in observation and collaboration, as well as an understanding of the developmental theories and philosophies of early childhood education. A teacher must be knowledgeable in the areas of the early childhood curriculum including art, music, literature, and science. Teachers also need to have an aesthetic sense and to be skilled or able to get help from others to produce graphic designs, journals, or recordings that communicate clearly the message of the documentation.

Loris Malaguzzi told Lella Gandini, "Teachers must learn to interpret ongoing processes rather than wait to evaluate results. In the same way, their role as educators must include understanding children as producers, not as consumers." He went on to say, "They must enter the time frame of the children, whose interests emerge only in the course of activity or negotiations arising from that activity. They must realize how listening to children is both necessary and expedient . . . [and] that it is possible to engage in the challenge of longitudinal observations and small research projects concerning the development or experiences of children. Indeed, education without research or innovation is education without interest" (Malaguzzi in Edwards, Gandini, & Forman, 1998, p. 73).

THE MANY FORMS OF DOCUMENTATION

Documentation can be created in many media. It can be a series of photographs and written observations recording the developmental sequences or experiences of the children as they unfold. Depending on the topic and age of children, documentation may range from a simple photograph with an explanation and, perhaps, an example of a child's work, to a series of panels that illustrate the process followed in a lengthy project. Documentation also may consist of a display of the children's work with written comments of the creation process, or it may take the form of written observations and photographs collected in a portfolio to give a comprehensive and detailed account of some aspect of the curriculum or child development. Documentation also may take the form of a daily journal or log written by the teacher including exact quotes of children's ideas as they work and talk, sketches of children's theories or work in progress, photos of children's work, and teacher comments about the process. In some cases, children may dictate their summaries of what were important discoveries or events of the day to the teacher, and illustrate the teacher's print with their own drawings. The journal may connect with other graphic representations in the classroom such as children's individual journals and wall panels.

There may be reciprocal use of teachers' journals and children's journals in documentation, with variations on the way children's journals are used. In some classrooms such as Patti Cruikshank-Schott's and Pam Oken-Wright's, children's journals are used whenever children want to explore some idea with their sketches or writing. Sometimes, teachers have specific expectations about the children's use of journals as in the suggestion Patti makes to the children in the coming section about the exploration of age; sometimes there are no specific expectations as Pam comments that in her classroom, some children never write or draw in their journals, and some write and draw and revisit the journals all the time. An interesting idea comes from Pam and is derived from the Sabot School about the children's journals. Pam invites families to begin the journals the summer before their children enter her classroom so that children already have something of themselves to bring to this new experience. To this kind of children's journal, teachers may add photographs of children working or their comments about the process. They also may excerpt from children's journals to illustrate their documentation about ongoing ideas and interests, as Patti did when sharing the story of the age project with the families.

In other classrooms, the journal becomes a kind of memory book created by the teacher for children and their families. For example, in Ann Pelo's classroom, the teacher may add a copy of some of the passages related to a particular child's explorations or activity from the teacher's notes so that children have a growing record of their play and work. In the toddler classroom at Lakewood, the journal consists of notes written personally three times a week to each child by the teacher, commenting on their activities and growth; teachers also add photographs and artwork, creating a memory book for children and parents. In the two-year-old classroom, teachers write one letter to the parents every day, and make copies for the children's memory books. The teachers at First Baptist Kindergarten have transformed their old newsletter procedure of basically summarizing events for families; instead, specific dialogs and quotes recorded by teachers become part of the daily documentation shared for parents' reflection. The daily observations and reflections are continually shared in journal or newsletter form with families, and kept for teachers' further reflection. It is important to realize that this daily documentation is an important component of whatever later form of panel or book documentation teachers create.

At times, if the children are active, the teachers may choose to videotape the experience. On other occasions, if the children are stationary and the area is quiet, the teachers may decide to audiotape the children's conversation. Many teachers audiotape routinely as children work or meet for discussion so that they have an opportunity to transcribe and listen for interpretation. Carlina Rinaldi reminds that observation involves not only perceiving reality, but also "constructing, interpreting, and revisiting it" (Rinaldi, 1998, p. 120). Whatever methods are used to "leave traces of a competent observation" (p. 121), it is important to remember that all methods are only partial and limited, and biased by whatever methods used in documentation. This suggests a reason for having multiple documents and media, open to many interpretations. A teacher like Pam Oken-Wright, who is simultaneously taking notes, making audiotapes, and taking photos of children at work, has more data to interpret in later reflection.

Documentation is also a useful tool in learning and understanding child development. Through the process of documentation, teachers act as researchers, studying, describing, and defining children's learning processes and making connections between developmental theory and real children. They document in ways

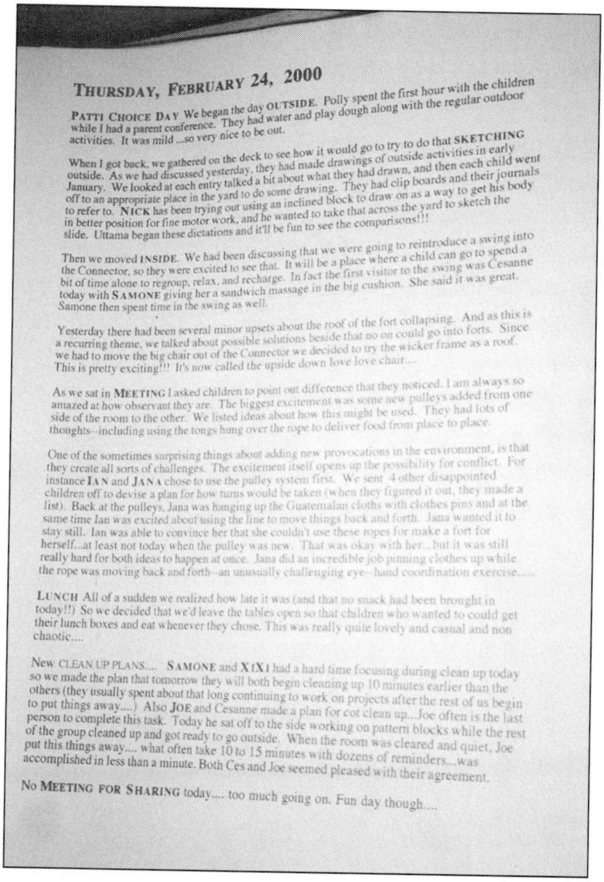

THURSDAY, FEBRUARY 24, 2000

PATTI CHOICE DAY We began the day OUTSIDE. Polly spent the first hour with the children while I had a parent conference. They had water and play dough along with the regular outdoor activities. It was mild ...so very nice to be out.

When I got back, we gathered on the deck to see how it would go to try to do that SKETCHING outside. As we had discussed yesterday, they had made drawings of outside activities in early January. We looked at each entry talked a bit about what they had drawn, and then each child went off to an appropriate place in the yard to do some drawing. They had clip boards and their journals to refer to. NICK has been trying out using an inclined block to draw on as a way to get his body in better position for fine motor work, and he wanted to take that across the yard to sketch the slide. Uttama began these dictations and it'll be fun to see the comparisons!!!

Then we moved INSIDE. We had been discussing that we were going to reintroduce a swing into the Connector, so they were excited to see that. It will be a place where a child can go to spend a bit of time alone to regroup, relax, and recharge. In fact the first visitor to the swing was Cesanne today with SAMONE giving her a sandwich massage in the big cushion. She said it was great. Samone then spent time in the swing as well.

Yesterday there had been several minor upsets about the roof of the fort collapsing. And as this is a recurring theme, we talked about possible solutions beside that so on could go into forts. Since we had to move the big chair out of the Connector we decided to try the wicker frame as a roof. This is pretty exciting!!! It's now called the upside down love love chair.

As we sat in MEETING I asked children to point out difference that they noticed. I am always so amazed at how observant they are. The biggest excitement was some new pulleys added from one side of the room to the other. We listed ideas about how this might be used. They had lots of thoughts–including using the tongs hung over the rope to deliver food from place to place.

One of the sometimes surprising things about adding new provocations in the environment, is that they create all sorts of challenges. The excitement itself opens up the possibility for conflict. For instance IAN and JANA chose to use the pulley system first. We sent 4 other disappointed children off to devise a plan for how turns would be taken (when they figured it out, they made a list). Back at the pulleys, Jana was hanging up the Guatemalan cloths with clothes pins and at the same time Ian was excited about using the line to move things back and forth. Jana wanted it to stay still. Ian was able to convince her that she couldn't use these ropes for make a fort for herself...at least not today when the pulley was new. That was okay with her...but it was still really hard for both ideas to happen at once. Jana did an incredible job pinning clothes up while the rope was moving back and forth–an unusually challenging eye–hand coordination exercise.....

LUNCH All of a sudden we realized how late it was (and that no snack had been brought in today!!) So we decided that we'd leave the tables open so that children who wanted to could get their lunch boxes and eat whenever they chose. This was really quite lovely and casual and non chaotic....

New CLEAN UP PLANS.... SAMONE and XIXI had a hard time focusing during clean up today so we made the plan that tomorrow they will both begin cleaning up 10 minutes earlier than the others (they usually spent about that long continuing to work on projects after the rest of us begin to put things away...) Also JOE and Cesanne made a plan for cot clean up...Joe often is the last person to complete this task. Today he sat off to the side working on pattern blocks while the rest of the group cleaned up and got ready to go outside. When the room was cleared and quiet, Joe put this things away.... what often take 10 to 15 minutes with dozens of reminders....was accomplished in less than a minute. Both Ces and Joe seemed pleased with their agreement.

No MEETING FOR SHARING today.... too much going on. Fun day though....

Figure 6–2.   Documentation may take the form of a daily journal or log. (*Courtesy:* Patti Cruikshank-Schott.)

that allow parents and others to understand and marvel at the developmental learning process. Documentation allows adults to reframe their images of children.

Development in childhood is a visible process that can be captured in photographs, written observations, or examples of children's work. This kind of documentation illustrates the changes that take place in a single child or in a group of children over a period of time. Documentation can be made of a child's artwork, showing his progress through the stages of art development from the earliest uncontrolled scribbles at the toddler stage to the detailed, representational work of the four- or five-year-old child. At times, it is helpful to explore the development of a complex process such as social play. In this case, teachers could keep a written and photographic record of a group of children as their play evolves from playing alongside other children using the same materials, in the first stage of social play called parallel play, to the later stage in which children role play, called sociodramatic play.

The teachers in one child care program (Quadra Island Day Care) spent a long time trying to decide how they could record the stories the children were telling one another as they swung back and forth on the swings in the playground. In this case, they decided that the only way would be to have an additional staff member write the conversations down. Another teacher (Quadra Island Preschool) is fortunate to have parents who assist her each morning. She placed an exercise book next to a fish tank filled with tadpoles that one of the children had collected. Anyone who was near the fish tank wrote down questions the children asked or comments they made as they watched the tadpoles changing into frogs. The teacher and helpers encouraged the children to draw their predictions and their observations as the process unfolded. These drawings were added to the written comments in the book, together with photographs taken of the children as they examined the tadpoles in the tank of water. The staff then discussed information in the notebook throughout the experience to gauge the children's level of interest in the topic and to get ideas for possible directions to follow the next day.

Student interns were used in another classroom (Carolina Friends School) to record individual children's dictated explanations of the drawings they had made illustrating their theories about how people who were the same number in age—6 years—could, in fact, be older or younger than another child of the same age. This allowed the teacher, busy with another project, to have written materials to read to the children in the next day's meeting to encourage revisiting and refining the theories.

Documentation is an ongoing process that is developed over a period of time. It often begins at the initial stages of an investigation that Forman and Fyfe (1998) have termed the design phase, when the observer asks key questions as the children and teachers begin to explore a topic. At this stage, the observer might record the provocation or what got the topic started, the predictions that teachers make, and the questions the children and teachers ask as the investigation progresses. Later, the documentations will show the work in progress as the topic unfolds. Finally, on completion, the documentation should communicate the story or the discourse, as Forman and Fyfe have termed it, in the context of the children's experiences.

The final documentation, regardless, whether displayed in a portfolio, a book, album, or on wall panels, should convey the following:

- a title stating the topic of the documentation

- an overall theoretical or philosophical statement; for example, the activity with tadpoles described above could be related to Vygotsky's theory by explaining how it moved children to a higher level of mental functioning

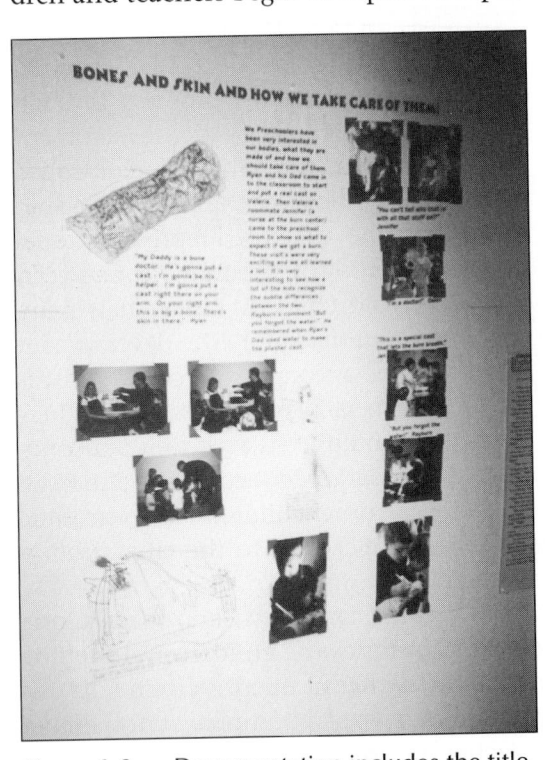

Figure 6–3.   Documentation includes the title of the investigation, children's work and words, photos to illustrate the process, and teacher reflections. (*Courtesy:* Lakewood Avenue Children's School.)

- an indication of the purpose or rationale of the activity or topic that is being documented

- an illustration of the experiences covered such as in photographs or written commentaries

- a description of the process of development or learning that has been observed and recorded

- a record of the experiences and voices of the children and teachers

- a display of the children's work

- an analysis of the experience in light of theory and philosophy

- a statement of implications for future work

- a concluding statement

THE DOCUMENTATION PROCESS

Observation

It is vital to realize that documentation is much more than observation. It involves reflection, connecting the observations to a knowledge base of theory, and communication. Doc-umentation involves a co-construction of an experience, and consequently, is far removed from the objectivity and implied accuracy of traditional child observation. But having said that, observation and recording are key beginning points for documentation.

Documentation begins with observation. Children are observed in many different situations and for many different reasons. They may be observed individually as they engage in solitary activities, as they collaborate in a group on a project, or as they participate with other children in play. They may be observed as they separate from their parents on arrival at school and enter the group or as they work on activities during the day. Selecting the best tool for observing children depends on the kind of information the teacher is seeking. The decision to carry out observations is often the result of a question that has arisen about a child or a group of children and their behavior or activities in the center. The decision to carry out documentation also can arise from the teacher's interest in following the path of a learning experience. In making the decision about which method to follow, however, it is essential that teachers collaborate to ensure that the documentation has input from all the people involved.

Teachers, with practice, optimally learn to be objective in their observations of the children's behavior. They learn not to make assumptions that might bias the recorded information. For example, they avoid using phrases in their recording such as "she likes to play" or "he is happy when . . ." Phrases such as these may be

Figure 6–4.   Frazer examines the
                      sand on the fence.

inaccurate statements of the child's real feelings. Teachers learn to be selective but truthful in what they record so that the information captures the essential qualities they are looking for in their observations. The use of descriptive language also helps teachers describe in detail the behavior they are recording. The following observation of a child looking up at sand spattered on a fence provides a rich source of information about the child's intellectual abilities such as his awareness, his curiosity, and his thoughtful, reflective style of investigation. It also provides the teacher with clues for a follow-up discussion.

> Frazer stood in front of the fence bordering the large sand area in the playground. He stood gazing up at patches of sand stuck to the boards of the fence. He had a puzzled expression on his face. Picking up a small shovel, he reached high up above his head to trace with the tip of the shovel the pattern made by the sand on the boards of the fence. He touched the pattern carefully without destroying it and then stood examining it for a few more minutes.

The educators from Reggio Emilia have taught us to be alert for opportunities such as this to see whether children might be interested in pursuing topics further. The observer who recorded this incident might want to see if Frazer could put his thoughts about the sand into words. Did he have any questions that might lead to further investigation? Could any other children be drawn into the conversation? Would there be any interest in doing more experiments with the properties of sand and observing transformations when sand is combined with water? Where else do we see examples of sand stuck on surfaces? Would the children be interested in sketching their ideas about sand? How many different media could be used to make visual representations? Perhaps it was the pattern that the sand made on the wooden planks that captured the child's interest. Where else do we see patterns? What patterns can we make and in how many different languages? These are the kinds of questions an observer would list and share later with the other teachers to decide how or whether they should proceed further.

The fundamental skill in all documentation is the ability to observe and record the children's behavior. Teachers who explore the Reggio Emilia approach perceive the child as "rich in resources, strong, and competent" (Rinaldi, 1998, p. 114). This image of the child has a profound effect on observation. The image becomes a lens through which observers view children as active participants in the co-construction of knowledge in the classroom. If the children are appreciated for their contributions and perceived as imaginative thinkers who ask interesting questions and can provide unexpected solutions to problems, teachers will be motivated to observe children closely, to find out what they are thinking and to listen to, and record their conversations to try to capture their ideas. Because collaboration is an important principle in the Reggio Emilia approach, these observations will need to be discussed later with colleagues to gain deeper insights into the children's behavior or thinking. Teachers, as a group, also can revisit the experiences they have recorded to discuss different approaches or to make predictions about how the topics that seemed to interest the children in the observations could be further developed.

Figure 6–5.   Illustrating the Reggio Emilia principles of documentation.

Teachers use a number of different methods to observe children. The tools for observation range from simple ones such as pencils and notepads, to more sophisticated electronic equipment such as digital cameras, audio recorders, video recorders, and laptop computers to record on-going dialog. The choice of method depends on the situation and on the focus for the observations.

Running Records.   The running record is probably the most frequently used observation method. The running record is used to capture a comprehensive record of the children's behavior as it is occurring. The observer writes down exactly what she sees or hears over a period of time. This can be as flexible as the situation warrants. The observations are usually recorded in a stenographer's notebook or on a laptop computer. The first column on the page can be used for the running record of observed behavior; the second column may be used later to recall important points, to make interpretations, or to note relationships to theories. Observation using the running record method is time consuming but gives a comprehensive, detailed account of the children's behavior. It allows for flexibility because it can be done spontaneously or any time something of interest is happening in the room.

Time Sampling.   Time sampling provides an observer with a snapshot of behavior occurring within a preset time frame at regular intervals throughout the period of observation. It is a more formal method of observation than the running record. The advantage of time sampling is that it is efficient. Teachers know exactly when they will be recording their observations and can make plans for a colleague to cover their absence from active participation with the children in the classroom. Time sampling also provides an unbiased account of what is occurring in the room during repeated intervals of time. A teacher interested in learning children's interests might plan to observe the children at intervals throughout the day to see if any specific topics come up repeatedly in their conversations. In this case, the teacher also might turn on a tape recorder at regular intervals to record the children's conversations.

Event Sampling.   Event sampling is designed to record the frequency of occurrence of a particular behavior during the day. The teacher might use this method of recording to assess the amount of interest the children show in a predetermined topic. For example, the teachers, after using a provocation with the children, could record the number of times the children engage in follow-up activities. This would indicate the amount of interest the children have in the topic and help the teachers decide if the topic is worth pursuing.

Anecdotal Records.   An anecdotal record provides a more in-depth account of an incident (either an event or an activity) that occurs in the classroom. The process is similar to that used for the running record, but the time of recording is limited to the duration of the incident, and the recording is most often done from recall at a later time. The teachers observe the children as they engage in an activity, and later analyze the information to discover ideas or directions they could take in developing the project further. For example, the children at the Vancouver Child Study Center collected snails on a field trip and made a home for them in a fish tank. After the children examined the snails in the tank for a few days, all the snails were emptied onto a tray, and an observer recorded the children's conversations as they observed the snails moving about on the tray. When the observer's notes were shared with the group, it was interesting to note how often the children referred to the elasticity in the snails' bodies. The teachers wondered if this attribute could be something worth exploring further with the children, either in music and movement using their own bodies, or in discovering other things that also stretch and shrink such as earthworms and elastic bands.

Tape Recordings.   A tape recording of children's conversations is useful because it provides the observer with a detailed account of exactly what they say. When an observer matches a taped conversation with a written record of a conversation, it is surprising to see how much detail is missing in the written version. On the other hand, a tape recorder is nonselective so the observer often has to listen to a lot of unnecessary data before getting to a segment of conversation that is useful. It is also a challenge for a teacher to make an audiotape of children in conversation that is clear and easily understandable. There is often too much background noise and the children move out of hearing range too quickly to catch what they are saying clearly. Frequently, the speech on the tape is meaningless when it is heard out of context. To tape children's conversations successfully, the teacher may find it helpful to review the following set of questions.

- What is the purpose of the observation?
- What will be the focus of the observation?
- Whose conversations will need to be recorded?
- Where might the conversations take place?
- When and for how long will they take place?
- What questions, objects, or materials will provoke discussion?
- What factors need to be considered to tape clear, "on topic" conversation?

For example, if the teachers who observed Frazer examining the sand on the fence thought that his curiosity about the pattern of sand could be further investigated, they would need to make a plan to test their hypothesis. Answers to the above questions would give the teachers some direction for putting their plan into action. Taping a conversation with Frazer and a small group of other children who also are interested in the topic might be their first step in this process. The teachers could move a small table out of the main classroom to a quiet area where there are few distractions so that they could tape a conversation between Frazer and the other children. On the table, the teachers could display a photograph of Frazer examining the pattern of sand on the fence and materials such as sandpaper and objects with raised decorative motifs to provoke discussion. A later analysis of the transcription of the taped conversation would indicate whether Frazer or any other children showed enough interest or enthusiasm to pursue the topic of sand and/or patterning further. It is important that all the teachers involved collaborate in analyzing the transcription of the tape so that discussion is as rich as possible and everyone has a shared understanding of the process if it proceeds further.

Pam Oken-Wright, working in a large classroom and studio space, routinely tapes work sessions and meetings with children. This allows her to make exact transcriptions of children's words in her daily log for further reflection. It also allows her to have her assistant and sometimes parent volunteer assist in documenting other activities elsewhere in the large space. Sarah, a teacher at Sabot School, also uses tape recorders regularly to document each small group activity. She comments that she is constantly astonished when she reviews the tapes to hear things that had slipped by her the first time around.

Photographs. Once teachers have developed an idea for creating documentation, they need to choose between a number of photographic techniques: black-and-white, color, Polaroid, or slides as well as computer printouts from a digital camera or video recorder. The documentation, if it is to tell the complete story of the experience, should record the process from the beginning to the end. The first step is to decide what kind of photographs would most clearly communicate the ideas being conveyed by the documentation. Sarah Felstiner remarks on the importance of getting the photos of the children's trip to the water tower in the Thinking Big project developed quickly, so they could be available for discussion as children were revisiting and representing their trip. The photos themselves represented another opportunity to explore the experience. Sometimes, teachers may wish to have two cameras loaded with different kinds of film. Because direction can change in the middle of a project, planning must be flexible. The group of teachers at the Vancouver Child Study Center who were working with the children on the Three Little Pigs project (described in Chapter 5) realized, while it was still in progress, that parents would be interested in seeing how the project was being developed. They decided to take slides to show at a parents' meeting in addition to the photographs that were being taken for the wall panels.

Videotapes.   If the topic involves a great deal of activity, a videotape might be the best form of documentation. For example, a group of early childhood education students at Douglas College observed that the children who visit their classroom once a week were acting out a camping theme in their play. The following documentation, taken from extracts in their journal, illustrates how the children and students developed the topic of going camping over a period of six weeks into a project on volcanoes. Interest in volcanoes is often high among children who live on the west coast of Canada, perhaps because many volcanoes are close to where they live.

> A tent was set up with authentic materials such as a Coleman lantern, cooler, branches of trees, sleeping bags, fishing rod, and food items like beans, juice, and pots and pans. Children used the camping equipment and materials to pretend that they were up in the mountain camping by a cave. The children began to discuss the types of animals that lived in caves, such as bats and bears. They then used their imagination to pretend to be the bears and bats that live in the cave. This play developed further into a camping trip. The children began to use the flashlights to explore the cave; later they sat around the rock fire pit, and used the pots, pans, and canned food to pretend to cook over a campfire. We asked the children: "What else can we do on a mountain?" This led into a conversation about how we could build a pretend mountain, and together with the children we decided to build a large papier-mâché mountain. We built the frame with chicken wire and masking tape to seal off the edges. We laid out papier-mâché made out of flour, water, and white glue. Children started to explore the papier-mâché through sensory exploration. Some of the children were more interested in touching the material than putting paper on the mountain. The next time we will build on ideas developed by the children.
>
> We decided to decorate the mountain using paint and different sorts of media such as toothbrushes, rollers, and sponges. The children explored different ways of getting the

sand onto the mountain. Pouring glue and then pressing handfuls of sand seemed to work the best; other exploratory ways were to dip the paintbrush into glue and then into the sand and rub it on the mountain.

The children's sensory exploration of the natural materials with the glue and paint resulted in lots of conversation and language. The language focused on the texture created by mixing the paint and glue with the sand and the way it made the mountain look. One child mixed the sand with red paint and glue, and while applying it to the mountain using a paintbrush, told us that this was the hot lava flowing out of the volcano.

From now on the artwork the children did began to express the notion of the mountain being a volcano erupting. The children made many sketches and clay representations of their ideas of volcanoes and volcanic eruptions (Students' journal, Douglas College).

From observations and recordings of the children's conversations, the students realized that the children had converted the papier-mâché mountain into a volcano. This sent the students on a search for information about volcanoes to share with the group. The children soon decided they wanted to make the mountain they had built out of papier-mâché explode like a volcano. The students carried out a series of experiments with the children to figure out how they could simulate a volcanic eruption. They investigated things that would safely explode in the classroom. This led to making popcorn and watching it "explode."

Figure 6–6.   The papier-mâché volcano.

Eventually, the students and children decided that the best way to simulate a volcanic explosion in the classroom was by mixing vinegar and baking soda together in a container placed in the hole at the top of the papier-mâché volcano, and pretending that the foam it made was lava pouring down the sides of the mountain.

The students videotaped the experiences each week and analyzed each segment. They then used this analysis to plan the following sessions. The students compiled written commentary and photographs of the key experiences in a portfolio. They then shared the portfolio with the children's teachers and parents.

Finally, the students made an edited videotape of the project and showed it on many occasions to groups in the community.

During this project, the students learned about the value of listening to children and helping them realize their ideas. They had experience in collaborating with one another and with the children. They gained a sense of accomplishment from staying with the same topic over a long period of time and exploring it in depth. The documentation of the experience on the videotape, photographs, and written observations at each stage of the process helped them analyze and revisit episodes to discover different approaches or new directions, and discuss where they could have gone deeper into their investigation with the children.

In their concluding comments in the portfolio, the students wrote:

> If we had more time with the children we would discuss what happens when a real volcano erupts. We would talk about things like what would happen to the trees, wildlife, and even the people who live near the volcano. As well, we would discuss the effects a volcano has on environments, such as all the smoke, ash, and pollution that travels through the air and where it lands. Then we would follow the children's leads by taking their ideas to move on to a new provocation.

Over a period of six weeks, the students and the children created an exciting and meaningful learning experience that was carefully documented with photographs, written observations, and videotapes. At each stage in the process, the students were able to use the documentation to go forward or to "change gears" and explore a different direction, as they did when the mountain became a volcano.

Interpretation of Observations

An analysis of the data collected from the observations is an important step in the process of documentation. The more data available, the more valid will be the interpretation of the information. All the data collected during an experience, including written observations, tapes, and photographs, need to be shared with colleagues throughout the learning experience. During the analysis, which is also done in collaboration with all the teachers involved in the project, any philosophical points and relationships to theory should be noted. At intervals and on completion of the project, the points drawn from the analysis and interpretation will be organized and added to the other material compiled for the documentation.

At any stage, documentation may cause a shift in focus so that the whole project may go off in a different direction or be the starting point for the group to begin working on a new idea. In the Three Little Pigs project the children decided to build a house that the wolf could not blow down, a brick house made of clay. Some of the children worked on building the walls and the roof, while others experimented with the remaining clay on the table. An observer recorded the conversation of one child as he began to shape the clay on the table.

William: I am making a volcano.

I am making a bigger volcano.

Mine is up.

This is a volcano. Fire is coming out of it.

Now this is the . . . what is that called . . . the fire hole . . . lava comes out.

How does it get down?

Gloria (the teacher): What is lava like?

William: Hot and sticky and you can't get it off.

This is the lava coming down. . . .

It is red it has to be a volcano.

The volcano has to be erupting.

It is water lava because all the volcanoes have holes so they could erupt.

Later, the observer shared the above transcription with the child's teachers. This discussion showed the teachers that the project that had started off as building a house with clay bricks "that the wolf could not blow down" had now taken a different direction. The children, and William in particular, now seemed more interested in building a clay volcano with a crater and lava pouring down the sides. The teachers discussed this new direction and decided to bring in some books about volcanoes to see if the children were really interested in exploring the topic further. They could see that interest in building houses for the three little pigs had waned (the brick house was nearly finished), and it was now time to follow the children's lead to pursue a new topic. This decision would have been harder to make if the children had lost interest partway through the project. This is why it is so important to be sure, when embarking on a project with children, that it is derived from the children's ideas instead of being imposed on them by the teachers. It is also important that the project is open ended so that if children lose interest, the project can be brought to a satisfactory conclusion at any point during the process. The termination of a project, however, should never be done lightly, because once started, it is important for everyone involved that it reach a satisfactory conclusion.

On reflection, the teachers realized that although initial interest in the topic was high and enthusiasm for building the houses was maintained until just before the end, to reach a satisfactory conclusion all three houses had to be completed. This was a long and involved process, which might have resulted in the children giving up before the end. Fortunately, this did not happen, but it raised the notion about the careful thought necessary in selecting a topic to follow and evaluating the predictions the teachers make at the outset.

Analysis of the Documentation

The process of documenting the path of learning in the classroom requires adults to collaborate, share, and interpret observations, articulate their understanding of theory and research, and analyze the data they have collected. This means that teachers can no longer work in isolation, because it is impossible to capture the complexity of an experience unless they work as a team in planning the form and function of the documentation, in reflecting on the learning as it unfolds, and to develop the panels, portfolios, or other kinds of documentation. This transforms the teacher's role into what Brenda Fyfe terms a *collaborative action researcher.* She states that documentation is an essential component in the process of moving toward a co-constructed, negotiated curriculum. She states that this is not a linear but a cyclical process of action research that moves from observation to reflection, analysis, planning, and action, then back again to observation (Fyfe, 1998, p. 23).

Recognizing the importance of discourse in co-constructing shared under-standings, the staff at the Sabot School have taken deliberate steps to create an environment that allows teachers to collaborate on their documentation and reflection. Each year at the close of school, the teachers hold debriefing meetings to identify the research in their work with children they want to continue the fol-lowing year. One of their declared intentions has been to explain their work and

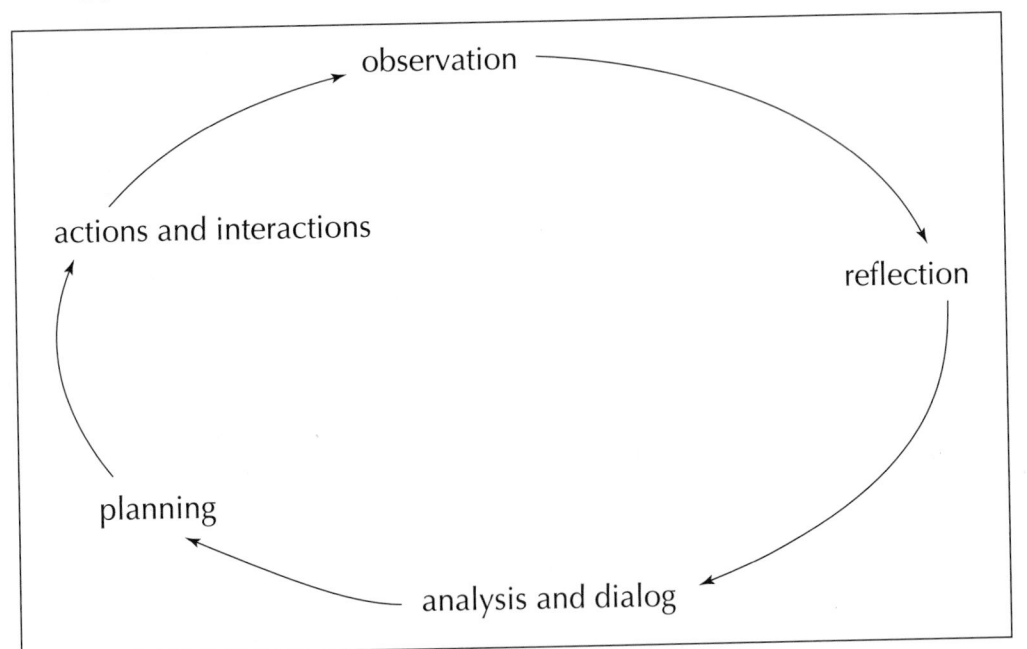

Figure 6–7.   This diagram illustrates how observation leads to reflection, reflection to analysis and dialog, on to planning, then to actions and interactions, and finally back to observation.

the work of children to parents. The classroom teaching teams have been increased from two to three, (actually four in a classroom with children with special needs), to allow more documentation of the work with small groups with teachers frequently tape-recording and taking notes. The budget allows for eight paid hours of staff communication time each week so that the whole staff can meet for an hour or so twice a week and individual teams can meet at other times. The school has separate studio space and a studio teacher who is available part of the time: the rest of the time, she is in a classroom. At 10:30 each morning, the school is declared open. This means that teachers and children may choose whether to be inside, outside, or in someone else's classroom. This sense of a seamless community allows children to work on multiage projects and teachers to collaborate on work and discussion with other colleagues. A visitor to the school leaves with a sense of a large learning community.

Collaboration with children, colleagues, families, and, at times, people in the community is essential in producing documentation that reflects a broad range of ideas and experiences. Brenda Fyfe states that "consideration of multiple perspectives will contribute to its [the documentation's] ultimate power to communicate. Since children and parents make up a large part of the audience that will read the documentation, it can be important to ask for their consultation in the process of organizing a panel or other form of public presentation of learning" (Fyfe, 1998, p. 20). Documentation that communicates the entirety of an experience needs input from all the participants. Everyone involved will have experienced the project in a slightly different way, and by sharing the individual experiences with the whole group, a more complete picture of the project will emerge.

The key points of the experience, the ones that will need to be shown in the documentation, become clearer as the group analyzes and synthesizes the material that the participants have accumulated. The group then needs to review previous decisions to decide whether the format for documentation is still appropriate. The next step is to delegate the work in producing the documentation. There are a number of different tasks such as printing the commentaries that explain the photographs, transcribing the children's conversations onto cards to be attached to the panels, labeling the children's work, and mounting the photographs. Individuals can carry out these tasks on their own once the group has made decisions about format, graphic design, and so on. Once the displays, portfolios, or videotaped documentation is complete, the group as a whole has a sense of ownership of the project. Whereas documentation can be said to be the gears that make the learning experiences grow and develop, collaboration is the fuel that drives the process.

Brenda Fyfe has developed four sets of questions, one for each stage of documentation, to help teachers produce documentation that captures the depth and breadth of an experience. The first set of questions is asked during the initial phase of documentation. These questions address practical, philosophical, and organizational issues. At this stage, teachers collaboratively answer the following questions as an investigation is beginning.

- What should we document?
- When and for how long should we document the experience?
- Who will do the documentation?
- Where will we do the documentation?
- What are the focus and rationale for the observation?
- How will the documentation be used?
- What tools and techniques will meet the purpose?

Once they have decided what, when, who, where, and why to document, teachers can move to the next phase in the cycle of collaborative action research, the *discourse phase*. At this stage, the following questions require reflection and interpretation.

- What does the documentation reveal about children's ideas, interests, feelings, opinions, assumptions, and theories?
- What does it show about environmental conditions and how they affect behavior, interactions, and relationships?
- What does it tell about connections with home and community?

At this point, teachers are using the documentation to consider whether there are new directions and possibilities for exploration beyond the initial starting ideas. Does the documentation to this point confirm the starting hypotheses?

In the next phase, the *design phase*, teachers draw conclusions from interpretations and reflections, design future observations, and make projections for learning experiences. The questions addressed in this phase include the following.

- What are the implications based on the interpretation of the data collected?
- What has surfaced that needs to be studied in more detail?
- What further ideas need to be explored?
- How can the documentation already collected be used to help children revisit their ideas and co-construct with others?
- How can we make children's ideas visible?
- How might parents become involved?

During the *documentation phase*, teachers are back to the beginning of the collaborative research cycle, thinking about how they can continue observation and documentation. They might ask the following questions.

- What tools and techniques will be needed to document the next set of observations and experiences?
- How will these be organized?
- How will the parents and community be involved?

Design, discourse, and documentation form a cyclical process in which teachers collaboratively revisit, reflect, and then reframe data in the process of negotiating the curriculum. Brenda Fyfe states that "documentation goes beyond telling a story to presenting a study" (Fyfe, 1998, p. 23).

CHALLENGES OF DOCUMENTATION

Making Time for Documentation

When teachers undertake documentation, they need time to plan the focus for it, then to reflect, analyze, and interpret once the documentation gets underway. Consideration of theoretical implications also takes time, as does the interpretation of the observations. Collection of the visual material such as photographs and videotapes is also time consuming. It then takes time to design and produce final documentation panels (if this is the method to be used). Therefore, documentation works best when the work is shared among a group of people. When the group collaborates, the work does not become too overwhelming for any one person, and the final documentation reflects the energy and enthusiasm of all the people involved.

Sometimes, however, teachers who work alone have no option but to carry out documentation on their own. Kathleen Laycock, a teacher in a public school system, describes the method she uses for documentation in a large kindergarten class:

> Last year I taught a total of fifty-nine children in kindergarten. Thirty-four of these children were in one class. I was anxious to start documenting their conversations using a tape recorder, as is done in Reggio schools. This soon proved frustrating for me because of the background noise, the actual technicalities of setting up a tape recorder in various spots of the classroom, and the way children would be distracted once I set up a tape recorder in their midst.

> One day I heard a conversation I wanted to document. I grabbed a paper and pencil and started to write. I was able to document the entire conversation. I then took a picture of the children at play to include with the written documentation. This worked so well for me that I started doing several a day. I would simply sit down with a group of children at play and document for a few minutes. Sometimes the conversations seemed insignificant, but I soon found that a great deal could be learned about the children from each and every conversation. The conversations were typed, matched with the corresponding photo, and placed in a binder for further study. Extra copies were made for the children's scrapbooks.

> Each photograph and the accompanying dialog was like a snapshot of that child's life at one particular moment in time. When I shared these documentation sheets with the parents at a parent-teacher conference, I was interested in the fact that parents were far more interested in the documentation than how the children were doing academically.

One parent was concerned that her daughter was monopolizing conversations and directing the play of the other children. As we studied all the documentation sheets that included her daughter, it was evident that her child was a team player as she worked with other children. In some cases it became apparent why their child had been experiencing difficulties with other children, or in other cases they were delighted to see their children sharing, helping, and playing cooperatively. Each of the documentations gave us very specific information to help us work with that child. Some parents were so excited about this glimpse into their child's life that they decided to start documenting their children's conversations at home.

The school speech therapist took a special interest in the documentations. As she studied conversations of specific children over a long period of time, she was able to see their development in the area of language usage. This became an important tool for her.

This type of documentation came to be known as *drop-in documentation*. It was an excellent description, because I would literally drop in on a conversation. The children became used to me doing this and would carry on their play without seeing me as an intruder. I would not contribute to their conversations unless invited to do so. I would merely document what I heard. These conversations became powerful tools in helping me understand the children in my class and in preparing lessons and activities that would be meaningful to them. The following is an example of one of my sample sheets:

Adventure Under the Sea

The children in my class took me on a surprise adventure. Let me explain how they did that. One day, I heard three boys playing at the water center. Rather than interrupting their conversation with a series of questions (which teachers are prone to do), I simply sat down beside them and wrote down their conversation and took a photograph of them playing. Their conversation posed some interesting questions about sharks and some creative answers.

The next day, the same three boys checked some books about sharks out of our school library. More questions were posed about sharks, sharks' tongues, and sharks' jaws. Once again, I noted their dialog without any attempt to direct it.

As these children sought answers to their questions, more and more children became enthralled with sharks or other sea creatures. A project was born.

I learned that a child's conversation has the power to lead you and your class to the tops of the mountains or to the depths of the sea. Listening to the children just may be the beginning of a new adventure.

Corey, Connor, and Mark playing at the water table:

Corey: Pretend you saw a baby shark and then a crab came.

Mark: The submarine catches the shark. Get the submarine out before it kills the shark. The shark is going crazy, it's hungry and wants to eat octopus.

Corey: The shark ate the food in the clam.

Mark: I see blood on the shark's tongue

Connor: Do sharks have tongues?

Mark: Yes, but I think they are different than ours.

Corey: Why are they different?

Mark: They are different because sharks don't talk.

Corey: Well let's make this tank a special tank for baby sharks.

Patti Cruikshank-Schott is another teacher who works alone. Patti has developed a method of documentation that allows her to document the interesting dialogs of children at work, discussing their ideas and insights with one another. During her meeting time with the group of children before and after their morning work, she sits with her laptop computer. Skillful enough at touch-typing that she can participate in the conversations while maintaining eye contact, she records the children's ideas nearly verbatim. Often, these ideas are read back to the children so that they can continue to represent their thinking in drawings or expand in further discussion. The computer printout is then added to children's drawings or accompanying photographs for display on the walls, for conferences with parents, and for further reflection. In fact, the daily journal record is then available to be sent to parents by e-mail, generating lots of reciprocal questions and dialog. Because Patti is using the journal for her on-going active reflection and communication with parents, the journal contains factual descriptions and her own thoughts and interpretations, often expressed in parentheses. The documentation includes classroom experiences and the layers of reflection about them. Therefore, the documentation offers glimpses into children's developing understandings, provides opportunities for children to continue working on their theories, and provides a vehicle for the teacher to reflect on her glimpses into children's minds and begin a dialog with parents.

An example of this is presented in an on-going project titled I Guess We Take Our Own Opinions. The meaning of this title will become clear in this section from her journal.

. . . Almost as soon as the morning meeting got started, we got sidetracked in the most interesting way . . . I don't remember what got said to begin this conversation . . . or argument . . . or investigation . . . but the gist was that Ian suggested that Joe couldn't be 6. Several children disagreed . . . They HAD all just been to Joe's birthday. But Ian insisted that since he—Ian—was 6, Joe couldn't be 6 because Ian was older . . . and would always be older . . . "He has to have another birthday to turn 6 . . . Then I'll be 7. He was 5 now he's $5\frac{3}{4}$ . . . no, $5\frac{1}{4}$. He doesn't automatically turn 6. See, we were in the downstairs and we were 5, now we are upstairs and I turned 6. But Joe wasn't downstairs so he has to turn 5 first." Ian continued with these kinds of

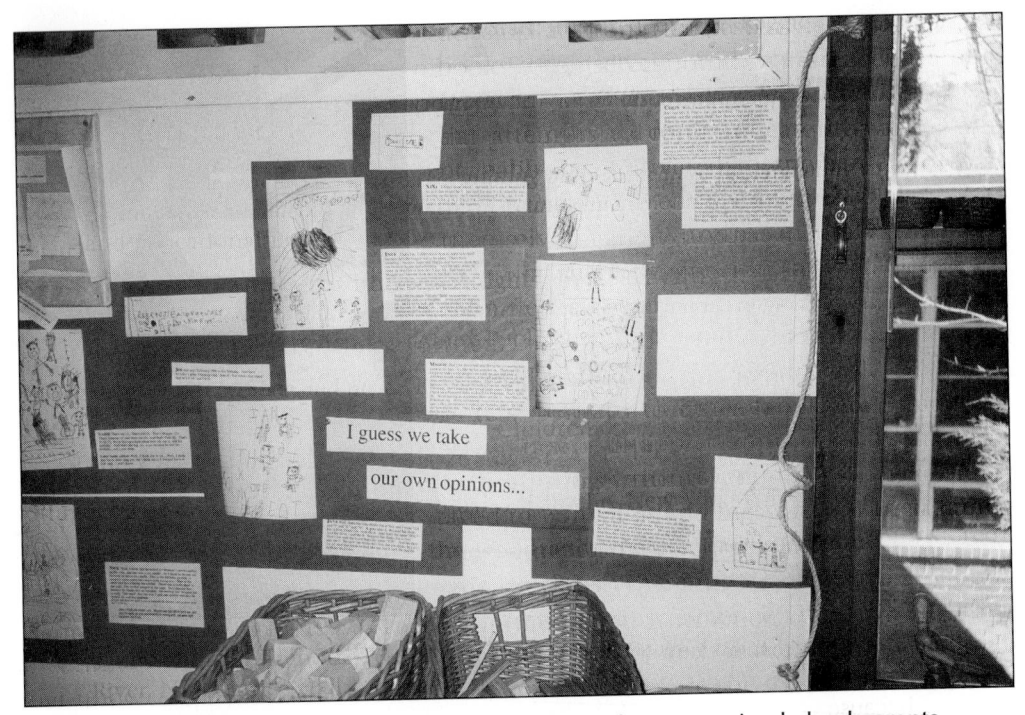

I guess we take

our own opinions...

Figure 6–8.   The "I guess we take our own opinions" documentation helped parents, teachers, and children reflect on the interesting topic of age.

comments. And children listened, disagreed, or agreed. Joe was definite about being 6, but didn't protest too vigorously about the discrepancies in Ian's figuring. When I pointed out that not everyone was agreeing with him, Ian said: "I guess we take our own opinions." Sadie tried to suggest: "You can go to $6^3/_4$." Ian replied: "I'm obviously a lot older." Joe looked sad at this. Ian noticed that and added, "Joe is . . . is $^1/_2$ older . . . he waited because I turned $5^3/_4$ then 6."

Herbert arrived with XiXi and I explained that he was a mathematician and knew lots about this kind of disagreeing, and might be able to give us some advice about how to work together with people even when you disagree. Herbert smiled and said: "I'm 6-2!" That caused a minor uproar: obviously XiXi's father wasn't 6 at all. It happened to be his height, and for me this comment was all the proof I'll ever need that Herbert is a genius. When we stopped laughing, I sent the children off to explain their theories in their journals. Before I share that, let me digress just a bit.

Looking for the heart . . .

Now you may be wondering why I didn't just explain the discrepancy in Ian's reasoning and get on with it. But for me, this is one of the most joyous moments in working with children. It has never been the "teaching" that inspired me, but rather the opportunities to get glimpses into children's minds, to wonder with them about how the world works, to begin to see with them how the world might be figured out and made manageable. I am not attached to facts and figures and passing on information, especially at this age. What I AM interested in is letting children know that they have marvelous minds, and that I'm interested in their ways of thinking about things. A prospective parent was visiting this morning and kept wanting me to explain my curriculum and objectives. I was trying to explain; I showed him the threads I had listed in yesterday's journal and also pointed to what was happening at the moment: an activity emanating from a child's theory, then exploring where the various minds in the class might go from there. But no, I had no planned ahead curriculum before the year began. But he said there must be some middle ground. Of course there is middle ground, and there are right answers, but for me this is not where the beauty is, nor the heart.

So the children worked in their journals and then met with Lauren [a student intern] to do dictation . . .

Meeting for Sharing

Nick's Dictated Theory:

"Well, I think that he turned 6 because I saw 6 candles on the cake, and one was a 6 candle. So I think he turned 6 because he has a 6 candle. This is the birthday picture (It includes 5 regular candles and a large 6 candle blazing away.) . . . I'm writing 'Joe' because Joe is right. This says that Joe was 5 and one quarter and then he turned 6 and two quarters. (Notice in the drawing that there are small boxes to represent the quarters, and an arrow from the 5 to the 6.)

Jana: "I think Joe could, um, maybe Joe can talk in Ian's ear and say 'I'm really 6 and you're really so wrong, and we were right because Joe IS 6.'"

Colin's Dictated Theory:

"I would be 6—see my name there. That is Joe—see he's 5. That is Joe and one quarter-see the quarter there. And there is Joe and 2 quarters. When he was one quarter, I would be seven, and when he was two quarters, I would be eight. And that's Joe at three quarters. And that is a box-you would take a five and a half and switch it with a five and 3 quarters. I'd call that square rooting but I'm not sure. This is Joe: 6. I would be like 10. I already did 5, and 5 and one quarter and two quarters and three quarters, and now Joe needs to do it. (And based on Colin's theory about him gaining a year for each $\frac{1}{4}$ that Joe turns, he WOULD be 10 when Joe turned 6. This is so impressive to me . . . and to think of boxes in relation to square roots, and he has a box for each quarter accurately notated!!!!)

Nick: "I know: well, probably if Joe was 6 we would be 7. We think Colin is wrong, because Colin would be 6 and Joe would be 6, and me and Ian would be 7. And that's why Colin is wrong." (So Nick knows he and Ian have already turned 6, but Colin hasn't, but will in a few days, and perhaps he knows that he and Ian will in fact turn 7 while Colin and Joe are still 6. Interesting. But another issue is emerging, which is that when the word "wrong" is used, which it has been twice now, there is much wincing on the part of the person claimed to be wrong. So I try to address this, suggesting that they might be able to say things like "I don't agree" or "this is my idea" or "I have a different answer.")

Nick: "Well in my opinion, Colin is wrong." Colin is aghast.

When Ian finished his drawing, he jumped up: "I got it!!! Joe has to be $5\frac{1}{4}$. If I'm like um 5 downstairs, and $5\frac{3}{4}$ upstairs. Then I turn 6. Joe has to go through the quarters too, so he's $5\frac{1}{4}$. If he was 6, I'd be 7—see. You see when I was downstairs and I turned 2, I got a quarter, and then when I turned 3, I got a quarter, and then when I turned 4 I got a quarter. Then I collected my quarters and turned 5 and $\frac{3}{4}$ and then 6. Joe has to do it too. Joe has to collect his quarters."

Samone: "You don't get quarters when you get older and older. You don't get quarters. You just get clothes or something, if it's your birthday. You don't get quarters and dollars."

Nick: "She doesn't know what kind of quarters."

Sadie: "I think what Ian means is you have to collect the quarters but not real quarters. Pretend, like if you're $5\frac{1}{2}$, you have a quarter, $\frac{2}{4}$ you have a quarter, $\frac{3}{4}$."

Samone: "I heard Ian say that in his journal." (It's so clear here that children are listening carefully and processing all this information in relation to their own experiences. This is co-construction of knowledge.)

XiXi's Dictated Theory:

"Ian said, Joe's not 6 because if he is 6, Ian would be 7. Ian said Joe was $5\frac{1}{4}$ when he was writing on the table. So I started counting $5\frac{1}{4}$, no $1\frac{1}{4}$, $1\frac{2}{4}$, $1\frac{3}{4}$, $2\frac{1}{4}$, $2\frac{2}{4}$, $2\frac{3}{4}$. Isn't that funny, because I said it all with quarters."

Indy's Dictated Theory:

"That's Ian. I didn't know how to make him small because he's the biggest kid in the class. That's them shouting!!! because Sadie and Maggie and Samone think he's 6 because he just had a birthday. And Ian said, when he came he was 5 so now he's $5\frac{3}{4}$. And Sadie and Maggie and Samone think he's 6 but that's not right. I think Ian's right. That's Maggie and Sadie and Ian and Joe and me. That's Joe because he's the smallest in the class."

Sadie: "I like the people."

Patti: "Why?"

Sadie: "Because they're neat. Nick and Ian, look you're the tallest."

At this point Joe begins to cry.

Ian: "It's not my fault."

Joe: "I'm not the smallest in the class."

Ian: "Then who is?"

Maggie: "I am." (She smiles at this as if being the smallest wouldn't be a problem at all.)

Nick: "No, Indy." (Indy looks quickly at Nick and her lower lip begins to quiver immediately.)

Now we have to stop at this point because Lauren has to leave for class, and also because a huge upset occurs over who is the smallest in the class. It's a long and very interesting story I'll type up later. It involved trying to line up according to size and Leah and Indy crying hard over this. It's about Indy's love for Nick, and Leah's fear that she'll be the smallest (and she is, which is even worse.) We'll continue to share these theories at Friday's meeting when Lauren will be here again to help. Look for copies of the sketches with the dictations displayed in the classroom.

The theories continued to be explored and documented over an extended period, and then resurfaced in a naptime conversation noted by Patti on April 12, nearly two months later. What an opportunity for teacher and families to gain insights into their children's thinking through this kind of documentation. Teachers who work alone are particularly challenged to find documentation methods that fit into their available time.

Time is also an issue for teachers who do not work alone. Dee Conley at Quadra Island Day Care describes how her staff works to find time for documentation:

We have weekly staff meeting for two hours. The first hour we discuss specific children and other items on the agenda. The second hour is dedicated to discussing documentation and children's interests and sharing our ideas. We use our communication book extensively throughout the week to share our thoughts and insights with each other. When a provocation is set up in advance, it is helpful to discuss beforehand who will document, who will facilitate the experience, and how each staff member can support the process. Another teacher at the same center: Time is set aside at meetings to do documentation, and sometimes a large part of the meeting will be spent organizing photos and deciding on text together. We read through each other's observations and comments, and make suggestions on how we can use them. We sort through all transcriptions and make separate files of topics that have generated interest over several sessions. We keep a file we call "other" in which we collect transcriptions of conversations or experiences that seemed more than usually meaningful but did not lead to extended activity.

However teachers create solutions, time is certainly an issue related to documentation. But recognizing the centrality of documentation to the reflective process it is an issue that must be met. "When asked once how the early childhood institutions in Reggio Emilia had time to work so rigorously with pedagogical documentation, Loris Malaguzzi answered, 'We prioritize'" (Dahlberg et al., 1999, p. 18).

Finding Space

Teachers need space for meeting with one another and parents to collaborate on the planning, design, and development of the documentation. They need wide, flat surfaces to work on the large panels that often are a major form of documentation. Storage space is essential, both for work in progress and for storing the documentations that have been completed. It is interesting to note that in the schools in Reggio Emilia, the documentation stays on display in the classrooms for years, even after the children involved have left the school. This gives newcomers a sense of the history that has gone on before. It also may give suggestions to newly enrolled children about activities they can do in the classroom. Sometimes, teachers will need to revisit documentation from previous years and a system for storing material is essential. Classrooms also need shelves or cabinets for filing photographs, children's drawings and paintings, and the large documentation panels developed in the course of a project. A visitor to Reggio Emilia commented on a portrait she had seen a child drawing of her teacher on a previous visit. She was astounded when the atelierista was able to go to the file and give her a photocopy of the portrait she had seen the child drawing two years before. This demonstrates the value of having a system in place for filing material so that it can be quickly and easily accessed.

American classrooms using practices inspired by Reggio make a number of adaptations that allow them to work around the space and storage issues. Many programs are using staff lounges or whatever studio space they have as teacher documentation areas. Sometimes, notes, observations, photos, and other artifacts related to a completed project are kept in loose-leaf notebooks. These can be stored on a shelf for later revisiting, or sent home with children in the evening to be shared with their families. Other teachers use individual rings to gather collections of art or photos and hang them on the wall where they can be taken down and paged through at length. One teacher displayed just one photo and comment of past projects to trigger recall. A creative suggestion was made by a teacher on the Reggio list: use community sites that will welcome documentation displays such as public libraries, churches, banks, pediatricians' offices, and other places where families may visit. Such a display would have the added advantage of enhancing community awareness of the capabilities and learning style of young children, and of what good early childhood education looks like.

Finding Funds

Documentation can be expensive in the time it takes to produce and in the materials it requires. When budgets are prepared for early childhood programs, the people responsible need to be sure that teachers are given the resources they need to produce documentation of the highest quality. Documentation is worth the cost

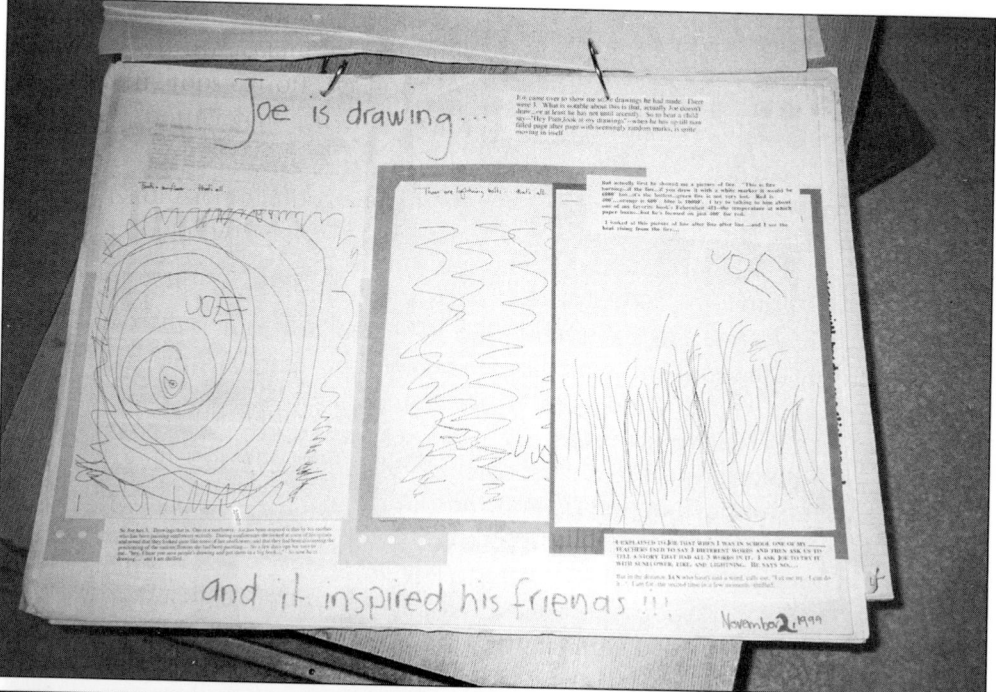

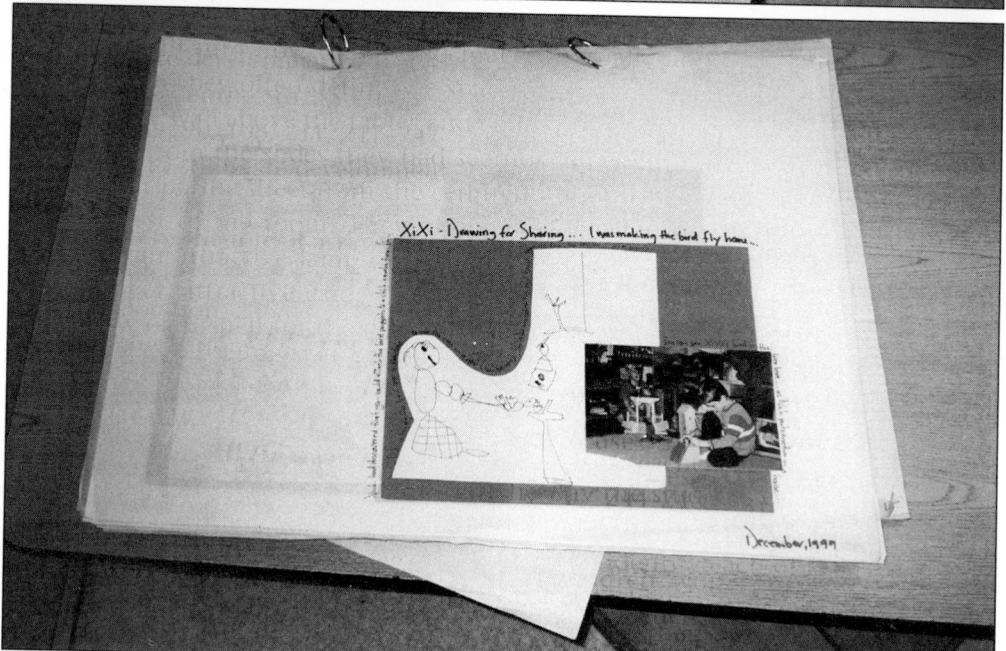

Figure 6–9. Collections of art or photos, gathered by large rings, allow for much work to be stored on one hook, to be paged through at length. (*Courtesy:* Patti Cruikshank-Schott.).

because it makes the program, especially the children's experiences, visible to the families and the wider community. It allows parents to be part of their children's experiences at school. It shows the teacher's commitment to providing an educational program that matches the learning potential of the children in the group. It also demonstrates that preschool education is a serious and an enjoyable experience.

Programs have found different and often creative ways of helping to defray the expenses of documentation. Quadra Island makes double prints of photos, and displays the second set for parents to purchase for fifty cents a picture. This helps to cover the cost of film and processing. Lakewood has a luncheon and silent auction at the end of the year, selling documentation panels to always-eager families; these proceeds pay for the supply of matte board and other materials for documentation the next year. First Baptist Kindergarten asks parents to donate 12-exposure films for teachers' use; parent volunteers assist the secretary in typing up notes and transcripts. Sabot School has asked their board to restructure the budget to support paid teacher time for documentation and computers for each team. The staff at the University of Vermont Campus Children's Center, in trying to raise money (not so much for documentation but for staff trips to Reggio), decided to use their teaching talents and offer workshops and classes to others interested in the Reggio approach. And many teachers are using their own resources: Pam Oken-Wright's father bought her digital camera for use in documentation.

Creative solutions combined with determination help teachers find documentation methods that fit their situation for expense of money and time. Ann Pelo and her colleagues at Hilltop have devised a fast and inexpensive method of daily documentation. There are nine headings on the Curriculum Board outside her classroom:

1. Community happenings
2. Social learning
3. Antibias learning
4. Sensory and physical knowledge
5. Sociodramatic play
6. Art and symbolic representation
7. Stories and emerging literacy
8. Logical and mathematical thinking
9. On-going projects and emerging interests

Under each heading is stapled a clear plastic protector the size of a standard sheet of paper. Each day at naptime, teachers write a story about children's play and work that highlights one of the curriculum headings. The stories include reflection and analysis to help illuminate underlying themes and learning. The teachers have made a commitment to families that they will add at least one new write-up to the board every day. Some days, one teacher writes several pages about one heading; other days, several of them will write a simple short piece, or make a photocopy of children's work with a couple of sentences of reflection added, or add a photo and brief caption to the board. When the write-ups are replaced with new ones, the teachers make copies of what they have written and place those copies in the children's journals, along with photos and other sorts of documentation. Ann comments that the teachers create other displays and books about project work, but the families are most consistent about keeping up with reading the daily documentation. "It's a powerful way to communicate that our curriculum is the daily life of the classroom, with all its meanderings and conflicts and discoveries, not just the projects that we do or other eye-catching happenings." Documentation is a way of drawing others in to the process of reflecting on the potential of ordinary moments.

Encouraging Parents to Read Documentation

Many teachers who have begun to use documentation as a part of their implementation of ideas from the Reggio approach have expressed initial discouragement that parents seem uninterested: "They just don't read it!" they protest. This can engender fairly strong teacher emotion, given the amount of time and reflection that have gone into the creation of the documentation. Teachers who have been on the Reggio journey for a longer time are comforting in describing changed responses. Jeanne Goldhaber, nearly 10 years into the Reggio journey, recalls that in the beginning, there was a great deal of talk about parents not reading the documentation. "But it's about creating a culture. Now parents see that the culture is to read the boards, to get involved in an exchange of information and reflection together—it's just what happens. And you can see the difference. Now parents are engaged in the intellectual lives of their children. The questions aren't just about what kind of a nap he had." Pam Oken-Wright, who sends her daily documentation journals to parents by e-mail, concurs: "Parents adore the logs. I am blessed year after year with incredibly supportive and 'present' parents (Not always the case historically, by the way). I think I have observed a cycle of positive energy, with parents reading the logs and talking with their children about what's going on, then coming in to see first hand what they've read about." Jane Watkins, whose children in a half day program arrive and leave primarily by car pool, reports that they have to leave the building open during regular business hours and on weekends so that parents can come in and read the changed documentation they have been alerted to in a newsletter, often bringing grandparents in as well.

How have teachers helped parents get involved in reading the documentation? Margaret Edwards displays the daily journal on a music stand set up prominently in the middle of the cubby area. Patti Cruikshank-Schott's journal is right beside the sign-in sheet, and parents on e-mail are sent it at home or office. The First Baptist newsletter is composed of quotes from the teachers' transcripts, linking the dialog to documentation which parents are invited to come and view. Other creative ideas from the Reggio list include:

- Post on the door (or near the car pool pick-up zone) a photo or sketch or two with a couple of quotes from transcription with the invitation to come inside and see more. Parents notice pictures.

- Teach the children to show the panels to their parents at the beginning of the day or at pick-up time, perhaps starting by showing a picture of them or a piece of work by them once a week.

- Take a good look at the halls of the school, trying to see them as a visitor or a newcomer, to make sure there is not too much background clutter. Simple displays draw the eyes. Teachers may pack too much into panels and make them overwhelming to approach.

- Try asking parents at the beginning of the year to create a panel/poster about their own child (what they are interested in, who is in their family) and let those be the first things you put up. Teachers should create panels too, as a way of introducing themselves to the community. Parents and children will be drawn to see themselves, and then to look for friends. Then, at the first parents' night, ask parents about how they approached the task, what they thought about, what they wanted people to know about their child. That gives them the experience of revisiting and reflecting about an experience. Then explain that that same thing will be happening through the year, revisiting experiences with the children and that you would like the parents to "revisit" these panels with their children.

- Take a project history book containing photos, transcripts, samples of children's work, reflections, and so on, on home visits in the fall. Parents can read this while teachers can focus on the visit with the child.

- Put up an "under construction" sign periodically with nothing on the board. That will let parents look forward to what's coming up next. If there's always something up, it is easy not to notice new work.

Teachers find that after a time, parents come to expect that this new reporting is much more meaningful evidence of engagement in learning than the typical newsletter or bulletin board was in the past. Then it seems they cannot get enough.

These are not the only concerns of teachers who begin the documentation process. Many teachers have not been prepared to use some of the computer and video technology that is used with the production of panels. While this is difficult, it is not insurmountable, with appropriate kinds of technical support. A larger issue may be the emotional reluctance to go public with one's work and reflections. Preparation for becoming comfortable with this is not generally part of professional training. However, as teachers collaborate with others, comfort will grow.

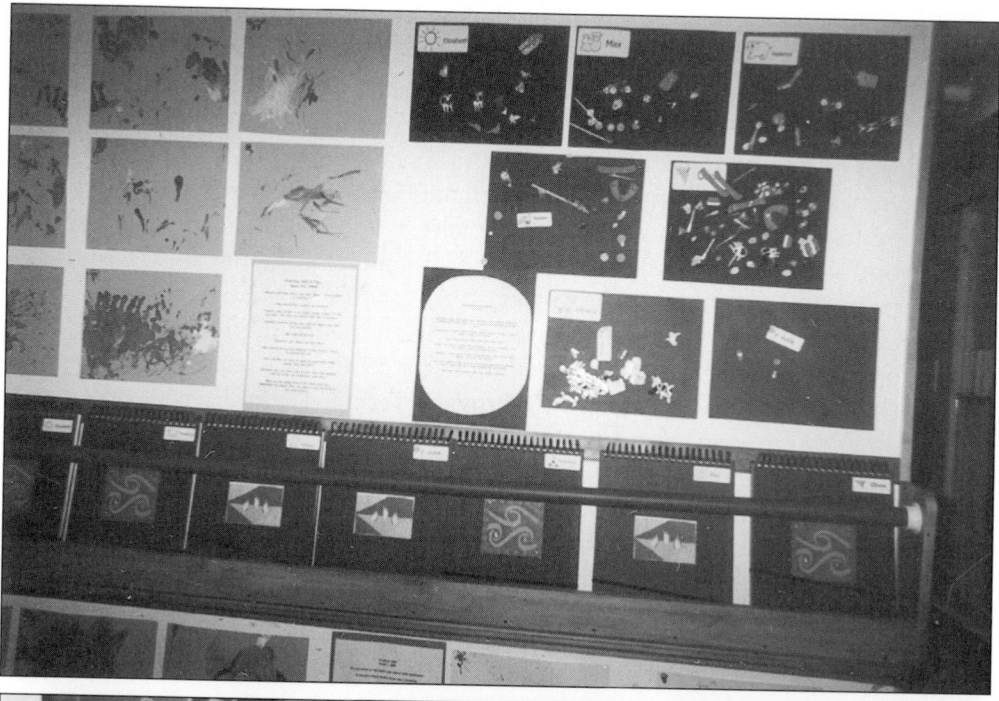

Figure 6–10.   Attractive documentation everywhere helps create the culture of parents reading documentation. (*Courtesy:* Lakewood Avenue Children's School.)

Whatever the issues teachers identify related to documentation, they must be met.

All teachers realize that to explore ideas from the Reggio Emilia approach successfully, some form of documentation is essential. Documentation addresses many levels of the program. For the children, it acts as a memory device, enabling them to revisit previous experiences and make connections to past, present, and future events and experiences. It gives teachers opportunities to help children move from unassisted to assisted learning and achieve a higher level within the zone of proximal development (Vygotsky, 1951, p. 103). It enables children to use higher mental functions such as focused attention, deliberate memory, and symbolic thought as opposed to the lower functions of reactive attention, associative memory, and sensorimotor thought (Bodrova & Leong, 1996).

Documentation also expands the role of teachers and provides a tool that enables them to be more effective in their work with children. It requires them to become critical thinkers and researchers in the classroom. Documentation displayed in the classrooms and entranceways gives teachers more credibility in the outside community. As parents and visitors to the center read the information and see the work the children are doing in the program, they can understand how much serious consideration teachers give to all aspects of the program, especially to the task of learning. Documentation serves as a communication channel from the center to the outside world. It is, therefore, an important tool in building relationships among the teachers, the parents, and the outside community. Documentation makes apparent the teachers' commitment to high-quality preschool education for children.

Carlina Rinaldi speaks of how documentation becomes a "place of listening," making listening visible and shareable. Documentation makes the process of learning visible to the children, to the teachers, and to the families. Perhaps what is most revolutionary about the Reggio Emilia construct of documentation is the idea that it actually modifies the structure of the learning process. Documentation is an "ongoing process of education and growth for children and adults together" (Rinaldi, January 1999).

Chapter **7**

Negotiating the Curriculum

The educational institution is, in fact, a system of communication and interaction among the three protagonists [children, educators, and families] integrated into the larger system. Given this system in its complexity, it can be understood why the potential of children is stunted when the endpoint of their learning is formulated in advance.

—Carlina Rinaldi

Questions to Consider:

- What are the differences in theme, emergent, and negotiated learning approaches to planning curriculum?

- How do teachers negotiate learning in the preschool curriculum?

- What is a provocation, and how is it used?

- What communication strategies are needed to set the process of negotiated learning in motion?

- How do teachers collaborate with children in making predictions?

- What does it mean to "expect the unexpected"?

- What are the differences in planning and implementing this approach to curriculum?

- What are the challenges in using this approach to curriculum?

THE TEACHER-DIRECTED CURRICULUM

There have been a number of changes in the way early childhood educators have approached the planning of curriculum over the last 20 years. During this time, the focus of the curriculum has changed from being teacher-directed to becoming more child centered. Now, as they have tried to use ideas from the Reggio Emilia approach in their programs, teachers have woven the principles of reciprocity and collaboration into the planning process, meaning that the approach to curriculum has changed yet again to become "child originated and teacher framed" (Forman & Fyfe, 1998, p. 240).

When the curriculum was solely teacher-directed, educators often wrote their teaching plans in advance for the week or month, and sometimes even for the whole year. Teachers knew what the theme was for each week, what they would be doing each day, what supplies they would need, and what preparation they needed to do. Teachers would plan the activities for Fall and Halloween, when they set out all those pumpkins for carving, followed by Thanksgiving and the winter holidays. Soon it was spring and time to plant seeds in styrofoam cups. Finally, the teachers would plan a summer picnic before packing up the curriculum boxes for another year. The problem with this approach was that children often had different ideas. For example, they were more interested in the new funnels in the sandbox than in discussing why leaves change color in the fall. The teacher's dilemma was how to reconcile the two ideas about curriculum: in this case, completing the teacher-planned activities related to the theme of Fall or allowing the children to pursue their own interests and investigate what happens to the volume of water when it trickles out of a funnel.

In the 1960s and 1970s, when governments invested money in early childhood education such as Head Start and other intervention programs, accountability became increasingly important. Early childhood programs were required to demonstrate that they were well-organized, able to set clear goals, and able to evaluate the program. This procedure was felt to be essential in justifying the expenditure of taxpayers' money on programs for children before school age. Early childhood educators needed to show that preschool education was a serious endeavor, and that it had short-term and long-term benefits for children.

Accountability became even more important in the 1980s when, owing to a recession in the economy, funding became increasingly scarce. As working families in the 1980s and 1990s more frequently used child care, demands from parents paying the fees often escalated requests for demonstrable learning in children. One way to demonstrate accountability was to make the organizational structure of programs clearly visible. Many early childhood programs attempted to demonstrate accountability by announcing a theme for each week or month of the year, setting goals and objectives, identifying the concepts that children needed to learn, deciding on appropriate activities, and evaluating the outcome to ensure that the goals and objectives had been achieved. This was the preferred method of program planning taught in most early childhood teacher preparation programs in the past two or three decades.

The teachers often mapped out the themes they chose on a chart which they displayed in the classroom or printed in the newsletter sent home to parents. Many teachers based their themes on the belief that it is important to encourage children to develop a positive self-concept, and heighten their awareness of themselves and the world around them. In many early childhood programs, the year often still begins with a theme of self and others. Included in this theme will be activities to do with body image, awareness of the senses, and expression of feelings. This theme then may be expanded to include activities that encourage children to get to know the other children in the class, their families, and the wider community. Often, teachers will arrange field trips so children can learn about the neighborhood such as visiting the fire station or grocery store. Seasonal change and holidays throughout the year also are popular themes in preschool programs.

Although many preschool programs still base their planning on a theme approach, teachers often find that the experiences that actually happen in the classroom have little relationship to the written plan posted on the wall. They find that children sometimes come up with more interesting ideas than those of the teachers. Teachers find themselves caught in the dilemma of sticking with the theme or abandoning it, and following the children's interests. Many teachers have found that theme planning is too rigid and that more flexibility is needed to provide children with experiences responsive to their ideas.

It is an unfortunate fact that teachers in the United States today feel the very real pressure launched by both school systems and parents for school achievement, too often narrowly viewed as only the end of grade test results often published for public perusal. The emphasis on test scores has led to many curriculum practices that focus too specifically on covering material to prepare for tests instead of "uncovering" the curriculum interests and learning style of children and the adults in their lives. Even preschool teachers feel this pressure, ignited by parents' anxiety that their child be ready for the academic rigors of kindergarten. Rather than feeling that negotiated curriculum is an impossible dream, given the current situation, the example from Reggio may be useful in providing a model of real learning for American teachers. Both parents and teachers in Reggio are fully aware of the traditional, test-driven methods their children will encounter later in the Italian school system. But they believe that the active, in-depth explorations of the preschools' negotiated curriculum will help children learn how to be confident, capable learners. They refuse to give up their strong beliefs in creating their appropriate curriculum in the preschool, believing this is the best way for children to become "ready" to cope with later academics. They continue to engage in dialog with the community and the school system, and to raise questions about the later methods. The image of this persistence in the face of pressure may be an important example to remember when we consider negotiated curriculum.

THE EMERGENT CURRICULUM

In recent years, theme planning has begun to give way to a view of the curriculum as emergent or arising out of the children's interests. "Curriculum is what happens," write Jones and Nimmo. "In early childhood education, curriculum isn't the focus, children are. It's easy for teachers to get hooked on curriculum because it's so much more manageable than children. But curriculum is *what happens* in an educational environment—not what is rationally planned to happen, but what actually takes place" (1995, p. 12).

An emergent curriculum begins with observation of the children and their interests. Teachers observe the children in the classroom, listen, record their ideas, and then select from these observations one or more topics that seem to interest the children. Teachers, either individually or as a group, then create a web on a large sheet of paper. They write the topic in which the children are interested in large letters at the center of the web. Next, they brainstorm the possible directions that they and the children might take in pursuing the topic further. They then write these subtopics on lines that branch off in different directions (see Figure 7–1). The words in circles represent the children's ideas; the words in squares are adults' suggestions. Teachers add new ideas and suggestions to the web as they emerge during the experience. A thick colored line may trace the path on the web that the experience actually follows as it unfolds. Teachers find that the advantage of this kind of planning, as opposed to theme planning, is that it is more responsive to the children's interests, and it enables teachers to be more flexible and creative in the planning process. The experiences mapped out on the chart can change direction at any time in response to new ideas and suggestions. Therefore, the project remains fresh and exciting for the teachers and children (Jones & Nimmo, 1995).

In this discussion of emergent curriculum, it also is important to state that sources beyond children's ideas and interests may offer topics that emerge from responding to the interests, questions, and concerns generated within a particular environment by a particular group of people at a particular time (Cassady, 1993). Both adult and child initiative may influence curriculum directions. Besides children's play, comments, and questions, other sources for curriculum explorations may come from adult interests and passions; things, events, and people in the environment; developmental tasks; family and cultural influences; issues that arise in the course of daily living together; serendipity, or what just happens; and curriculum resource materials that give ideas for adaptations (Jones & Nimmo, 1995).

THE NEGOTIATED CURRICULUM

The educators in Reggio Emilia perceive the curriculum as emerging from the interests and ideas of the children, but they also believe that there should be negotiation between all those involved in the development of the curriculum and in the planning and projects as they unfold. This perspective of curriculum is based on the theory that children co-construct knowledge within their social group. George Forman and Brenda Fyfe state that "this theory holds that knowledge is gradually constructed by people becoming each other's student, by taking a reflective stance

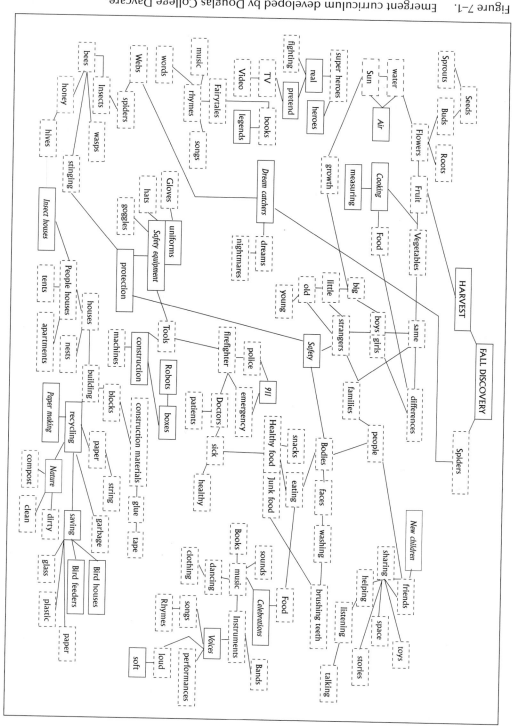

Figure 7-1. Emergent curriculum developed by Douglas College Daycare.

toward each other's constructs, and by honoring the power of each other's initial perspective for negotiating a better understanding of subject matter" (1998, p. 239). Negotiated learning, therefore, begins with observations of the children and by listening closely to their conversations. However, it goes beyond observation "to uncover the children's beliefs about the topics to be investigated. . . . [The teacher's] analysis reveals the reasons behind the children's interests, the source of their current knowledge, and the level of articulation about its detail" (Forman & Fyfe, 1998, p. 240). Teachers then share this information with other adults. Perhaps the teachers will see in this discussion that there is the germ of an idea that might become the topic for a future progettazione. All those who will be involved in the project then discuss the possibilities and the many ways in which the project could evolve. They write down their hypotheses and predictions for future directions the topic may follow. They discuss the possible choices the children will make and where these choices might lead. The team then will need to decide whether the idea for the topic will sustain the children's interest for a long period of time. If they agree that the topic has long-term possibilities, they begin to prepare for subsequent stages of the project (Rinaldi, 1998).

In the discussion about negotiated curriculum, teachers also may need to consider whether they are omitting key people and ideas from the negotiation (New, 1999). If the idea from Reggio is accepted that "no one has a monopoly" on what children need or need to know, then others beyond the teacher and child also must be involved in negotiating curriculum. Children's families, other teachers, and community members all have important ideas about what is important for children to learn to connect them with their future lives within their sociocultural context. When these people are missing from the discussions on negotiation, it is entirely possible that teachers' views of what and how children should learn may be too limited. In a statement in the Reggio Internet discussion reported in *Innovations*, Rebecca New says that it is a teacher's challenge to be able to "zoom in and out of the classroom context, incorporating what she knows about those particular children, believes and values about children in general, learns from their parents, and understands about the pressing issues in our society" as a part of the negotiating of curriculum decisions (4[1]).

In taking a negotiated learning approach to curriculum, teachers move beyond simply providing children with experiences. They probe further, either by asking questions or by engaging the child in discussion, to discover why children are deeply absorbed in exploring a material, or they try to figure out what children are thinking as they touch, taste, examine, or explore the texture of interesting objects.

It is important to realize that, in negotiated curriculum, all participants have important roles. The focus is not the issue of being either child-centered or teacher-directed: it is whether the curriculum is "child originated and teacher framed" (Forman & Fyfe, 1998, p. 240).

George Forman and Brenda Fyfe have identified the three components as *design, documentation,* and *discourse* to define negotiated learning (see Chapter 6).

Design Phase

The design stage begins when the teachers and other adults, from observations and transcriptions of the children's conversations, have decided on a subject that they believe will be of long-term interest to the children. Teachers use various methods of planning curriculum, but one that works well is similar to the method for planning an emergent curriculum described above. On a large sheet of paper, the teachers make a web with the main topic at the center. Then they brainstorm as a group to identify possible directions the project may follow and write their predictions on the chart, drawing lines from the topic to the subtopics that may possibly evolve from the main subject as the project unfolds. The chart also includes a list of ideas for provoking the children to think more deeply or broadly about the topic. These provocations might be questions that a teacher plans to ask the children to find out how well they understand a topic and to provoke them to further investigation. Or they might be plans for arranging equipment and materials in the classroom to encourage children to see relationships and develop deeper understanding of a subject or experience, such as a visit to a water tower in the community (see Chapter 8).

A term that may be useful to consider when thinking about this phase in planning an exploration is *reconnaissance* in place of planning (Edwards, Gandini, & Forman, 1998). This seems to identify the active going before and checking out of possibilities that adults do in considering the extent and possible directions of the learning activities. It is by this thinking through process that teachers can identify learning potential to deem if the interest offers rich enough possibilities to warrant beginning the exploration. The design phase also offers teachers the opportunity to consider whether developmental and program goals can be met by facilitating learning in these directions.

Children are also involved in the design phase of the project. Teachers may select a small group of children who have shown real interest in pursuing the topic. At each stage, they encourage the children to discuss and symbolically represent their ideas about the subject so that the teachers can assess their level of understanding of the topic. "*Design* refers to any activity in which children make records of their plans or intended solutions. A drawing can be a design if it is drawn with an intent to guide the construction of the items drawn, or to guide a sequence of steps" (Forman & Fyfe, 1998, p. 241). When children sketch or represent their thinking, their knowledge and ideas may become clearer to the teacher, and, in fact, be expanded by the process. Their drawings may become blueprints to suggest directions for constructing the project. Teachers share and discuss these representations with the other children and adults in the group; with input from others, the representations tend to become more detailed and elaborate as the investigation proceeds. They also become part of the core material for the documentation that is developed as the project unfolds.

Documentation Phase

Documentation is a central component of negotiated learning. In the early stages, the teachers will have met to decide on the possible forms the documentation will take such as written observations, transcriptions of audiotape, slides, photographs displayed on panels or in portfolios, and videotapes. Whatever media the teachers choose, the documentation will be used to describe the process the teachers and children follow as they negotiate the learning that takes place during the project. Forman and Fyfe state that "when teachers document children's work and use this documentation as part of their instruction with the children, the net result is a change in the image of their role as teacher, a change from teaching children to studying children, and by studying children, learning with children" (1998, p. 240). Documentation also provides the group with a means of revisiting previous experiences and discussing future directions the project may take.

Discourse Phase

When communication is conceptualized as *discourse*, interaction goes beyond just listening and talking to children. It includes the added dimension of reflecting on and analyzing what is being heard and said. Discourse requires teachers to pay careful attention to the language they hear and speak, to ask questions to uncover the meaning behind the words, and to try to figure out the reasons for the child's comments. Transcribing the children's conversations, and then examining and analyzing them with the other adults is essential in developing a project. "Treating talk as discourse causes teachers to look for theories, assumptions, false premises, misapplications, clever analogies, ambiguities, and differences in communicative intent, all of which are pieces to be negotiated into shared meaning by the group" (Forman & Fyfe, 1998, p. 247).

In planning the next phases in an investigation, care must be paid to careful analysis in order to follow the true intentions of the participating children. Too often, teachers might decide on an idea and follow it, no matter what the behaviors and words of the children were telling them. Sarah and Ann offer an example of using discourse to inform the direction of a project in the "Thinking Big" video.

As they watched the children continuing to explore the possibilities of building tall structures and heard their comments about height and power, the teachers pondered where to go from there. One idea they had was to see if the children would be interested in exploring birds, because birds could get really high, too. They brought in branches, nests, and little bird figures, and continued to observe the children at play. As they analyzed, they commented that it seemed clear from what the children were saying that their play was still about being tall, being up high.

"I'm pretending I'm standing on those big long branches."

"Let's tie things high up in the tree—we'll need the step stool."

"Look at me—I'm taller than the trees."

The teachers decided that what was important about birds was that they could get to the tops of trees. The children still were most interested in being up high and building tall things, so the discourse phase of this negotiated curriculum helped the teachers realize that their planning should be about experiences that could help continue the exploration of height, and not be sidetracked by feeling they should introduce new curriculum ideas.

Educators also use transcriptions of the children's conversations to remind them of thoughts and ideas they expressed earlier, and to help children extend their understanding of a subject. For example, a teacher might observe a child's continuing interest in the movements of the snails in the tank. Reflections on the transcriptions of the child's talk the previous day might lead her to provoke the child to think further about the subject. "Yesterday, you said the snails reminded you of an elastic band because their bodies stretched and contracted. Look at this snail upside down on the lid of the tank. How does he stay up there? Could an elastic band do that?" Used as a provocation, this question might lead, as it did at the Vancouver Child Study Center, to a short project investigating snails and their habitat. In the early spring, the children collected snails in the forest and constructed an environment for them in the classroom, planting moss and ferns to make it look like the place where they had found the snails. The children fed the snails fresh fruit and vegetables every day. Many of the children sketched and made three-dimensional representations of the snails. One morning, the children were delighted to find that the snails had laid a mass of eggs at the bottom of the tank. Before the children left for the summer holidays, they carried the snails back to the forest and placed them where they knew they would be safe. The children and teachers were concerned that the children who attended the class in the afternoon would wonder what had happened to the snails. They decided that they would draw a map to show the afternoon group where they had set the snails free in the forest. On their return to the classroom, Vivian, one of the teachers, noticed Neilson sitting at a table with another child and drawing shapes and long lines on his sheet of paper.

Neilson: I am going to do the Snailish trail after I have done the Spanish trail.

Vivian: Would you like to write the word? It starts with an S. Are you drawing the map so the afternoon children will know where the snails are?

Neilson: I did! X—that is where they [the snails] are.

Vivian (pointing to the shapes on the paper): I like the way you drew the horsetails—now they will know where to look for them.

(Earlier on the walk, the children had placed the snails near a patch of coarse, green plants that Neilson had told us were horsetails. "But," he had said, "there is a problem. Horses can't eat them for food. I don't know why they are called horsetails.")

From the observation and recording of the child's talk above, the teacher inferred that Neilson was making a map that included a drawing of the plants that grew near where the snails had been released in the forest. His question about why the plants were called horsetails when horses, in fact, did not like to eat them, is an example of what Loris Malaguzzi called expecting the unexpected. If there had been enough time left in the school year, this child's comment might have been an interesting idea to follow up. Horsetails are fascinating plants in themselves, but they were also the dominant plant species during the dinosaurs' time on earth. Many of the children in the group, like most children, are fascinated by everything to do with dinosaurs, so the teachers could have considered investigating horsetails with the children, which, in turn, might have led to a project on dinosaurs and their environment.

Listening attentively to what children are saying and being able to follow up with questions that uncover the child's level of meaning are essential skills in implementing a negotiated learning approach to curriculum. Both skills take practice. An image of the child who is competent and full of ideas is central to listening attentively to what children say. When teachers expect children to say interesting things and to contribute ideas, they will be much more likely to pay attention to what children have to say. When children know that their ideas are appreciated, they will be more willing to share them. Slowing down and taking the time to really hear what the child is saying and then trying to see it from the child's perspective is important. Reflecting on the child's responses to questions also helps a teacher learn what kind of questions are most effective. If the kind of questions the teacher poses elicit one word or no response, the questions the teacher is asking may be too direct. A question that is more reflective may encourage a more elaborate response. A question phrased as, "I wonder what is happening here?" encourages the child to think about what he is doing and to make a response that provides a teacher with unexpected insight into what he is thinking. Reflecting what is understood from the child's comments is also helpful, as in "I think I am hearing you say. . . . Is that right?" This response also may help clarify the child's thinking. Rejoicing in the child's competence with comments and questions such as "That is amazing! How did you do that?" will probably encourage the child to further effort and may even generate some explanation of the child's thinking. Sometimes a teacher may need to encourage children to clarify or go deeper saying, "I don't quite understand what you mean by saying that. . . . "

Giving the child many opportunities to engage in authentic conversations is important. An authentic conversation is one in which the participants engage in a dialog that has a purpose and is of genuine interest. This kind of talk is more likely to happen when teachers respect children, view them as competent, and are genuinely interested in hearing what they are thinking about. Sometimes, children have ideas but they have not developed enough vocabulary to express them clearly. This is why it is important that teachers establish close relationships with the children. When a teacher knows a child well, she is more likely to be able to infer what the child is trying to say and provide the child with the missing words. Margaret Mead tells the story of taking her grandchild for a walk. As they passed a display of pussy willows in a florist shop, Margaret Mead heard her granddaughter say "pussycat," and she knew immediately that the child had connected the branches of pussy willows to a poem she had taught the child's mother years ago.

I'm a little pussy

But I'll never be a cat

'Cause I'm a pussy willow

And that is that!

From the one word the child uttered, Margaret Mead was able to access the child's meaning, and the two of them went on down the street reciting the poem together. To be able to engage in meaningful dialog with children, teachers need to do the following.

- establish an environment that values communication in all its different forms; verbal, gestural, symbolic, and so on
- establish a close and trusting relationship with the child
- hold the image of the child as competent and filled with ideas
- be genuinely interested in what the child is saying
- listen attentively
- slow down the pace of the talk and reflect before responding
- probe to uncover meaning
- scaffold the child's ability to express ideas by supplying the missing words
- encourage the child to think about thinking (metalinguistic knowledge)
- encourage the child to use a wide range of language techniques such as metaphors, analogies, and hypotheses
- accept the inevitability of conflict and view it as a positive dynamic in moving ideas forward

In the following transcript of a conversation, Susan Emery, a teacher at the child care center on Quadra Island, shows how she used some of the above suggestions in a conversation with Grant to help him come up with a mutually satisfying solution to their problem.

There are many silver strips hanging down from the skylight, reflecting light on the floor and walls. I am holding a strip that has fallen down. Grant comes over.

Grant: What are you doing with that?

Susan: It fell down and I'm wondering how to put it back without going and getting a ladder.

Grant: Stand on a chair.

Susan: I'll try that. (I'm a long way from reaching the skylight.)

Grant: Now JUMP off the chair and REACH UP and stick it on!

Susan: I'm worried I might hurt myself if I do that.

Grant: You won't. Go on. Jump!

Figure 7–2. Silver strips of foil hanging from the skylight.

Susan: Well, Grant, I'm thinking of how I could reach it up there without breaking my ankle.

Grant: A big stick.

Whatever he'd said—within reason—I would have tried, but he saved me the trouble by coming up with a workable solution himself. I got a broom and stuck the silver strip back on the skylight with the handle.

Susan: Your idea worked fine, Grant.

Learning to listen and communicate in meaningful dialog are skills that need practice and attention. Students in early childhood education professional development programs that have been influenced by Reggio practices—Douglas College, the University of Vermont, the University of New Hampshire, and Virginia Polytechnic University (Virginia Tech)—are encouraged to be deliberate and thoughtful as they work with children. Reflection on carefully recorded and transcribed conversations develops these skills. The students observe and record one another communicating with the children. They then analyze the transcripts to see what kind of responses the children made to their questions and comments. They learn to avoid using "pop-quiz questions" such as "What color is that stop sign?" and questions with a hidden agenda such as "How many chickens can you see?" They learn that judgmental comments such as,"What a beautiful painting" or "I like the man you drew" are comments that close down rather than open up the conversation. They discover that questions that arise out of the teacher's agenda such as "Tell me about your picture" are one-sided comments that do not foster a negotiated learning approach. They begin to understand that teachers ask questions only when they are genuinely interested in the answers. With practice, they begin to realize the value of listening to children. They learn that when they really hear what children have to say, a meaningful dialog develops. Conversation becomes discourse when teachers begin to use dialog to collaborate with children in co-constructing theories about subjects they and the children are interested in discovering more about.

Design, documentation, and discourse are essential components in planning and implementing a negotiated learning approach to curriculum. These three components do not necessarily occur in a linear fashion but are interwoven throughout the process as the project evolves. Each one affects the others. Documentation informs the discourse, and discourse the documentation. Design forms the structure on which the project grows.

NEGOTIATED CURRICULUM AND LONG-TERM PROJECTS IN REGGIO EMILIA

Perhaps one of the most distinguishing features of the curriculum in the schools in Reggio Emilia is the long-term concentration of children and adults engaged in explorations that may last for weeks or even months. As Lilian Katz (1998) points out, such long-term investigations are not new to preschool or primary education, since Dewey's Progressive education movement featured project work in the early 20th century, and the ideas were picked up again in British Infant schools and American open education in the 1960s and 1970s. Katz herself, along with her colleague Sylvia Chard, had advocated project work in *Engaging Children's Minds: The Project Approach,* published in 1989, before most American educators had heard of the Reggio approach. But the Reggio projects represent the concept of negotiated curriculum at perhaps the most complex level yet seen. Many are now familiar with some of the long Reggio projects through viewing the exhibit "The Hundred Languages of Children" at some place in its travels through the United States or Canada, by viewing some of the videotapes of Reggio work, or even by visiting the schools themselves on one of the delegations. It is useful to consider the projects themselves to further explore the three phases of negotiated curriculum. It is through this consideration that the true interconnectedness and cyclical nature of the three phases can be understood.

Design in a Reggio Project

Loris Malaguzzi's own words explain the importance of design in beginning project work.

> It is true that we do not have planning and curricula. It is not true that we rely on improvisation . . . We do not rely on chance either, because we are convinced that what we do not yet know can to some extent be anticipated . . . We use projects because relying on the capacities and resources of children expresses our philosophical view . . . In trying to make a good project, one has to have, above all, a pertinent expectation, shaped in advance, an expectation also felt by the children. This expectation helps the adults in terms of their attentiveness, choices, methods of intervention, and what they do concerning the relationships among participants (Malaguzzi, 1998, p. 89–90).

It is these "expectations" that inform the design of the project work. As Malaguzzi said, each project has a kind of prologue phase during which the members of a group share information and ideas. These initial conversations help the adults to form predictions and hypotheses about what could happen as children bring their different understandings and experiences. But it is definitely a collaborative experience, possible because the children in Reggio classrooms have enormous amounts of collective experience in discussing in small and large groups.

> So ideas fly, bounce around, accumulate, rise up, fall apart, and spread, until one of them takes a decisive hold, flies higher, and conquers the entire group. Whatever it turns out to be, the adopted idea in turn adopts the children and the teachers (Malaguzzi, 1995, p. 10).

The delightful, long-term project of building the Amusement Park for Birds was undertaken by children and adults at La Villetta School in 1993. The progress through this project has been documented in the book *The Fountains* (1995), and in the videotape, "An Amusement Park for Birds" (1994).

The school sits in the midst of a wooded yard, and the children had previously enjoyed watching the birds. In past years, one group of five-year-olds had explored the meadow from a bird's perspective, and another group the next year had built birdhouses and watched birds playing in the water. So the teachers begin the design phase by asking the children what they remembered of these two earlier experiences. As the children consider caring for the birds, they get the idea of making a lake where birds could drink. But birds that are thirsty must have other needs such as being tired and hungry. In the preliminary discussions, new thoughts develop. Refreshment and renewal could mean houses in the trees, swings for baby birds to ride, and elevators for the less agile, older birds. But then why not Ferris wheels and other rides, a haunted house needing a ticket booth? And why not water skis? And why not fountains? Big, real fountains, and lots of them so the birds would not argue? One child comments: "I am sure the birds are listening and think these children have a wonderful idea!"

The project is born. In this initial design phase, children's ideas are quickly translated into drawings to illustrate the profusion of ideas. The adults hypothesize which of the subjects raised by the children have the potential of strong interests to follow. As the adults listen and converse with the children, they help them structure the theme of the project and plan first steps in meeting their objectives which then will lead to further meetings to refine the design.

As Malaguzzi explains in his answer to what makes a good project, there are two elements that come together in the design phase: the initial observation of ideas that "warm up" the children, and the adults' awareness of what could be done. First drawings and graphic representations of the ideas become the first blueprints for subsequent activities.

Documentation in a Reggio Project

A Reggio project is carefully observed and documented. Teachers record the children's discussions with a tape recorder and written notes, as well as cameras and/or video cameras to record the visual images. All the teachers, along with the atelierista and the pedagogista, will discuss and analyze the process of learning using the documentation. Parents also are involved in the discussion. As children revisit their own documentation, using their work to discuss their insights and frame their questions, the design is refined and the discourse deepens.

In the amusement park project, the teachers plan several field trips to take small groups of children to explore the real fountains in the city. Both children and adults take photos, and children sketch what they see and report all their explorations back to their classmates. The conversation continues of fountains the children have seen, their appearance, and functions. They explain their drawings to one another, raising questions with each other that trigger revisions. From these first representations of fountains, children begin to form their preliminary sketches into versions made of clay, often a daunting task when the children want to reproduce delicate statues, multiple sprays, and sources for the water to come out. Each step is carefully documented so that children can be assisted in remembering their original ideas, and helped to formulate new questions and theories.

How do the fountains work? The original photos and drawings are revisited to form theories to answer this question. Amelia Gambetti, the project teacher, sits with children and encourages them to explain their ideas to her, challenging them to consider the inconsistencies in their answers and encouraging them to discuss their ideas with other children. The teachers assist the children in using the photos and acetate overlays to draw their own theories of how water flows through the pipes to make them work. A slide of the photo of the fountain is projected on a Plexiglas easel so that children can draw the inner workings of the fountain. The documentation offers opportunities for observation and rethinking, adults and children working together. The documentation also helps teachers decide which steps might be most fruitful next. The curriculum is emerging through the analysis of the project.

In the case of the amusement park project, the next step was to create an elaborate waterworks with taps, pipes, waterwheels, and inclines that allowed the children to play and work with water, and to verify their ideas about the movement of water. Gradually, practical knowledge was translated into more representational knowledge as children constructed their own understandings. The documentation panels are part of the legacy of the project, representing the layers of experience through children's words, drawings, and photos that allow participants and observers to return to their own experience both during the process and afterward.

Discourse in a Reggio Project

Discourse is the communication that occurs when children work and think together, as they reconcile different experiences and ideas, as they negotiate and argue, and as they frame new questions and theories all supported by their teachers. Malaguzzi said that one of the "what to do's" of teachers is "to help children recognize the enrichment that comes from the negotiation of ideas and actions, to see the value of sharing and changing points of view, the growth in organizational abilities, knowledge, and linguistic and communication skills" (Malaguzzi, 1995, p. 20).

The videotape record of this project shows how the activities of the project allowed children to have genuine discourse. There are occasions when children, as they explain their drawings or theories to others, correct their own ideas when they hear their own words. There are times when teachers repeat children's words back to them, hoping they will catch the inconsistencies, and probing them more deeply when they do not: "How can this be? I don't understand." There are long discussions recorded as children are encouraged to discuss their work with their friends, and to ask questions of one another, what George Forman refers to as "the pleasure of exchanging ideas." These are not heated or defensive exchanges, merely interested. And then there is the memorable exchange between Simone and Giorgia when they are figuring the numbers of wires for Giorgia's clay sculpture in two different ways.

"No, no, no, do not count this way."

"Please do not shout."

"You are making a mistake."

"I did three."—"I don't understand."—"Wait a second." (In this exchange, both children are talking at once.)

"You should have explained to me before."

"I explained it a hundred times."

Giovanni, the atelieriste, waits with interest as the children continue the exchange, then moves in to help further the discourse: "What is the problem?" And after each child has explained the individual point of view, he concludes: "So you all agree, right?" This is discourse at its best, with new abilities to express oneself, probe for meaning, and develop understandings as a result. The adult in the discourse is developing understanding as well.

> Discourse connotes a deep desire to understand each other's words . . . Discourse connotes a more reflective study of what is being said, a struggle to understand, where speakers constructively confront each, experience conflict, and seek footing in a constant shift of perspectives (Forman & Fyfe, 1998, p. 241).

Through such discourse, adults can frame the course for a curriculum project. Through such discourse, children integrate the ideas of other children and grow in understanding. This is co-construction at work. This extended project, and other Reggio projects, demonstrate the three aspects of negotiated curriculum.

A REGGIO-INSPIRED PROJECT ON BRIDGES

One spring, teachers Chava Rubenson and Pat Breen, and children at the Vancouver Child Study Center, began an investigation about the building of bridges that carried on until school closed for the summer holidays at the end of June. Since school began in September, the teachers had observed that both the morning and afternoon groups of children seemed particularly interested in the construction materials in the classroom. Many of the children spent much of their free play time building in the block area or using the small blocks set out on tables in the room. Earlier in the year, the morning group had built the houses for The Three Little Pigs project (described in Chapter 5). The afternoon group also had shown a strong interest in construction. Previously, they had built swimming pools, the first one out of Styrofoam and other recycled material, and the second out of clay bricks. In both groups, the children's interest in construction continued to grow as the year progressed. One day, a teacher read the story "The Three Billy Goats Gruff" during circle time. Later, the teachers observed the children building

Figure 7–3.   The first bridges the children made using blocks.

bridges in the block corner. The teachers decided to see whether the children would be interested in an in-depth investigation of building bridges.

The first step in the process (the design phase) was to find out what the children already knew about the subject. The teachers encouraged the children to draw their ideas and make pictures of bridges with shapes cut out of construction paper and popsicle sticks of various sizes and widths. From these representations, the teachers were able to see what the children's present level of understanding was of bridges and how they were built. From their initial explorations with the children, they found the following misconceptions.

- Some children thought that bridges are built along the side of a river.
- There was misunderstanding of how traffic gets up onto the bridge deck. Some of the children had not realized the significance of having a ramp leading onto the bridge.
- None of the children had much understanding about the different supports a bridge needs to span a wide expanse of river.

Once they identified these misconceptions and gaps in knowledge, the teachers planned activities that would enable the children to further their understanding of bridges. The teachers decided that they would use written observations, anecdotal records, and photographs to document the learning experiences as they unfolded. Once the preliminary work was complete and the teachers had discussed the possibilities of doing a project on building bridges, they and the children embarked on a journey of investigation together.

The teachers encouraged the children's interest in building bridges in the block corner by setting out the animal characters on the carpet in front of the blocks. The carpet on which the children played had a pattern on it of roads and a river. The teachers placed a truck loaded with small blocks on the carpet as a provocation. A few children began to build bridges across the river on the carpet and hop the toy animals over them.

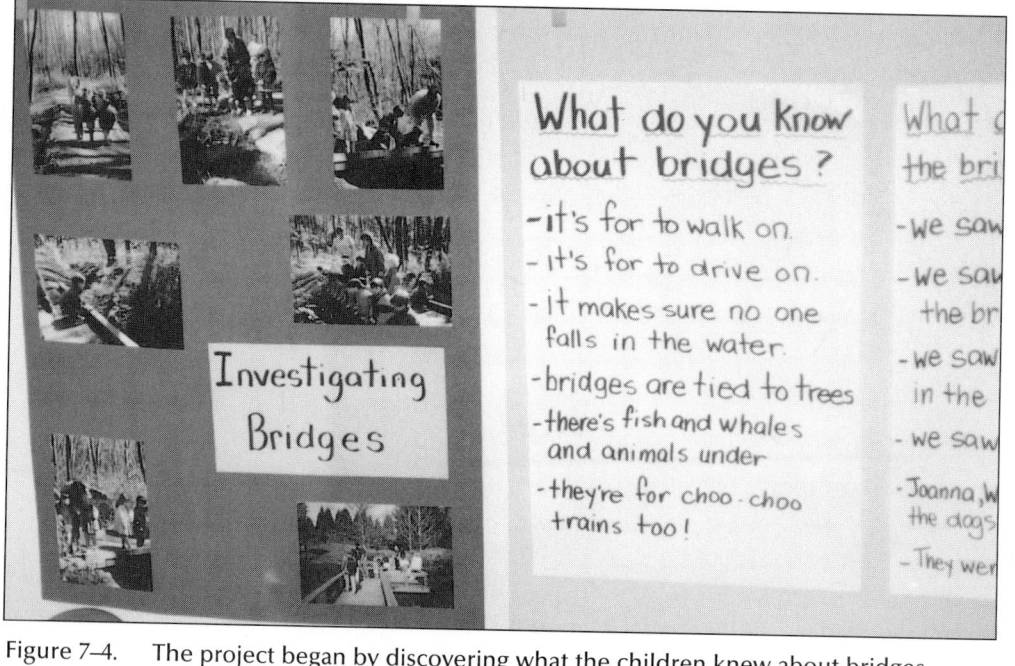

Figure 7–4. The project began by discovering what the children knew about bridges.

Figure 7–5.   Bridges have railings.

The teachers decided to take the children on a walk through the forest that surrounds the school to look for bridges. One child, when coming to a small bridge across a stream, shouted, "Look, Gloria, a bridge!" The children used a variety of materials such as felt pens, construction paper, and popsicle sticks to represent their understanding of bridges. The teachers arranged a field trip to Van Dusen Gardens to show the children the many different kinds of bridges that had been built there. A newsletter went out to the parents asking them to take their children to visit a local bridge and to draw the children's attention to bridges when they crossed them while out driving or walking. Vancouver is situated at the mouth of a river that has many bridges. Many of the children crossed at least one big bridge every day as they traveled with their parents around the city. The teachers visited the library and brought back a selection of books about bridges which they displayed prominently in the classroom. At circle time a few days later, the teachers, wanting to discover how much knowledge the children had of bridges, asked them to tell the group what they had learned about bridges.

Noah: Bridges have railings because we don't want to fall off in the water.

Aaron: Some bridges wiggle like floating bridges; they are broken.

Julie: A car is sometimes like a bridge.

Sally: Some bridges are made of stones and bricks.

Douglas: Some bridges are strong and some are not strong. You don't want to go in the water—that is why we need a bridge.

Teacher: What do people who build bridges do before they start building the bridge?

Aaron: They need to think.

Patrick: They need a barge.

Teacher: Yes, you need a barge to take out the supplies.

The children seemed particularly interested in the topic so the teachers gave them glue, pieces of wood, rocks, and clay, and encouraged them to build bridges. The children began by building arches. The documentation of this stage showed that the children were struggling with the problem of getting the supports for the arches of the bridge to stay upright. Note how Pat, one of the teachers in the afternoon group, was able to scaffold the children's efforts:

> Pat: Is it sticking? Maybe you could count to ten. Now what about the other side? We don't want it to fall over on the other side.

At this stage, the children did not think about creating ramps at either side of the bridge.

The teachers met to discuss which materials would help the children develop their notions of bridge construction further. They decided to paint a blue river with narrow and wide sections on a large sheet of plywood and to challenge the children to build a bridge across the river.

> They introduced the river to the group during circle and asked the children to suggest how to build a bridge across the river.
>
> Pat: What have we here?
>
> Children: A river. Yes, let's call it the Beautiful Blue River.
>
> Aaron: I know we are going to build bridges.
>
> Pat: Yes, let's pretend we are bridge builders and we must decide where we should build a bridge across a river.

Figure 7–6.   Working together to design a river crossing.

Many children scramble to point out a place where they could build a bridge.

> Pat: Just a minute. Let's cut a piece of ribbon to cross the river. Gillian, show us where you would build a bridge.
>
> Gillian: Across here. (She points out the spot.)
>
> Pat: Think carefully about where would be the best place to cross the river. (Aaron points out a narrow place in the river.)
>
> Pat: Why did you choose that spot, Aaron?
>
> Aaron: Because it wouldn't take as much.
>
> Pat: You mean it wouldn't take as many materials. Why?
>
> Aaron: Because it is smaller.
>
> Pat: Yes, it is a smaller distance. See, the river is narrower here and broad over here.

The teachers handed out pieces of string of various lengths and asked the children to estimate the width of the river and choose a piece of string that would be long enough to cross the river. The teachers put out small colored blocks and Kapla blocks beside the painted river, and six children remained after circle time to construct bridges with the blocks.

The next day at circle time, Pat and Chava again placed the plywood sheet in the center of the circle.

Pat: I remember yesterday that many of you used blocks to build across the river.

Chava: What do real engineers use to build a bridge?

Aaron: Stone. Only stone is strong enough.

Chava: Yes, bricks and metal too.

Pat: We also have to make mortar. Now we are going to take our beautiful blue river and experiment to make bridges—a footbridge . . .

Chava, adding to the list: A truck bridge, a man bridge or a bicycle bridge.

Chava and Pat placed the painted river on the plywood sheet on the floor and set out wood, string, toilet paper rolls, rocks, tongue depressors, and clay nearby. Many of the children began by constructing an arch out of three pieces of wood. They had trouble stabilizing the structure; on setting it upright, the arch swayed back and forth. Douglas sang "London Bridge Is Falling Down" as he watched Sally's arch collapse.

Chava: This is not an easy task. You will have to make your bridge so it doesn't fall down. Sometimes bridges have a support in the middle of the river and boats can go on either side. Is this the only material we have, or are there other things we could use?

Sally then began to build a pillar to support the bridge in the middle of the river.

Pat, emphasizing the need for collaboration, encouraged the children to help one another: Work together. Real bridge builders work together.

Douglas, after watching the children's difficulties with the swaying arches, solved the problem by making balls of clay, placing them on top of each other to form two towers on either side of the river, and strengthening them by driving short sticks downward to hold the balls of clay together. He used two tongue depressors as extensions to provide a wider foot for the ball of clay at the bottom of each pillar. He then placed a strip of cardboard between the two towers, pressing the surface down hard onto the clay to make a bridge of the right size to span the width of the river.

Chava, to the children sitting round the plywood sheet: How would you get over this bridge?

Sonja: Maybe an elevator.

Liselotte: Jump. Everyone has to jump.

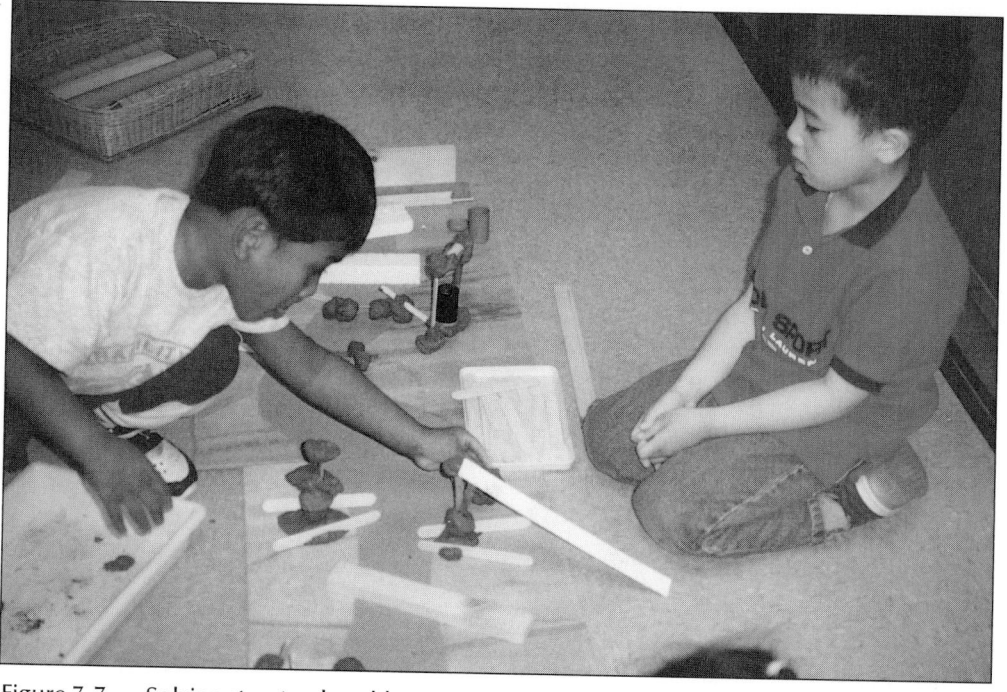

Figure 7–7.   Solving structural problems.

Douglas: I have an idea.

Douglas tried different materials to form the ramp on each side of the bridge deck eventually deciding to use two thin strips of wood at either end. Aaron also made the pillars for his bridge out of balls of clay, but he used two tongue depressors as braces to support them. Julie began by looking at the picture of a suspension bridge in a book propped open on the table. She selected a long, narrow piece of cardboard for the bridge deck and then returned to examine the picture.

Pat: Have you seen a bridge like that?

Julie: You know, the animal bridge.

Pat: You mean animals go over the bridge?

Julie (laughing): No, no, the one with the lion.

Pat: Oh, do you mean the Lions Gate Bridge?

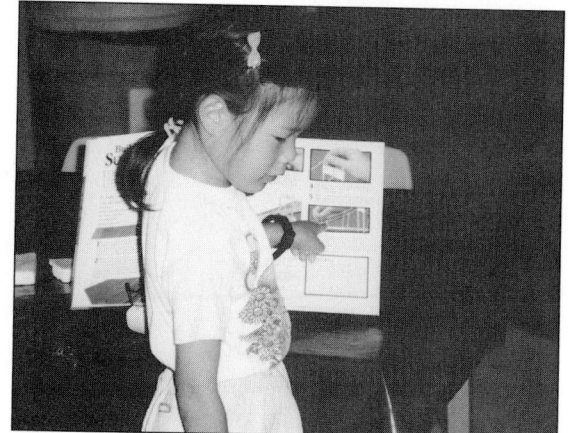

Figure 7–8.   Julie investigating how a suspension bridge is made.

Julie: Yes, yes.

Pat: I see you have a bridge deck. What else do you need for the Lions Gate Bridge?

Julie pointed to the cables in the book.

Pat: Yes, you will need cables. I could get you some string.

She left and returned with string and scissors, and cut off some lengths of string.

Julie placed the deck over the river and contemplated how to tie the string. She returned to look at the book.

Pat: Do you see that the cables are attached to big supports? Let's see what you could use for supports.

Pat looked in a tray of materials and found pieces of wood, rocks, popsicle sticks, and tongue depressors. Julie selected popsicle sticks and began. When she spotted colored popsicle sticks, she exchanged hers for matching pairs. She attempted unsuccessfully to stand popsicle sticks at the end of the bridge.

Pat: Perhaps you could use something to support it, to hold it up. We have rocks, clay, and wood.

Julie selected a ball of clay to hold up the popsicle sticks. In the process she discovered that she had to provide support on both sides. When she finished installing supports at both ends of the bridge, she began to tie string to each end. She examined the

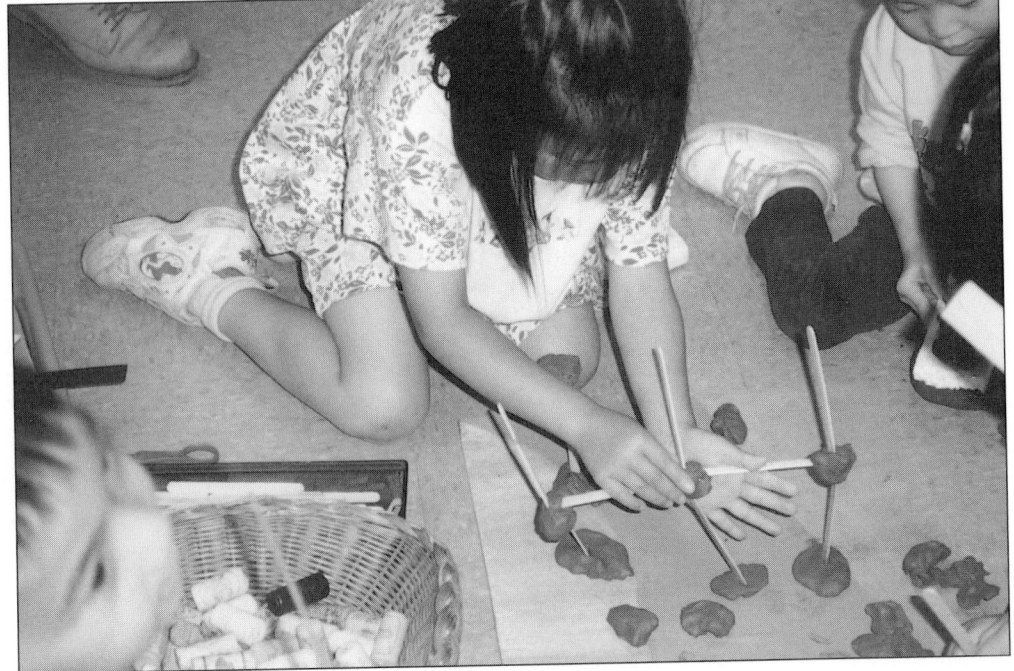

Figure 7–9.   Julie figuring out how to stabilize the structure.

results and looked puzzled. She returned to the book to look at the cables. When she returned she pressed the string down in the middle of the span.

Pat: I wonder how you could hold it down. Perhaps you could try a piece of clay.

Julie: I know.

She cut a piece of string and anchored both string cables in the middle by tying a piece of string around the deck. She smiled at her accomplishment. Pat reminded Julie that the Lions Gate Bridge has two stone statues of lions at one end of the bridge. Julie spent the remaining time making two lions out of clay and installing them at one end of the bridge.

On discussing all the methods the children had used to make a bridge to cross the painted river, the teachers decided that the next day they would encourage the children to work collaboratively in extending Julie's idea of constructing the Lions Gate Bridge. Earlier, the children and teachers had seen an idea for

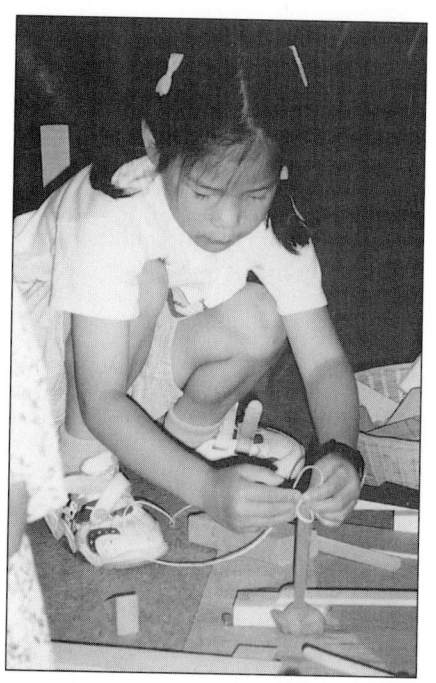

Figure 7–10.   Julie building a suspension bridge.

building a suspension bridge in one of the books on bridges they had borrowed from the library. The teachers worked with the group of children to build a suspension bridge in the classroom by using chairs and sheets of cardboard as in the illustration they had seen in the library book. The group placed two adult-sized chairs back to back and a cardboard deck between the chairs. They tied two ropes to join the backs of the chairs.

Gillian tested the construction's strength by pulling on the rope. The chairs tipped.

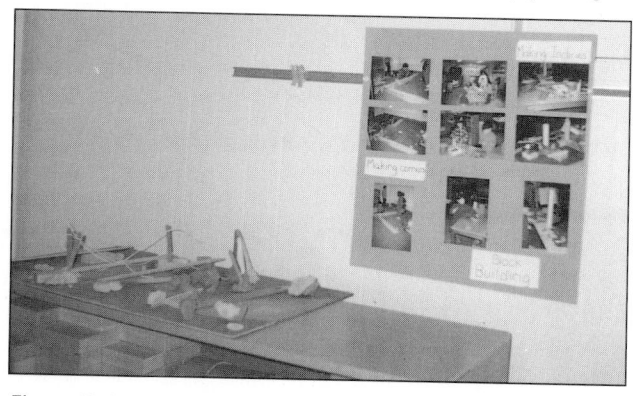

Figure 7–11.   Documentation of the bridge construction

Sally (shouting): Put a brick on the chair!

The chair tipped again.

Aaron: Try two bricks.

The chairs still tipped.

Chava: Here is some more rope.

She tied the rope and pulled it taut. Gillian tested it again, the chair did not tip.

Chava: I would have to sit here and hold it all the time.

Julie: How about putting the brick on it?

Chava: Let's tie it (the brick) to the rope.

They tied another rope at the end of the bridge, and several children went to the other end of the bridge to tie two more ropes to the top of the chair and then anchored the ropes to bricks. The children had difficulty pulling the ropes taut, owing to space restrictions.

Chava: Tell me, is this bridge finished?

Noah: We need to fasten this down. (He points to the bridge deck.)

Douglas: How will the people get up?

Chava: That is a good question.

Cole: You could climb the ropes.

Aaron: But you would FALL OFF!

Noah returned to his concern about the unstable bridge deck: You need more rope.

Chava: What if you put a rope here? (between the cable and bridge deck)

Figure 7–12.   Noah and Gillian helping to build a suspension bridge in the classroom.

Noah: You need a drill to make a hole.

Aaron (wondering how the cars would get up on to the bridge deck): We need some long blocks.

He ran off to fetch them.

When the children drove a car up the ramp and over the bridge deck, the deck sagged in the middle.

Chava: How can we solve this problem?

The children suggested many ways to anchor the bridge deck. For instance, the children built a tower of blocks up from the floor to provide support underneath the bridge deck. They also tried putting blocks on the cardboard, blocking one end of the bridge deck.

Chava: How will cars drive through?

Chava reminded the children of Noah's earlier suggestion of using more rope. Some children tied ropes from the cables joining the backs of the chairs to the bridge deck. The idea evolved that this was indeed the Lions Gate Bridge, and the children ran to find lions to decorate the bridge. The discussions about the real Lions Gate Bridge prompted the children to drive many vehicles across their bridge. When the bridge became busy with traffic, Pat asked the children to suggest how to avoid collisions. They discussed traffic lanes and directions, and a teacher helped the children to make arrows and center lines with tape. Pat reminded the children of the signs used to control traffic on the Lions Gate Bridge. She offered to write a sign for the children to copy. Four children made signs. For some, this was their first attempt at writing words other than their names! The teachers taped their signs to the bridge, and the children made many other signs and taped them to the bridge. (Observations and transcriptions by Pat Breen, Vancouver Child Study Center)

Figure 7–13.   Building a ramp for the bridge.

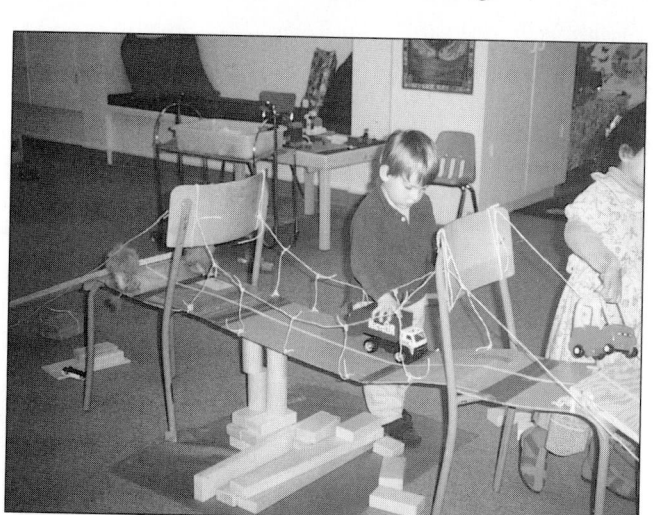

Figure 7–14.   Noah driving his car across the bridge.

Exploration followed for many days with the suspension bridge the children had built in the classroom. The children continued to take walks to visit the bridges that cross the stream that flows through the forest surrounding their school. As spring turned into summer, the weather improved, and the teachers set out construction materials in the large sand area in the playground. The teachers helped the children dig a river which they filled with water. For many days, the children spontaneously built bridges, complete with ramps and reinforced pillars, over their river in the sand.

This project was an attempt by the teachers to implement a negotiated learning approach to curriculum and to carry out a project that was sustained over a long period of time. The teachers tried to incorporate many of the principles they had learned from the educators in Reggio Emilia. They documented the process and dis-

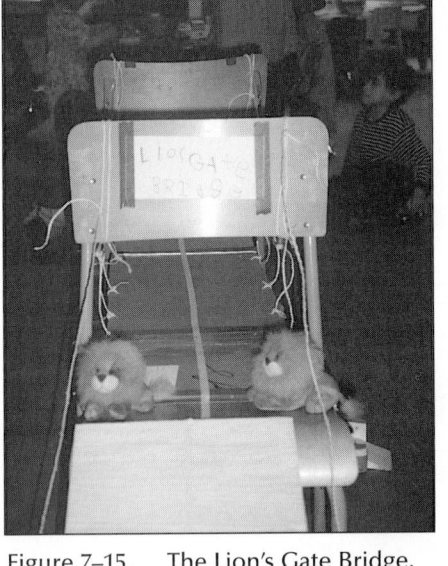

played panels of photographs and observation materials throughout the classroom. The children, teachers, parents, and community collaborated in the project. The children worked as a group in constructing the suspension bridge in the classroom. Parents became involved by taking their children to visit bridges and discussing with them how they were built. An expert from the community brought in interesting materials for the children to use in building bridges over the river they had dug in the sand area of the playground. The teachers encouraged the children at all stages to make symbolic representations of their ideas. It was interesting to see how their drawings developed from simple representations of a square arch at the beginning to more complex drawings, showing their understanding of ramps, buttresses, and supports for the bridge deck of central pillars or cables, suspended from

Figure 7–15.   The Lion's Gate Bridge.

tall towers at either end of the bridge.

On completion of the building of bridges project, the teachers reviewed the observation data and reached the following conclusions:

> With more experience [with the Reggio Emilia approach] there are things we would do differently next time. Perhaps holding discussions with smaller groups would ease the

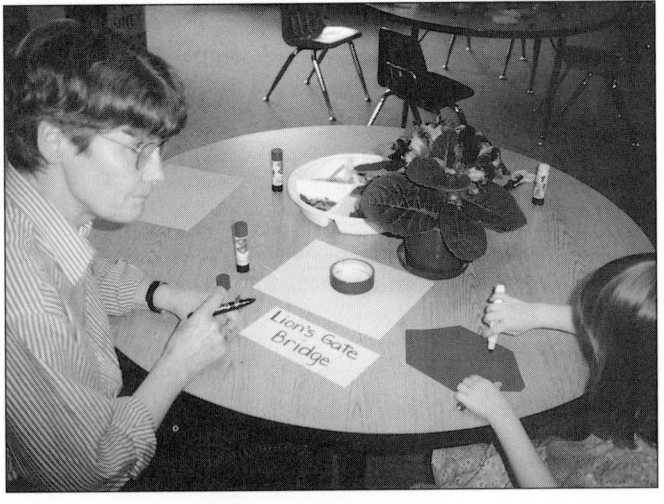

Figure 7–16.   Making traffic Signs.

facilitation and documentation of the discussion since the larger the group, the harder it is to honor each child's contributions, comments, and queries. It would be easier if we had a homogenous age group, as they do in Reggio Emilia. Many of our children also do not speak English as a first language, and this makes it difficult for them to be part of a long discussion. The above documentation does not capture all of the discussion, nor does it represent the totality of the discussion, as "bridges" was a spontaneous topic of conversation throughout the days and weeks of our investigation. It would be better on selected occasions to videotape or audiotape the discussion to complement the written transcription in an effort to be more accurate. We can see, however, that there were times we missed opportunities to encourage the children to expand or extend their thinking. For instance, when Pat asked Gillian to show us where she would build a bridge. Gillian pointed and said, "Across here." We missed the opportunity to ask her why she chose that spot. The

Figure 7–16.   Documentation of the bridge project.

next day, Chava asked, "What do real engineers use to build a bridge?" Aaron answered, "Stone. Only stone is strong enough." Perhaps at this point we should also have asked for other opinions from the children. The reality is you always lose opportunities in an attempt to keep on track when trying to manage 16 or 18 children. One of the difficulties of large group discussions is if you wait too long for an individual child you lose the attention of many of the other children. This reminds us of the need to help children stay focused and get used to discussions. In some instances a teacher may elect to forego an opportunity to continue discussion with several dominant discussion participants in favor of drawing in a younger or more reluctant contributor, even if this means missing the chance to advance the depth of discussion. We are still learning. The bridge project was undertaken early on in our exploration of the Reggio Emilia approach.

CHALLENGES IN NEGOTIATING THE CURRICULUM

There are many challenges in moving to a negotiated learning approach in all early childhood education programs. One of the most important factors is the image of the child held by the teachers. If teachers see children as competent, inventive, and full of ideas, it follows they will value the children's ideas, see the importance of listening to children, and provide them with opportunities and the

materials they need to represent their ideas. Another crucial factor is the establish-
ment of trusting relationships among teachers, children, and their families. Good
relationships are essential in a curriculum that is co-constructed. As the outcome
of a project is unknown initially, it will become apparent only through negotiation
between children, teachers, and other adults along the way. Today, many communities require particular kinds of learning for young children, often assessing children on their mastery of particular skills and cognitive concepts before they are
accepted into educational programs. It is difficult to change thinking when so
much emphasis has been placed on achieving a measurable product. Many may be
anxious when the emphasis is on process rather than product. It will take time for
teachers to be able to assuage the concern about the process, and to help other
adults become comfortable with the many kinds of learning that occur in a negotiated curriculum. A third important factor is communication. For negotiation to
be successful, children and teachers need to be able to carry on discussions and to
understand the importance of listening to one another. They need to know how to
sustain conversation through turn-taking, and asking and answering questions
that enable them to probe deeper into a topic. To help parents and others in the
community become aware of the learning that is occurring, teachers will have to
frame careful explanations and documentation to answer questions and concerns.
As teachers take the initiative to communicate, the depth and meaning of the curriculum will become more apparent. Finally, a negotiated curriculum depends on
"offering contexts that facilitate learning, creating enriching situations, and
helping the children to be the direct agents and constructors of their own learning
processes" (Spaggiari, 1997, p. 10).

Chapter 8

The Investigating Classroom

We see the child as strong, capable, full of resources: how serious the child is in wanting to grow, how strong a researcher, a semioticist, asking "Why am I here?"
—*Carlina Rinaldi*

Questions to Consider:

- What are the ingredients necessary to promote investigation in a preschool classroom?

- What theoretical information do teachers need to help them understand how young children learn?

- How do children construct theories to interpret reality?

- How much emphasis should teachers place on fantasy and reality in the child's investigations?

- What is the role of the environment as a third teacher in the child's search for knowledge?

- What is the role of play in promoting learning?

DISCOVERING THE INVESTIGATING CLASSROOM

Most of us can discern immediately on entering a classroom whether or not it promotes investigation. There are a number of clues, some obvious and some more subtle, that tell a visitor whether children in the room are encouraged to be active agents or passive recipients in their learning. The classroom, in the way the environment is planned, in the materials selected for children to use, and in the work on display, makes a strong statement about what kind of activity is valued in that space. If the visitor sees that there are areas in the classroom that are designed to encourage small groups of children to work together, that there is a wide variety of materials that are easily accessible, and that the materials are of the kind that allow children to transform them, then she knows that she is in an environment where children are encouraged to be active participants in their learning. Environments that encourage investigation are orderly without being rigid, and are free of strict rules forbidding children to take materials from one area and use them somewhere else. In a classroom that encourages investigation, children can carry sand from the sandbox over to the art area and use it with the glue if they have a specific purpose such as determining if sand can add texture to their designs.

Besides having the usual materials of paint, clay, and drawing tools for art, the investigative classroom also has equipment for sand and water exploration, and science equipment including balance scales, magnifying glasses, and tools for measurement. In a classroom that fosters curiosity, many different materials are arranged to provoke an element of surprise. In the preschools in Reggio Emilia, visitors see children using many unusual materials and equipment. The children may use antique brass scales to weigh an assortment of nuts and real fruit. The classroom environment should have about it a quality of expecting the unexpected. This kind of environment draws children and adults in, intrigues them, and sets them off on a journey of investigation. An interesting resource to promote investigations is the science room at First Baptist Kindergarten. The school has a science room and science resource teachers who function much like an atelierista by provoking and sustaining children's explorations of animals and other natural phenomena. With 30 animals in the room, there is nearly always something interesting to watch, feel, explore, measure, or otherwise document.

In a classroom that promotes investigation, the children have many opportunities to engage in the sensory exploration of materials, and to learn about the properties of the materials. Later, they can move beyond sensory experience and use the materials more purposefully as a means of investigation or as a medium to represent their ideas. Carol Anne Wien describes an incident during her visit to Reggio Emilia in which she observed a child's attempts to solve a structural problem using clay. The child struggled "to get his rather large knobbed antennae to stand up in the air, attached." The teacher, noticing his difficulty, scaffolded the child's learning by first providing him with a piece of curved bark to act as a support for the insect's body, and then later helped him find a photograph in a reference book that he used as a guide to accurately position the insect's antennae (Wien, 1997, p. 36). In this example, the child, with assistance from the teacher, achieved two things. He discovered that wet clay has limitations and that unlike a more rigid medium, a thin, cylindrical piece of clay, when placed in an upright position, does not have the strength to support a heavy knob of clay. He also learned, with scaffolding from the teacher, about the body parts of an insect and how they are connected.

The teacher's interactions with the children in the classroom also indicate whether investigation is encouraged. Does the teacher encourage the children to ask questions and embark on a search for answers? Does she model curiosity and excitement in response to the children's ideas and suggestions? Is she resourceful in helping children find ways of furthering their knowledge? Does she encourage children to use a wide variety of materials to represent their ideas and to make visible their thinking? Does she encourage children to share their questions and ideas with other children to support co-construction of knowledge and small group investigations? If the answer to all these questions is yes, then it is probably true that the children in the classroom are encouraged to be active agents in their construction of knowledge.

THE THEORIES BEHIND THE INVESTIGATIVE ENVIRONMENT

Teachers in a classroom that promotes investigation usually take a cognitive developmental approach to learning. They follow Piaget's belief that children construct knowledge through actively exploring the environment. Children between three and six years, who are still in the preoperational stage of development, will bestow magical qualities on phenomena in their environment. Their thinking is transductive, meaning that they draw conclusions based on disconnected observations. They may state that there is snow in their garden but not in their neighbor's because the fence surrounding their yard keeps it in.

By the time children are in kindergarten, they are moving closer to the concrete operational stage and are able to pursue a more logical train of thought. Their thinking is less influenced by immediate perceptions based on sensory information, and they are able to take other perspectives into account. At this stage, they begin to understand volume, size, and area. Children in the concrete operational stage of development are able to consider a number of reasons why snow remains in their yard and not in the neighbor's. They may think about factors such as sun and shade or exposure and sheltered spaces in thinking through the problem. At this stage, they are able to consider more than just one aspect of a situation. They are able to perform simple mental operations such as reversing their thinking in order to reach a more logical conclusion. This development in the thinking of children at the concrete operational stage also enables them to make more accurate, detailed, and realistic representations of their ideas.

In more recent years, teachers have begun to take the theories of Vygotsky into account. They have come to understand how knowledge, in addition to being self-constructed, is also co-constructed with others in the group. Teachers have learned from studying Vygotsky that when children collaborate with others, especially with more knowledgeable or skilled partners, they can increase their level of ability. Vygotsky terms the range of ability between what a child can achieve on his own and what he can achieve when assisted by others the *zone of proximal development*. The understanding that children can achieve a higher level of functioning when given support has heightened awareness of the importance of teacher-child and child-child interaction in the classroom. William E. Doll notes that as we have become more aware of how intelligence is co-constructed, "a sense of community is placed in a new light. More than being merely a pleasant frame in which to work or in keeping with our democratic beliefs, community—with its sense of cooperation and critical judgement—may be essential to meaningful deep learning" (1993, p. 105). He also notes that when people share their ideas, conflicting opinions often arise in the group, but that instead of acting like a road block, the conflict can become a source of energy that enables the group to change direction or find creative solutions to problems. He writes that "we need to realize that much of human learning comes from this interaction—via the conflicts that create the dilemmas which generate growth" (p. 120).

Howard Gardner defines intelligence as "the ability to solve problems or fashion products that are valued in at least one cultural setting" (1983). He has broadened our view of intelligence by identifying the different kinds of intelligences children may possess. Gardner's list of types of intelligence serves "to help us change our sense of what an intelligence is and to help us to recognize the diverse skills that are valued in societies all over the world" (Krechvesky, 1993, p. 8).

The first intelligence Gardner identifies, which he calls *linguistic intelligence,* is an awareness of the structure of language including sounds, grammar, and syntax, and the functions of language including semantics, meaning making, and pragmatics. We find this intelligence in verbal children who enjoy reading and writing, playing with words, and inventing imaginative stories. The second intelligence Gardner calls *logico-mathematical intelligence,* demonstrated by people who have the ability to use logic in their reasoning and who excel in science and mathematics. Young children who are interested in discovering patterns and noticing the relationships between numbers are probably demonstrating this kind of intelligence. *Musical intelligence,* a heightened sensitivity to rhythm, sound, tone, and so on in music, develops early and is often apparent by the age of two or three. *Spatial intelligence* involves "the ability to match patterns, to perceive similarity in rotated forms, and to conceptualize spatial relationships" (Krechevsky, 1993, p. 8). This kind of intelligence is often seen in children who produce complex constructions with three-dimensional materials such as blocks or Legos in preschool. *Bodily-kinesthetic intelligence,* the fifth in Gardner's theory, is the ability to use one's body in effective and creative ways. Children who are observed using their athletic ability to make the fullest use of the playground equipment or moving expressively and rhythmically to music are demonstrating bodily-kinesthetic intelligence. The sixth and seventh intelligences are two personal or social intelligences. *Interpersonal intelligence* involves an understanding of others, and *intrapersonal intelligence* involves an understanding of oneself. The child who demonstrates interpersonal intelligence is particularly sensitive to emotional cues and to the dynamics of the social environment. Children who demonstrate intrapersonal intelligence are in tune with themselves; they know their likes and dislikes and their strengths and weaknesses. In the preschool environment, these are the children who make choices easily and who seem to know instinctively exactly what activities they will enjoy doing. More recently, Gardner has identified an eighth intelligence, *natural intelligence*. This describes the child who seems particularly in tune and sensitive to the natural world.

Krechevsky notes that "everybody who is normal has significant proportions of all of them [the intelligences described above]. But people differ in their particular configurations of intelligences. Furthermore, one never finds an intelligence in isolation. Most roles, tasks and products involve a combination of intelligences." She goes on to say that "the interesting challenge in education is to understand different intellectual profiles and to figure out how to build on them" (1993, p. 8).

PROMOTING INVESTIGATION IN THE CLASSROOM

Teachers who create classrooms that promote investigation have a broad vision of how children learn, accept a wide range of abilities, value the many dimensions of intelligence in children, and provide them with many languages with which to express their ideas. By having a sound understanding of the kind of environment that promotes learning in young children, teachers help them to grow intellectually. They understand that children need many opportunities for acting on materials and transforming them in order to grow intellectually. These teachers know the importance of giving children access to materials so that they can use a variety of media to represent their ideas. They understand how to scaffold children's learning and how to create an environment that encourages children to work with others in the co-construction of knowledge. They ensure that there is enough flexibility in the organization of the room so that children are free to use materials and equipment in creative ways. Most important, they know how to listen to children, and to recognize and support the big ideas that emerge from the children's thoughts about a topic. They then know how to open up an experience by asking questions, helping the children see relationships, expanding on their ideas, extending their thinking, and scaling down the elements to make the project manageable. They understand how to negotiate with children and are sensitive as to when it is appropriate to take the lead and when to follow the children's ideas.

Children are able to build theories about subjects that are of interest to them when teachers encourage them to be active learners, to use a variety of media to represent their thoughts and ideas, and to participate in the co-construction of knowledge with teachers and other children in the classroom. The following example describes the process in which the children, with the support of their teachers at the Vancouver Child Study Center, co-constructed their knowledge of how snails reproduce.

One day in the spring, the teachers and children returned from a walk in the forest with some snails. They kept the snails in a terrarium in the classroom for the next few weeks and examined them each day. Eventually, the children discovered the snails had laid eggs under the leaves at the bottom of the tank. They examined the mass of little white eggs with magnifying glasses and discussed the differences between these and chicken eggs. The following documentation, compiled by the teachers reveals how the children co-constructed a theory about how snails hatch from eggs.

> At meeting time we had a chance to talk some more and reflect about releasing the snails. All of the children knew now that the snail eggs had been discovered in the fish tank. We had put out four different kinds of magnifiers to look at the snails, the eggs, and the cottonwood tree catkins. (The children may have thought the catkins were seedlings.) I wrote out two questions: "What are these?" (next to the catkins) and "The snails have laid eggs. What will happen next?" Some children offered answers during their investigations with me, and others offered answers at meeting time.

> *Stewart:* They will hatch.

> *Godfrey* (who speaks English as a second language): Like a chicken.

> *George:* Baby snails will come out.

> *Paige:* When they crack open, they won't crack open because they don't have beaks. (Paige was recalling a story, *Bluebird Seven,* which we had read earlier in class.)

> *George:* They will use their antennas to hatch out.

> *Spencer:* When they hatch out, we'll have a birthday party to help them grow.

> *Rachael:* Their mother will sit on them to help them hatch.

> *Neilson:* When they have their birthday party, they can go bowling with their eggs.

The teachers realized from this documentation that some of the children were getting confused between how snails and chickens hatched from eggs, and that there were many gaps in the children's knowledge.

Through a similar process, the same children began to build a theory about how bridges are constructed (see Chapter 7). At the beginning of the project, the children thought bridges stood upright because they were tied to trees, and that to get up to the bridge deck, the cars would need to take an elevator (one child said, they could jump "one, two, three!"). The children, through group discussions, opportunities to represent ideas in a wide variety of media, ongoing documentation, and field trips in the community, learned that there are many kinds of bridges and many ways in which they are constructed. Throughout the bridge-building project, the children demonstrated their increasing knowledge of bridges by making more detailed and accurate pictures of bridges including foot bridges, floating bridges, and suspension bridges. During their investiga-

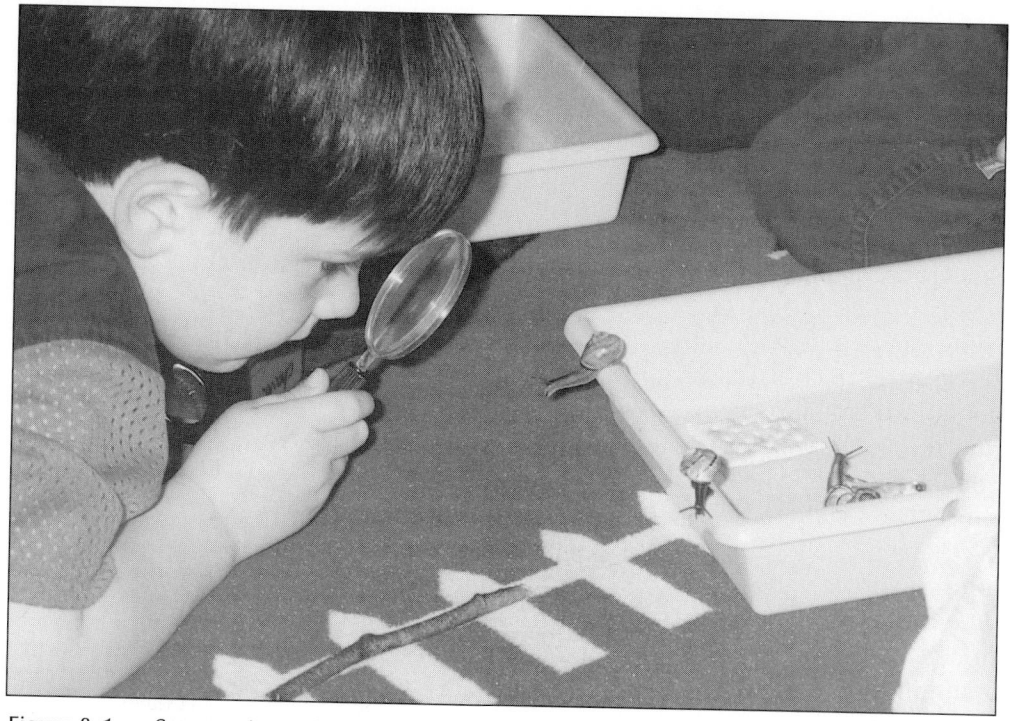

Figure 8–1.   Spencer investigating the snails.

tions, they corrected some of their own misunderstandings about how bridges are constructed.

The children in Pam Oken-Wright's classroom at St. Catherine's School had been involved over time in creating a playground for worms after finding worms in their play yard. The worm playground they created was wonderful with carefully constructed clay swings, monkey bars, snack area, and so forth, all colorfully painted. As the time neared to put the playground out in the yard for the worms, the children developed concern that birds might come and find the worms at play. They decided on two courses of action: one was to create a separate area that would be attractive to birds, and the second was to make signs warning the birds away. The small group working on the playground discussed the issue of whether birds could read, and one suggested that birds could read a sign that said, "Tweet, tweet," though others were dubious. When the children were invited to write a sign that birds could understand, a variety of different ideas appeared. Some of the children wrote musical notes. Another child theorized that birds could read our alphabet if there were dots on the letters, like musical notes; several of the other children accepted this idea as plausible and adopted the technique. Another theory was that birds would understand a variety of languages, including musical notes, letters with dots, cursive (surely a foreign-feeling language to a five-year-old), and pictures. Another child wrote "Prlak" and asked the teacher what she'd written. When Pam told her how the word would sound, she seemed satisfied that the word was not from our language, and wrote "Prlak" all over the page, apparently believing that the criterion for legibility for birds is that it is not in our language.

The children also came up with a variety of messages for the signs: "No Birds Allowed;" "Birds Allowed" on the bird attraction at some distance from the worm playground; and a very mischievous "No Worms Here." The following day, they revisited their ideas. After discussion, they went on to create final plans for the signs, each on her own clipboard, with one child popping up to get a song book to model her musical notes after correct ones. Another child changed her theory about bird language from the idea she had had on the day before, now adding the dots to her letters; Pam commented in her journal entry of the day that this was a good example of co-construction, and the reason they often revisited an idea a few times. The children then collaborated on painting the final signs on pieces of slate with one pair choosing to create a sign that used people language on the left side and the bird language—notes and a picture of what they wanted the birds to do when they read the sign—on the right. Together, the children co-constructed an understanding of how best to protect the worms on their playground, and how to communicate in comprehensible ways.

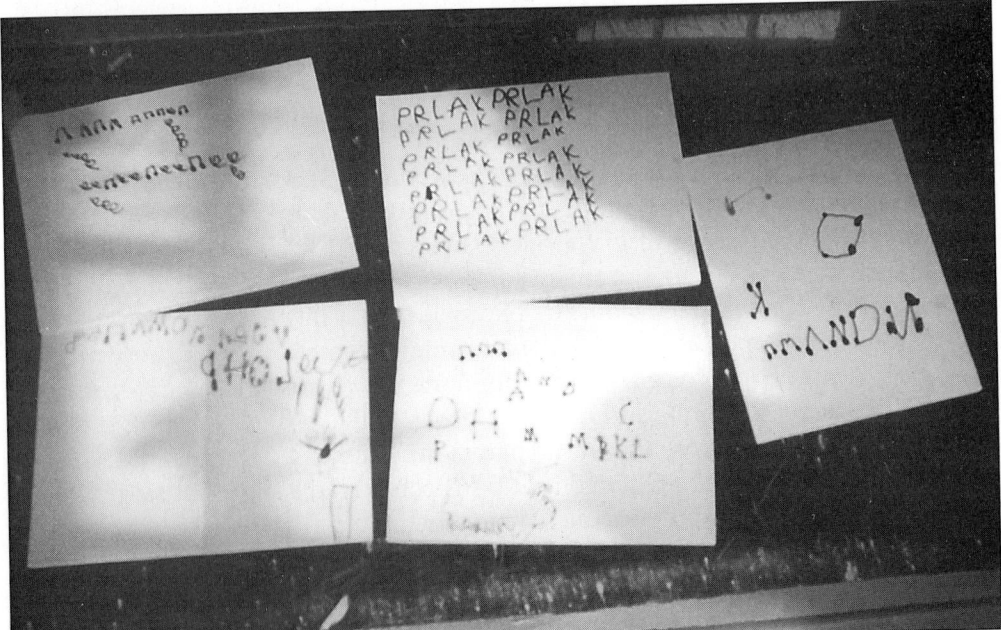

Figure 8–2.   Children involved in the worm playground project created signs to communicate in language that the birds could comprehend. (*Courtesy:* Pam Oken-
Wright, St. Catherine's School.)

In a comment to the Reggio list some months before this experience, Pam had noted that this group of children, new to her classroom this year, had not engaged in conversation before to construct theory, had no particular disposition toward collaboration, and did not engage in extended project work. But she noted their drive for relationship, and it was that drive that formed the foundation for this later group work of investigation. Again, it is important to note the intricate interconnections of the various Reggio principles; relationship, collaboration, and the use of "the hundred languages" in pursuing an emergent curriculum project rich with ideas to investigate.

Howard Gardner writes that "a human intellectual competence must entail a set of skills of problem solving—enabling individuals to *resolve genuine problems or difficulties* that he or she encounters when appropriate, to create an effective product—and must entail the potential for *finding or creating problems*, thereby laying the groundwork for the acquisition of new knowledge" (1983, pp. 60–61).

FANTASY AND REALITY IN THE CURRICULUM

The question arises during a systematic investigation such as the bridges project of whether children are being given enough time and encouragement to use their imagination and engage in the fantasy play typical of preschool children. The importance of play has been the foundation of early childhood education philosophy since Froebel wrote *The Education of Man.* In this book he stated that,

> Play is the purest most spiritual activity of man at this stage, at the same time typical of human life as a whole—of the inner hidden natural life in man and all things. It gives, therefore, joy, freedom, contentment, inner and outer rest, peace with the world. It holds the source of all that is good. A child until physical fatigue forbids will surely be a thorough, determined man, capable of self sacrifice for the promotion of the welfare of himself and others. Is it not the most beautiful expression of child life at this time a playing child, a child wholly absorbed in his play? ([1887] 1974, p. 55)

Some educators like Gretchen Reynolds have wondered what degree of importance the teachers in Reggio Emilia place on the role of play. On a recent study tour in Reggio Emilia, she asked whether the teachers document the children's play. Antonia, the pedagogista in Neruda School replied, "We believe observation is an attitude. That attitude does not regard only projects. It's a way of listening that takes in the whole day. This morning in the playground some things were happening. I make ongoing observations of how the children move in the playground outside." Antonia then described an episode in which a group of children tried to include another child who was having a hard day. She went on to say, "I believe the role of the adult is to make sure children listen to themselves but also listen to others. Because what you observe are children who have been together a short time and need to learn to do this" (Reynolds, 1998, p. 7).

Reynolds inferred from this answer that the educators value "relationship, dialog, exchange, and communication" in play. She went on to say that Antonia

> watches play carefully, she reflects on its meaning so that she can understand the children's motivation and she tells stories to explain it to others. As the children's teacher, Antonia is in a relationship with them. Over the year a shared understanding has developed among them. From this particular place of understanding, Antonia knows her role as teacher—to observe, give comfort and coach when necessary, and to remain in the background of the play. As they learn to understand and support each other, solidarity and a strong sense of community develops among the children (1998, p. 7).

As we think about Froebel's belief in the value of play and his view that a child in play is "capable of self sacrifice for the promotion of the welfare of himself and others," we can match these ideas to those of the educators in Reggio Emilia, especially in the importance they place on reciprocity and relationship in the play of young children, and in the role of the teacher in children's play. Whereas educators in other parts of the world stress the principle of learning through play, the educators in Reggio Emilia emphasize learning through the relationships that are promoted through play. The teachers in Reggio Emilia do not worry so much about finding a balance between fantasy and systematic investigation in preschool programs. Instead, they concentrate on fostering and valuing the relationships that children have with teachers and other children as they play and as they investigate their world. The relationship between children and teachers becomes more equal as teachers become partners in both the play and the children's investigations. When a partnership develops between children and teachers, the teacher's agenda disappears and the children are free to follow a more natural path that may alternate between systematic investigation and imaginative play. Children are then able to use their imaginations, express their ideas, and move through periods in which their thoughts are more influenced by "magic" than by logic. Gradually, with the scaffolding of adults and other

Figure 8–3.   Des, the veterinarian.

children, they begin to refine their theories and ground their ideas in reality as they try to figure out how the world works.

The children in the Quadra Island center experienced this process after visiting the local veterinarian's office. In the days that followed, the teachers set up an animal hospital in the classroom, with a desk, laboratory equipment, toy animals, and cages. The following documentation of the children's play and conversation indicated to the teachers the children's level of understanding, as well as gaps in their knowledge of what happens to animals at the vet's office.

Dee (the teacher): Do you know what is wrong with that puppy? We have an injured puppy.

Grant: It is bleeding everywhere.

Des: O.K. I have an idea. There are things you take pictures. I am just trying to put it . . .

(He puts the animal in a box that he was pretending was an X-ray machine.) I think his heart wasn't working very well . . . special thing stuck on here and water will make it go down. We have got special medicine. (Des brings medicine over and injects it into the toy animal.) A small piece of dirt that got in his mouth. See you next time.

(Des sits at the desk, looking at a magazine about animals. He asks the teacher to put a mask on his mouth.)

Barb (teacher): What would a vet use a mask for?

Des: To stop germs getting in mouth. (He takes off the mask.) . . . I will check his blood. (He presses a syringe against the dog's body and pretends to put blood in a bottle, which he places on a tray.) I'm checking for germs. . . . We have to get that kitty into the dishwasher. I guess you can lift her up.

Barb: How will she like that?

Des: We have to put her asleep for a long time because we have to do things that hurt a lot. We have to put blankets on her so she stays asleep.

(Susan Fraser, Quadra Island Day Care)

The teachers read through the documentation later and were surprised at how much Des had learned from his visit to the vet. They discovered that he had learned many details about the procedure a vet follows in the course of his day's work. Des showed from his conversation that he understood why the vet followed certain procedures such as taking an X-ray, putting a mask over his mouth, and taking a blood sample. The teachers also analyzed their interactions. They noted the initial provocation the teacher made when she entered the play by asking the children, "Do you know what is wrong with that puppy?" They noted that she was successful in engaging the children with the materials. They discussed whether the questions they asked were open-ended and furthered the children's understanding. They pondered whether the question about the mask was appropriate, wondering whether it furthered the children's play or interrupted their thinking. They noted how Des demonstrated his concern for the animals and how the teachers supported his empathetic responses with questions that helped the children reflect on their actions, such as, "How will she like that?" The play continued for over three weeks. A documentation panel at the entrance to the center kept the parents informed about the children's growing understanding and co-construction of knowledge of a veterinarian's role in caring for animals.

A classroom that fosters investigation provides children with materials to explore the physical, social, and natural world and helps them build theories on topics of interest to them. It is an environment in which teachers view the child as competent, inventive, and full of ideas. It is a classroom in which teachers focus on the children's strengths instead of on their needs, and use the kind of language that fosters investigation.

The Thinking Big Project

An extended investigation by the children in the preschool classroom of Ann Pelo and Sarah Felstiner began with play centered around building tall structures. The teachers believe that the theme of the play was so central to the issues that four-year-olds are working on developmentally that the investigation lasted for many months and came to involve all the children in the class.

The story began in the block area where the teachers noticed the children involved in building really tall structures. The structures were not particular buildings such as castles or office buildings. The children just seemed to be building to reach as high as they could, using all available materials. Height was the essence. The children stacked cubes to reach even higher, and used a small step stool. Initially, the teachers had to do some collaborative rethinking about typical preschool classroom restrictions on building higher than shoulders or climbing on objects to get higher. They also had to change the physical environment to allow building on such a grand scale. But as they observed, they came to trust the children's abilities and skills, and to see how important this building was to them. The children were so intent on being able to reach ever higher they suggested getting a taller step stool. Responding to this interest, the teachers took the children to the local hardware store where children seriously and carefully tested out the various options and selected a stool to assist their height work. Their daily goals were to "build something to the lights or the ceiling."

During this time, Ann and Sarah listened carefully, taking a lot of notes, to try to discover the theme of the children's play, what the play was about.

"I'm the highest, I'm the king."

"I'm as high as the light."

"I'm taller than anyone."

"If this falls, it will bump this one. It will all come down."

"I'm in the crow's nest. I can see pirates ahead and treasure."

"I can see the moon; I can see the stars."

The teachers decided the emerging themes were about changing perspectives and being powerful. They paid attention to what the children were building and how they were building, and by really listening, the teachers came to see why the children were building as tall as they could.

Next, the teachers began to see more representational building, a shift from the earlier work. They created a bulletin board display with pictures of tall buildings from Seattle where the school is located. Then they added pictures of the children themselves, building tall towers. Taking the provocation, the children built a cityscape right underneath the pictures of the tall buildings. Another teacher addition was a mirrored platform on which to build. As the children built on the mirror, the buildings almost doubled in height. The children's comments noticed this unusual new perspective.

"It seems like it's getting lower to the ceiling."

"It's going to touch the ceiling inside that mirror."

"We're building on the bottom."

"Upside down and not upside down."

Ann and Sarah were intrigued at uncovering this strong interest of the children. They began to use their weekly naptime meeting to talk about their notes and other documentation for the "height project" as they had begun to call it. They were trying to decide where to go with the children from there in the investigation. It was at this point that they hypothesized that a possible next path might be birds, so they brought in branches, nests, and little bird figures. But continued careful attention to the play convinced them that this was not the direction to pursue. The teachers believed that the children's recorded words made it clear that the play was still about being tall, being up high.

"I'm pretending I'm standing on these big long branches."

"Let's tie things up high in the tree—we'll need the step stool."

"Look at me; I'm taller than the tree."

Apparently, the most important thing about birds was they could get to the tops of trees. The children were still interested in being up high and building tall things; the teachers decided to continue to support the height work.

They brought in a book with pictures of tall buildings. The favorite was the Empire State Building which the children called the "United States Building."

One of the children knew that it was the tallest building in the world and, as Ann says, "It became an icon for all the tall buildings." The children continued to build tall, with blocks, No Ends®, unifix cubes, and their own bodies. They made and measured long rows of unifix, wondering if it would stretch from floor to ceiling. When it was lifted up carefully, it did! Ann says, "Math work with a meaningful context."

The teachers decided it was time to extend the investigation into the community. They arranged to visit a water tower in a nearby city park. They arrived early and wandered around, looking up at the tower, imagining how to get up to the top. Some children suggested climbing on each other's shoulders or bringing a rope. Mostly, they wondered how the tower got built so high. The teachers invited the children to draw with pencil on their clipboards; they commented that this was their first attempt at asking the children to draw at teacher request. Their sketches indicated that the children were at very different places in developing representational skills. The teachers' roles were to help the children really look at the water tower and notice particular aspects. Many of the drawings showed the details that had been discussed.

The tower gave them a rigorous climb, and the children counted all 107 steps. From the top, the children could look out and see the Space Needle, a Seattle landmark. This gave the children a new dimension to draw: what could be seen from the tower. Back at school, the teachers invited the children to join groups of three or four to draw on a poster-sized paper. This experience gave opportunities for co-construction as children had very different perspectives on the tower. Some were more experienced with drawing whereas others were just learning how to represent their ideas. (Ann comments that this was a time they were pleased to have the quiet of the separate studio space they had created so that children could really concentrate on their work.) The children first compared their drawings and noticed the differences. Then they planned together to create a poster that would include all the important details. Being inside the tower had helped. As they drew, the children were able to change scale and represent height, and to show what they had seen from the water tower. The children's conversation was about how powerful they had felt up so high and how different things looked. The drawings were posted on the wall so the classroom was surrounded by images of the water tower.

The photos from the trip were developed quickly and brought to the class meeting. The children told and retold stories about the trip. The photos helped spark their memories, their language, and their understanding.

"The tower looks like a big bagel."

"It wasn't as tall as I thought it would be."

"We couldn't get in the door and we tried to climb up—what if we stood on everybody's head—then I could go to the top."

The teachers tried to recreate that conversation, problem-solving with a miniature tower and miniature figures. The children even tried to figure out how to get in using their own bodies. A few days later, Sarah brought some climbing equipment in and put it in the dramatic play area where children pretended to scale mountains and towers. Later, they took the ropes to the park and tried scaling there.

More building continued with No Ends® with children now trying to build the curved water tower itself. The teachers gave them clipboards to draw the recreated tower. One child couldn't resist: he brought the beloved step stool over and climbed the "water tower."

Sarah and Ann planned to give the children more opportunities to revisit and rerepresent their understandings of the water tower. Since the children had made both small and large black and white drawings, the teachers now offered blank paper, their earlier sketches of the water tower, and watercolors, and invited them to paint. Their thinking was that as each child has the opportunity to transfer their concept from one medium to another, they also might make a transformation of their ideas and actually expand their understanding.

Next came another medium for children to use to explore the water tower. The teachers offered clay, and the children began to build the water tower brick by brick. For over a month, a number of children worked in the studio, first making the bricks, and then using the bricks to build the water tower. It was hard, painstaking work, but the children were really motivated. As they built, they compared their sketches and referred to the other drawings like blueprints.

A next teacher decision was that going to see the Space Needle was the next logical step. Many of the children in the class had never been to the top. Ann and Sarah checked with the children whether or not they felt like going up—completely an option—allowing them to reconsider their decision when actually there. They took the elevator up and experienced real height and a different perspective.

"The cars look like toy cars—so small I could pick them up."

"The ferry boat looks long and skinny."

The interest in investigating height, power, and changing perspectives was still strong. The clipboards were again available to document the new understandings.

Ann and Sarah decided on one more opportunity for children to represent their ideas. They provided sugar cubes and glue for children to build tall structures. Some decided to build the Empire State Building and made initial sketches. For some children, it was important that the sugar cube building be as tall as the sketch and taller than all other sugar cube buildings being constructed. They put up a sign "Please don't build your structure taller than ours." And they got a response: "We want to build our tower taller than your Empire State Building. We don't agree with your idea."

The teachers perceived that interest in the investigation was winding down and it was time for the project to end. The perfect ending was provided when a parent invited the class to the building downtown where he worked. It was one of the tallest buildings in Seattle, looking down on both the water tower and the Space Needle. The children's investigation had truly taken their understanding to new heights.

Barb Gerst, a kindergarten teacher in Canada, describes how she has found the Reggio Emilia approach "a wonderful inspiration." She notes that as she became increasingly familiar with the approach, she made fundamental changes in her program:

> I started to work with children as a collaborator. I knew that I had to let go of my previously held view of myself as a director in my environment. I became interested in helping the children deepen their understanding of whales and dolphins, our chosen area of study that fall. My new role as a collaborator allowed me to take on a variety of roles in my classroom that I had not valued before. Sometimes I was a nurturer supporting the children's growth. Other times, I became their partner in learning as we discovered a new fact about dolphins. I became a provocateur, challenging and probing the children to expand their abilities to think critically. (1998, p. 43)

Gerst also began to view her assistant and parent volunteers as collaborators who helped her, in particular, reflect on the children's conversations she had begun to record in the classroom. She recorded the words a child imagined the mother whale called out to prevent her baby from getting lost.

Pamela: They would actually say to each other, "Where are you?"

Pamela: He would answer, "I am in a group!"

Colleen: "I love my baby!"

Tanner: "Come here because I want to show you something!"

Colleen: "See my new calf!"

When Gerst played back the tape of this imaginary conversation, she observed how much greater the level of the children's interest and involvement in the whale project was, and "how much richer and detailed children's large group discussions" became. She concludes by stating that,

> The richness and depth of many conversations that took place during this Reggio-inspired project [on whales and dolphins] will inspire me to consider several ideas when having conversations with young children next year. Most importantly, I will continue to place a high value upon children's thoughts and convey interest in their words through my enthusiasm. I have become aware that meaningful conversations take place in quiet environments away from distractions. Additionally, I have discovered that placing an emphasis upon good listening skills and respect for others' ideas is crucial. I believe that reflections with parents and teachers about types of questions

that may stimulate discussion is valuable. Involving a parent during a conversation is important. A quick summary of the main points in a conversation helps children stay focused and interested in a topic. I have learned that tape recording conversations allows children's ideas to become alive in a classroom. (1998, pp. 47–48)

Gerst discovered that as she began to use ideas learned from the Reggio Emilia approach, the human relationships in the classroom became more equal and collaborative. In particular, the teacher's role changed from that of a director to a partner in the co-construction of knowledge. Communication skills such as listening became critical, but of most interest was the role that imagination played in taking the experience to a deeper level of meaning for the children in the class. Following the lead of the teachers in Reggio Emilia, she saw the value of the coexistence of both fantasy and reality in the children's experience with the whales and dolphins. She did not demonstrate a need to replace fantasy with scientific knowledge as so often happens in classrooms. In the whale and dolphin project, Gerst saw how imagination deepened the level of investigation.

EMBARKING ON AN INVESTIGATION OF PLANTS

Early in the spring, when the first daffodils were blooming in local gardens, the students at Douglas College began an investigation of plants. The inspiration for this investigation came from the segment in the video "The Creative Spirit" which documented the children in Reggio Emilia visiting a poppy field and then expressing in a mural the joy and excitement the experience evoked in them. In the investigation of plants workshop, the goal was to give the students a similar encounter to evoke similar feelings, and to expose the students to specific aspects of the Reggio Emilia approach. The hope was to help them appreciate that art should not be viewed as an isolated activity but as part of a broader experience that includes aesthetic awareness, scientific investigation, and schematic representation. In "The Creative Spirit," the children were encouraged to observe the poppies closely, then to do a series of detailed drawings before they began to paint the mural of them. The children were not learning to draw but drawing to learn, the goal of this student experience. Further, the experience enabled the students to follow an exploration from the initial provocation through to collaborating in the final task, as the children in Reggio Emilia did in expressing their collective ideas in a large mural.

Susan Fraser describes her experience in stimulating college students' investigation of plants:

A few weeks before the investigation of plants workshop, to prepare for the class, I soaked red runner bean seeds overnight and put the seeds on the inside surface of a large glass jar, pressing them firmly in place with layers of wet paper towel. Later, at intervals in the two weeks prior to the first class, I germinated more seeds by covering

Figure 8–4.   Douglas College
               students painting spring
               flowers.

them with wet paper towels on pie plates. I wanted the seeds to be at different stages of germination when we were ready to use them. By the time we began our investigation of plants, some of the seeds in the glass jar had grown into vines and had begun to form bright red flowers. I also picked a few branches of forsythia, quince, cherry, and plum blossoms, which I brought indoors for a few days to force them to be in full bloom for the class. On the day we began our investigation of plants, I arranged bunches of spring flowers—crocus, grape hyacinth, daffodils, and the flowering branches—in vases on each table in the classroom. When the students arrived the room was filled with the scent of the spring flowers and ablaze with color. The unexpected transformation of the classroom into a spring garden acted as a powerful provocation for the students to engage in exploring the plants. After they had time to enjoy the blossoms, I handed out paper and pencils and suggested that they fold and staple the pages together to make a small book. This book would become the documentation of their investigation of plants.

Once the students had constructed their books, I gave each student two beans: a dried bean from an unopened packet of scarlet runner seeds and one of the beans that had begun to germinate. I asked them to compare the seeds and to sketch the beans at different stages in their growth. At this point, I introduced a provocation by asking the students, before they opened up their beans, to draw a sketch of how they thought the inside of the bean would look after it was opened. I suggested that they begin to work together in small groups to share their ideas and keep a documentation of how these ideas changed as they examined one another's sketches and shared information.

Finally, they opened up their bean seeds, all of which were at different stages of germination, and compared what they saw to their previous sketches. I then asked the students to tell the class what they learned from this part of the investigation. Many of them were intrigued by the different patterns they discovered on the outside skin of their beans, others by the difference in size between the dried bean and the germinated seed. Most students were amazed at the complete little bean plant they found growing between the two cotyledons when they opened up the seed. The students then had time to complete their books. They became quite excited by their investigation and were inspired to write imaginative stories or to draw realistic or imaginative pictures of a bean plant, using the bean vines I grew earlier as a model for their sketches. Others wanted to find out more information on the plants in the classroom from the reference books. The students' books, when complete, were put on display in the classroom so we could all enjoy them.

In the second class, I taped large sheets of white paper onto the tables in the class-room. I poured acrylic paint (for painting on plastic surfaces) into glass jars with white paint added to some jars to make the pastel shades of spring blossoms. I also cut sheets of plastic to the same size as the paper on the tables and set them aside for use later. On each table, I provided a bowl of flowers, soft pencils, erasers, a tray of paint in clear glass jars, and brushes of various widths. There were also the vines growing in the glass jars and some dried vines and pods laid out in baskets.

We began the class by watching the section in the video "The Creative Spirit" in which the children in Reggio Emilia visited the poppy field and then made murals of the flowers and insects they saw in the field. The students, inspired by the children's murals, began in groups of three or four to design their own murals. They drew their motifs from their earlier investigation of bean seeds and from the spring flowers dec-orating the room. Once each group was satisfied with their basic outline for the mural, they laid the plastic sheets over the paper and used the design they drew on the paper under the plastic as a guide in painting the mural on the plastic sheet. When the murals were finished, we hung them in the windows in the classroom. The effect of the spring sun shining through the transparent murals was breathtaking. We cre-ated a video and photographic documentation of the experience so that the class could revisit and reflect on the experience. The following examples are from the tran-scription of the students' discussion in the debriefing that followed the second class.

Melanie: The fresh flowers [were a provocation]. I felt it put me in the mood to draw flowers and having the smell of flowers too!

Chelsea: Colors [were a provocation] . . . the variety of colors; we could mix the colors. No stipulation of what you had to do with the colors.

Marsha: I get really involved in the picture I am doing. And I like to pay close atten-tion to details. It was really nice after not having painted for a long time to get kind of sucked into what you are doing and being able to express that in detail.

Kim: I also think too . . . the approach where everyone works as a group—it doesn't put pressure on you to actually have to create something of your own. When you work together, like they say [in Reggio Emilia], you create one big picture, and it is better than one individual's art. So the whole creation of all of us working together makes for such a beautiful result instead of each being individualized.

This experience is an example of how the principles learned from Reggio Emilia have been implemented in the early childhood education program at Douglas College. The principles that were most in evidence in the investigation of plants were aesthetics, collaboration, reciprocity, and the use of natural materials. Aesthetics were important in how the classroom was prepared and in the choice and presentation of the materials. At all stages of the experience, the instructors tried to ensure that students were aware of the underlying value of aesthetics.

Students experienced the principles of collaboration and reciprocity throughout their investigation of the bean seed and in their creation of the spring murals. Reciprocity was evident in the way students shared their knowledge of seeds and plants, and in the way they worked collaboratively in designing and painting the murals. Natural materials were used throughout the experience, especially as a provocation to capture the students' interest and to motivate them to investigate and represent their ideas about plants. This provocation was particularly effective in the spring after a long cold winter.

Baerbel Jaeckel, a teacher from Quadra Island Preschool, came to Douglas College to take part in the investigation of plants workshop. She wanted to try out some of the things students were doing at Douglas College with the children in her preschool. In a documentation panel, she said about the workshop, "I could sense the energy from over there—there was this calmness and this concentration and I could not believe what I saw—how everyone was so involved and the paintings that came out of it were really beautiful—and see how the sun makes the red [shine through the plastic up on the window]." She returned to Quadra Island inspired to try out an investigation of plants with the children in the preschool.

On her return, she provided the children with sunflower seeds to plant in small plastic cups so they could observe the growth of the plants through the clear plastic of the cup. In the next few weeks, each time the children came to school, they examined the plastic cups and noted how the roots were beginning to fill the lower part of the cups with "squiggly white lines." She encouraged the children to represent their ideas verbally, and in drawings and paintings of the seeds as they grew. In group time, the children moved their bodies, stretching their arms and wriggling their fingers to show how their seed was growing into a sunflower. The parents helped the children make a garden by digging and adding compost to a flower bed in the playground so that they could plant some sunflowers outside as well.

When the seeds in the plant pots had grown to be about three inches tall, the children gathered around the table to shake one of the plants out onto a pie plate. They carefully examined the roots, discussed how they were connected to the stem, and speculated on when the flower would appear. Baerbel suggested that the

Figure 8–5.   Observing the germination of sunflower seeds.

children use the Plasticine she had put out on the table to make three-dimensional pictures of their sunflowers in bloom. The pictures that the children made captured many of the details they had observed as the seed grew into a sunflower. They used thin strips of Plasticine for the stem and a few children captured the fragility of the stem by making curves in the Plasticine. They placed the leaves carefully two by two up the stem, exactly as they had seen them on their own plants. Some children rolled fine threads of Plasticine to join to the end of the stem for roots, and placed a cluster of leaves at the tip of the stem to represent the stage of growth their plant had reached. Other children went further and made a flower with a round center and petals radiating outward, just like the sunflower they had seen on the seed packet and like the one that would appear on their plant in a few weeks.

The children's abilities in rendering their ideas in a three-dimensional medium to represent realistically what they had observed and what they predicted would happen to the flower were remarkable. Their achievement reinforced the idea that, in following the Reggio Emilia approach as best as possible without the assistance of an atelierista, children can be encouraged to produce detailed representational art at a much younger age than previously believed possible.

In the fall, when the children returned to school, Baerbel took them outside to examine the sunflowers they had planted in the garden in the spring. She helped the children pick a sunflower head and brought it over to a rug on the grass, where they examined the flower.

Baerbel: How do you get started? You poke your finger inside.

Figure 8–6.   Examining the roots of the sunflowers.

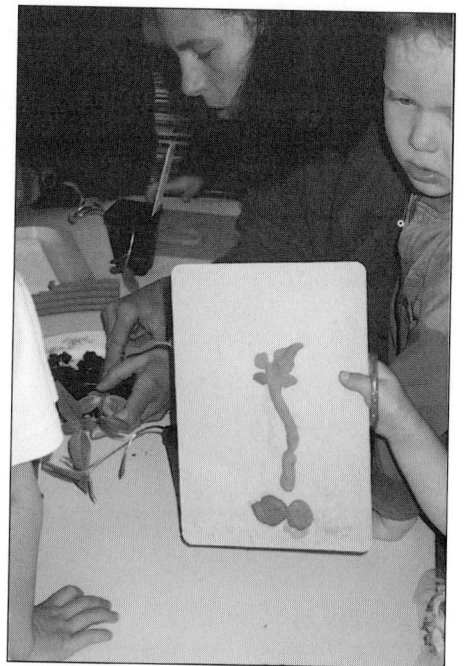

Figure 8–7.   Symbolic representation of sunflowers.

Emma: I just want to get a seed out . . . nothing inside.

Baerbel: I wonder why there are no seeds inside?

John: We could shake them all out.

Kelsey (discovering an insect): Bug! Bug!

Baerbel: That bug needs to live—there is lots of room. . . .

Jamie: We could put seed heads on the blanket and shake it.

Amanda: Mine has one little one and one big one.

Baerbel had brought out a book called *Backyard Sunflower* by Elizabeth King (1993) which she looked at with the children. They recalled how they had planted the sunflower seeds in the spring. Looking at the pictures in the book, they began to compare them with their own experiences with sunflowers.

Emma: It needs earth to grow. It has to have roots, the roots make it stand up, they attach it to the ground. The water goes into the roots and makes it grow. The plant needs water to grow just like people.

Amanda: I took my seeds and my plant home. It grew up 'til it was so big we couldn't touch the seeds. It was growing slow. It had lots of time to grow tall. We were giving it water.

Kelsey (picking out the seeds from the sunflower head): I know! I can plant these then next year I will have lots of seeds.

Baerbel compiled photographs and transcriptions of the conversations in an album to create a documentation of the project, from planting the seeds in the spring to harvesting the heads in the fall. The documentation demonstrated the depth of understanding that the children had developed over the seven months. From the conversation among Emma, Amanda, and Kelsey, it can be seen that in a classroom that supported investigation, the children had built a fairly accurate theory of how a plant goes through the cycle of growth, from seed to plant and back to seed again, from their observations, their actions on real materials, and the books they had read.

FACTORS THAT PROMOTE INVESTIGATION IN THE PRESCHOOL CLASSROOM

Teachers

- see themselves as equal partners in the learning process
- pay attention to the child's thinking instead of feeling responsible for teaching facts or concepts

- encourage children to make their thinking visible, either verbally or by drawing, painting, or using three-dimensional material such as Plasticine or clay

- provide a wide variety of materials that can be used in representing ideas and thoughts

- discover the child's intent and provide help (scaffolding) in realizing these intentions

- keep a trace of the children's experiences in the classroom through documentation

- welcome and learn to expect the unexpected

- slow down and give children the opportunity to explore topics in depth

- extend topics into all curriculum areas such as art, science, math, social studies, and literature

Figure 8–8.   Examining the seed heads.

- identify interesting questions ahead of time to provoke children's thinking
- question, rather than give answers
- model a sense of inquiry and curiosity
- encourage the use of imagination

Materials

- are of good quality, in a wide variety, and easily accessible
- can be used flexibly and in many creative ways
- are arranged in unusual configurations in the classroom so they capture attention and provoke thinking
- are presented and used to reflect the principle of relationship
- are stored and presented to evoke the principle of transparency
- can be transformed by children

Environment as a Third Teacher

- invites investigation
- provokes investigation through the arrangement of materials and equipment

- reflects the principle of aesthetics in the planning of the space
- reflects transparency at many levels
- provides documentation for the purpose of information and as a means of revisiting previous experiences

Chapter 9

Aesthetics
in the Program

There are many remarkable things about the municipal preschools of Reggio Emilia, Italy. What seems most remarkable to me, however, is the educators' deep understanding of the power of materials and of words to shape experience. Alongside this is a respect for the complexity and beauty of the natural world, and for the intelligence and creativity of young children and the adults who work with them.

—*Louise Cadwell*

Questions to Consider:

- What are the underlying values in a program of creative arts that is based on the principles learned from Reggio Emilia?

- What is the role of aesthetics in preparing an environment for creativity?

- How does consideration of aesthetics influence the presentation of art materials in the classroom?

- How does the principle of relationship affect the arts program?

- How important is technique in the creation of art, especially in drawing, painting, and working with clay in a Reggio Emilia-inspired program?

- What is the role of the teacher in the arts program?

- How can the community be effectively involved in a preschool arts program?

A WALK THROUGH THE CLASSROOM

Walking through any preschool classroom, the visitor can see from the art displayed on the walls the kinds of experiences that are provided for children in that environment. The children's artwork indicates whose head and hands have been busy in the room. If there are a dozen or so identical pictures on the wall, the visitor knows immediately that the teacher or parent helpers' hands have probably cut out the shapes, and they have told the children how to use them. When this kind of structured art is on display, there is no indication that the "intelligence and creativity" that Louise Cadwell refers to in the opening quote to this chapter is valued or encouraged in the classroom.

On the other hand, there may be drawings and paintings on display that show the developmental stages children pass through in art. These pictures may be scribbles with random marks zigzagging or circling on the page, illustrating children's work at the earliest stage of development. There may be examples of children's drawings on display at a later stage of development, with well-formed ovals, circles, and lines that become suns and people, the typical shapes found in the drawings of three- and four-year-old children. Some of the children probably will have begun to use symbols to represent objects that the visitor can recognize. Art that shows samples of children's work at different stages of development indicates that the teachers believe in providing children with an unstructured, developmentally appropriate art program, one that allows the children's art development to unfold naturally. A visitor to this classroom will probably see from the art displayed that the children also have had many opportunities to finger paint, manipulate playdough and clay, and use paper, paste, and glue, along with a wide assortment of collage materials. Children in a classroom with teachers who believe in fostering development will have spent much of their time using their senses to explore and learn about colors, shapes, and textures of materials. They will not be expected to create representational art until they are about five or six years old.

The art on display in the classrooms in the municipal preschools in Reggio Emilia is very different from that in either structured or nonstructured art programs in traditional preschools in other parts of the world. Visitors to Reggio Emilia are amazed at the overwhelming beauty of the work the children have created and are challenged by the complexity and high level of maturity apparent in their art. Children in Reggio Emilia produce very detailed, representational work, as in the mural the children painted on large sheets of clear plastic of the poppies and insects they had seen in a field on a visit to a poppy field. Visitors are also amazed at the level of skill needed to create much of the art such as the large clay pieces of the fountains that the children in La Villetta school made for their Amusement Park for Birds, or the intricate wirework that is part of the traveling exhibit "The Hundred Languages of Children."

The skill and complexity of work such as this have led educators from other parts of the world to think about the artwork children produce in their own schools, and perhaps to question whether preschool children should be allowed to be entirely free and creative in their art. Teachers wonder whether they are doing the right thing by standing back and letting the children's art development unfold without adult interference, or whether they should expect children to use skills and art techniques at such a young age.

Teachers who are trying to explore ideas learned from Reggio Emilia become aware of some fundamental differences in the approach to the role of art between traditional thinking and the programs in Reggio Emilia. In Reggio Emilia, art is more than just a curriculum subject. It is one of the essential tools, one of the "hundred languages," that children use to enhance and represent their learning. In

Figure 9–1.   The detailed paintings and wire work seen in Reggio Emilia raise questions about children's creative abilities.

the preschool years, children are continually learning to use language to make sense of the world. Children, when encouraged to use art as a tool for communication, become much more practiced in using it as a means of expression, in much the same way as children become increasingly expert in using language during the preschool years.

George Forman makes an important distinction when he notes that the children in Reggio Emilia "draw to learn as opposed to learn to draw" (Edwards, Gandini, & Forman, 1998, pp. 1–7). In his description of "the intelligence of a puddle," he explains how the children in Diana School put their skills in drawing representational figures to work to learn about the difference between shadows and reflections. The teachers noted that one day after a rainstorm, the children observed that only the upper torso of their bodies was reflected in the water as they approached a puddle in the playground. When children in the preschools in Reggio Emilia notice something that puzzles them, the teachers encourage them to draw their theories about it. In this case, a teacher placed a mirror on the ground and encouraged the children to experiment with their reflections in the mirror. The children began to compare the reflections they had seen earlier in the puddle of water and the images they saw of themselves in the mirror on the ground. The teacher then encouraged the children to draw and cut out figures to place on and around the mirror. The children noted what happened to the image in the mirror when they placed it in different positions and viewed them from different angles. The investigation was carried further by giving the children a flashlight so they could discover the difference between the reflection and the shadow of an object. This project reveals that the educators in Reggio Emilia take a different perspective of the role of art in their program. In Reggio Emilia, art has a broader purpose that goes beyond sensory exploration and self-expression, and becomes a tool for learning, a means of communicating ideas, and one of the "hundred languages" of children.

Children's creative representation in Reggio Emilia, whether drawings, paintings, clay, papier-mâché, or other media, is for the purpose of using *"graphic languages"* (Rinaldi, 1991) . . . "to record and represent their memories, ideas, predictions, hypotheses, observations, feelings, and so forth in their projects" (Katz, 1998, p. 28). Katz suggests that one idea resulting from examining the creative works of children in the Reggio Emilia preschools is that many in North America may have seriously underestimated the representational abilities of young children and the depth of intellectual work the representation may produce.

Ann Pelo describes how thinking about art used in the schools has transformed her understanding of art:

> I used to see art as an important creative process for kids, but was "hands-off" and "anything goes," comfortable with messes and exploration and the sensory aspects of art, but not drawn to offer particular skills or coaching about the use of materials and tools. I still highly value the exploratory, sensory aspects of art, but now weave those aspects together with teaching about how to use a range of media. I do this so that the children are competent and confident with a variety of media (the Reggio idea of "hundred languages"), and able to communicate their theories, understandings, and visions with clay, wire, paint, black pen, etc. I emphasize the idea of representation and re-representation, in in-depth project work, of course, but also in many small moments each day. For example, a couple of kids invented a "catapulter machine" to put away the Kapla blocks a couple of days ago. After they got all the blocks in the Kapla bin, I asked them to create instructions for their machine, so that other kids could build it and use it. I wrote down their verbal description of how to build and use the machine, and then asked them to illustrate each step. This set of instructions is in the Kapla bin now, so that other kids can read it and recreate this machine. This isn't something I would have done before I encountered Reggio; now it's a part of every day life in my classroom.

Early exposure to art media also enables children to create the high-quality art seen in the preschools in Reggio Emilia. Children who have attended the infant–toddler centers will have been given paint, clay, and other art materials to explore before entering preschool. They will have learned a great deal about the possibilities inherent in the many art materials available for use even before they are three years old. This exposure and exploration was termed "learning the vocabulary" of the various representational languages by a teacher at the Sabot School when she described the deliberate attempts to teach two-year-olds techniques of how to explore and use various art media. Many children, therefore, will have passed through the stage of needing to explore the materials in a sensory manner and be ready by the time they enter preschool to learn the skills and techniques for producing more elaborate artworks that represent their ideas and learning.

The high value placed on aesthetic awareness in the preschools in Reggio Emilia also fosters children's artistic abilities. This emphasis reflects the value placed on aesthetics in the Italian culture as a whole. Italian children absorb the beauty of the culture around them when they are out in the community, whether walking with their families and looking at the goods so beautifully displayed in the shop windows or experiencing the stone carvings in the streets and piazzas. When children are taken to visit places such as the poppy fields, or the fountains and sculptures around the city, they are encouraged to notice and experience the aesthetic details that surround them. In the Reggio Emilia preschools, beautiful objects, potted plants, and bowls of flowers are displayed on shelves and tables, and light is everywhere shining through colored strips of plastic or reflected in the many mirrors in the room. The beauty so apparent in the classrooms is designed to inspire children to become more visually aware and motivate them to create beautiful artwork themselves. In turn, the teachers show their appreciation for the quality of the children's work by mounting and displaying their art on the documentation panels on the walls of the classrooms and entrance halls. All this makes a strong statement about the value of aesthetics in the preschools in Reggio Emilia. The children and the parents can see that children's art is valued and respected.

In contrast to typical American practice where parents inquire "Didn't you make me a pretty picture today?" and teachers feel an urgency to make sure children have produced some artwork to take home at the end of the day, at best to decorate the refrigerator briefly, artworks in Reggio Emilia become the basis for discussion, for explanation, and for later revisions. The artwork itself is preserved as a means for deepening understanding and recording the process. Sometimes, works are displayed years after the completion of the project activity of which the art was an integral part. A teacher at First Baptist Kindergarten commented that not taking art home every day represented one of the most fundamental changes they made in their thinking and program, moving art from the realm of creative self-expression to the realms of representing ideas.

The educators in Reggio Emilia have made it a priority to provide the space and resources necessary for a high-quality art program. In each school, an area is set aside as an atelier—studio—filled with art materials and equipment. There are cupboards, ample storage space, and shelves on which materials are attractively displayed and accessible to the children. Large surfaces on tables and easels provide sufficient space for children to work comfortably. Sinks are located nearby for easy clean-up. Children are given many different tools to use in creating their artwork such as high-quality paintbrushes of various widths, lead and colored pencils, felt-tipped pens, chalk, pastels, charcoal pencils, and tools to model clay. Many different colored paints are mixed in glass jars which are set out on trays or carts beside the easels. Paper is available, including transparent papers to use on the light tables, colored tissue, and cellophane paper. The children also are provided with many less common materials such as wire, plaster of Paris, materials from nature, and recycled materials. Clay is provided in abundance, and children work with it using a variety of techniques.

All of these materials are available in the atelier which Loris Malaguzzi described as a

> place where children's different languages could be explored by them and studied by us in a favorable and peaceful atmosphere. We and they could experiment with alternative modalities, techniques, instruments, and materials; explore themes chosen by children or suggested by us; perhaps work on a large fresco in a group; perhaps prepare a poster where one makes a concise statement through words or illustrations. . . . What was important was to help children find their own styles of exchanging with friends both their talents and their discoveries" (Malaguzzi in Edwards et al., 1998, p. 74).

The success of the atelier encouraged the educators in Reggio Emilia to provide mini-ateliers adjacent to each classroom. The mini-atelier provides a space where a smaller group of children can work with a wide assortment of art materials on projects that are less complex than those carried out in the main atelier. Some of the schools also have an outdoor atelier, used in good weather. In the Reggio Emilia preschools, children are given the time and space that allow for careful, uninterrupted work, and the support of an atelierista who has specific training and can help the children interpret their ideas in a variety of art media.

Many American Reggio-inspired schools are envious of the space available in Reggio preschools to dedicate to a studio; resources to hire a teacher designated only for studio work also are beyond most programs. Nevertheless, they recognize the contribution each of these components makes to the quality of children's art experiences and do their best to work with what they have available. Pam Oken-Wright was able to get her school administration to create a glass-walled studio space when she convinced them the window would enhance her ability to supervise children in a large classroom space. Other schools have converted a teacher lounge into a kind of studio that can be used for display, storage of materials, and for teachers to take small groups to work. The Sabot School was able to hire a part-time studio teacher. Attention to organization and display of materials creates the feel of a studio space within the classroom.

The words of Marty Gravett of Sabot School echo the feelings of many American teachers:

> It was the images of the artwork of the children of Reggio Emilia and the exquisite aesthetics of the classrooms and buildings that originally attracted me to these remarkable schools. I already had a personal bias toward the use of art with young children. But what I did not have was the knowledge of how powerfully, how intentionally, children could wield these media. (And I use art in the large sense meaning The Arts.) I did not understand that children, given exploration and scaffolding, could develop the skill to represent their thinking. The fall-out from this thought alone has influenced myriad aspects of the program. We now use the concept of studio-laboratory to set up the environment both inside and out; we consider our own and the children's interests and intelligences (in the Gardner sense) when we stock our environment; we seek artists to educate us on how to use clay and music and other media; we strive to perceive the children's art as a window to their thinking, not as a product; and we delight in framing the children's work with our own reflections and perspectives.

THE REGGIO EMILIA APPROACH TO ART

Principles fundamental to the Reggio Emilia approach such as respect, relationship, collaboration, transparency, reciprocity, and documentation also are apparent in the art activities in the preschools.

Respect

The respect that the Reggio Emilia educators show for children and the image that they hold of the child as rich, strong, and powerful seem to encourage the children to create art beyond what was believed possible in the past. Educators also show respect for children's abilities by giving them materials of the same quality as those an artist would use, and by presenting them in a way that makes them appealing and accessible. The children's artwork is richly documented in panels that describe in great detail the process the children followed.

Relationship

The educators in the preschools in Reggio Emilia have made relationship a basic principle in their approach to art. Art is not considered in isolation but is integrated into the program as part of the "hundred languages" children use to investigate and represent their world. In many preschool programs in other parts of the world, paints, collage materials, playdough, and sometimes clay are available for the children to use each day, but teachers seldom encourage the children to use the materials other than for sensory exploration and self-expression. In the preschools in Reggio Emilia, however, the children use the materials, often in collaboration with other children and teachers for an investigation and communication of ideas.

In the project of the Amusement Park for Birds, for example, the children and the atelieriste, Giovanni Piazza, worked together with clay to create the prototypes for building a waterwheel and fountains for birds. Teachers also provide support, or scaffolding, for children by helping them explore in greater detail the objects they are representing. In The Amusement Park for Birds project, the teachers projected a slide of the angel fountain onto a light panel to enable two children working together to trace the outline of the fountain and make a schematic drawing of their theories about the fountain's inner workings.

Figures 9–2a,b,c,d,e.   Reggio-inspired classrooms display creative materials with aesthetic care and attention, to invite thoughtful use. (*Courtesy:* (a, b, and c) Patti Cruikshank-Schott; (d) Lakewood Avenue Children's School; and (e) Pam Oken-Wright, St. Catherine's School.)

(c)

(d)

(e)

The principle of relationship is also evident in the way art materials are presented in the classroom. For example, teachers set out clay on a table on which they have arranged other natural materials such as wood, rocks, shells, and dried grass. The unexpected arrangement of different materials captures the children's interest and focuses their attention on the aesthetic qualities of texture, form, and color inherent in the objects themselves. Visitors to the Diana School saw the children working with clay on a table on which there were displayed feathers and a bird's nest with a tiny toy bird peeking out of the nest. The teachers placed these materials together, perhaps to provoke the children

Figure 9–3.   The juxtaposition of fresh flowers with art materials creates a provocation to create. (*Courtesy:* Lakewood Avenue Children's School.)

to think about how birds use mud in building their nests or to suggest how the children could use the clay themselves.

Collaboration

Collaboration, essential to all aspects of the Reggio Emilia approach, is also evident in the approach to art. Teachers and children collaborate in developing many of the projects. The teachers discuss ideas for the projects and decide with the help of the atelierista which art media will be appropriate for representing their ideas. Children often work in a group on an art project as they did in creating the large murals of the poppy field mentioned earlier. The space in the classrooms is designed to encourage small groups of children to work together. Easels are wide enough to allow three or four children to paint at the same time on one large sheet of paper.

The creation of the artwork and the explanation of the product to others often generate further creativity as ideas are challenged. In the video "Amusement Park for Birds," viewers see where Andrea explains his waterwheel to others. The waterwheel has been drawn, then constructed in a paper model. As he explains how it works, he comes to understand the error in his logic about how the wheel will move. He corrects himself and transfers his new understanding as he renders the idea in a clay model. The collaboration with others using the artwork as a basis for conversation has deepened his own understanding and enriched his later artwork.

Transparency

The use of light as an art medium is an example of the principle of transparency woven into many aspects of the program. Overhead projectors, light tables, and mirrors allow children to experiment with light, shadow, and reflection. The children often use cellophane and tissue paper in their artwork. Some visitors observed the children in Diana School pressing bunches of different colored tissue paper into wire mesh that had been shaped into balls that were later hung from the ceiling to make a display of the planets and the sun. In La Villetta School, the children arranged objects on an overhead projector within a checkered pattern they had previously drawn on a sheet of acetate. The children experimented with various sizes of objects by placing them on the grid and then observing the pattern they projected onto the wall. One child placed a fern on the grid and arranged the objects around it so that it looked like a Christmas tree when projected. Louise Cadwell relates how Vea Vecchi, the atelierista at Diana School, projected pieces of blue acetate onto the walls to simulate the sky and then made a cloud which the children "blew out of the window" (1997, p. 28). In the video "The Creative Spirit," a slide projected on the classroom wall shows the children dancing among the brilliant red poppies during their visit to the poppy field.

Reciprocity

The relationship that develops between the children and teachers during the three years they spend together in the preschools in Reggio Emilia also helps children create art of such high quality. The trust and respect that develop from this long-term relationship enable the children and teachers to learn from one another, and to share their ideas and skills as they collaborate in creating artwork.

Documentation

The documentation of the process the children follow in doing their artwork enables teachers, children, and visitors to see each step in the development. The teachers and children can revisit each stage of the experience and think about what equipment, materials, and skills they needed to express their ideas, what they could do differently next time, and what they learned from the experience. This process enables the children and teachers to refine their skills and techniques and to gradually build expertise in creating art.

The approach to art and aesthetics in Reggio Emilia is inseparable from consideration of the other ideas about learning. Pam Oken-Wright made the following comments about the influence of aesthetics on a Reggio-inspired classroom:

> Aesthetics in general—in the classroom, but also in the world around—have become so much more central in my life since I began to explore the principles of Reggio Emilia. There is no separation between what you are calling art and all other learning. Media become languages as children learn to use them for expression, communication, and to explore ideas and figure things out. Each time we represent a thing or an idea in a new language, our understanding grows and deepens. This process becomes

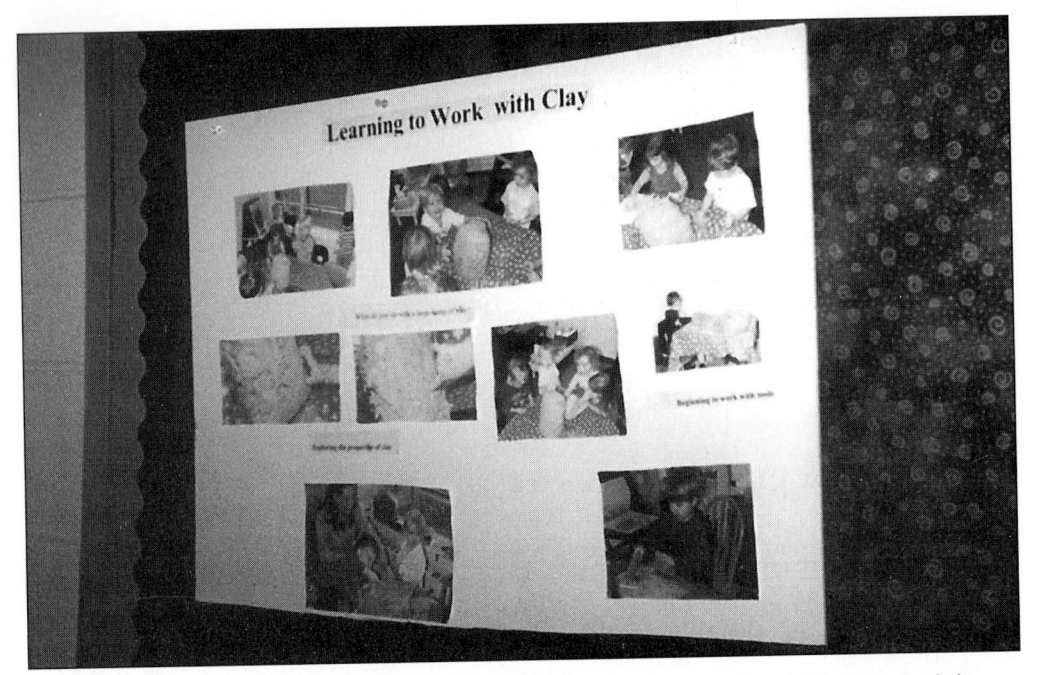

Figure 9–4.   Documentation of the process of using materials helps children and adults revisit the experience. (*Courtesy:* Sabot School.)

central to learning in a Reggio Emilia-inspired classroom. We cannot think of "art" as even a piece of the program, for it is all of one piece. Some things that might change when one makes this shift in thinking: Media are not rotated in and out. Children need time to learn the affordances (George Forman, 1994) of media; only when we know a medium can we use it as a language. If we put watercolor out for a week and put it away for months thereafter, or if we put it out every Monday only, children are not as likely to develop proficiency with the medium, nor is it likely to become a language for them. We also may broaden the palette of media available, making sure to include media for three-dimensional as well as two-dimensional work. Our choice of media to offer may be affected by this larger purpose as well. I choose earthenware clay over playdough for my five-year-old students, because I know that as they come to want to represent complex ideas, clay is more likely to satisfy the children's intent. Also, because of the in depth studies and exquisite observation ability the children develop, we have all, I think, become more aware of the world around us, and of its beauty. Our curriculum is the rainbows that dance on our classroom walls. It is the worm that the children believe keeps presenting itself to them as they dig in the dirt—and the playground they made for it and its friends, and the attraction for birds nearby so that the birds will not bother/eat the worms at the playground. (We heard more about this project in Chapter 8.) It is the intricacies of and relationship with trees arising out of the desire of one child to make a tree in clay. We expected that the children would become more aware of and more connected with the beauty of the world around us. We hadn't expected that we, as teachers, would as well.

PUTTING THE PRINCIPLES
OF AESTHETICS INTO PRACTICE

The teachers in early childhood programs on Quadra Island and in the Vancouver Child Study Center attempted, each in their own way, to implement the principles they learned from the educators in Reggio Emilia in their approach to art. Each program adapted the principles in a unique way and focused on different aspects of art. Although the teachers felt satisfied that they had made some progress in implementing the approach, the teachers all realized that they still had much to learn before being able to provide children with a program that would foster the high standard of creativity seen in the preschools in Reggio Emilia.

Building a Puppet Theater

Early in the fall, the teachers in the Quadra Island program focused on the principle of collaboration. They collaborated within the center and with a local artist. The teachers were interested in exploring ways in which an artist could share skills and scaffold the children's art experiences, and they hoped that this experience would make up in a small way for the lack of an atelierista in their program. They invited Lesley Mathews, a local artist who they knew was comfortable working with children, to the center. She had volunteered a few years before when her own children were enrolled in the program. Lesley was enthusiastic about sharing her skills with the children and agreed to come once a week to participate as she had before.

On her first visit, Lesley brought along a collection of papier-mâché figures and masks she had made. Displayed in the entrance hall at that time was the documentation of a visit the children had made to the Campbell River Museum to see the work of First Nations artists. Lesley also knew that many of the children would have visited the museum on Quadra Island to see the ceremonial regalia, especially the famous transformational masks made by artists of the Kwagtiulth nation who

Figure 9–5.   Learning how to make papier-mâché.

Figure 9–6.   Children's drawings of their ideas for making puppets.

Figure 9–7.   The forms for the
                     puppet heads.

live on the island. She thought that the children might be interested in making masks themselves. Lesley met the children at group time and as a provocation, passed around some masks she had made for the children to try on. After the children examined the masks, she explained how she had made them out of papier-mâché. The children were interested in the masks, but from the teachers' observations it became apparent that they were more interested in how the masks had been made out of papier-mâché than in the masks themselves.

On a later visit Lesley, the teachers, and the children discussed what else they could make out of papier-mâché. The children suggested making puppets and a puppet theater. The teachers brought out paper and pencils, and the children began to draw their ideas on a large sheet of paper.

Once the children had made representational drawings of how they wanted their puppets to look, they began to work on making a structure on which to build the puppet's head. Lesley, the teachers, and the children discussed how they might make a shape on which to build the rounded heads the children had drawn in their sketches. They considered how they might make a shape into

Figure 9–8.   Designing the puppet theater.

a tight ball, twist the free end to fit into a toilet paper roll, and then keep it in place with masking tape. Not all the children used this method to make puppet heads; one child made a snake puppet by using a long, tightly rolled sheet of newspaper as a base for the papier-mâché. The children were then able to apply

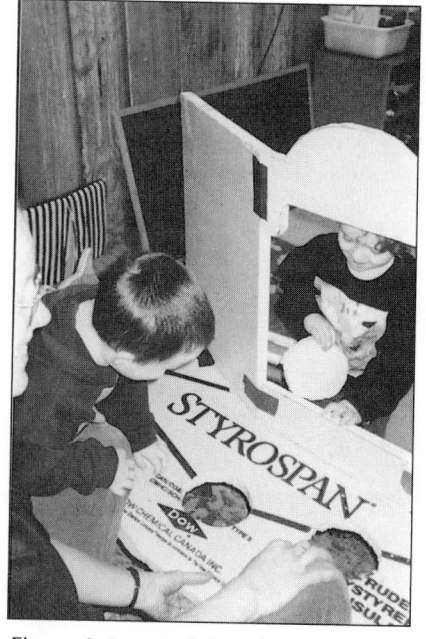

Figure 9–9.   Building the puppet theater.

their skill in using papier-mâché to make puppet heads. Then they placed the puppet heads upright in cottage cheese cartons to dry. The cartons also held the puppets upright so the children could paint them later and add hair, fur, and in one case, an elephant's trunk.

In the meantime, Lesley began to work with a small group of children who were interested in designing and building the puppet theater. Together, they discussed what they needed to construct it and decided on the dimensions. Lesley drew a pattern based on their ideas on a piece of paper. She then helped the children follow the pattern in marking the correct measurements on large sheets of Styrofoam. The children, again with Lesley's help, began to assemble the structure using duct tape to join the upright walls to the base. When the construction of the puppet theater was complete, the children

Figure 9–10.   Plastering the walls.

worked with Lesley to cover the Styrofoam sheets with papier-mâché.

Eventually, when the whole structure was covered and the papier-mâché was dry, the children began to paint the puppet theater. They had a long discussion about how they would paint the walls and decided to use blue, yellow, pink, and green paint. The children painted a large pink crown covered with jewel-like dots in the arch above the window. They covered a section of one wall in a pattern of horizontal pink and yellow stripes that looked like a ladder going up one side of the building. The predominant features were a large star outlined in pink with a solid blue circle in the center, and a bright yellow sun that Lesley painted on the wall opposite the star the children had made. The children then surrounded her sun with dots similar to those on the crown above the window. When the children had finished painting the puppet theater, the bright colors and folk art images resembled paintings on circus structures.

Figure 9–11.   The finished puppet theater.

The puppet theater was placed on a table and a curtain was draped across the front to hide the legs. The collaboration with a local artist, which lasted many months—from October to March—had created a beautiful piece of equipment that they and future generations of children attending the center would use for many years. At the end of the project, the teachers reviewed the photographs they had taken to document the project and felt satisfied that they had successfully implemented at least two of the principles learned from Reggio Emilia. First, they collaborated successfully with an artist in the community who understood how to support children in doing art without taking over too much of the control herself. Lesley demonstrated many of the qualities of an atelierista in Reggio Emilia, knowing intuitively when to follow the children's lead and when to take the lead herself. She was particularly skilled in listening to children, then helping them figure out how to carry out their ideas successfully. She was able to share her skills without imposing expectations that were too high on the children. Second, she and the children had created a beautiful object that demonstrated the value of aesthetic experiences in the education of young children.

Creating a Mural

A beautiful mural decorates the walls of the kitchen entry into Lakewood Avenue Children's School. It is the result of a lengthy collaboration between the preschool class, a kindergarten class from a local public school, and an artist in the community. They had wanted the artist to work on a joint project with the two classrooms, one, for the fun of it, and two, to meet goals of the teachers. The teachers wanted the preschoolers to get some exposure to kindergarten, to prevent being overwhelmed by the transition to "big kids school" the following year. And they wanted the kindergartners, at the bottom of the ladder in their elementary school, to get a little ego boost by being bigger than somebody else. The artist, Joel Bergquist, was hired with grant funds to plan a joint project for the children. He decided the best project would be oil paintings—16 in all because there were 16 children in each class—with each oil painting a joint project between two children, one from each of the two schools. The plan was that on some occasions, the preschool children would travel to the kindergarten to work on their projects, and sometimes the kindergarten children would travel to the preschool. Other times, Joel would carry the canvases back and forth to show each child what the partner had done, and ask the other to take the next step. Before starting the paintings, however, Joel wanted to take some time to get to know both groups of children so he spent about a day a week in both schools, working and playing and doing art with the children in that school.

This was how the mural at Lakewood developed. Joel and the children decided they wanted to do a project together, and jointly decided on the mural in the kitchen. Since the kitchen is the entrance to the school, they felt their parents would

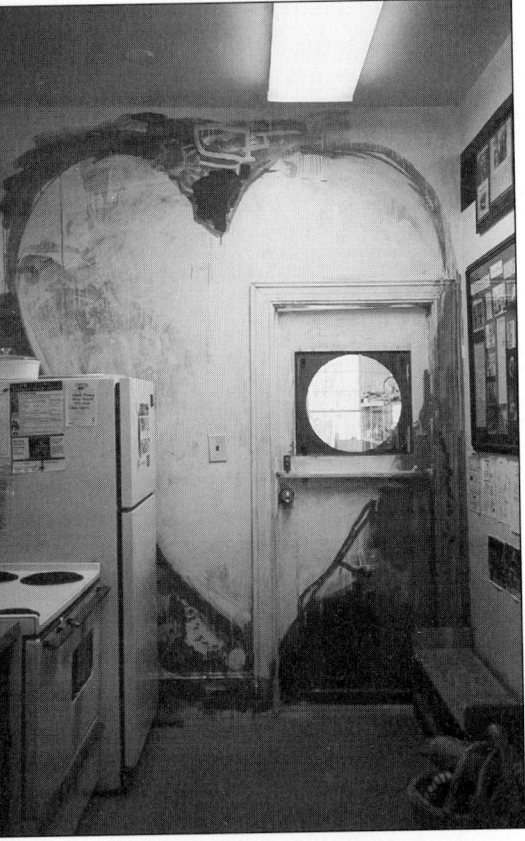

Figure 9–12.   After much exploring, the final
                 mural adorns the entrance.
                 (*Courtesy:* Margaret Edwards,
                 Lakewood Avenue Children's
                 School.)

like to see their work first thing when they walked in. As the children worked, the ideas emerged, almost like graffiti. Tentative ideas and paintings would be worked on, and then scribbled out as new ideas developed. The parents got to watch all the various stages of the project, and found the scribbling and not having a specific plan for the end product or a timetable for finishing rather unsettling. The children communicated that anxiety to Joel who was confident that everything would be all right. He let the children know that one does not always know the end point of a project, but when the end point came, they would all know and be happy about it. "Don't worry, we'll know when it's done." As Margaret Edwards said, "It was really quite amazing how Joel was able to communicate the confidence that he feels in himself as an artist to the kids. I used to love sitting in that little office off the kitchen and listen to their conversations. The kids sure were learning more than just art skills and techniques!"

So they continued to work on the mural. At last a day came when they stood back and considered the wall. Together, they all announced, "It's done." Today, the mural at Lakewood adorns the walls, a testimony to the skills and artistic sense that came from the collaboration of an artist with the preschoolers and kindergarteners.

Weaving Experiences

At Quadra Island Preschool, Baerbel Jaeckel began to implement Reggio Emilia principles in her approach to art almost immediately after school started in the fall. Early in September, the children became interested in the spider webs that are seen everywhere in autumn. Baerbel wondered if the children would make a connection between spider webs and weaving looms. She hoped that encouraging this connection would help her to introduce the principle of relationship into her approach to art.

The children drew their theories of how spiders spin their webs on large sheets of paper. Many of them had drawn circular shapes with crisscrossing lines, but when they examined the web closely, they were interested in how the spider uses two branches as a frame to attach the silk thread, first

Figure 9–13.   Constructing the loom.

making a Y, then weaving strands of silk in a spiral to form a web. Baerbel discussed with the children how they could build a loom in a window in the classroom, like the spider, by using two branches and strings between them. The children helped her lay out the string on the floor and made about 30 loops measuring about five feet long. She then cut the string at either end and helped the children tie the strands to the branch they had hung from the top of the window frame. Then they

Figure 9–14.   Tying the string on the branches.

tied the ends to the second branch that hung just above the ledge at the bottom of the window. Once they had made the loom, the children worked singly or in small groups to weave strands of different colored wool back and forth between the strings of the loom. Baerbel or one of the parents who regularly assists in the preschool would often sit with the children as they worked on the loom, giving them help if necessary. The loom stayed in the window the whole time the children were in preschool, and by the time school ended in June, the children had woven about 10 inches of cloth on the loom.

In reviewing the project, Baerbel felt that although she still had more to learn, she had been successful in implementing some of the Reggio Emilia principles in the art program. She had tried introducing the principle of relationship in presenting the art materials such as in the way she helped children make connections between the spider's web and a loom for weaving. She had encouraged a great deal of collaboration between children and adults in many of the art projects they had done throughout the year. She ensured that there were opportunities for discussion between her, the parents, and the children, and that the adults provided support if the children needed help in mastering a skill such as learning how to weave. Overall, Baerbel's greatest strength was her skill in making aesthetics a strong value in all aspects of the art program: in the arrangement of the room, in the presentation of materials, and in the beautiful artwork that the children created.

Painting Lupines

The teachers and children at the Vancouver Child Study Center carried out many projects that were inspired by the Reggio Emilia approach to art. One project in particular, the lupine painting, was clearly inspired by a video the teachers had seen, "The Creative Spirit" (1991) that showed the children's paintings in Reggio Emilia of poppies. In early summer, on one of the field trips to find out more about bridges, the teachers and children discovered fields of lupines growing wild in the grass on the way to the park. The children were thrilled by the lupines, squealing with delight as they danced in the grass, losing one another in the brilliant mass of purple and mauve flowers. The teachers took photographs of the children holding hands and running through the field of flowers. Bridges were forgotten as the children hid and chased each other in the lupines, some of which were taller than the children's heads. They decided to collect a few bunches of flowers to take back with them to school. The next day, Pat and Chava, the teachers, mixed paint in shades of purple. They poured the paint into glass jars and placed them next to a jar of green paint on a tray on the table so that children could see the different shades of color available for them to use. They also placed the photographs of the field trip and a large bowl of lupines on the table to trigger the children's memory of their experience in the park. All through the afternoon, a steady stream of children came to paint at the table. All of them produced paintings of the lupines with tall green stems that filled the page, and small

Figure 9–15.   A child paints his impressions of lupines.

purple and mauve oval shapes running down each stem. They frequently stopped to examine the photographs and look at the lupines in the bowl. The children seemed totally absorbed in their paintings and said very little. The experience seemed to reach to the roots of aesthetic awareness in the children, helping them to bring their keen sense of color, shape, and texture to the surface as they expressed symbolically their delight in the lupines.

EXAMINING ART MEDIA

Reggio Emilia has inspired the teachers in all these programs, as well as many others in the United States and Canada, to reexamine their approach to art for young children. Teachers inspired by the Reggio approach have come to view art as one of the "hundred languages" that children use in representing their ideas and investigating the world. They also come to understand the importance of helping children develop the skills and techniques needed to effectively use the various art media they are offered for graphic representation. The teacher from Sabot School who made the comment about providing experiences to the youngest children that allowed them to learn the "vocabulary" of the "hundred languages" talked about the process of helping children develop techniques. "We deliberately slow down to teach them how to use the materials—how to put caps back on the markers, how to use glue sticks, how to explore the properties of a block of clay. When children have the time and support for learning discrete skills with the various media, they can later use these skills for artistic expression as they grow cognitively and have new ideas to express."

Teachers also deepen their appreciation of the value of providing experiences that encourage children to develop aesthetic awareness. Teachers try to understand the complex process that enables the children to create the art on display in the preschools in Reggio Emilia and in the exhibit "One Hundred Languages of Children." In particular, teachers have come to realize that they need to have a deep understanding of how children create art, especially when drawing, painting, modeling with clay, and using light. These four art media are fundamental to the art programs in Reggio Emilia preschools.

Drawing

Teachers recognize that children spontaneously use drawing as a language to represent their ideas and express their emotions. The educators in Reggio Emilia have helped to show how important drawing is in communicating the thinking of young children who have not yet developed an adequate vocabulary to convey the same information through words. The images children draw, either from reality or from their imagination, make the meaning visible. The marks they make on the

Figure 9–16.   Drawing a kingfisher and a hooded merganser after visiting a bird sanctury.

paper become the invented symbols that hold meaning for them, and act as markers on the page to help them keep in mind the ideas or the series of events they are drawing. This process is known as *schematic drawing.* As the children in Pam Oken-Wright's classroom were developing their ideas of how to protect the

worms in their worm playground from hungry birds, their drawings of the bird language they would use in their warning signs made visible their understanding that birds do not communicate the same as people.

The work from Reggio Emilia demonstrates the importance of encouraging children to make representational drawings. Teachers encourage the children to look carefully at the objects they are drawing, to take

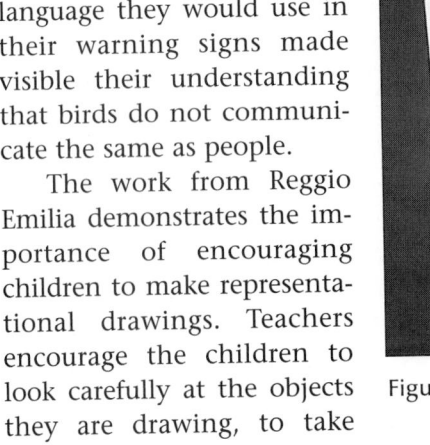

Figure 9–17.   Spencer's final drawing of the kingfisher and hooded merganser.

time to study the details, and to think how best to represent the information. Children often collaborate in this process so that they can share ideas and learn from one another. For the teachers, the children's drawings are a reflection of what the children are thinking. In examining the drawings and discussing them with the children, the teachers can discover any disequilibrium in the children's thinking or any gaps in understanding that they need to address. The teachers then can use this information to decide on possible directions they might follow in furthering the children's learning.

In the project on bridges described in Chapter 7, the teachers realized that the children had not included ramps on the bridges in the pictures they made. The teachers discussed with the children their theory of how people and traffic get up onto the deck of the bridges in their pictures. They realized that the children needed to observe how bridges are constructed more closely so they took the children to see bridges, and together they discussed their observations. Representational drawing led to further investigations in other media.

In the project Thinking Big (described in Chapter 8), the teachers gave the children numerous opportunities, beginning with sketching, to represent their understanding of height and perspective. At their trip to the water tower in the city park, they invited children to draw the water tower using the clipboards and pencils they had brought along. Back at the school, they invited children to collaborate on drawing on a poster-sized paper, comparing their initial sketches and planning together to include important details. As the project continued, children themselves began to get out the clipboards, to sketch the tall structure others had built in the classroom. Later representations moved to watercolors, building with clay, and building with sugar cubes and glue. With each opportunity to represent, children were able to demonstrate their increased understandings of height and perspective.

Painting

When first introduced to paint, children use it primarily to explore its physical properties. They are fascinated by the way it drips down the page and how it can be applied to the paper with smooth sweeps or short, stabbing movements of the brush. They discover the way colors change when they overlap on the paper. Paint gives children many opportunities to explore elements such as line, color, and texture. They discover the many ways they can use paint to make lines that are thick and thin, straight and curved, and looping and zigzagging all over the page. Many children also spend long periods of time in sensory exploration of the color and texture of the paint. They may make patch paintings in which they lay circular patches of solid color side by side, or in horizontal or vertical stripes to see the effect. Then they may experiment with texture by making brush marks on the surface of the wet or dry paint. Later, they make schematic or representational paintings, just as they do in drawing.

Children in the preschools in Reggio Emilia, just like children everywhere else in the world, follow this same process in using paint. The educators in Reggio Emilia, however, have encouraged teachers to go beyond simply putting paint out for children to use. They have shown the value in providing children with more in-depth experiences with different kinds of paint besides tempera such as translucent inks and acrylic paints. The teachers also provide the children with a wide range of colors of paints, often arranged in glass jars on carts beside the easel. At times, however, the teachers may limit the choice of paint to tints and shades of only a few colors. This heightens the children's awareness of gradations of color. Louise Cadwell, on her return from Reggio Emilia, describes how she selected specific colors of paint at the College School in St. Louis, Missouri, to heighten the children's aesthetic awareness of fall colors:

> During our investigation of leaves, we mixed colors we had noticed outside from quarts of a wide range of tempera colors. Many children had the opportunity to paint at the easel and to use these colors. I wanted to offer the children the chance to make stronger connections with their experience in the midst of this brilliant season through autumn hues in painting (1997, p. 73).

In this project, children were given the opportunity to respond aesthetically to the autumn colors and to use paint as a means of investigation. Louise Cadwell describes how her experiences in learning to be an atelierista in Reggio Emilia changed the way she presented paints to children:

> When I saw even very young children in Reggio Emilia painting with three or four gradations of yellows, pinks, blues and green, on easels outside in the spring air, or 4-year-olds investigating and then painting the variations of violets and greens in the wisteria blooming on the trellis outside their school, I felt that surely even those of us with much experience and background could learn a great deal from this way of introducing young children to paint (1997, p. 78).

The educators in Reggio Emilia have increased our understanding of what preschool children can learn with a great deal of exposure to various kinds of paint and with the appropriate scaffolding from adults. It appears that children, with the sensitive support of adults, can develop more advanced skills in painting. The large murals painted by children in Reggio Emilia are an example of the advanced work children can create with this kind of support. Further, the educators and atelieristi in Reggio Emilia teach us to respect art materials such as painting, to offer them displayed in a way that indicates this respect and fosters aesthetic awareness, and to expect children to use them, as would an artist, with thought, care, and attention.

Clay

As with paint, teachers encourage children to explore the clay and discover for themselves the many possibilities inherent in the material. The children discover how clay becomes more malleable as they add water, and how, when it dries, it becomes difficult to manipulate. Spontaneously, they discover that they can use their hands to control the shape the clay takes, and they pinch it to form little balls, roll it into coils, and flatten it with their hands to form a slab. They discover that they can make imprints in the clay with objects or embellish the clay by adding small pieces of clay to the surface.

Later, the teacher can build on these early experiences to help children learn techniques such as coiling and building forms with slabs of clay. Children learn how to join two pieces of clay by using a stick to roughen the edges and then applying slip, a mixture of clay and water, before pressing the edges together and smoothing the seam. If the children decide to build clay forms that need support, the teacher can show them how to use wire as an armature, or if the children want to make the clay into rounded forms for heads or pots, how to crunch up newspaper into tight balls to act as a support for the clay as they mould it into rounded shapes. The children can, if they wish, embellish the clay forms they have made by adding small pieces to form features (using the method described above for joining clay) or by using textured objects to indent the surface of the clay.

When the piece is finished, it needs to be dried slowly to prevent the clay from forming cracks, either by covering the clay with a wet towel for a few days or by wrapping it in plastic and letting it dry for a couple of weeks. If children want to keep working on their clay at a later time, it can be wrapped in plastic; however, it will need to be sprayed with water occasionally.

Often, children view their work in clay as a process and are willing to roll up their clay into a ball when they are finished working with it, but sometimes they want to keep their work. In Reggio Emilia, the large clay forms that the children made were covered in shellac to preserve them. It is preferable, however, to fire the clay if the children want to keep the clay pieces they have made. The dried clay pieces can be fired either in an electric kiln or in a pit fire if no kiln is available.

The preschoolers in Marty Gravett's classroom at Sabot School were very busy with clay work this year. A dominant theme was caves, with various methods of creating the caves, from carving out the space inside the cave to making a flattened piece of clay curve enough to create the enclosed space. Marty noted how children learned their technique from each other, and how their conversations all indicated that they were using the clay to explore the Big Ideas of preschoolers' lives related to safety and danger.

Light as an Art Medium

Perhaps one of the most powerful memories that visitors to the preschools in Reggio Emilia take away with them is of the use of light as a medium in art. In the preschools in Reggio Emilia, there are many different ways for children to explore the possibilities of light. Children manipulate light by arranging transparent

Figure 9–18. A flower arrangement on top of a light table invites a different view for creativity.

objects and pieces of colored tissue or cellophane paper on the surface of light tables or overhead projectors. A light table consists of a wooden box with two strips of cool fluorescent light tubes fastened to the bottom and a sheet of opaque Plexiglass covering the top. The inside of the box is painted white. Besides arranging transparent objects and paper on the surface, children can use colored inks to paint and felt-tipped pens to draw on tissue or transparent paper on the surface of the light table. Sunlight shines through the murals hanging in the classrooms which children have painted on sheets of plastic. The principle of transparency is evident in the creative use of light in the classroom and especially in the many different ways that children use it in their artwork as one of the "hundred languages" to investigate their world and represent their ideas.

Light in creative work has also come into American classrooms inspired by Reggio. In Pam Oken-Wright's classroom, children worked with colored disks, creating patterns projected on the wall by an overhead projector. The children tried to duplicate a colored design they had created on the nearby computer. In another area, a flower arrangement was displayed on top of the light table along with pastel watercolors to reproduce the flowers.

Multimedia

In Reggio Emilia, the children are encouraged to represent their ideas using more than one medium. For example, children created the fountains in the Amusement Park for Birds project using a variety of media. They drew sketches for fountains with colored pens and ink, traced the drawings on a light panel, and created three-dimensional models in clay. In this way, children are encouraged to think about different aspects of a problem or idea. Forman (1994) suggests the Reggio idea that children learn more deeply when they represent the same concept in different media. With each opportunity to express their understanding, the multimedia use leads to deeper and broader thinking. A sequence of activities across media is desirable. The teachers in Reggio Emilia are more likely to supply the techniques children need to represent their ideas by helping them build wire armatures to support their clay structures. Carol Seefeldt (1995) describes her observation of the teachers in Reggio Emilia showing the children how to construct vertical clay structures by cutting strips from the base and pulling them up. Art experiences are cumulative, unlike the one-shot art activities so often provided for children in other parts of the world.

PREPARING TEACHERS

Early childhood education students need to experience firsthand in their classes the approach to art learned from Reggio Emilia. The most difficult barrier to break through in trying to adopt the principles in teacher education probably is integrating art into all other aspects of curriculum. Courses may need to be rescheduled so that the curriculum subjects can be taught together. This, in turn, requires instructors in the different curriculum areas to collaborate and teach subjects such as art, music, literature, science, and social studies as a team.

Sue Fraser describes experiences in working with early childhood education students to enhance their understanding of creative representation:

> At Douglas College, we have found that by making Children Teaching Teachers the core curriculum course, content for all the other subject areas can be drawn from instructors' observations of the students and children as they participate in the course. In one session, for instance, the students had put out balls of clay for the children to use with water in a cottage cheese carton on the table. One of the first children to show interest in using the clay was a three-year-old boy. He sat down at the table and immediately poured the water over his ball of clay, flooding the table and turning the clay into liquid mud. The students made a quick decision to clean up and pack the clay away. I could see, as the instructor observing the session, that in our next class, I would have to give the students more information about how to introduce clay as an art medium. I also saw that we needed to discuss how the experience with the clay might have been used as an opportunity to help the child, if he were interested, discover more about the properties of clay and how it is transformed as water is added. We would also need to discuss broader issues, such as development, and review the typical behavior of a three year old on encountering a new material. We would have to revisit Vygotsky's theory and discuss how the zone of proximal development can be nudged upward when the adult scaffolds the child's learning. It becomes impossible, therefore, to teach art as a separate curriculum subject. At Douglas College we have found that it makes more sense to integrate all curriculum areas, but this means that instructors have to work, like the students, as a team.
>
> In implementing the Reggio Emilia principles in the program at Douglas College, our approach to art has changed profoundly. First, our image of the student has changed, just as our image of the child has changed. We now begin with an image of the student as competent, inventive, and full of ideas. Second, we have tried to ensure that

aesthetics are part of every aspect of the art program, such as in the way the materials are prepared and presented in the classroom, and in the respect we show in displaying the students' work. We have come to value and often capitalize on the unexpected things that happen. We are, in fact, learning to expect the unexpected, to be more flexible and use these experiences as opportunities for taking a different direction or embarking on a new course of action. We have also learned to slow down and explore ideas more thoroughly. We hope to help the students get in touch with their own creative processes and become confident in expressing themselves through art. Once the students have experienced each stage in the process of working with an art material, including deciding which techniques are needed, what possibilities there are in using the material, and the importance of building on experience, we hope they will be more confident in sharing their skills and will be better prepared to provide children with a high-quality art program.

THE ROLE OF THE TEACHER IN ART PROGRAMS

As teachers gain more understanding of the Reggio Emilia approach, they come to view art as one of the "hundred languages" of children. Their goals expand from merely seeing the importance of providing children with developmentally appropriate art activities that foster sensory exploration and creativity to making art a part of the total experience, a means of expression, a tool for investigation, a medium of communication, and above all, a way of making thinking visible. The relationship of teachers to children's art changes when they view art as another language children use in making sense of their world. To help them explore the Reggio Emilia principles, teachers can ask themselves the following questions.

- Are aesthetics considered at every stage of the process, from preparation of the art materials to presentation of the materials to the children?
- Is respect shown in the way the materials are used and displayed in the classroom?
- Is relationship evident in every aspect of the program such as in the way in which materials are presented and in how the children's work is documented by the teachers?
- Are there opportunities for the children to use the materials on their own and in collaboration with other children and adults?
- Are children encouraged to use a wide variety of media to represent and communicate their ideas?
- Are children encouraged to make schematic drawings of their ideas and representational drawings of real objects?
- Are children encouraged to use drawing as a means of making their thinking visible to others?

- Are there opportunities for adults to share their skills in creating art with children?

- Are there opportunities for children to share their ideas with adults and other children?

- Is the principle of transparency woven into the art program in the visibility of materials provided for the children to use, in the use of light as a tool and a medium of expression, and in the documentation of the children's work?

- Have natural materials been used in the preparation of the environment and made available for the children to explore and use in their artwork?

- Have the teachers established links with the community by inviting people to share their art or skills with the children?

In the following descriptions, Arolynn Kitson, a kindergarten teacher, explains the changes she made to the physical and interpersonal environments in the classroom after being inspired by the schools of Reggio Emilia.

The environment is referred to as "the third teacher" in the schools of Reggio Emilia. It is with this concept in mind that I began to look at my surroundings in a different light.

I made three specific environmental changes in my classroom. The changes included the physical environment, the interpersonal environment, and activities to stimulate development in the environment.

The Physical Environment

The first environmental change I made was to set up a more appealing art studio. My initial art studio was full of materials placed in a semi-organized manner.

My first attempt at a more appealing art studio was a simple one. It involved coordinating the drawing tools by color and presenting them in clear jars. Although this was a simple idea prevalent in the schools of Reggio Emilia, I began to see how the children and I began to look at the materials in different ways. I also began to introduce the children to higher quality materials, including various drawing pencils, fine line markers, charcoal, and watercolor pencil crayons. We talked about how they were responsible for choosing the right tool for their work. Comments overheard in the art studio included: "I need a big black felt because I need a big line" and "You shouldn't use the charcoal in your Life book because it will smear."

This organizational change promoted decision making, as the children were not only given the opportunity to choose their own tools but were expected to do so.

A surprising outcome of this organization was that the children began to show more respect for their tools. We talked about how artists cared for their tools. The children always put their tools back properly. I was not to see another dried-out glue stick.

Parents as Partners

I have always valued and respected the important role the parent has as an advocate and participant in their child's education. Although I appreciated and was grateful for the help that the parent gave in the classroom, by working with children and helping to make materials, I was uncomfortable at the same time. I felt the parents should have a more pronounced influence on their child's program, but at the same time I did not want the parents to feel that my role as the teacher was compromised by asking for their input. Inspired by the invaluable partnership that is honored in the schools of Reggio Emilia, I decided to take a somewhat intrepid step into forging a better relationship between the parents and myself. I asked the question: Are there any artists out there? To my delight, one parent stepped forward, and we slowly began to talk about how she could share her skills with the children.

A most magical thing happened when the parents simply painted with the children. The children worked on one painting for a complete hour. One child in particular chose to continue his painting at snack time. It was his words that I will always remember: "See I'm a little bit of an artist." This was the same child who never chose any activities that required him to hold a drawing or painting tool. Another comment that was equally important to me was the parent who commented, "It was really fun! I hadn't painted for a long time."

Activities to Stimulate Development

The children and I talked a lot about taking our time and really looking at things, whether it was observing our crabs, worms, and plants or photographs of real objects. In my previous kindergarten class I had never given the children the opportunity to draw from either real objects or photographs. I was delighted to see how the children responded to using these materials. The children were observed paying close attention to their models and spending increased time periods drawing. Amy spent an hour drawing her grasshopper. She shared with myself and her peers many things she learned while closely observing and drawing this grasshopper.

Creating an atmosphere and environment to support children's artistic sensibilities and abilities is part of the extended cycle of Reggio ideas related to learning and representation of that learning. Art and aesthetics are present to help individuals find their best voice within the "hundred languages" open to them. American teachers inspired by Reggio work understand the importance of the arts in their classrooms. When asked about aesthetics in her program, Patti Cruikshank-Schott answered:

Sometimes I think that aesthetics is the only thing my work is about: I think children deserve to be totally surrounded by beauty, and that one part of the beauty of the universe is its order. Here is a short list of beauty in the classroom, by no means all.

1. Use natural materials, with as little plastic as possible. (I think this means disposing of all educational catalogs). Use baskets of seashells and stones for counters instead of plastic teddy bears.

2.   Arrange materials with an eye to "like with like" and size. This way of arranging all the baskets in a row, from big to tiny, is just really beautiful; and it is the beauty of mathematics, which is also a sight to behold. Even 5 screwdrivers arranged on the wall in descending size in the woodworking area look good.

3.   Display real art. Display children's art. Display it like you would in your own home. Use beautiful photographs. I tend to use the Japanese concept of clustering things in odd numbers and asymmetry in arranging things. (Don't use cartoons or juvenile pictures.)

4.   Include everyday objects as much as possible, especially from different cultures. I think the whole thing about real stuff may be the point. I use "real" art supplies, and arrange art materials in baskets and clear containers.

5.   Realize that you will spend more time at school than you do at home. I also surround the children with beauty because I spend all day there and want to enjoy the sights.

6.   Choose a color theme and use it. Choose 2 or 3 colors near each other in the spectrum, and limit yourself to those, with the addition of black and white. This is about interior design rather than playroom mentality.

7.   Consider beauty when you purchase educational materials. There are memory card games that are gorgeous—UNICEF children's faces, museum of modern art sets, classical buildings.

8.   Collect beautiful children's literature and take good care of the books.

9.   Find a place for each item and put it in its place at the end of the day. Set aside some time to tidy the room each day. Managing clutter is an important and time-consuming task

Creating a beautiful space is part of the Reggio-inspired classroom that contributes to children's aesthetic sensibility and artistic ability.

Chapter 10

The Hundred Languages of Children

The child has a hundred languages
(and a hundred hundred hundred more).

—*Loris Malaguzzi*

Questions to Consider:

- What ingredients are necessary to foster the child's imagination in a preschool classroom?
- How do children make meaning of their world?
- What role does the environment as a third teacher play in the child's search for meaning?
- What is the role of play in promoting early literacy and math skills?
- How can adults increase the child's awareness of the community and culture in which they live?

One of the most important contributions Loris Malaguzzi and the educators in Reggio Emilia have made to preschool education in other parts of the world is in extending the awareness of how many languages children can use to express themselves and represent their world. Just as Howard Gardner has broadened our view of intelligence beyond valuing only the logical mathematical and linguistic aspects of intelligence, so have the educators in Reggio Emilia increased our understanding of how children use graphic, verbal, literate, symbolic, and imaginative play "and a hundred hundred hundred more" languages in making meaning of the world.

From birth, children are meaning-makers, intrepid explorers, and researchers learning about the world around them deliberately through their actions and interactions. Young children have not yet settled into the fairly narrow range of methods of communication used by the adults around them. The challenge for adults is to learn to recognize, listen to, and respond to what children are expressing. The "hundred languages" is a metaphorical expression of the number of ways that children can find to express themselves. If they are in a context where they can find a medium that suits their style and message, they can express their initial ideas. If they continue to explore their ideas in any one of a variety of other media as George Forman (1994) points out, they may find one that better expresses the idea, or they may find whole new ideas or ways of thinking as they work. Truly, the possibilities seem limitless, "a hundred, hundred, hundred more."

One of the greatest joys for a preschool teacher is being a part of the early experiences of young children as they make meaning of their world. What could compare to sharing in the discovery that the marks the children make in their early attempts to communicate in drawing and writing hold meaning for other people, or to being one of the first people to read or tell stories to children that as Bruno Bettelheim says, scatter seeds.

> Some of these will be working in his conscious mind right away; others will stimulate processes in his unconscious. Still others will need to rest for a long time until the child's mind has reached a state suitable for their germination, and many will never take root at all. But those seeds which have fallen on the right soil will grow into beautiful flowers and sturdy trees—that is, give validity to important feelings, promote insights, nourish hopes, reduce anxieties—and in doing so enrich the child's life at the moment and forever after" (Bettelheim, 1977, p. 154).

What a privilege it is for a parent and a teacher to realize that through choosing and reading stories to young children they can sow small seeds that may grow and help them make meaning of their lives. By sharing books and encouraging early literacy in the preschool years adults also have the ability to foster in children a life-long love of reading and writing. "Stories told and stories heard: all develop individual 'pools of knowledge' as unique as fingerprints" (Goodman, 1998).

The Language of Imagination

Herbert Kohl, in his foreword to Gianni Rodari's book *The Grammar of Fantasy*, notes that Rodari envisions the teacher as "an adult who is with the children to express the best in himself or herself, to develop his or her own creative inclination, imagination, and constructive commitment" (1996). Rodari, a friend of Loris Malaguzzi, was influential in making the imagination a strong ingredient in the education of young children in Reggio Emilia. Rodari, an exceptionally creative children's author and teacher, had a great deal to say about imagination and creativity in school. "We have many intelligent theories about play, but we still do not have a phenomenology of the imagination, which gives life to play" (1996). Rodari states that when there is something wrong with society and it needs to be changed, "to change it, creative human beings are needed, people who know how to use their imaginations" (1996, pp. 110–13). The power of these ideas shows in the kind of early childhood education provided in Reggio Emilia. When imagination is valued and encouraged in all aspects of the curriculum, the classroom comes alive with the creative input of children and teachers. The result is rich and stimulating early childhood education.

There are many ways in which teachers can encourage imagination in their classrooms. They can make an assortment of fairy tales, folk tales, and picture books available to children. There are so many wonderful children's authors to choose from. The list is endless; every classroom teacher has favorites. Some might include *Color Dance* by Ann Jonas, *Mr. Gumphy's Outing* by John Burningham, *Boxes, Boxes* by Leonard Fisher, *Mouse Paint* by Ellen Walsh, *Mr. Rabbit and the Lovely Present* by Charlotte Zolotow, *Martin's Hats* by Joan Blos, *Pretend You're a Cat* by Jean Marzollow, *I See a Song* by Eric Carle, *Max Found Two Sticks* by Brian Pickney, *Jenny's Hat* by Ezra Jack Keats, and *Five Live Bongos* by George Lyon. Such books tickle children's imaginations in delightful ways. There also should be an assortment of materials for dressing up and playing out themes that are important in the children's lives. The old favorites are the housekeeping materials and the equipment for playing doctors, nurses, and firefighters. Then there are the dress-up clothes: the crowns and capes that the children use in dramatizing the characters they are introduced to in fairy stories. Perhaps best of all is a variety of "loose parts"—open-ended items, often "beautiful stuff" (Topal & Gandini, 1999), that can be used to represent any object the child needs for imaginative play. It is the scarves, sashes, old hats, and other odd cast-off household bits that lend richness to children who use their imaginations to transform and create an idea. It is the old saddle that a teacher added to the playground or a collection of baskets of all sizes that become the catalyst for pretending.

The teachers in the Quadra Island center transcribed the songs and stories the children made up as they swung on the swings in the playground. These transcriptions gave the teachers insight into what the children were thinking about that would allow them to plan the props they would set up later for the children's play.

Chloe: I am a princess. How about my name is Sunflower Rose and my big sister and the witch go in my car.

Serena: Sister! I am at McDonald's. We are almost at the ferry; turn off the car.

At a meeting that evening, the adults noted how there were all the ingredients for a fairy tale in this dialog. With the addition of props, including a crown and cape for the princess, a hat for the witch, a large box for the car, and perhaps even the materials for the restaurant scene from McDonald's, the children's conversation could be developed further in their play. They also discussed whether there might be enough interest in the topic of fairy tales to make puppets of witches and princesses so the children could create their own puppet show of a fairy tale. One of the teachers suggested putting out the fairy tale characters and the flannel board to see if the children were interested in using the flannel characters to tell or create their own fairy stories. They made the following recording as three girls, on one of many occasions in the next few weeks, used the flannel board to tell each other imaginative fairy tales.

The three girls were sitting in front of the flannel board, and Serena told a fairy story.

Serena: How about the prince be sleeping beauty? She growed and growed. She [the witch] got burnt by the candles.

Serena made the flannel figure of the prince, who had now become the sleeping beauty, chase the witch onto the candelabra above.

Serena: She [the witch] got burned by the candles. The end.

The children listened to many fairy stories that the teachers had read. It was interesting to see how the children were able to use the elements of a fairy tale in creating their own characters, a plot, a surprising transformation, and then to end, like in many fairy tales, with a victory of good over evil in the end.

It was about this time, in the spring, that the teachers in the program were joined by a practicum student, Barb, who is married to a local carver, Max Chickite from the Kwagiutl Nation. She brought in many books of native legends from the west coast of Canada and read them to the children. It was a wonderful extension from listening to fairy stories that originated in a land far away to hearing legends that had been created by the people in the place where the children lived. One day, the practicum student invited her husband to visit the center and bring in some of the drums, shakers, and masks he had carved to show the children. The following are excerpts from the student's documentation of the visit. (Each of the comments in the documentation of the experience is illustrated with photographs, all of which are compiled and attractively displayed in a folder.)

Max told us that the button blanket represents the Big House and when "you dance in one for 20 minutes wearing a 30-pound blanket, it gets heavy."

Martyn: We got to try on this stuff [the button cape, apron, white fur hat, and masks].

Kevin: I like the sound of the shells rattling on the apron.

Max showed us how the rattle is used by the first dancer, checking out the space before the other dancers begin. The rattle is for protection. He showed us his drum. Max told us that the drum represents the mother's heartbeat (or mother earth). It is sometimes calm, sometimes anxious. When it goes from a regular beat, a change or transformation is coming. All the children had a turn to play the drum.

Serena: If you wipe the drum, it makes a killer whale.

Max performed a dance for the children, demonstrating how the rattles and drum were used in traditional native dances. He then offered to stay and show the children how he made a carving. Everyone was thrilled.

We all watched as Max took his chainsaw and began to cut the piece of wood he had found on the beach. As he carved, the wood

Figure 10–1.   Max, the carver, visits the children.

began to take on the shape of an octopus. He told us that the octopus means change. It can change to the color of the rocks if something is after it. He asked us if we had ever seen one in the water.

Barbara: No, but I know they are real!

Max: What do you guys think I should do with this?

Martyn: Paint it!

Max: If I leave it here would you all keep care of it for me?

Frazer: Yeah!

The carving of the octopus, painted with traditional Kwagtiulth designs, is now on the shelves with the other treasured objects that the teachers and children have collected over the year. It has become part of the beautiful display that the teachers were inspired to make after seeing slides of the environment in the preschools in Reggio Emilia.

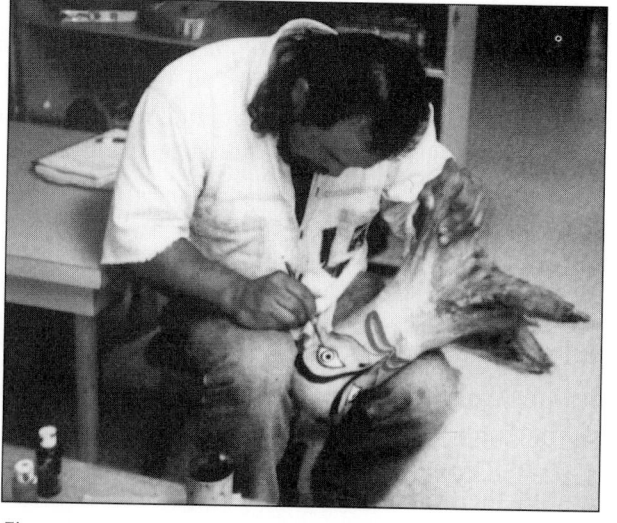

Figure 10–2.   Carving the octopus.

Figure 10–3.   The finished carving on display.

The ingredients necessary for fostering imagination in a preschool classroom are an understanding of the value of rich fantasy play in a child's life, the provision of a wide variety of materials in all aspects of the program including literature, music, art, science, and dramatic play, and a stimulating program that broadens children's horizons and gives children opportunities to experience creativity and imagination through art, music, and literature. But perhaps what is even more powerful is for children to see for themselves someone, like Max, the carver, using imagination and creativity in his own work.

Bringing Imagination to the Classroom

Inspired by the work of Gianni Rodari and by the imaginative approach to early childhood education in Reggio Emilia, the instructors in the professional development program at Douglas College have tried to ensure an emphasis on the power of imagination in the preparation of teachers of young children. Herbert Kohl, in his foreword to Gianni Rodari's *The Grammar of Fantasy*, writes, "There is no imagination curriculum or pedagogy of the imagination in our schools. Yet, if as the poet Wallace Stevens wrote, 'the imagination is the power of the mind over possibilities of things,' then to neglect the imagination is also to impoverish children's worlds and to narrow their hopes" (1996, p. ix). When we neglect the imagination in early childhood teacher education, we impoverish children and the students who will become teachers of young children in the future.

We have tried to encourage students to become aware of how valuable it is to use their own imaginations in planning curricula for young children, especially in the art, literature, music, science, and social studies classes, and in the core curriculum course Children Teaching Teachers. As a result, the instructors have tried to model for the students the value of using imagination in our own approach to teaching the courses at the college.

Just before the students begin their first session of Children Teaching Teachers and when the weather is still good in the fall, we take the students to a small park called the Friendship Gardens two blocks away from the college in New Westminster. These gardens are part of a small park that a particularly imaginative landscape architect designed in recognition of the New Westminster's sister city, Moriguchi, Japan. The park has many unexpected features such as a bridge that seems to end in the middle of the stream but then takes a sharp right turn to reach the far bank, and a miniature mountain that provides a secret lookout over the stream that flows through the gardens. There is a sign at the entrance to the park that says "Let Peace Prevail on Earth," and it is here that we begin our walk with the students. We follow a small stream that flows down the hill and tumbles over small waterfalls into tranquil pools of water. Mallard ducks swim among the lily pads and dragonflies skim the surface of the water. The banks of the stream are bordered with unusual trees such as a weeping mulberries and flowering fruit trees. There are no blossoms at this time of year, but many of the branches of the trees hanging over the banks of the stream are adorned with spider webs.

In preparation for our visit to the park, we read the children's book *Who Hides in the Park?* by Japanese author Warabe Aska to the students. The story, which takes the reader on a magical journey through Stanley Park in Vancouver, is a wonderful way to provoke the students to use their imagination as they explore the park. We give each group of students two assignments that are written on a sheet in the form of a provocation and are handed out to them as they set off on their walk through the park.

Provocation 1: Walk downhill along the bank of the stream and stop at one of the duck ponds. Think of ways you might cross the stream without wading across. Be as imaginative as a child might be in thinking up solutions. Appoint a recorder to keep track of your ideas, then sketch the ones you find most interesting.

Provocation 2: Discover at least two unexpected things about the park. The landscape architect, for example, designed some unusual ways of crossing the stream himself.

Predictions: Draw up a flow chart similar to the one the teachers in Reggio Emilia created of the adult predictions for the Amusement Park for Birds, and predict how you may use some of these ideas with children as you plan your next session of Children Teaching Teachers.

Responses to Provocation 1. The students suggested many imaginative ways of crossing the stream. They thought they might be able to ride across on a duck's back or perhaps stuff a cushion with the duck feathers lying on the banks of the pond and float across. They were inspired by the way the spider webs stretched over the surface of the water to spin their own webs to cross the stream. Some groups thought of using the branches of the weeping mulberry tree to weave a rope ladder and make a swinging bridge across the stream. Someone suggested weaving a small basket and asking a dragonfly to carry them across in the basket.

Figure 10–4.   Students work on finding imaginative ways to cross the stream.

Predictions.   Each group drew up a flow chart listing their predictions of topics they thought the children might be interested in pursuing when they visited the college (see Figure 10–5). The experience in the park stimulated the students to think of activities they could prepare to promote the children's exploration of topics of possible interest such as water, air, plants, insects, and birds. The students also were inspired by the aesthetics in the design of the park. This increased their own awareness of the importance of aesthetics in planning the environment and art materials for the children.

Documentation.   The students returned to the college with the sketches they had made of their imaginative ideas for crossing the stream. Each group developed documentation that incorporated their sketches, the written transcriptions of their discussions of their ideas with the other students in the group, the web they had drawn up showing their predictions of how they could use the ideas with children, the activities they developed in their sessions with the children, and the photographs taken at each stage in the process. The documentation panels were displayed outside the classrooms so all the people involved in Children Teaching Teachers could see the process the students had followed in their planning and presentation of experiences for the children.

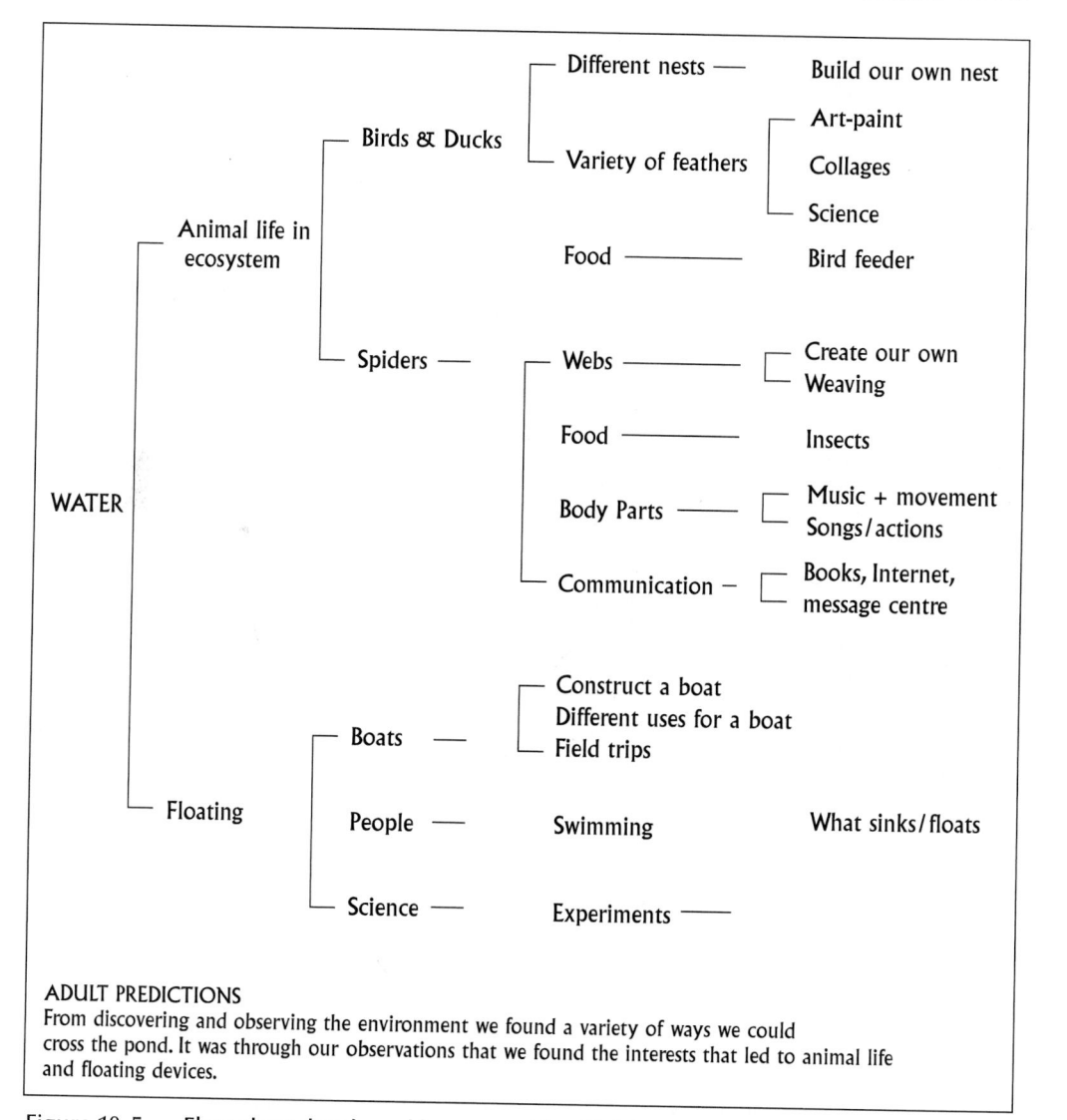

Figure 10–5.   Flow chart developed by group 4 for Children Teaching Teachers: Adult
predictions in their initial meeting together.

We believe that Gianni Rodari would have been happy to know how his suggestions for "thinking outside the box" had inspired us to encourage the use of
imagination in the preparation of teachers.

Other ways the instructors at Douglas College have devised to encourage students to consider broader horizons to offer children is described here. Students in
the early childhood education program at Douglas College come from all over the
world: India, Africa, China, the Caribbean, South America, and many parts of
Europe. Creating an atmosphere of community and collaboration is a principle of

the Reggio Emilia approach. To help everyone connect with one another's lives, one instructor developed an experience called "the world tea party." For this occasion, the classroom was transformed physically into a multicultural tea room, alive with teacup clatter and personal storytelling, and the tables were dressed up to reflect the various cultural heritages of students and faculty.

It began several years ago with a proposed field trip with students to an interactive art installation called World Tea Party. The idea was that tea is a medium to unite cultures blending art and tradition, and celebrating diversity and human connectedness. The students liked the concept and wanted to take part, but they were more interested in hosting their own world tea party at Douglas College.

For the past several years, this event has been held as part of the curricular studies. The world tea party experience affords each class the chance to look at a piece of the image of who they are collectively in the group. The importance of looking at ourselves is a Reggio Emilia principle, and this is one way it is played out in the program at the end of the third semester.

The students organize themselves in small groups, and each group chooses a specific culture to feature at the tea party. They collaborate by gathering materials, designing the table settings, and planning how to present their ideas to make it interactive and aesthetically engaging by using a variety of media.

A recent tea party featured stories and festivities from Italy, Sweden, India, China, the Philippines, Scotland, and Quebec. A highlight was the guest visit by the grandmother of one of the students who told her story of coming to Canada from Italy and described Italian weddings to the tearoom audience. She made antipasto and sponge cake for the tea table, and showed a video of her family members' recent vacation in Italy.

At another table, a student spoke about the hierarchy of pouring tea in her family's tradition. She also talked about the custom of foot binding of Chinese women and the reasons for doing it. She played some contemporary music from China; everyone remarked on how Western it sounded. A faculty member read the works of Scottish poet Robbie Burns from a book that has been in her family for generations. She recalled how her brothers had to be dressed in their kilts to sit down for dinner each night in her parents'

Figure 10–6.   The World Tea Party.

home. The tradition seemed even more surprising when she explained that her parents' home was not in Scotland but in South Africa. One student told about her family's potlatch that lasted for days and consisted of singing and dancing, drumming, and gift-giving. Whether a west coast potlatch or an Italian wedding party, the world tea party has given students a context for widening their worlds and building a sense of community. The instructors hope that such experiences will help them see the potential for widening the worlds of children beyond their classrooms.

THE RICHNESS OF CHILDREN'S WORDS

Children, in the early years, work hard to make meaning of the world around them. It is often in the preschool years that they first show an interest in encoding and decoding the written word. One of the first indications of an emerging interest in learning how to read and write is children's recognition of environmental print, in letters such as the M for McDonald's restaurants and words such as STOP on traffic signs. At about the same time, they begin to assign meaning to their scribbles and may even expect adults to be able to read their "writing." These early attempts at writing usually emerge spontaneously from the child's drawings. Bob Steele outlines the connection between a child's drawing and writing, noting how adults can support this process. He writes,

> Drawing evolves from single configurations into elaborate pictures. Human subjects are depicted in action and placed in environments. At this point pictures now become the pathfinder for using single words to describe complex situations. . . . 'This is Mom holding my hand. We are crossing the street.' Drawing is a rewarding language activity in its own right, but its value to literacy is heightened when children and parents (and teachers) talk and write (print) single words and short sentences about the drawing's content. This can happen only when adults take the time to be involved. (Steele, 1996)

As children become more aware of the need to use conventional symbols for writing, their drawings become dotted with shapes and approximations of the letters of the alphabet. The most recognizable letters are often those they have learned to print when writing their own names. Gradually, children begin to grasp the concept of signs, written symbols that can convey meaning. They combine mock letters and later more conventional print to form words. At first, the children use invented spelling to express their ideas; it is only later that they become aware of the need to use conventional spelling in their attempts at writing (Clay, 1975).

The attitude of adults is a critical factor in fostering young children's literacy. Children whose parents have read to them since they were infants will probably

Figure 10–7.   Drawing evolves
                into elaborate
                pictures.

develop a strong interest in learning to read books themselves. And children who have received an enthusiastic response to their initial attempts to communicate in writing will probably be motivated to try harder to learn how to use conventional print in expressing themselves. Parents and teachers also help children in their progression toward becoming fully fledged readers and writers by providing them with many authentic literary experiences. They can encourage the child to "write" letters, perhaps to other family members who they know will appreciate the child's attempts at beginning writing. Children can be encouraged to write lists and messages for their family or the teacher at school (Harste, Woodward, and Burke in Asseline, 1997). In preschool, teachers can enrich the children's play environment with literacy materials. They can provide note pads beside the toy telephone, recipe cards by the stove, and a receipt book by the cash register. At one center, the teachers set up the writing area as a newspaper office, and encouraged the children to pretend to be reporters and interview one another and the teachers. The next morning, one of the families woke up to find their young son already out on the sidewalk, notebook in hand, interviewing the workmen who were repairing their street!

In many classrooms, each child has an individual journal, and the teacher creates an expectation that children will have things to write about and will want to write. The availability of clipboards, prepared with blank paper and attached pencils, suggests a similar expectation of written communication. Teachers writing their observation notes as they sit beside children busy at work, provide the daily model of adults writing with purpose.

There are many opportunities for including early literacy experiences in projects such as the building of bridges project discussed earlier. The children, in this case, had many opportunities to practice their writing skills as they made signs for controlling the traffic on the bridges they built in the classroom and outside in the playground. The children in Pam Oken-Wright's classroom making the signs to warn the birds away from their worm playground were incorporating their understandings about literacy and different forms of communication. In Patti Cruikshank-Schott's classroom, the children who dictated their explanations of their theories about age that they had drawn in their journals were seeing their words in print recorded by an adult. Roskos and Vukelich state that teachers should "encourage 'littering' the play environment with print. If print 'flows through' the play world of young children, then there is greater likelihood that children will become familiar with it in ways that are not only informing but also pleasurable and motivating" (Roskos & Vukelich, 1991, p. 33).

Setting up message centers like those the teachers have created in the preschools in Reggio Emilia is another way of encouraging early literacy in young children. Visitors to the schools in Reggio Emilia notice how much careful thought goes into designing the space and materials in the message centers in the classrooms. The space allows a small group of children to work together. The children all have their own mailboxes which are labeled with a graphic symbol and their name. On shelves nearby are good quality paper and writing tools for the children to use in writing their messages. There are photocopies of pictures of animals and other objects, and copies of the children's photographs in a variety of sizes, so children who are not yet readers and writers can send messages to one another using pictures. On a display board above the desk, the children may pin a random selection of their written messages to one another. In addition, a computer and a typewriter are set on low shelves for the children to use.

The message center provides children with the incentive to read and write in an authentic way. As children write notes to one another and receive messages from their friends, they become increasingly aware of the need to use conventional symbols as a means of communication. The message center enables children to co-construct knowledge, as children with assistance or scaffolding from teachers and more knowledgeable peers produce representational work ahead of their independent level of performance; that is, they achieve more with assistance than on their own (Vygotsky, 1962). The message center enables children to perform higher-level mental functions. For example, they move from reactive attention to more focused attention, and they begin to use deliberate memory for learning the conventional symbols in writing letters, words, and eventually, sentences. "Written speech is not just oral speech on paper but represents

Figure 10–8.   Thank-you letter to the Day Care Fairy.

a higher level of thinking. It has a profound influence on development because 1. It makes thinking more explicit . . . 2. It makes thinking and the use of symbols more deliberate . . . 3. It makes the child aware of the elements of language" (Bodrova & Leong, 1996, p. 102).

The teachers at Quadra Island created a communication center in the classroom by setting up a cupboard with slots for mailboxes beside a desk with a drawer full of an assorted writing materials. Carrying on with the interest that the children had shown in fairy stories, the teachers, who hoped to provoke the children's interest in literacy, wrote a note to each child from the day care fairy. The children found these notes in their mailboxes the next day when they came to school. They decided to write their own replies as well as a group thank-you note to the fairy on a large sheet of paper.

THE LANGUAGE OF NUMBERS

Often, in Reggio Emilia, the communication center is used as a center for mathematics. On the wall are hung large graphs made of small, colorful pictures of fruit pasted in horizontal lines to show how many children liked each fruit. A number of tape measures hang down from a shelf. One visitor sees two children measuring real fruit and nuts in a beautiful, antique brass balance scale and recording the weight on a sheet of paper.

A visitor to La Villetta School noticed numbers carefully written and taped to each step in the tall building. There were numbers on the steps going up, and different numbers on the steps going down, as children explored ideas of tall buildings, and realized that counting steps going up and down produced the same total, but the steps had different numbers each way.

The book *Shoe and Meter: Children and Measurement* shows vividly how a group of children in the Diana School constructed an understanding of numbers and measurement through their project of helping in the building of a table for their classroom. As Loris Malaguzzi points out in the introduction, modern life is full of mathematical languages. "Children of today are constantly confronted with names of numbers, pictures of numbers, and words expressing quantity and measurement, and they use these words even before knowing their meanings, values, roles and purposes" (Malaguzzi in Castagnetti & Vecchi, 1997, p. 16). Learning to use the language of numbers is learning one of the "hundred languages."

The teachers at the Vancouver Child Study Center also were interested in expanding children's early attempts at using conventional symbols in writing to using numerical symbols for expressing simple math concepts. They also wished to find out more about how well the children understood concepts of time. They decided that although many of the children knew the purpose of a calendar, they were unsure whether the children understood the measurement of time on a calendar. The following information is taken from the documentation of a project on making calendars at the Vancouver Child Study Center.

At the end of the year, the teachers brought in a number of old calendars and left them in the library corner as a provocation. Many of the children were fascinated by the calendars, and during the next two or three weeks, the calendars often were the most frequently chosen item from the bookshelves. For many days, the library corner had calendars strewn all over the floor as the children examined each page and discussed the pictures, the printed numbers, and the letters for the days and months with their friends. Often, they asked the teachers to help them find their birthdays on the calendar. The teachers decided to see if the children would be interested in using their early literacy and math skills to make their own calendars. They began by asking the children in group time what they knew about calendars and listed their responses on a chart as follows.

Calendars:

- have pictures
- have numbers
- have pages
- have letters
- have a hole to hang them
- have twelve pages

The teachers put out a variety of materials in the writing area such as construction paper, white paper on which to draw pictures, fine-tipped felt pens, and small squares of paper cut from an old calendar, with the date on each square. The teachers also added small, blank squares of paper on which the children could write their own dates. On the table they placed a card with the year printed on it for the children to copy, if they wished. The children drew many interesting pictures for their calendars, some of which seemed to have been inspired by the pictures of scenery they had seen on the old calendars. There were pictures of mountains and trees, and one child drew a snow scene with a perky snowman perched on the side of a steep hill and people skiing down the ski slopes. Once the children had pasted their pictures on the large sheets of construction paper, they began to paste the small squares of paper with the dates. Some of the children chose to write their own numbers, using either conventional or invented symbols, on the squares; if they could not find the printed number they were looking for, they sometimes wrote their own and placed it on the calendar. Most children pasted their squares in random order all over the construction paper, but a few of them put the dates in order. Only one child got as far as pasting the numbers in correct order from 1 to 11, but he placed the dates vertically, moving up the page instead of in a line across or down the page.

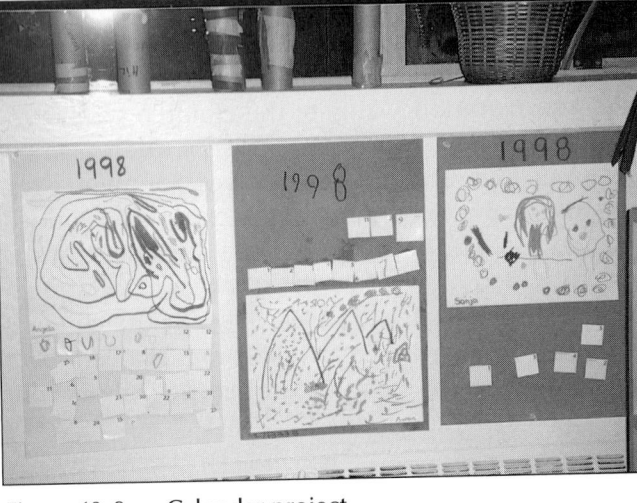

Figure 10–9.   Calendar project.

Most children copied the year from the card on the table and placed it in a prominent position on their calendars.

The calendar project, as seen by the children's enthusiastic response, was a successful experience. The teachers were surprised at the deep level of interest the children showed in the topic of dates and calendars. The teachers also were amazed at how much information the children already had about calendars and how much they understood about the concept of measuring time with a calendar. Many of the children could find the date of their own birthday and other special dates on the numbers printed on small squares of paper. The interest in calendars lasted for nearly a month, from the time the children discovered the calendars in the library corner to the time they made their own calendars to display in the classroom. From this project, the teachers learned how important it is to follow the children's interest. They realized that if they were to repeat the experience, they would need to slow down and explore the topic in more depth. In this way, they also might give the children who were slow to show an interest more time to get involved.

CREATING A MESSAGE CENTER

The students at Douglas College are encouraged to set up a message center as part of their presentations for the children during Children Teaching Teachers. This is especially important in the third semester when some of the children who participate in Children Teaching Teachers come from the first grade class in the local elementary school. The instructors ask each group of students to generate a list of materials and equipment they think they will need to create a message center such as the following.

- a small table, and chairs or desks that can be placed against the wall

- shelves on which to set up small boxes so each child will have his or her own mailbox. Transparent boxes with a slit in the lid are best but are difficult to find, so students may use shoe boxes with windows cut out of the front and covered with acetate. One group of students used clear plastic soda bottles with the tops cut off, set horizontally, and attached to each other with duct tape. Another center used a clear plastic shoe bag, labeling each shoe pocket with the child's name and symbol.

- labels for each mailbox such as stickers with a symbol chosen by each child, a Polaroid photograph, or a self-portrait labeled with the child's name
- shelving units
- a typewriter or a computer with a printer (optional)
- a wide assortment of pens, pencils, paper, cards, and small pads
- envelopes and stamps
- an alphabet or ABC books

The instructors encourage the students to consider principles such as aesthetics, reciprocity, and collaboration in setting up the centers.

Aesthetics

In planning the physical layout for the message center, the students put considerable thought into how they could make it visually appealing and inviting for the children. They often define the space by draping a length of fabric from the ceiling to the wall above the tables and chairs. One group of students, taking their inspiration from the slides they had seen of the environments in Reggio Emilia, hung a clear plastic sheet from the ceiling to floor to separate the message center from the rest of the room. They often included items such as a small bowl of flowers or an attractive lamp on the writing table. The students provided good quality paper, attractive cards, and writing tools in glass or pottery jars set out attractively on a shelf for the children.

Reciprocity

The principle of reciprocity is evident in the way the students establish a process that children can follow in sending messages and writing responses. One group of students helped the children draw a symbol to identify each of the mailboxes. They then photocopied these symbols and put them into a small container labeled with each child's name. The children can then use these symbols as stamps. If a child decides to send a message to a friend, she can find the symbol for the friend's name, paste it on the envelope or on the message, and then match it with the one on the mailbox.

Collaboration

The message center provides many children with opportunities to share their literacy skills as they assist one another in writing names and words on their messages. The principle of collaboration is much in evidence as the students practice their skills in scaffolding the children's emergent writing abilities and in helping them read the messages they receive in their mailboxes.

The instructors, in debriefing the experience with the students, discuss what the benefits are to providing a message center for the children. The students have often observed how the center encourages positive social behaviors such as sharing and taking turns. They often comment on how it gives the children a means of relating to one another and the teacher in a small group. They find that during the first session especially, one of the students needs to stay in the center while the children are using it to demonstrate the procedure. For example, at first they need to help the children select paper and writing tools suitable for their purpose such as pencils and paper for messages, or colored felt pens for invitations or birthday cards. The students find that the children often ask them for help in writing words and sentences for their messages. Sometimes, they need to remind the children to sign their names and then help them find the recipient's box. The students find that as they work with the children in the center they learn a great deal about emergent literacy. They learn how to identify the different stages of emergent writing, and they practice helping children write letters, words, and even sentences. Some of the younger preschool children sometimes need help in writing their own or their friends' names on their letters. The message center seems to encourage a sense of belonging in the group. It provides children and teachers with a natural way to form relationships with one another. Later, the children themselves begin to suggest ideas for the message center. One group of children suggested writing messages in bottles and then floating them across the water play table.

In later sessions, if the children's interest seems to flag, the students discuss ways they can vary materials to make the message center more inviting for the children. One group of students solved this problem in a creative way. They designed and built a double-sided telephone booth so that a person on each side of the booth could use a telephone, made out of two tin cans connected by a string, to speak to the person in the booth on the opposite side. The telephone booth had a number of additional features that encouraged the children to develop their communication skills as they played with the telephones. Inside the booth, the students had pasted a telephone directory on the wall listing the emergency numbers for the police, ambulance, and fire station. The students made a number grid for the children to use as a dial to punch in telephone numbers. On a shelf beside the telephone, the students provided note pads and pencils so the children could take down messages. The following extracts are taken from observations in the students' journal of the children using the telephone booth.

> To extend and expand on the children's interactions and language development, and early literacy skills, we introduced a phone booth to the dramatic play area. The children used problem-solving skills, expressive and receptive language, sharing, and turn taking and practiced social skills in learning how to conduct conversations. The children, in writing messages, were given the opportunity to develop emergent writing.

> *J:* I'm J. You can call me J.

> *I:* What are you doing?

> *J:* Nothing. I don't know.

> *I:* What are you doing?

> *J:* I'm going to a friend's house.

> *B:* Hi.

> *J:* Who's that?

> *B:* It's B.

> *J:* I'm J.

> *B:* I'm busy. I have to go.

> By adding the telephone we wanted to explore other forms of communication. We hoped to provide opportunities for the children to develop relationships and build their social and communicative skills.

For all of us, making meaning of our world is a lifelong endeavor. How we do this depends on our stage of development and on the tools we bring to the task. For Piaget, knowledge is primarily constructed through active interaction with the physical environment. According to Vygotsky, however, "cognitive construction is always socially mediated; it is influenced by present and past social interactions" (Bodrova & Leong, 1996). The social context, therefore, profoundly influences how and what we think. Both Piaget and Vygotsky stress the value of play in the child's growing ability to make sense of the world. They both emphasize the value it holds for symbolic representation and action. For Vygotsky, however, there is the added value in the opportunities play provides for children to develop self-regularization through their social interaction in the group. From the educators in Reggio Emilia, we have expanded our awareness of the many languages children use to make meaning of their world, and as teachers, we have learned from them the importance of our role as mediators of the physical and social environment in the lives of children.

In the words of Loris Malaguzzi, the child has one hundred languages and more: "a hundred hands, a hundred thoughts, a hundred ways of thinking, of playing, of speaking, . . . of listening, of marveling . . . a hundred worlds to discover, a hundred worlds to invent, a hundred worlds to dream." But the danger lies in the environment that fails to recognize the limitless potential. Malaguzzi goes on to say, "They steal ninety-nine. The school and the culture separate the head from the body. They tell the child to think without hands . . . to understand without joy . . . that work and play, reality and fantasy, science and imagination, sky and earth, reason and dream are things that do not belong together." Those who are inspired by Reggio must say, along with the child, "No way. The hundred is there."

Afterword

THE ROAD AHEAD

For the past decade or so, educators all over North America have been involved in dialog and discussion about the programs in Reggio Emilia. Where are we, and where do we go from here? There is certainly no answer to such a general question; the answers are as many as there are educators involved. Sue Fraser reflects on the progress of her own journey by saying:

> To embark on a journey, we first have to begin somewhere, and second we need a map. In the case of the Reggio Emilia approach, the map must be one that shows many possible routes. The map we used both in the teacher education program at the college and in the centers in the field was one on which the principles of the Reggio Emilia approach such as the image of the child, the environment as a third teacher, documentation, and relationship were marked on signposts to help us on our journey. There were also many interconnecting routes we had to travel to discover important aspects of the approach such as aesthetics, transparency, reciprocity, provocation, and collaboration. We could not have embarked on our journey without taking along as a guide the work of theorists such as Vygotsky, Piaget, and Dewey. So six years ago we began, and two years ago the teachers in the preschools joined us on our journey. This book is a story of this journey, of how we crisscrossed the map, visiting each major signpost and traveling down the interconnected paths. We encountered many unexpected things and traffic jams on our journey, and learned to use them, as Carolyn Edwards showed us, as a source of energy to resolve conflict and move ahead.
>
> There are still many roadblocks that we need to cross before we can move along some of the routes on our journey. We have not, for instance, figured out how we can support teachers to nearly the same degree as in the schools of Reggio Emilia.

Without this level of support, teachers find it hard to achieve the quality in documentation and in the program that the preschools in Reggio Emilia have achieved. As well, we have to overcome our lack of an atelierista who works with the teachers in the preschools in Reggio Emilia as a curriculum consultant. All I can say at this point is that our journey in implementing the Reggio Emilia approach has not ended. I cannot even tell from our perspective how far along the road we have come. But we can say for certain that we have been inspired by the principles learned from Reggio Emilia, that we have done our best to interpret them in our own context, and that we have attempted to implement them in many, but not all, aspects of our programs.

Most of the teachers whose work is described in this book would identify with the metaphor of the journey of exploration, using the signposts that have been offered by the examples of the schools in Reggio Emilia. Many might avoid terms such as "implementing the Reggio Emilia approach," heeding the cautions that the complexity and cultural significance of the approach prevent a wholesale implementation in North American settings. Not only that, as Lilian Katz has pointed out, it would take any of us a very long time to be worthy of that name, and "if we implement the Reggio Emilia approach insufficiently or inadequately, we might unwittingly and inadvertently give it a bad name, cast doubts about it, and give the impression that it is just a passing fad" (Katz, 1994, p. 17). But there is no question that the inspiration to study, reflect, and analyze our own practices has come to many teachers from the light of the shining example offered in the schools of Reggio Emilia. The very fact that the approach cannot be imported and implemented with the ease of any other prepackaged and readily available curriculum resource makes what we learn more powerful stimulation for us to work to make it our own.

Each teacher and each group of teachers has to identify the values and ideas that most resonate with meaning in view of her/his teaching philosophy, experiences, and context. In the case of most American educators, the shared theoretical base allows them to appreciate the full beauty of the practices chosen by Reggio educators to embody the ideas of Dewey, Piaget, Vygotsky, and others. The model is there, to appreciate and to ponder, to consider its separate elements and the holistic, living creation. The separate elements can be pulled out for the sake of discussion, but never in the reality. And then comes the consideration of how to fine-tune our own practice, keeping our best ideas and impulses while enriching our work with the infusion of new breadth and energy that comes with a profound appreciation for the Reggio model. All the while, the educators in Reggio remind us that their work, even after 50 years, continues to evolve and grow. The journey will continue.

Some of the most valuable practices begun by the educators in this book are time consuming and beyond the realm of typical experience and training for many educators. The most outstanding example of this is the process of documentation, of making public the process of classroom collaboration for teachers' and children's learning. Traditional constructs of the teacher as professional left no room for the tentative, reflective stance that is revealed in documentation. Yet the communication that is supported by such revelation forms the basis for the rich, deep relationships and collaboration that we admire in the Reggio system. Here is authenticity, a way of living together without certainty, open to the moment, with potential for all involved. This is also the motivation for the restructuring and reconceptualizing teacher education programs and moving toward a collaborative model for helping new teachers understand through experience what becoming a reflective practitioner means. Education becomes, for them, a co-creating of the culture of the future instead of simply transmitting what has gone before. Herein lies the hope that has enticed so many educators currently working on examining their individual practice in the light of Reggio.

Change is never easy, and the very complexity presented by the intricate circle of necessary principles involved in the work of Reggio Emilia can be daunting. Brenda Fyfe (1994) described the process of professional development related to Reggio practices undertaken with a group of fifty educators in the St. Louis area in the early 1990s. She noted the importance of collaboration, of having a support system for discussion, reflection, and interpretation of their work of change. Following this experience, she highlighted several areas of advice for teachers just beginning their study and work with practices from the Reggio Emilia approach.

Approach Old Activities in New Ways

When teachers study new ideas, they often begin by feeling incompetent. Teachers who have succeeded in making changes have generally moved at a pace that was slow enough to allow change to happen gradually, and connected to their earlier knowledge and practice. Moving too quickly may create a void; moving more gradually allows teachers to adapt their former methods of teaching. For example, using a camera to document children's activities in the fall field trip to the farm that the teacher has always planned may lead to new opportunities for revisiting and reflecting on what is truly interesting to the children about the experience. The activity was part of the teacher's traditional way of doing things; the opportunity to extend learning by beginning to document the process and reflect on its implications was the new idea.

Trying things out, assessing the result, adjusting, listening, giving a bit more time, and eventually changing a little: these are the baby steps toward comfort and competence.

Explore the "Hundred Languages"

As representation becomes a more dominant part of the teachers' work with children, teachers and children may need to spend time together exploring the various media they can use. Becoming familiar with the properties of each medium, and learning how to support developing skills to use the material effectively, are all part of teachers' understanding how to scaffold children's ability to represent their ideas. This investigation of the "hundred languages" may be an important entry into collaborative explorations with children that allows teachers to begin dialog with other teachers and community resources.

Plan for Emergent Curriculum

For many teachers, beginning the process of following children's leads in uncovering threads for further investigations may be disconcerting as they move into the area of hypotheses rather than certain teacher plans. Because the process of interpreting children's words and actions as clues on how to scaffold further learning is often unfamiliar, teachers can benefit by having others with whom to consider possible directions for projects. The brainstorming process builds relationships and supports teachers in moving into unfamiliar territory.

Reconsider Time

One of the loudest laments of teachers attempting to work with Reggio ideas is that there is just not enough time for the kinds of collaboration that supports collegial reflection. While this is certainly a reality in the present scheduling and structuring of staff interaction in most early childhood programs, it may be that teachers are going to have to use the opportunities they do have as they watch children at play. When collaboration is the priority and considered to be a necessity, not just a nice idea, teachers may find new methods of organizing time for dialog and reflection.

Persevere in Collaboration

Most American teachers have not developed the disposition or skills to work effectively with others. Many teachers have worked independently in their classrooms, with contact with other teachers perfunctory at best and not viewed as an essential element of the teaching-learning process. It is not usually part of the American culture to engage comfortably in the kinds of debate, argument, and differences of opinion on which the participants in Reggio Emilia seem to thrive. As Fyfe says; "We find it very difficult to deal with hard critique, let go of ownership of ideas, and question our certainties" (p. 28). It will be hard, and there will be tears, but getting past the hard places is critical to success. Learning to respect and accept differences is an important part of the journey, and learning to use the conflict for growth is vital.

Involve Parents

Another difficult but necessary part of the change process relates to bringing parents into the heart of the process of change and into the heart of the classroom. Again, when communication with families has been pleasant but superficial, teachers and parents are moving on to new ground. Learning can become reciprocal when parents and teachers can both offer their perspective as equal partners. When parents are involved in the change process, they can become part of the support system, not part of the opposition. (Ideas from Fyfe, 1994.)

Supports for the Journey

As teachers decide to move out on their journeys, there are aids to support them. The bibliography will suggest print and video resources for teachers who want to read and see more. There is also a special interest discussion group on the Internet. The Reggio list offers opportunities for discussion about its approach with those new to the exploration and those who have already taken some steps. Past discussions are kept in an archive, organized by thread and date, so that those wanting to get others' ideas on a particular topic may search there. Viewers may subscribe to the discussion group by following these steps:

1. Send an e-mail message to the listserv address.
2. Leave the subject line blank.
3. In the body of the message, type subscribe listname firstname lastname, as in subscribe REGGIO-L Carol Gestwicki.

The address for REGGIO-L is listserv@postoffice.cso.uiuc.edu. The archive may be accessed at the ERIC Reggio web site: ericeece.org/reggio.

The web site also has:

- ERIC digests related to the Reggio Emilia approach
- bibliographies of citations from ERIC database on the Reggio Emilia approach
- a list of videos
- links to Internet sites
- contact information
- a calendar of conferences and workshops related to Reggio Emilia
- the calendar for the traveling exhibit, The Hundred Languages of Children
- information on the two newsletters related to Reggio: *Innovations in Early Education: the International Reggio Exchange* and *Rechild: The Reggio Children Newsletter.*

In addition, the web site has a listing of schools self-described as Reggio Emilia-based schools. The schools are self-nominated as based or inspired by the approach used by the preschools in Reggio Emilia, and are not reviewed or sanctioned by any agency. The list is provided as a service for those interested in locating preschool programs that are in some way related to Reggio ideas. It could provide teachers with resources for visits or discussion in their communities. The list can be accessed at ericeece.org/reggio/reschool.html.

All of these resources could benefit teachers who are beginning to explore the philosophy and practices of the schools in Reggio Emilia, and the related practices by other American educators. There is no limit to the numbers and kinds of school where educators are exploring the ideas from Reggio in relation to their own practice in their own classrooms. Reggio-inspired classrooms can be found in Head Start programs and inner city subsidized childcare programs (Haigh, 1997; Sheldon-Harsch, & Wagner, *Innovations* 4[2]; in full day programs (Saltz, 1997, as well as Hilltop School, Lakewood Avenue Children's School, and the Carolina Friends School described in this book); public kindergartens and primary classrooms (Tarini & White, 1998; Cadwell, 1997; Katz et al., 1998; Breig-Allen & Dillon, 1997; Forman et al., 1998); private kindergartens (Oken-Wright, 1998); private preschools (Geiger, 1997, as well as Sabot School and First Baptist Kindergarten from this book); college laboratory schools (Williams & Kantor, 1997, as well as Virginia Tech child development lab school and University of Vermont Children's Center described in this book); middle and high school classrooms ("The Great Duck Pond Project" video); and infant-toddler programs (Sanderson, 1999). Since this list is only a beginning, it is probable that each state has programs that could be listed under any of these categories. There is a powerful wealth of energy and resource to be tapped by teachers beginning an exploration.

Perhaps the greatest support will come from other teachers moving at their own pace on the journey of exploration. Hear the words of Alex Doherty, director of the child care center at Loyalist College in Belleville, Ontario, describing the influence of the ideas of Reggio Emilia in transforming their work.

CONCENTRIC CIRCLES OF ACQUAINTANCE

An environment for children is a reflection of all the relationships of the individuals who come in contact with each other: the children, the teachers, the families, the classroom, and the school. In this relationship, the individuality of each person (as well as the individual as part of the whole) also should be evident and transparent throughout. People often ask us how we did what we have done. To answer that, we have to go back and reacquaint ourselves with the developmental process. A metaphor for the development of our schools is that of a pebble in a pond. As the pebble drops into the middle of the pond, concentric circles of relatedness form and begin to ripple into larger circles as the ripple makes its impact on the pond.

The first part of any relationship is the acquaintance process. We are constantly in a state of becoming acquainted, but this is heightened in the early stages. The acquaintance process was an enviable position to have, in the beginning: a new school, new faces, new relationships. Meeting all the new staff, the children, and the parents for the very first time and making their acquaintance, becoming familiar, and welcoming them into our new school nine years ago was a position of great perspective. It is difficult, and almost awkward when you meet people for the first time. The foremost perspective is to offer a sense of being welcome; the welcoming that begins should never end in our school or any school. As each teacher or parent comes to our school each day, they should feel a sense of belonging, a sense of welcoming, and knowing where they belong, where others belong, and the roles and the intricacies. The flow of relationships are clear in every conversation, every moment of meaning, each resonance of the "one" and the "all."

The acquaintance process now, from a different perspective, appears to us as a time of becoming more resourceful, inwardly and outwardly. Resourcefulness means being aware of the many possibilities of what can be and of what is, and finding a means of expression as we become more familiar and thereby more confident in expressing ourselves, either through children, through curriculum, through documentation, or through our environment by having resonance of the children in our school.

In the beginning, a child's responses are framed by the teacher's curriculum. One has to look in all the nooks and crannies of our school at how the children go through the process of becoming familiar, of feeling isolated, feeling alone, or of reaching out and extending themselves toward something that is unknown. It is a feeling that ripples back to us from time to time but with particular poignancy in the early years. In the beginning, we had to become acquainted with the faces of children, become observant of who they were in the context of their own family, and how they would express themselves in a new environment for all of us.

We also needed to become acquainted with what it felt like to be with others, new children, and new colleagues, and begin to understand that we all had a different way of expressing ourselves, and we had to develop a way to understand the many languages of ourselves. The many voices and the many expressions often made moving past the acquaintance process difficult; understanding many children and many children's rights was difficult to assimilate into one chorus, and also becoming fluent in understanding colleagues' ideas, concepts, and languages often made coming to a collaborative perspective challenging.

In this time of becoming acquainted, all of the individuals could be perceived as pebbles in ponds and all the concentric circles, because of the vibrations of each, would accept each other but would not necessarily connect. That highlights again the concept of isolation, the concept of nonconnectedness, the concept of not feeling that one belongs, that one is still in the perspective of reaching out and shaking hands, and making eye contact and not quite having achieved the level of mutuality, the level of connectedness that would make one feel truly as though one belonged, as though one were embedded into an environment, embedded into a relationship, embedded into our school.

Although the metaphor of the pebble in the pond fits the idea of how something beautiful yet simple can have an impact on a greater whole, it does not go far enough to show that what we all need and want, and what children rightfully deserve, is a feeling of connectedness, a feeling of being embedded.

Relationships and Reciprocity

The process of acquaintance and relationship made us realize throughout the years that we were certainly on a developmental adventure that often was similar to the developmental process that was evident in our young children as they began to learn and became more confident with the acquisition of skills and knowledge. Once we began to see this reflection and as we began to do new and challenging things, we began to develop a deeper understanding of how our children acquired knowledge from their own base of curiosity and the idea of "I wonder how" became a percolation of how the foundation of everything began.

We began to explore the image of children—how the reflection of each child was received and perceived within our own eye and how each child was reflected differently in each of our eyes. We also explored how the image of ourselves as individuals was reflected in our own eyes and in the eyes of the children, our colleagues, and the parents. We also had to look at the meaning and the image of us—was it who I worked with, the children who I worked with, or was it the group as a whole? How did we all see ourselves? The last image that began to come to us was the image of our school. How did we see our school, and how did our school see us? This last question we thought was a very provoking but almost silly concept, but if we see the school, the school must see us in some fashion.

The relationship, reciprocity, or mutuality phase of our development of the children or with the children is an ongoing one. At times we perceive and are more sensitive to the children or ourselves, our sense of us, or our sense of school, and we do have times in which we are more responsive to those particular areas, but they are ongoing, a kind of bedrock of our foundation. The environment is a reflection of the values of the teachers and their image of themselves and their children. This touchpoint offers us oneness; everyone is simply a "one." Often, life seems more special when oneness is celebrated by all; a simple example is a birthday party. It is a very special day to celebrate the day you came into this world and were welcomed by your friends and family. We all celebrate the wonderfulness of you. It would be very sad if you had to celebrate your birthday all by yourself with no one else to celebrate with you, and that is what working in environments, in classrooms, that do not reflect who you are or who the children are, is like: lonely and not very validating.

Reciprocity affords us an image of ourselves. When I had the opportunity to become acquainted first with colleagues, I saw a rich potential that sparkled in their eyes of the promise offered by the new opportunity. I see that look in the faces of the children who come through the doors of our school every day. Every day brings a sparkle to their eyes, a grin on their little mouths, and an exuberance in their bodies, saying, I can hardly wait to get to school today. I feel that teachers need and have the right to feel that way most days when they come to school, and so we as educators have to look at ourselves as rich with potential, rich with possibilities, as resourceful. We see the child as full of possibilities to be explored each day. We should embrace colleagues in the same way we nurture our children, not looking at weaknesses as negative and strengths as vehicles for conflict. In the beginning, working as a team and being a collaborative group was simply a process of paying lip service to the idea of being a team, but we were insensitive to each other and we did not listen to each other, so weaknesses led to tension and conflict—not the kind of tension and conflict that solved problems, but the kind that created more problems.

Letting Go

One of the hardest things that we did and that I encourage others to do is to let go of those practices that make us feel so safe. Once a relationship has been built with perhaps one other or a few other colleagues, you will begin to understand that your colleagues will catch you if you stumble. A metaphor that we use to describe this particular junction in our development is that of a "cart." A "vehicle" of expression is described from the perspective of one of our team members who always felt that there was a cart and there was a particular person driving, and there was a particular person navigating, and the rest of the team sat very comfortably in the back of the wagon. This colleague felt that she was always on the very tip of the back of the wagon and she felt that every bump knocked her off the wagon. She would stumble off, and she felt that everyone always had to stop and come around, pick her up, and put her back on the wagon. She always felt very apologetic for the fact that she did not perceive that she was moving along with curriculum and environment the way everyone else was. What we had to show to her was that the driver will get tired of driving and will want to take a rest in the back of the cart, and the navigator will get tired of navigating and it will be someone else's turn. What we have found in the last five years is that we do have valleys, and we do have large mountains that the cart goes up and down, and we do take turns. Sometimes the trip is fast and sometimes it is slow, but the trip is always together.

Creating our program meant letting go of the things that we held dearest to us—the idea that we were the most wonderful teachers, that we were following curriculum specifically and correctly, that we were taking care of children to the utmost of our ability and that the children in our care were very safe, clean, and well educated. We almost strangled the wonder out of each of our days, and out of the children's days. The parents had entrusted us with the most important years of their children's lives, the first five years which are filled with wonder, curiosity, and the acquisition of everything wonderful such as learning to walk for the first time, learning that water is wet and trickles down your nose when someone splashes you, learning how it feels to dress up very fancy and be the king and queen, and having all your friends welcome you each day when you come to school. By holding on so tightly to a prescribed curriculum that was preset by teachers rather than encompassing the right of the child to have their interests reflected each day, we almost suffocated our school, and I see that suffocation in many child care centers that I visit. We began to trust each other and ourselves to be open to the interest in the curriculum that came from the children. Once teachers felt that trust, they could reflect it with the children. Once our children felt more trusted, they became more expressive, and as we were more open and the children felt more empowered, our curriculum began to emerge. We could see for the first time all the sprinklings of wonder that we could help capture with our children. From security in our relationships with ourselves came a relationship with the image of the child within us.

Reflecting

From this point, our reflections, relationships, and reciprocities began to become transparent to us and we felt we could offer these to the children. As the children received this mode of feeling, it became reciprocal. It was almost like a ball was being bounced back and forth from one to another. Sometimes it was a quick process and sometimes it was slow. We began to feel more resourceful about ourselves, our children, our curriculum, and our environment. We began to listen to our children and to ourselves. When we looked at our corners, and our nooks and crannies, we found that there was no image of us in our school, and we began to take photographs and study what each corner meant to our children and to us. Then we began to really watch and listen to what play patterns, what opportunities, and what activities would occur in specific areas of time and record our observations through writing or through pictures. What occurred to us was an extremely powerful moment of reciprocity in which the children described to us through their actions an environment that they felt they rightly deserved. When we began to really listen and watch the children, we began to make transformations with them and for them. Once we began to trust the information the children were giving us, the children felt more trusted to express to us more and more of what they felt they rightly deserved.

As we worked with the children, many things were difficult and challenging, and many things were a joyful process. The stripping-down process is ongoing, like the concentric circles that I spoke of earlier. The power of feeling listened to for the first time moved us to begin to listen to the children with our ears wide open and to begin to ask questions.

As we began to hear clearly, we began to ask more precise questions, and to immerse ourselves in transcribing and translating the stories of the children each day. As we became good listeners, we could help translate the expressions of the children, even for our youngest babies and toddlers.

When we began to share the many stories, we began to understand the importance of writing them down for others to share, and we began to explore recording our observations and our resonances of what we had seen and heard. We began to tell our stories on white pieces of Bristol board with the aid of pictures and written information which we shared with our parents and our students.

When we began to look at our stories, we began to understand through reading of the documentation and reading of other literature. This reflecting became important to us as a team because we then began to refer and build a dialog reciprocity and acquaintance. We had now become connected and were able to translate each other's languages and understand each other's expressions. This became something we enjoyed. We didn't talk at each other anymore, we spoke with each other, and many languages were being heard. We became more competent in listening to the children.

Discussions about the day, the stories of our children, and moments with each other or with our children's parents became almost "camp fire" experiences for us. We would sit for hours, regaling each other with successes and competencies of the children and ourselves each day. We have stories that we have told for five or six years that we enjoy as much today as we did when we first discovered a particular moment of magic.

Touchpoints

A specific document that was offered to us as a foundation or touchpoint was a simple article entitled "Building Wonder in Your Environment" by J. Greenman (1993). Yes, your environment is wonderful, but is it wonder-full? And when we began to look at questions of whether our school smelled good, felt good, looked wonderful, or felt wonderful, we began to let go of something else that we felt was very important, a teacher-directed environment. We began to wonder what every corner looked like from the perspective of a child. Another simple touchpoint that was helpful to us, was what we called 20 questions. In making any transformations or in implementing any curriculum, we asked ourselves 20 questions about why we were doing something, what we were doing, and how. If we were resourceful enough to respond confidently to good questions about the underpinnings of what we were doing, we felt we could go ahead because what we were doing was resplendent with observation and resonance, and the images of us and the children were transparent. We ask ourselves 20 questions with everything from moving a shelf to hanging documentation, to talking about an emerging project or interacting with each other. It is kind of like working with the two-year-olds when they ask you why, why, why; and to every response you give them, ask why again, and so it reacquaints us with the developmental process that is emerging within our own children through their natural curiosity. We need always to be familiar with the tools of our children so that we may offer them proper and specific tools, whether they are tools in a play space or tools for asking questions and being a good listener.

Symbolic Transformation

Once we began to strip down our environment, to ask good questions, to observe our children, and to transform the environment in keeping with the image of the child and the image of the school, we began to look at congruency to make sure meaningfulness was evident in our school and in our classrooms consistently. One of the specific areas that we looked at was our symbolic play area. Some individuals would call it a dramatic play area, a dress-up area, or a housekeeping area. We, in the beginning, were a school that received a lot of new toys, and we enjoyed the stage of going through catalogs and choosing all the wondrous things that when we were a "have-not" school we could not afford to have. Consequently, our infant, toddler, and preschool rooms were full of many brightly colored Fisher-Price® and Little Tykes® items. These props were very prominent in our symbolic play area next to our play stove and our play fridge where we would have the Fisher-Price® frozen peas and pretend hot dogs. We began to look at whether play is the work of the child and what kind of work we could accomplish in a kitchen that has tools similar to the ones that we propose for our children. We began to ask ourselves questions about whether we would give children a paintbrush of poor quality at an easel, and answered no because we felt it was an expressive medium. But do our children not express themselves in the most wondrous and magical ways in the dramatic or symbolic play area? We answered yes, so we felt that we needed to give our children tools that were expressive and not limiting. Who knows what is in a pot of soup bubbling on a four-year-old's play stove? It could have a boot, a rock, some spaghetti, and a rolled-up sock, but because we offer them the frozen peas or the pretend hot dogs, we don't allow them to express all the magic of what their soup is like. By offering them a real ladle, real china bowls, and a real spoon, suddenly we allow them to transform their play to a symbolic language they could express, of who they are, who they think they are now, and who they wish to be. Play is transformed to wishful thought, and from there the children can springboard into many wondrous and magical areas, simply by being offered specific tools.

We then began to embark on a quest to make all our symbolic play areas similar. We began to weave that concept throughout other areas in our school, and we began to look through this process at meaningful units—at what was meaningful to us and what was part of our value system. When we began to explore this together and with our children, we began to discover our culture and to become reacquainted and reconnected with who we were and what was important to all of us.

Through simple concepts such as congruency, reciprocity, and acquaintance, it is as if you embark on a quest or a process in which there is no formula or right way of doing things. When something comes around full circle, you know you have begun the concentric circles of acquaintance. You have begun to know your children, yourself, your families, and your school, and you have begun to have a little sense of the enigmatic magic of what Reggio Emilia inspires you to achieve.

The Reggio Emilia approach cannot merely be studied and transplanted at home. It is a living, organic system growing in a culture very different from our own. Can it take root here and grow? If so, what kind of plant will emerge? The answers depend on us all. Let the conversations continue.

Appendix **I**

Children
Teaching Teachers

Ten years ago, the Early Childhood Education (ECE) program at Douglas College in New Westminster, British Columbia initiated an innovative method of preparing teachers to work in early childhood centers. Still part of the curriculum today, preschool children from local child care centers and first grade children from the elementary school across the street from the college are invited to participate for two hours, one morning a week, with the early childhood students in a core curriculum experience called Children Teaching Teachers (CTT). The class is divided into six groups of five or six students. Each group is paired with a sister group that collaborates in preparing an environment, and taking turns in observing and presenting activities to the visiting children. Sister groups jointly write up a journal that includes reflection and documentation of their experiences. Early childhood faculty and students observe and videotape each session, and later debrief and analyze the videotapes with the students. This documentation is used as the basis for planning the following week. Each week, the students photograph the children as they participate in each session and compile documentation of some aspect of their experience in CTT of particular interest. Students may, for example, document the process of creating a communication center and adapting it as they gain a deeper understanding of early literacy over the six-week period they work with the children.

RATIONALE

Piaget stressed the importance of active learning and social transmission as critical factors in the learning process. Children Teaching Teachers provides the students with many opportunities to work directly with preschool and elementary children, and collaboratively with fellow students, sharing ideas and giving one another suggestions and feedback.

Vygotsky believed that learning does not take place in isolation and that knowledge is co-constructed by members of a group in the process of collaborating and working together. This principle is evident in Children Teaching Teachers as students plan, initiate, and evaluate one another's experiences after each weekly session. The instructors also participate in this process as they observe the students working with children. The early childhood curriculum is not static and emerges through the actions and interactions of children, students, and instructors. Students negotiate the curriculum for each session of CTT in the process of working with the children and with one another. The children's regular teachers are invited to observe each session and provide feedback for the students. The instructors also participate in this process by observing and reflecting on their observations in a debriefing with each group of students at the end of the weekly sessions. The instructors collaborate and base their lecture content for the following weeks on observations and information from the debriefing sessions. Courses are no longer taught in isolation as content is increasingly integrated and courses often are team-taught.

GUIDING PRINCIPLES FOR CHILDREN TEACHING TEACHERS

1. *Active Learning.* Students learn by exploring curriculum materials, working directly with children, and getting immediate feedback from the children, peers, and instructors.

2. *Collaborative Learning.* Students work closely in groups and with their sister group in planning, presenting, and evaluating activities for young children.

3. *Observation.* Through Children Teaching Teachers, students practice and refine their skills by observing, recording, analyzing, and evaluating curriculum experiences and child development.

4. *Interpersonal Skills.* Students are continually learning and improving their ability to work and relate to others as they collaborate in their groups.

5. *Guiding Children's Behavior.* Students have many opportunities to practice guidance with the support of other students in their groups.

6. *Integrating Curriculum.* Students learn to provide children with a play-based, well-rounded curriculum experience that is developmentally appropriate and based on the children's individual needs and interests.

The Reggio Emilia Approach
in Children Teaching Teachers

In the last six years, the ECE faculty has introduced the Reggio Emilia approach into the early childhood program, and the students have been required to implement principles learned from Reggio Emilia in planning the environment, preparing experiences, and interacting with the children who visit the campus once a week.

Collaboration

Collaboration is a key principle in the Reggio Emilia approach and in the CTT program. Students collaborate with fellow students, with the children, and with the children's regular teachers. Instructors observe the students' presentations and collaborate in preparing course content for future weeks of class. Courses in the early childhood program are increasingly team-taught.

The Image of the Child

Collaboration in planning curriculum experiences presupposes a shared understanding of the image of the child. Students begin the semester by exploring their own image of the child. Based on these observations, discussions, and participation in a group exercise, the students create a visual representation of their image of the child. One group of students wrote in their journal, "The way we created our poster was for us to think like a child, to be spontaneous and inventive, and to have fun. Our poster was unstructured; we each took the initiative to express ourselves, and we came together as a team to make our final product—a poster of our image of the child." The students, by observing, listening, and conversing with children, discover how competent and inventive the children are. They then plan an environment that supports their image of the child.

The Environment as a Third Teacher

Prior to planning their environments in the classroom for Children Teaching Teachers, each group of students chooses one aspect of the environment such as transparency, relationship, aesthetics, or bringing the outside in and the inside out. Then they create a display illustrating the principle they chose. The students visit each group's display to learn and get ideas from one another. This activity helps them set up an environment to act as a third teacher for Children Teaching Teachers in the following weeks.

Documentation

Documentation of the experiences in Children Teaching Teachers is carried out by the students using a number of methods such as recording observations in writing, videotaping, and using tape recorders and still photography to capture the experiences in the weekly session. The journals developed jointly by sister groups provide a detailed record of the process. CTT provides students with many opportunities to practice their skills in documentation and to experience how important documentation is for sustaining topics and negotiating the curriculum with children. The documentation of the children's experiences has become an important means of informing the parents, staff in the centers, and the community about Children Teaching Teachers.

Provocation

Students are encouraged to think of innovative ways of provoking the children's thinking or further investigation of a topic of interest. Students might provoke the children to investigate a topic or material by setting up an area of the room as a mini-atelier filled with art or science materials to stimulate the children's exploration, creativity, and interest in carrying out symbolic representation. Provocation also may occur during the course of a conversation with children, or in setting out materials or equipment in unexpected ways or in unusual relationships. Sometimes, a successful provocation will develop into a project that extends over many sessions of Children Teaching Teachers. Before CTT begins in the fall semester, the faculty and ECE students visit a small park near the college and explore together how a provocation is put into practice. After this experience, students have a better understanding of how to plan and initiate provocations when they work with the children.

HOW CHILDREN TEACHING TEACHERS WORKS

First Semester Overview

Courses:
- Child Growth and Development: Infants and Toddlers
- Methodology and Classroom Planning
- Observation Skills

The principles of Reggio Emilia introduced during this semester include:
- relationships
- respect for children

- aesthetics
- collaboration
- the environment as a third teacher
- observation
- documentation

Family Days.   Families with young children are invited to spend two mornings with the ECE students who set up mini-environments for infants and toddlers. The students plan and implement a developmentally appropriate setting for children, observe and record the activities and experiences, and document their findings. This is the beginning of the students' journey in early education using the principles of Reggio Emilia such as collaboration, relationship, and aesthetics.

Second Semester Overview

Courses:

- Child Growth and Development: Preschool Children
- Methodology and Classroom Planning
- Curriculum: Art, Literature, Music, and Movement

The principles of Reggio Emilia are expanded during this semester to include the following:

- relationships
- the image of the child
- respect for children
- aesthetics
- provocation
- environment as a third teacher
- learning through play
- observation and recording
- documentation

Children Teaching Teachers is introduced in this semester. After each session, the faculty ask the students the following questions:

- What went well for you today?
- What was difficult, and how would you change it?
- What did you learn from the children?

The observation, analysis, and documentation compiled by each group in each session are used to plan for CTT the following week.

Third Semester Overview

Courses:

- Child Growth and Development: Primary Children and Language Arts
- Methodology and Classroom Planning
- Curriculum: Science, Mathematics, and Social Science

The principles of Reggio Emilia are expanded to include the following:

- relationships
- image of the child
- respect for children
- aesthetics
- transparency
- taking the inside out
- bringing the outside in
- sociocultural environments
- communication and message centers
- provocation
- the environment as the third teacher
- learning through play
- observing and recording
- documentation

Children Teaching Teachers provides students with the following skills:

- collaboration
- cooperation
- communication
- analysis
- problem-solving
- conflict resolution
- evaluation
- documentation

The campus child care center and a local elementary school bring the children to the college for six consecutive sessions in which the students set up environments developmentally appropriate for older preschool and first grade students. Communication, conversation, and language are emphasized. Projects, problem-solving, and conflict resolution are important components in these sessions with the children. At the end of each session, instructors ask the students the following questions that have been designed to develop analytic and critical thinking skills:

- What went well?
- What did not go as planned?
- What was demanding?
- What interests of the children were observed, and how will you build on these interests?
- What did you learn from the children, and what action will you take as a result of this learning?

At the conclusion of each session, the students document their findings using photographs and text to describe the experience and learning. The analysis, observation, evaluation, and documentation are used to plan for CTT the following week.

Children Teaching Teachers is a process in which students, faculty, and children learn from one another. Children lead the students who are discovering and applying the principles of Reggio Emilia in a safe, secure setting in which everyone collaborates, cooperates, and respects individual differences and universal similarities.

(This material was based on a presentation for the National Association of Young Children Conference, Toronto, November 1998 by Susan Fraser, Elva Reid, and Cathleen Smith.)

Appendix **II**

Audiovisual Materials

A Message from Malaguzzi. Produced by George Forman and Lella Gandini. 1993. A one-hour video of an interview with Loris Malaguzzi. Available from:
Reggio Children USA
1341 G Street, NW
Suite 400
Washington, D.C. 20005-3105
(800) 424-4310
(202) 265-9090

To Make a Portrait of a Lion. A long-term project of children in one of the municipal preschools in Reggio Emilia. 1987. Available from:
Reggio Children USA
1341 G Street, NW
Suite 400
Washington, D.C. 20005-3105
(800) 424-4310
(202) 265-9090

Childhood. PBS. 1991. Short segments on Reggio Emilia in parts three and four of this multipart video. Available from:
Ambrose Video Publishing
1290 Avenue of the Americas
Suite 2245
New York, NY 10104

Detroit Head Start Inspired by the Reggio Approach. 1996. A 16-minute video that focuses on a staff development project launched in consultation with Reggio Children, and sponsored by the Merrill-Palmer Institute of Wayne State University and the Head Start Division of the Detroit Human Services Department. Available from:

    The Merrill-Palmer Institute
    Wayne State University
    71-A East Ferry Avenue
    Detroit, MI 48202

The Long Jump: A Video Analysis of Small Group Projects in Early Education as Practiced in Reggio Emilia, Italy. George Forman and Lella Gandini. 1991. Available from:

    Performanetics Press
    19 The Hollow
    Amherst, MA 01002
    (413) 256-8846

An Amusement Park for Birds: A long-term project at the Villetta School in Reggio Emilia. George Forman and Lella Gandini. 1994. Available from:

    Performanetics Press
    19 The Hollow
    Amherst, MA 01002
    (413) 256-8846

The Hundred Languages of Children. A 30-minute video filmed at the Hundred Languages of Children exhibit at Dominican College, San Rafael, California. 1995. Available from:

    M. S. Lyon
    101 Lombard Street, 608W
    San Francisco, CA 94111
    Fax: (415) 397-8211

The Creative Spirit. PBS. 1992. Segment on Reggio Emilia in part two of this multipart video. Available from:

    PBS Video
    4401 Sunset Boulevard
    Los Angeles, CA 90027

Setting Sail: An Emergent Curriculum Project. The story of one in-depth emergent project for preschoolers based on ideas inspired by projects in Reggio Emilia. Ann Pelo and Sarah Felstiner. Available from:

    Harvest Resources
    P.O. Box 22106   and
    Seattle, WA 98122   Redleaf Press
    Fax: (206) 720-0494   (800) 423-8309

Thinking Big: Extending Emergent Curriculum Projects. The work of two teachers working with children on a long-term investigation with comments about the teachers' thinking processes and practices inspired by the Reggio approach. Ann Pelo and Sarah Felstiner. 1999. Available from:

Harvest Resources
P.O. Box 22106
Seattle, WA 98122
Fax: (206) 720-0494

The Great Duck Pond Project: A learning community venture inspired by the Reggio Emilia approach. Describes long-term investigations by a number of teachers working at various educational levels, all exploring how the principles of Reggio Emilia could inform their work. Available from:

Lynn Hill
Department of Human Development
Virginia Tech
Blacksburg, VA 24061
Fax: (540) 231-7012

Bibliography

Aska, W. (1986). *Who hides in the park?* Montreal: Tundra Books.

Asseline, M. (1997). Bridging the gap: Family and community literacies. *Canadian Children* 22, 2:23–29.

Baumrind, D. (1967). Child care practices anteceding three patterns of preschool behaviour. *Genetic Psychology Monographs* 75:43–88.

Bettelheim, B. (1977). *The uses of enchantment: The meaning and importance of fairy tales.* New York: Vintage Books.

Biber, B. (1972). Learning experience in school and personality: Assumptions and application. In S. J. Braun & E. P. Edwards (eds.), *History and theory of early childhood education,* Belmont, CA: Wadsworth.

Biber, B., E. Shapiro, & D. Wickens. (1971). *Promoting cognitive growth: A developmental-interaction point of view.* Washington, DC: NAEYC.

Bodrova, E., & D.J. Leong. (1996). *Tools of the mind: The Vygotskian approach to early childhood education.* Englewood Cliffs, NJ: Merrill.

Brazelton, T.B. (1981). *On becoming a family: The growth of attachment.* New York: Delacourte/Seymour Lawrence.

Bredekamp, S. (1993). Reflections on Reggio Emilia. *Young Children* 49:13–17.

Breig-Allen, C., & J. Dillon. (1997). Implementing the process of change in a public school setting. *First steps toward teaching the Reggio way,* J. Hendrick (ed.), Upper Saddle River, NJ: Prentice-Hall.

Bronfenbrenner, U. (1979). *The Ecology of human development: Experiments by nature and design.* Cambridge, MA: Harvard University Press.

Bruner, J. S. (1986). *Actual minds, possible worlds.* Cambridge, MA: Harvard University Press.

———. (1996). *The culture of education.* Cambridge, MA: Harvard University Press.

Cadwell, L.B. (1997). *Bringing Reggio Emilia home*. New York: Teachers College Press, Columbia University.

Cassady, D., & C. Lancaster. (1993). The grassroots curriculum: A dialog between children and teachers. *Young Children* 48, 5:47–51.

Castagnetti, M., & V. Vecchi. (1997). *Shoe and meter*. Reggio Emilia, Italy: Reggio Children.

Ceppi, G., & M. Zeni (Eds.). (1998). *Children, spaces, relations: Metaproject for an environment for young children*. Washington, D.C.: Reggio Children.

Clay, M. (1975). *What did I write?* Aukland, Australia: Heinemann.

Dahlberg, G., P. Moss, & A. Pence. (1999). *Beyond quality in early childhood education and care: Postmodern perspectives*. London: Falmer Press.

Dewey, J. (1897). My pedagogic creed. *The School Journal* 54, 3.

———. [1915] (1956). *The school and society*. Rev. ed. Chicago: University of Chicago Press.

Dixon, G. (1994). The first years of kindergarten in Canada. *Canadian Children* 19, 2:6–9.

Doll, W.E. (1993). *A post-modern perspective on curriculum*. New York: Teachers College Press, Columbia University.

Edwards, C. (1998). Partner, nurturer, and guide: The role of the teacher. In C. Edwards, L. Gandini, & G. Forman (eds.), *The hundred languages of children: The Reggio Emilia approach—advanced reflections*, Norwood, NJ: Ablex Publishing Corporation.

Edwards, C., L. Gandini, & G. Forman. (Eds.) (1993). *The hundred languages of children: The Reggio Emilia approach to early childhood education*. Norwood, NJ: Ablex Publishing Corporation.

———. (1998a). *The hundred languages of children: The Reggio Emilia approach—advanced reflections*. 2nd ed. Greenwich, CT: Ablex Publishing Corporation.

———. (1998b). Conclusion: Final reflections. In C. Edwards, L. Gandini, & G. Forman (eds.), *The hundred languages of children: The Reggio Emilia approach—advanced reflections*, Norwood, NJ: Ablex Publishing Corporation.

Erikson, H.E. (1950). *Childhood and society*. New York: W.W. Norton & Co. Inc.

Filippini, T. (in collaborations with S. Bonilauri). (1998). The role of the pedagogista: An interview with Lella Gandini. In C. Edwards, L. Gandini, & G. Forman (eds.), *The hundred languages of children: The Reggio Emilia approach—advanced reflections*, Norwood, NJ: Ablex Publishing Corporation.

Forman, G. (1994). Different media, different languages. In L. Katz & B. Cesarone (eds.), *Reflections on the Reggio Emilia approach*, University of Illinois, Urbana: Eric/EECE.

———. (1996). Negotiating with art media to deepen learning. *Child Care Information Exchange* 3:56–58.

Forman, G., and B. Fyfe. (1998). Negotiated learning through design, documentation and discourse. In C. Edwards, L. Gandini, & G. Forman (eds.), *The hundred languages of children: The Reggio Emilia approach—advanced reflections*, Norwood, NJ: Ablex Publishing Corporation.

Forman, G., J. Langley, M. Oh, & L. Wrisley. (1998). The city in the snow: Applying the multisymbolic approach in Massachusetts. In C. Edwards, L. Gandini, & G. Forman (eds.), *The hundred languages of children: The Reggio Emilia approach—advanced reflections,* Norwood, NJ: Ablex Publishing Corporation.

Fraser, S. (1992). Talk to play and play to talk. *MCmulticulturalism/multiculturalisme* XIV, 2/3:27–30.

Froebel, F. [1897] (1970). *The education of man.* Trans. W. Hailman. Reprint, New York: Kelly.

Furth, H.G. (1969). *Piaget and knowledge: Theoretical foundations.* Englewood Cliffs, NJ: Prentice-Hall.

Fyfe, B. (1994). Images from the United States: Using ideas from the Reggio Emilia experience with American educators. In L. Katz & B. Cesarone (eds.), *Reflections on the Reggio Emilia approach,* University of Illinois, Urbana: ERIC/EECC.

———. (1998). Questions for collaboration: Lessons from Reggio Emilia. *Canadian Children* 23, 1:20–22.

Gandini, L. (1994). Celebrating children day by day: A conversation with Amelia Gambetti. *Child Care Information Exchange* 100:52–55.

———. (1998). The experience of the infant-toddler center in Reggio Emilia: An interview with Cristina Bondavalli. *Innovations* 6, 1.

Gardner, H. (1983). *Frames of mind: The theory of multiple intelligences.* New York: Basic Books.

Geiger, B. (1997). Implementing Reggio in an independent school: What works? In J. Hendrick (ed.), *First steps toward teaching the Reggio way,* Upper Saddle River, NJ: Prentice-Hall.

Gerst, B. (1998). Further reflections upon the applications of the Reggio view in a kindergarten classroom. *Canadian Children* 23, 2:43–48.

Goldhaber, J., D. Smith, & S. Sortino. (1997). Observing, recording, understanding: The role of documentation in early childhood teacher education. In J. Hendrick (ed.), *First steps toward teaching the Reggio way,* Upper Saddle River, NJ: Prentice-Hall.

Goodman, V. (1998). The power of voice. *Canadian Children* 23, 2:49–50.

Haigh, K. (1997). How the Reggio approach has influenced an inner-city program: Exploring Reggio in Head State and subsidized child care. In J. Hendrick (ed.), *First steps toward teaching the Reggio way,* Upper Saddle River, NJ: Prentice-Hall.

———. (1999). Building collegiality: Reflections on organizational structure, collaboration and the impact of role definition, motivation and leadership on collegiality. *Innovations* 7, 2.

Harris H., S.B. Judy, & K. Steinheimer. (1998). *Windows on learning: Documenting young children's work.* Columbia University, New York: Teachers College Press.

Higgins, M. (1999). Come join the journey: Bringing Reggio Emilia to the college community. *Canadian Children* 24, 1:33–40.

Hunt, J. McV. (1961). *Intelligence and experience.* New York: The Ronald Press.

Author. Highlights from the Reggio e-mail bulletin board. *Innovations 4*, 1.

Jones, E., & G. Reynolds. (1992). *The play's the thing: Teachers' roles in children's play.* New York: Teachers College Press.

Jones, E., & J. Nimmo. (1995). *Emergent curriculum.* Washington, D.C.: NAEYC.

Katz, L. (1994). Images from the world: Study seminar on the experience of the municipal infant-toddler centers and preprimary schools of Reggio Emilia, Italy. In L. Katz & B. Cesarone (eds.), *Reflections of the Reggio Emilia approach,* University of Illinois, Urbana: Eric/EECE.

———. (1997). Can the Reggio approach be adapted? *Rechild—Reggio Children, newsletter 1.*

———. (1998). What can we learn from Reggio Emilia? In C. Edwards, L. Gandini, & G. Forman (eds.), *The hundred languages of children: The Reggio Emilia approach—advanced reflections,* Norwood, NJ: Ablex Publishing Corporation.

Katz, L.G., & B. Cesarone. (Eds.) (1994). *Reflections on the Reggio Emilia approach.* University of Illinois, Urbana: Eric/EECE.

Katz, C., P. McCadden, & L. Geismar-Ryan. (1998). The crab story. *Innovations 6*, 1.

Kaufman, P. (1998). Poppies and the dance of world making. In C. Edwards, L. Gandini, & G. Forman (Eds.), *The hundred languages of children: The Reggio Emilia approach—advanced reflections,* Norwood, NJ: Ablex Publishing Corporation.

Kennedy, D. (1996). After Reggio Emilia: May the conversation begin! *Young Children 51*(5):24–27.

Krechevsky, M. (1993). Today's children: Our keys to tomorrow. *Canadian Children* 18, 2:6–12.

Malaguzzi, L. (1993). For an education based on relationships. *Young Children* 49, 1:9–12.

———. (1995). The game of "what to do." In *The fountains: From a project for the construction of an amusement park for birds.* Reggio Emilia, Italy: Reggio Children.

Moran, M.J. (1997). Reconceptualizing early childhood teacher education: Preservice teachers as ethnographers. In J. Hendrick (ed.), *First steps toward teaching the Reggio way,* Upper Saddle River, NJ: Prentice-Hall.

———. (1998). The project approach framework for teacher education: A case for collaborative learning and reflective practice. In C. Edwards, L. Gandini, & G. Forman (eds.), *The hundred languages of children: The Reggio Emilia approach—advanced reflections,* Norwood, NJ: Ablex Publishing Corporation.

Mouzard, D.G. (1997). Building castles. *Canadian Children* 22, 1:38–39.

New, R. (1990). Excellent early education: A city in Italy has it. *Young Children* 45, 6:212–18.

———. (1994). Reggio Emilia: Its visions and its challenges for educators in the United States. In L. Katz & B. Cesarone (eds.), *Reflections on the Reggio Emilia approach,* Urbana, IL: ERIC/EECC.

———. (1997). Reggio Emilia's commitment to children and community: A reconceptualization of quality and DAP. *Canadian Children* 22, 1:7–12.

———. (1998). Theory and praxis in Reggio Emilia: They know what they are doing, and why. In C. Edwards, L. Gandini, & G. Forman (eds.), *The hundred languages of children: The Reggio Emilia approach—advanced reflections,* Norwood, NJ: Ablex Publishing Corporation.

———. (1999). What should children learn? Making choices and taking chances. *Early Childhood Research and Practice* 1(2):1–19.

Oken-Wright, P. (Winter 1998). How does the gosling get in the egg? Five year olds and the co-construction of theory. *Innovations* 5, 4.

———. (1998). *Reggio Emilia: Some lessons for U.S. educators.* University of Illinois, Urbana: ERIC/EECE, EDO-PS-93–3.

Parten, M. (1932). Social participation among preschool children. *Journal of Abnormal and Social Psychology* 55:825–30.

Piaget, J. (1952). *The origins of intelligence in children.* New York: International Universities Press, Inc.

———. (1971). *Science of education and the psychology of the child.* New York: Viking.

Prochner, L. (1994). A brief history of daycare in Canada: The early years. *Canadian Children* 19, 2:10–15.

Protagonists, La Villetta. (1995). *The Fountains.* Reggio Emilia, Italy; Reggio Children.

Reynolds, G. (1998). Reggio Emilia—an impossible dream? *Canadian Children* 23, 2:4–10.

Rinaldi, C. (1993). The emergent curriculum and social constructivism: An interview with Lella Gandini. In C. Edwards, L. Gandini, & G. Forman (eds.), *The hundred languages of children: The Reggio Emilia approach to early childhood education,* Norwood, NJ: Ablex Publishing Corporation.

———. (1998). Projected curriculum constructed through documentation—progettazione: An interview with Lella Gandini. In C. Edwards, L. Gandini, & G. Forman (Eds.), *The hundred languages of children: The Reggio Emilia approach—advanced reflections.* 2nd ed., Greenwich, CT: Ablex Publishing Corporation.

———. (1999). Visible listening. *Rechild—Reggio Children newsletter* 3.

———. (1999). The image of the child and of the child's environment as a fundamental principle in the infant-toddler centers of Reggio Emilia. *Innovations* 7, 1.

Rodari, G. (1996). *The grammar of fantasy: An introduction to the art of inventing stories.* New York: Teachers and Writers Collaborative.

Roskos, K., & C. Vukelich. (1991). Promoting literacy in play. *Day Care and Early Education* 19, 1:30–34.

Saltz, R. (1997). The Reggio Emilia influence at the University of Michigan-Dearborn Child Development Center: Challenges and change. In J. Hendrick (ed.), *First steps toward teaching the Reggio way,* Upper Saddle River, NJ: Prentice-Hall.

Sanderson, M. (1999). Reaping the rewards of project work with infants and toddlers. *Innovations* 7, 1.

Seefeldt, C. (1995). Art—a serious work. *Young Children* 45, 3:39–45.

Sheldon-Harsch, L. (1997). Detroit Head Start: Inspired by the Reggio Emilia approach. *Innovations 4*, 2.

Smilansky, S. (1968). *The effects of sociodramatic play on disadvantaged preschool children.* New York: Wiley.

Smilansky, S., & L. Shefatya. (1990). *Facilitating play: A medium for promoting cognitive, socio emotional and academic development in young children.* Gaithersburg, MD: Psychosocial and Educational Publications.

Smith, C. (1998). Children with special rights. In C. Edwards, L. Gandini, & G. Forman (Eds.), *The hundred languages of children: The Reggio Emilia approach—advanced reflections.* 2nd ed. Greenwich, CT: Ablex Publishing Corporation.

Spaggiari, S. (1997). *Shoe and meter.* Reggio Emilia, Italy: Reggio Children.

Steele, B. (1996). A cornerstone of literacy: Children draw to express their deepest thoughts and feelings. *The Vancouver Sun,* 26 August, A19.

Sturges, P. (1998). *Bridges are to cross.* Illus. G. Laroche. New York: G.P. Putnam's.

Newsweek. The 10 best schools in the world and what we can learn from them. 1991. *Newsweek,* 2 December.

Tarini, E., & L. White. (1997). Looking in the mirror: A reflection of Reggio practice in Winnetka. In J. Hendrick (ed.), *First steps toward teaching the Reggio way,* Upper Saddle River, NJ: Prentice-Hall.

Topal, C., & L. Gandini. (1999). *Beautiful stuff: Learning with found materials.* Worcester, MA: Davis Publications.

Wagner, M.B. (1997). Reflections on adopting and adapting the Reggio Emilia approach in my classroom. *Innovations 4*, 2.

Wien, C.A. (1997). A Canadian in Reggio Emilia, May 1997, study tour. *Canadian Children* 22, 2:30–38.

Williams, D., & R. Kantor. (1997). The challenge of Reggio Emilia's research: One teacher's reflections. In J. Hendrick (ed.), *First steps toward teaching the Reggio way,* Upper Saddle River, NJ: Prentice-Hall.

Vygotsky, L.S. (1962). *Thought and language.* Cambridge, MA: The M.I.T. Press.

Yeates, M., C. Warberg, D. McKenna, & K. Chandler. (1990). *Administering early childhood settings: The Canadian perspective.* Columbus, Ohio: Merrill Publishing.

Glossary

Many of the words used to describe components of practice and philosophy in Reggio Emilia are from the Italian language and are not easily translated. Others are terms used in a particular way in the context of discussions about the Reggio approach. It is hoped that the following glossary will help readers better understand the discussion of Reggio in this book.

Aesthetics   A component of the environment; the result of paying attention to the visual attractiveness and sensory pleasure in the furnishings, arrangements, materials, and displays in the classroom and school.

Asilo nido   An Italian phrase literally meaning "safe nest;" used to describe the centers for infants and toddlers, children from three months to three years, in the Reggio Emilia municipally supported programs. Different from crèches established primarily for physical care of infants of working mothers, federal legislation in 1971 instituted social and educational services for children under three years of age in Asili Nidi. In 1975, the federal government transferred the authority to municipal governments to establish their infant-toddler centers. The infant-toddler centers in Reggio Emilia had, in fact, been established before that time.

Atelier   A French word meaning studio. The atelier in a preschool or infant-toddler center in Reggio Emilia is a room where a variety of creative material is displayed beautifully for children's expressive use, where children are taught techniques of using various media, and where children's representational work on projects is done and stored. Malaguzzi described an atelier as a "space rich in materials, tools, and people with professional competencies" (Edwards et al., 1998, p. 74). In Reggio, the atelier is seen as far more than an art studio, and is recognized as a place for research that assists adults in understanding how children learn.

Atelierista/Ateleriste   An individual trained in visual arts who functions as a studio teacher collaborating with children on their work, and with teachers and pedagogisti in the process of progettazione. The ateleristi help teachers with the process of documentation. The role of atelerista is unique to the schools in Reggio Emilia and does not exist in other systems in Italy.

Collaboration A principle of the Reggio philosophy that places a high value on the working together of children with children, children with teachers and ateleristi, teachers with parents, with co-teachers, and with pedagogisti and ateleristi. More than mere cooperation, when this term is used in the Reggio philosophy, it implies the necessary interdependence of all parties.

Co-construction The concept of generating new knowledge by interaction, negotiation, creative confrontation, and conflict. In co-construction, each participant is seen as both teacher and learner, providing insights and psychological support for each other.

Design phase The phase of negotiated curriculum in which children make records of their plans or intended solutions. In design, materials are created that can communicate and lead to reflection.

Discourse phase A time of analyzing the communication and of attempting to understand the meanings of others in planning next steps for exploration.

Documentation phase Any activity or record that conveys the meaning of the exploration carried out. In Reggio, the process of documentation implies not only a finished product but also a dynamic source for teacher reflection and communication with others.

Emergent curriculum The learning explorations that develop as a result of the interaction of the particular people in a particular place at a particular time. The curriculum emerges from the interests and dialog of the individuals in a learning environment, and is, therefore, not predetermined. In emergent curriculum, activities and projects develop through teachers' careful observations of children's work and communication, and subsequent decision-making about appropriate directions and time frames.

Hundred Languages The Reggio phrase that describes the many media available to children to explore and to represent their learning. Examples of the hundred languages used in Reggio are paint, charcoal, colored pencils, pen-and-ink drawings, clay work, wirework, collage, paper sculpture, shadow play, drama, music, work with words and numbers, computers, and many others.

Hypotheses The theories made by children in describing their understanding of a subject and the predictions made by teachers in considering the possible courses of an investigation. In both cases, the ideas are tentative, and are open to change and growth as the experience proceeds.

Mini-Atelier The small studio areas that are part of individual classrooms in Reggio preschools. These allow children to work on representational projects apart from the classroom activities.

Negotiated curriculum The term used by some educators to describe the process of creating curriculum between teachers and children as teachers work to frame and direct the ideas originating from children's interests. Negotiated curriculum describes the process of social constructivism where teachers work to uncover what children know and believe about a topic in order to design meaningful learning experiences.

Pedagogista   The term used to describe a professional role in numerous school systems, particularly in northern Italy, of a curriculum coordinator/resource person. In Reggio, the pedagogisti have taken on a unique role of dynamic collaboration within the schools. Although they have some administrative functions in the overall system since there are no directors or principals, their unique functions include promoting dialog and reflection with teachers, parents, and ateleristi about most appropriate learning directions. In this capacity, they are involved in developing the projects in their particular schools, and part of the on-going teacher development and in-service training, reflecting together with teachers on their practice.

Piazza   The central gathering areas in the schools in Reggio Emilia modeled after the piazza or town square in most Italian towns and cities. The gathering area opens into other important areas in the schools such as the kitchen and dining rooms, the atelier, and the classrooms. There are comfortable places to sit in the piazza, interesting objects to explore or play with, and documentation about some of the activities and people in the school. Children from various classes, teachers, and parents may use the piazza.

Project   The term used to describe the long-term explorations that are central to the curriculum and learning style of the schools in Reggio. Sometimes undertaken by small groups of children and other times involving the whole school, the projects develop as children and adults together consider possible methods of exploring a particular topic of interest and work to represent their learning over time.

Progettazione   An Italian word that conveys a complex network of hypotheses, observations, predictions, interpretations, planning, and explorations. This describes the process of adult reflection, thought, and communication that precedes the development of a project as teachers try to anticipate all the possible ways that the activity could develop, and identify likely ideas and choices of the children. It also describes the process of following the activity in extended investigations, making room for changes and for unexpected directions, and is, in fact, part of the activity.

Protagonist   The word used in Reggio to describe the active role of the participants in learning. The trio of protagonists in Reggio includes the child, the teachers, and the parent. This word is deliberately chosen to convey the notion of strength and equal participation.

Provacateur   One of the roles of teachers in the Reggio philosophy. It conveys the sense of the teachers as deliberately creating "knots" or problems worthy of children's efforts and attention.

Provocation   The term used to suggest an activity, experience, or material that may be planned as a starting point in a project of investigation; designed to elicit interest, ideas, questions, and directions for further exploration.

Scaffolder   A term that has come from those discussing Vygotsky's theory of social construction of knowledge. In this theory, the term zone of proximal development refers to those activities that children can undetake when given assistance by a more knowledgeable peer or adult. That individual then assumes the role of scaffolder, supporting the development of knowledge that could not be possible without such assistance.

Social construction   Another term derived from consideration of Vygotsky's theory. The understanding is that individuals are assisted in constructing new knowledge through their interactions with other people.

Index